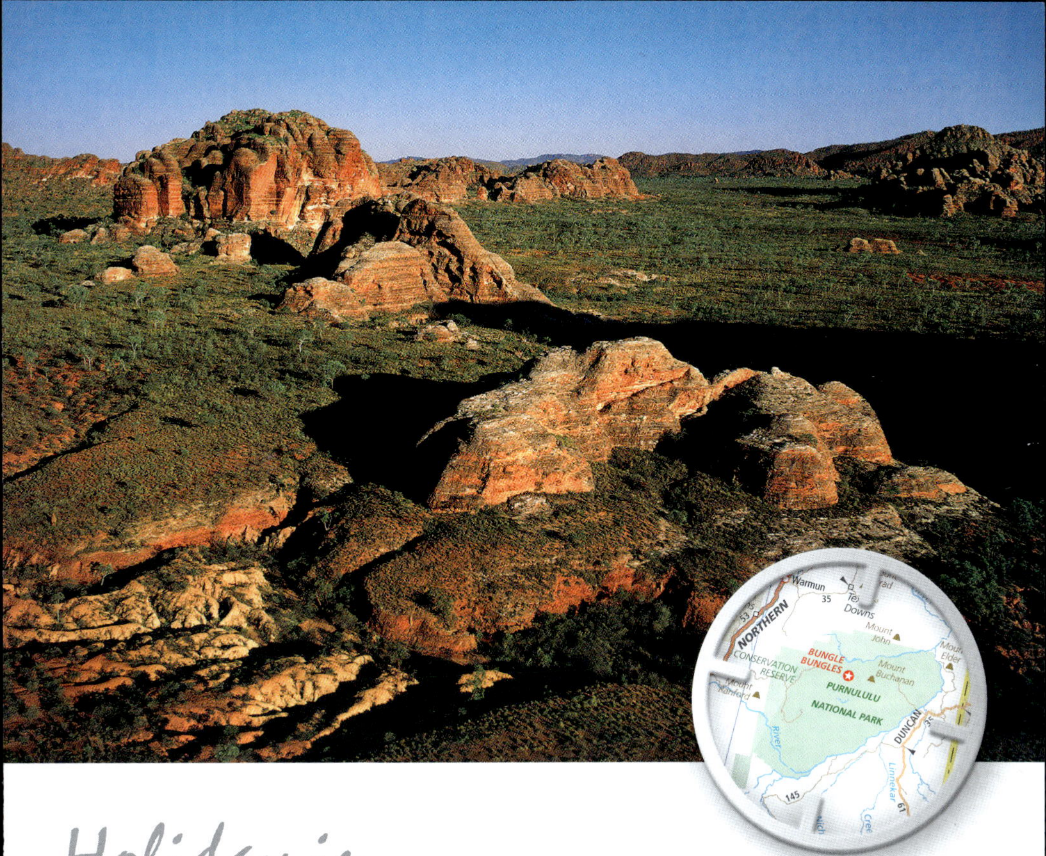

Holiday in

Western Australia

EXPLORE AUSTRALIA

CONTENTS

→ **INTRODUCTION** iv

→ **PERTH** 4

City Centre 8
Northbridge 11
East Perth 12
Inner East 13
Inner North 13
Inner West 13
Inner North-West 15
South-Western Beachside 16
North-Western Beachside 16
Inner South 17
South 18
Outer South 18
Fremantle 19
City Essentials 23

→ **REGIONS** 29

Rottnest Island 30
Darling & Swan 32
The South-West 34
Heartlands 36
Great Southern 38
Esperance & Nullarbor 40
Goldfields 42
Outback Coast & Mid-West 44
Pilbara 46
Kimberley 48

→ **TOWNS FROM A TO Z** 50

→ **WHERE TO EAT** 132

→ **WHERE TO STAY** 185

→ **ROAD ATLAS** 252

→ **INDEX** 270

WESTERN AUSTRALIA IS...

Spending a day at Perth's beaches, including **COTTESLOE** / Eating fish and chips on

FREMANTLE'S WHARF / Seeing magnificent beaches and searching for quokkas on

ROTTNEST ISLAND / Taking a camel ride along **CABLE BEACH**, Broome / Sampling

wines at cellar doors in **MARGARET RIVER** / Feeding dolphins at **MONKEY MIA** /

WESTERN AUSTRALIA

FISHING ALONG SHARK BAY, PERON PENINSULA

A scenic flight over the Bungle Bungles in **PURNULULU NATIONAL PARK** / Walking through giant stands of karri and tingle trees in the **VALLEY OF THE GIANTS** / A visit to **NAMBUNG NATIONAL PARK,** home to the moonscape of limestone pillars known as the **PINNACLES** / Swimming with whale sharks in **NINGALOO REEF**

WESTERN AUSTRALIA is defined by its size. Spanning an area of 2.5 million square kilometres, it covers one-third of the Australian continent. In dramatic contrast to its size, its population is just over two million, around one-tenth of Australia's total population. Over 72 per cent of Western Australians live in or around the capital city of Perth.

Within this great state there are incredibly diverse landscapes – an ancient terrain of rugged ranges and dramatic gorges to the north, towering forests to the south, arid deserts to the east and 12 889 kilometres of the world's most pristine coastline to the west. To match the huge variety in landscape are huge differences in climate, from the tropical humidity of the north and the dryness of the desert to the temperate Mediterranean-style climate of the South-West.

After driving for hours along empty highways, you will get a true feeling for the state's vastness. But you will be amply rewarded when you reach your destination. Western Australia boasts precious natural features, including the 350-million-year-old Bungle Bungle Range, the limestone sentinels of the Pinnacles Desert and the majestic karri forests of the South-West. There is the extraordinary marine life of Ningaloo Reef, the friendly dolphins of Monkey Mia and Rottnest Island's famous quokkas.

Western Australia's historic sites are also a highlight. The Aboriginal people who first inhabited the land up to 65 000 years ago left a legacy of distinctive rock art. Albany,

 fact file

Population 2 259 500
Total land area 2 529 875 square kilometres
People per square kilometre 0.8
Sheep and cattle per square kilometre 9.8
Nearest interstate city Adelaide, 2700 kilometres east
Length of coastline 12 889 kilometres
Number of islands 3747
Longest river Gascoyne River (760 kilometres)
Largest constructed reservoir Lake Argyle (storage volume 10 760 million cubic metres)
Highest mountain Mount Meharry (1253 metres), Karijini National Park
Highest waterfall King George Falls (80 metres), northern Kimberley
Highest town Tom Price (747 metres)

Hottest place Marble Bar (160 days a year over 37.5°C)
Coldest place Bridgetown (33 days a year begin at below 2°C)
Most remote town Warburton
Strangest place name Walkaway
Most famous person Rolf Harris
Quirkiest festival Milk Carton Regatta, Hillarys Boat Harbour
Number of wildflowers 12 500 species
Most challenging road Gibb River Road, the Kimberley
Best beach Cable Beach, Broome
Most identifiable food Pavlova (created at Perth's Esplanade Hotel)
Local beer Swan Lager

the site of the state's first European settlement in 1826, boasts well-preserved heritage buildings, while gracious 19th-century buildings in the capital city of Perth and its nearby port of Fremantle hark back to the days of the Swan River Colony. Remnants of great gold discoveries remain around Coolgardie and Kalgoorlie from the 1890s, which transformed Western Australia into one of the world's great producers of gold, iron ore, nickel, diamonds, mineral sands and natural gas.

SHEEP ROUND-UP, BOYUP BROOK

gift ideas

Gold nuggets (Kalgoorlie–Boulder) Visit the Australian Prospectors and Mining Hall of Fame to find gold nuggets in presentation cases and on chains as pendants. See Kalgoorlie–Boulder pp. 92–5

Cricket merchandise (WACA, East Perth) Cricket lovers will be thrilled to receive a memento from the world-famous Western Australian Cricket Association grounds. See Museums pp. 27, 6 D3

Ugg boots (Uggs-N-Rugs, Kenwick, Perth) This iconic sheepskin footwear is available around Australia, but in January 2006, Uggs-N-Rugs won a legal battle to remove an American company's trademark for 'ugh boots' from the Australian Trademarks Registry – a major victory for Australian manufacturers. 9 Royal St, Kenwick. 254 B3

Arts and crafts (Fremantle Markets, Fremantle) Over 150 stalls sell everything from local arts, crafts and clothes to fresh produce. See Fremantle Markets p. 21

Argyle diamonds (The Kimberley) Diamonds of unique brilliance in various colours, including the world's only intense pink diamonds. See Kimberley pp. 48–9, 266

Freshwater pearls (Broome) With its unique pearling heritage, exquisite pearl jewellery is available all over Broome. Willie Creek Pearls also have a showroom in Sorrento Quay, Hillarys Boat Harbour, north of Perth. See Broome pp. 58–61

Wine (Margaret River) There is an abundance of fine wine to choose from in this top wine-producing region. See Margaret River pp. 106–8

Jarrah, karri and marri woodwork (South-West region) Western Australia's unique woods are turned into handcrafted furniture, boxes, bowls, platters, salt and pepper grinders, to name but a few. See The South-West pp. 34–5, 225

Wood-fired bread, biscuits and nut cake (New Norcia) Made by New Norcia's Benedictine monk community. Their rich, intensely flavoured, panforte-style nut cake is also available at the New Norcia Bakeries at 163 Scarborough Beach Rd, Mount Hawthorn, and Bagot Rd, Subiaco. See New Norcia pp. 113–14, 257 B1, 258 B2

Quokka soft toy (Rottnest Island) Get a soft toy version of this small marsupial, which famously lives on 'Rotto', from the general store or gift shop. See Rottnest Island pp. 30–1, 254 A3

PERTH is...

Views across the city from **KINGS PARK** / **SWIMMING** at any of Perth's beaches / Eating fish and chips on **FREMANTLE'S WHARF** / Sipping a coffee on the 'cappuccino strip' of **SOUTH TERRACE**, Fremantle / Seeing black swans at **LAKE MONGER** / A cricket match at the **WACA** / A picnic

COTTESLOE BEACH

VISITOR INFORMATION
Western Australian Visitor Centre
→ Cnr Forrest Pl and Wellington St
→ 1300 361 351 or 1800 812 808
www.westernaustralia.com;
www.wavisitorcentre.com

on the **MATILDA BAY** foreshore / A visit to the **WESTERN AUSTRALIAN MUSEUM** / Eating out in **NORTHBRIDGE** / Browsing the eclectic offerings at the **FREMANTLE MARKETS** / A footy match at **SUBIACO OVAL** / Touring the forbidding **FREMANTLE PRISON**

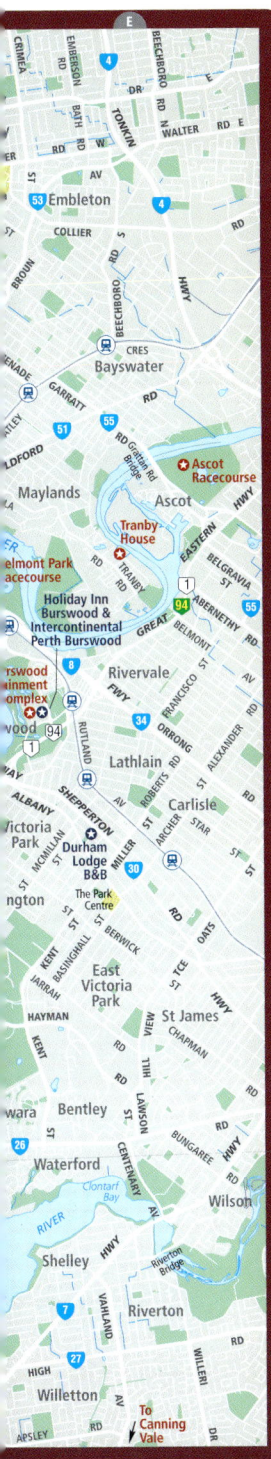

CAPITAL CITY

P erth is the most isolated capital city in the world, closer to Singapore than it is to Sydney. Its nearest neighbour, Adelaide, is 2700 kilometres away by road. Yet, it is exactly this isolation that has allowed Perth to retain a feeling of space and relaxed charm.

Claimed to be the sunniest state capital in Australia, Perth has a Mediterranean climate: hot and dry in summer, cool and wet in winter. This climate, and the city's proximity to both river and ocean, fosters a relaxed lifestyle for the population of 1 658 000. One of Perth's great attributes is that its water frontages are public land, accessible to everyone. Picnicking is a popular pastime, while cafes and bars spill their tables and chairs out onto pavements to make the most of the glorious weather.

Yet, for all Perth's coastal beauty, it is the Swan River that defines the city. North of the river is Kings Park and the old-money riverside suburbs with their grand homes; further on are the beaches and the newer northern beach suburbs stretching up the coast. At the mouth of the Swan River is the historic port city of Fremantle, with its rich maritime history, creative community and street-cafe culture. Upstream from Perth – where the river dwindles to a meandering waterway – is the Swan Valley, the state's oldest wine district.

CITY CENTRE

Perth's city centre is a compact mix of towering skyscrapers and elegant colonial buildings. It is bordered to the south and east by the Swan River, with stretches of grassy parkland fringing the riverbank. Perth's central business district (CBD) harbours the city's large pedestrian-only shopping precinct, made up of a series of malls and arcades. This is connected northwards to the Perth train station by an overhead walkway across Wellington Street. To the west, the ultra-hip King Street is renowned for its gourmet cafes, galleries and fashion houses. On the south side of the city is St Georges Terrace, the main commercial street – a strip of high-rise buildings interspersed with remnants of Perth's early British heritage. Just beyond it is the main bus depot, the Esplanade Busport, and at the river end of Barrack Street is the city's jetty at Barrack Square.

Malls, arcades & a touch of old England

Perth's central shopping precinct is in the blocks bounded by St Georges Terrace and William, Wellington and Barrack streets. These three main shopping blocks encompass the vehicle-free zones of **Hay Street Mall**, **Murray Street Mall** and **Forrest Place**. Between them, the two malls contain a swag of brand-name fashion outlets, bookstores and homewares shops. The big department stores of Myer and David Jones both have entrances on Murray Street Mall, and the western side of Forrest Place is home to the GPO. A series of arcades and underground walkways run from Murray Street Mall through to Hay Street Mall and on to St Georges Terrace, making it possible to shop in the city without ever crossing a street. **Carillon City** is a modern shopping centre between the malls, while **London Court**, an arcade with the appearance of a quaint Elizabethan street, runs from Hay Street Mall to St George's Terrace and is Perth's only open-air arcade. At the mall end, knights joust above a replica of Big Ben every 15 minutes, while St George and the Dragon do battle above the clock at the St Georges Terrace end.

King Street

This historic precinct of commercial buildings between Hay and Wellington streets dates from the 1890s gold rush. While the street has been restored to its turn-of-the-century character, its commercial interests are entirely modern: designer fashion houses, specialist bookstores, art galleries and gourmet cafes, such as the ever-popular **No 44 King Street**, with its homemade bread and extensive wine list.

St George's Terrace

The city's main commercial street is lined with modern office towers that overshadow a number of historic buildings. At the western end of the terrace is the **Barracks Archway**, the only remains of the Pensioners' Barracks, a structure that originally had two wings

LONDON COURT

and 120 rooms. This building housed the retired British soldiers who guarded convicts in the mid-1800s. The **Central Government Building** on the corner of Barrack Street marks the spot where Perth was founded with a tree-felling ceremony in 1829. Around 50 years later, convicts and hired labour commenced work on the building that stands there today. At one stage it housed the GPO, and a plaque on the building's east corner marks the point from which all distances in the state are measured. Other historic buildings along the terrace include the Cloisters, the Old Perth Boys' School, the Deanery, St George's Cathedral, Government House and the Old Court House *(see Grand old buildings, p. 24)*. As you are walking along the Terrace, look out for the commemorative plaques inlaid in the footpath which celebrate the achievements of over 170 notable Western Australians. This was

THE FUTURISTIC SWAN BELLS TOWER

a sesquicentennial project in 1979 celebrating 150 years since the foundation of the Swan River Colony.

City gardens

Two delightful city gardens are located in the block bounded by St George's Terrace, Riverside Drive, Barrack Street and Victoria Avenue. **Stirling Gardens** offer ornamental trees, well-kept lawns and plenty of shady spots. Along the footpath on the St George's Terrace side there are large statues of kangaroos – a great photo opportunity. Just nearby, within the gardens, is an ore obelisk, a memorial acknowledging the state's role as one of the world's foremost producers of minerals. Look carefully in the garden beds from the footpath on the Barrack Street side of the gardens and you will find small statues of May Gibbs' 'Gumnut Babies' nestled among the ferns. The gardens also house the oldest public building in Perth, now the Francis Burt Law Museum (see Museums, p. 27). The **Supreme Court Gardens**, further towards Riverside Drive, are a popular location for concerts on warm summer evenings, including the annual Carols by Candlelight.

Bells & a jetty

Barrack Square, at the water's edge south of the city, is where you will find the Swan Bells and the ferry jetty. The Barrack Street Jetty is the departure point for ferry services to Fremantle, South Perth, Rottnest Island and Carnac Island, along with various leisure cruises on the Swan River and to the vineyards of the Swan Valley. Behind Jetty six is the Willem de Vlamingh Memorial, which features a sundial indicating Amsterdam time and many historical references.

The Swan Bells consist of 18 'change-ringing' bells, which form the largest set in the world. Twelve of the bells, given to the state in 1988 by the British Government, come from London's Sant Martin-in-the-Fields church. The bell tower – which cost $6 million to build amid great controversy – offers galleries from which you can view the bellringers and the bells in action. A viewing platform at the top of the bell tower provides excellent views of the river and city. *Barrack Sq, cnr Barrack St and Riverside Dr; (08) 6210 0444; open from 10am daily, closing times vary seasonally (check the website, www.swanbells.com.au); full bell ringing 12–1pm Mon–Tues, Thurs and Sat–Sun.*

NORTHBRIDGE

Northbridge, which lies north of the city centre across the train line, is Perth's centre for the arts and the heart of the city's nightlife. This inner-city suburb is connected to the city centre via a walkway that crosses Perth Railway Station and leads directly to the Perth Cultural Centre. Bounded by Roe, Francis, Beaufort and William streets, the Perth Cultural Centre includes the state museum, art gallery, state library and Perth's institute of contemporary arts. William Street and the streets further west are packed with restaurants and bars that offer great eating, drinking and nightclubbing.

Art Gallery of Western Australia

The state's principal public art gallery, founded in 1895, houses collections of Australian and international paintings, sculpture, prints, craft and decorative arts. The gallery's collection of Aboriginal art is one of the finest in Australia. *Perth Cultural Centre, James St Mall; (08) 9492 6622 (24-hour information line) or (08) 9492 6600; open 10am–5pm Wed–Mon; general admission free; free guided tours available.*

Western Australian Museum

At this comprehensive museum you can see a 25-metre whale skeleton, the 11-tonne Mundrabilla meteorite and 'Megamouth', a rare species of shark. There are exhibitions concerning the state's Aboriginal people; the origins of the universe; and dinosaur, bird, butterfly, mammal and marine galleries. The interactive Discovery Centre is great for children. Within the museum complex is the **Old Gaol**, built in 1856 and used by the Swan River Colony until 1888. *Perth Cultural Centre, James St Mall; (08) 9212 3700; open 9.30am–5pm Thurs–Tues; admission by donation; free guided tours available.*

Perth Institute of Contemporary Arts

Commonly referred to by its acronym, PICA, the Perth Institute of Contemporary Arts is where you can sample the latest in visual and performance art. There is an ever-changing program of exhibitions. *Perth Cultural Centre, James St Mall; (08) 9228 6300; open 11am–6pm Tues–Sun; general admission free.*

EAST PERTH

East Perth is where you will find the Western Australian Cricket Association oval, known colloquially as the WACA (pronounced 'Wacka'), where cricket matches entertain the crowds over the summer months. Gloucester Park Raceway, with night harness horseracing on Friday nights, is nearby. Once the dead end of town – except when night matches or race meets lit up the night sky – East Perth is now an enclave of offices and hip inner-city apartments. There are two historically significant sites in this precinct, the Perth Mint and Queens Gardens.

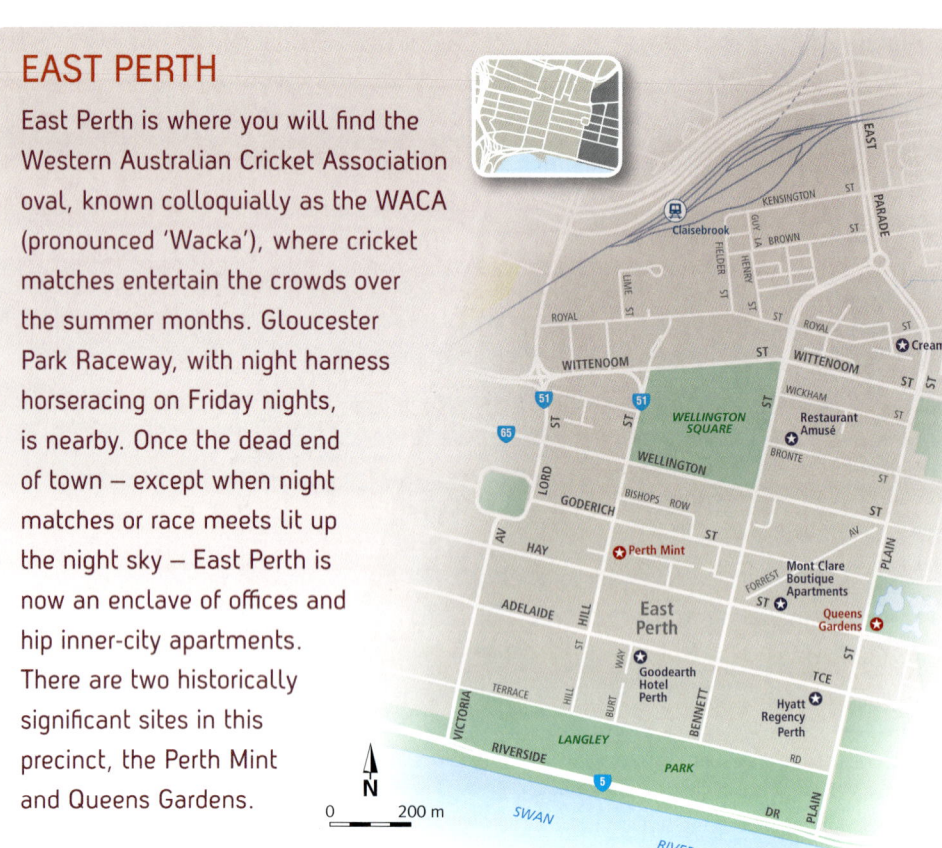

The Perth Mint

The Mint's imposing facade was built in 1899 from Rottnest Island limestone and is one of the best examples of Perth's gold-boom architecture. Here at Australia's oldest operating mint you can see the world's largest collection of natural gold specimens, including the 'Golden Beauty', a 11.5-kilogram nugget. Visitors can hold a 400-ounce gold bar, mint their own coins, take a guided tour and watch gold being poured. *310 Hay St (cnr Hill St), East Perth; (08) 9421 7277; open 9am–5pm Mon–Fri, 9am–1pm Sat–Sun and public holidays.*

Queens Gardens

The serene, English-style Queens Gardens feature a tranquil water garden complete with a replica of the famous Peter Pan statue that graces London's Kensington Gardens. These gardens were originally clay pits, where bricks were kilned for use in early colonial buildings such as the Perth Town Hall. *Cnr Hay and Plain sts.*

WACA

Across Hale Street from Queens Gardens is the WACA, the home of the state's cricket team, the Western Warriors. True lovers of the sport should visit the WACA's cricket museum *(see Museums, p. 27).*

INNER EAST

Burswood Entertainment Complex 7 E3

Built on an artificial island on the southern banks of the Swan River, this complex includes a casino, hotel, convention centre, tennis courts, golf course and Burswood Dome indoor stadium (the venue for the Hopman Cup). The Atrium Lobby has an impressive 47-metre-high pyramid of shimmering glass containing a tropical garden and waterfall. Burswood Park, the beautifully landscaped gardens that surround the complex, offers paths for walkers, cyclists and joggers, a heritage trail and a children's playground. *Great Eastern Hwy, Burswood; (08) 9362 7777.*

INNER NORTH

Tranby House 7 E2

Just beyond East Perth in the suburb of Maylands is historic Tranby House. Built in 1839 overlooking the picturesque Swan River, Tranby is one of the oldest surviving buildings from the early settlement of the Swan River Colony and is a unique example of colonial farmhouse architecture. A major attraction is the property's gardens which feature two century-old oak trees. The house has been beautifully restored by the National Trust. *Johnson Rd, Maylands; (08) 9272 2630; open 10am–4pm Wed–Sun (closed 24 Dec – 6 Feb).*

INNER WEST

Just minutes from the city centre, Kings Park is visited by millions of people each year. Beyond it at the end of Kings Park Road is the suburb of Subiaco, with its popular shopping, cafe and market precinct. Below Kings Park, Mounts Bay Road winds its way along the river's edge to the suburb of Crawley, passing the Old Swan Brewery site, now a riverside complex of up-market offices, apartments and restaurants. The distinctive clock tower of the University of Western Australia's Winthrop Hall is an easily spotted landmark. Across Matilda Bay Road from the university is the grassy Matilda Bay shoreline, with shady spots and views back up the river towards the city.

Kings Park & Botanic Garden 6 C3

The first stop for any visitor to Perth has to be Kings Park. Standing on top of Mount Eliza, you enjoy sweeping views of the city and the Swan River, with the Darling Range in the distance. Within this huge 400-hectare natural bushland reserve there are landscaped gardens and walkways, lakes, playgrounds, a restaurant and cafes.

Fraser Avenue, the main entrance road into the park, is lined with towering lemon-scented gums, honouring those who perished in war. The clock tower and bronze portrait bust at this entrance is a memorial to Edith Cowan, the first woman elected to an Australian parliament. A tireless advocate for women's rights and children's welfare, she now lends her name to one of Perth's universities.

Opened in 2003, the Lotterywest Federation Walkway is a combination of on-ground pathways, elevated walkway and spectacular steel-and-glass bridge, extending 620 metres through the Botanic Garden. It is a snapshot of Western Australia's famed flora; at ground level you'll pass boabs, boronias and tuart trees, while the walkway through the treetops takes you close to karri, marri, tingle and jarrah trees. The Botanic Garden itself is spread over 17 hectares and planted with more than 1700 native species.

The Botanic Garden's newest attraction arrived in July 2008 when a giant boab tree weighing 36 tonnes and estimated to be 750 years old was transported 3200 kilometres from the Kimberley town of Warnum and transplanted in the garden opposite Forrest Carpark. It joins long-time favourite attractions such as the State War Memorial precinct; the Pioneer Women's Memorial, with its water fountains which periodically shoot skywards; the nearby DNA Tower, offering spectacular views; the fantastic dinosaur and fossil creations at Synergy Parkland; and the child-friendly Lotterywest Family Area.

In spring, the annual Kings Park Festival showcases the best of the state's wildflowers, attracting over 500 000 visitors from around the world. This month-long event showcases all aspects of the park, with myriad spectacular events and activities. During summer the park is a favourite venue for live outdoor entertainment and moonlight movies (www.bgpa.wa.gov.au). *Fraser Ave; (08) 9480 3600; open daily; free guided walks from the visitor centre at 10am and 2pm daily.*

University of Western Australia 6 C4

With its distinctive Mediterranean-style architecture and landscaped gardens, the University of Western Australia is renowned as one of Australia's most beautiful campuses. Here you'll find **Winthrop Hall**, with its majestic clock tower and reflection pond and the **Sunken Garden**, backdrop for many a wedding photo. The **Lawrence Wilson Art Gallery**, home to the university's extensive collection of Australian art, includes works by Sidney Nolan, Arthur Boyd, Fred Williams and Rupert Bunny. *35 Stirling Hwy, Crawley; (08) 6488 3707; open 11am–5pm Tues–Fri, 12–5pm Sun; admission free.*

Also within the university grounds is the **Berndt Museum of Anthropology**, which houses one of Australia's finest collections of traditional and contemporary Australian Aboriginal art and artefacts. Currently in the process of relocating, the museum will be closed until the end of 2010. It will then temporarily reopen in the Lawrence Wilson Art Gallery building until its new, purpose-built home is finished. *www.berndt.uwa.edu.au*

Foreshore suburbs 6 B4

Extending along the river foreshore from Matilda Bay towards the ocean is a series of exclusive waterfront suburbs with charming village-style shopping areas, fashionable galleries and foreshore restaurants. **Nedlands** is the suburb closest to the University of Western Australia. **Dalkeith's** Jutland Parade takes you to Point Resolution, with magnificent views of the river to the south and west. Follow the walking paths down the hillside to White Beach on the foreshore, a popular recreational spot.

Subiaco 6 C3

Beyond West Perth is the popular shopping, cafe and market precinct of Subiaco, with its village-style main street, Rokeby Road (pronounced 'Rock-a-bee'). 'Subi', as it is known to the locals, is one of Perth's oldest suburbs, and there are some fine old homes in the back streets behind Rokeby Road. The word Subiaco rings a bell for AFL supporters too, as it is the home of **Subiaco Oval**.

Parliament House 6 C3
Go inside the corridors of power on a free, 45-minute guided tour. *Harvest Tce, West Perth; (08) 9222 7259; tours 10.30am Mon and Thurs.*

Scitech Discovery Centre 6 C3
This interactive science and technology centre has more than 160 hands-on exhibits. You can touch, switch, climb, crank and explore – all in the name of science. There's also **Horizon**, a state-of-the-art planetarium screening extraordinary journeys into space on the largest dome screen in the Southern Hemisphere. *City West, cnr Sutherland and Railway sts, West Perth; (08) 9215 0700; open 9.30am–4pm Mon–Fri, 10am–5pm Sat–Sun, school holidays and public holidays.*

INNER NORTH-WEST

Lake Monger 6 C2
Lake Monger, a large urban wetland 5 kilometres north of Perth's CBD in the suburb of Wembley, is the best place in Perth to see Western Australia's famous black swans. Ever since 1697, when Dutch explorer Willem de Vlamingh named the Swan River after the numerous black swans he found on its waters, the majestic waterbirds have been inextricably linked with Western Australia. The first settlement was named the Swan River Colony and the black swan became the official State Bird Emblem of Western Australia in 1973.

THE MEDITERRANEAN-STYLE ARCHITECTURE OF THE UNIVERSITY OF WESTERN AUSTRALIA

SOUTH-WESTERN BEACHSIDE

With pristine white-sand beaches stretching northwards up the coast, swimming and surfing are a way of life in Perth. Several stunning beaches, including Cottesloe, are close to the city. Scattered along these beach fronts are lovely cafes, restaurants and bars. Enjoy the sublime Perth experience of sipping a glass of Western Australian wine as you watch the sun sink into the Indian Ocean.

Cottesloe 6 A5

Cottesloe is distinguished by its towering Norfolk Island pines and the **Indiana Cottesloe Beach Restaurant**, a neo-colonial building of grand proportions that sits right on the beach. *91 Marine Pde, Cottesloe; (08) 9385 5005.*

The Spanish-style **Cottesloe Civic Centre**, once the private mansion of flamboyant millionaire Claude de Bernales, boasts magnificent gardens with sweeping views of the Indian Ocean. *109 Broome St; (08) 9285 5000; open daily; admission free.*

Claremont 6 B4

This up-market suburb is home to Perth's swankiest shopping area, centred around Bay View Terrace. The **Claremont Museum**, on Victoria Avenue, was built in 1862 by convicts and the Pensioner Guards as the Freshwater Bay School. It now offers an interesting social history display of more than 9000 items related to the district, including artefacts, photographs, oral history tapes and documents. The main exhibitions are housed in the schoolhouse, which has been carefully preserved to provide a glimpse into the colonial education system. Nearby is a children's playground and picnic area. *66 Victoria Ave, Claremont; (08) 9340 6983; open 12–4pm Mon–Fri; admission free.*

Peppermint Grove 6 A4

Peppermint Grove boasts some of Perth's grandest homes. A drive along The Esplanade takes you past grass-backed riverside beaches, natural bushland and shady picnic areas. Follow the road around to Bay View Park – another great place for picnicking – in Mosman Park, and up the hill for sweeping views of Mosman Bay, the Swan River and Perth city skyline.

NORTH-WESTERN BEACHSIDE

Scarborough 6 A2

Renowned for its beachside cafe society, the beach here is a top spot for surfers and sailboarders. The five-star Rendezvous Observation City Hotel dominates the landscape, reminiscent of the Gold Coast resorts. On weekends the Scarborough Fair Markets set up stalls just opposite the hotel, where you can shop for antiques, bric-a-brac, arts and crafts plus – of course – surf gear and hippie wear. *Cnr Scarborough Beach Rd and West Coast Hwy; open 9am–5.30pm Sat–Sun.*

Hillarys Boat Harbour 254 A2

This ocean-side complex houses a marina, a world-class aquarium *(see next entry)*, and Sorrento Quay, a 'village' of shops, cafes, restaurants and resort apartments. If the beautiful sandy beaches are too tame for you, try The Great Escape, a leisure park with water slides, miniature golf and trampolines. Ferries to Rottnest Island run from Hillarys and there are whale-watching cruises from September to November. If you visit in March, be sure to attend the Milk Carton Regatta, a fundraising event for the local telethon. Competitors in this

WESTERN AUSTRALIA → PERTH → **INNER SOUTH** **17**

SNORKELLING WITH TURTLES AND SHARKS AT AQWA

wacky boatrace build their craft entirely from milk cartons, then dress up to coordinate with their creative craft and paddle for glory. The day also includes a sand sculpture competition that produces amazing results and plenty of other beachside entertainment. *Southside Dr, Hillarys Boat Harbour, (08) 9448 7544; Sorrento Quay, (08) 9246 9788.*

Aquarium of Western Australia (AQWA) 254 A2

The highlight of this attraction, housing five different aquariums, is an incredible 98-metre underwater tunnel aquarium, surrounded by approximately three million litres of the Indian Ocean. Here you'll see thousands of marine creatures including sharks, stingrays, seals, crocodiles, sea dragons and turtles. For the ultimate underwater sensation, visitors can snorkel or swim with sharks. *Hillarys Boat Harbour, 91 Southside Dr, Hillarys; (08) 9447 7500; open 10am–5pm daily.*

INNER SOUTH

Perth Zoo 6 D4

Perth Zoo, with its shady gardens, walkways and picnic areas, is just a short ferry ride across the river from the city. Visit the Australian Walkabout for a close-up look at native animals in a bush setting. Other exhibits include the Penguin Plunge, African Savannah, Reptile Encounter and Rainforest Retreat. *20 Labouchere Rd, South Perth; (08) 9474 0444 or (08) 9474 3551 (recorded information line); open 9am–5pm daily.*

Old Mill 6 C3

This picturesque whitewashed windmill at the southern end of the Narrows Bridge is one of the earliest buildings in the Swan River Colony. The foundation stone was laid by Captain James Stirling, the first governor, in 1835. The mill, the adjacent miller's cottage and the recently established Education Centre review the development of flour milling in the early days of the colony. Coloured lights turn the

THE WHITEWASHED OLD MILL

huge Norfolk Island pine next to the Old Mill into a giant Christmas tree every December, making a festive display in the summer night sky. *Mill Point Rd, South Perth; (08) 9367 5788; open 10am–4pm Tues–Fri, 1–4pm Sat–Sun.*

SOUTH

Wireless Hill Park 6 C5

This natural bushland area boasts a magnificent springtime wildflower display. Three lookout towers provide views of the Swan River and the city skyline. A **Telecommunications Museum** is housed in the original Wireless Station and is open by appointment only. *Almondbury Rd, Ardross; (08) 9364 0158.*

Point Walter Reserve

This recreation area on the river is a pleasant spot for a picnic. Pick a shady peppermint tree by the water's edge to sit under and watch children paddling in the river. A kiosk, cafe, free barbecue facilities and children's playground area are nearby. Stroll out on the jetty to see what's biting, and walk out on the huge sandbar for great views both up and down river. *Honour Ave, Bicton.*

Point Heathcote Reserve

Cross the Canning River – a large tributary of the Swan River – via Canning Bridge and wind your way through the affluent suburb of Applecross to Point Heathcote Reserve on Duncraig Road. This hilltop playground and parkland area, which includes a local museum, art gallery, restaurant, kiosk and free barbecue facilities, is the best spot south of the Swan for sweeping views of the river and city.

OUTER SOUTH

Adventure World 254 B3

The state's biggest amusement park offers over 30 thrill rides and water slides, including the Turbo Mountain Rollercoaster, the Power Surge, the Shotgun and the Tunnel of Terror that corkscrews its way down Water Mountain. Nearby Bibra Lake is a great place to see black swans and other waterbirds. *179 Progress Dr, Bibra Lake; (08) 9417 9666; open 10am–5pm Thurs–Mon, daily in Jan and school holidays.*

FREMANTLE

Although now linked to Perth by a sprawl of suburbs, Fremantle ('Freo' to the locals) has a feel that is quite different in both architecture and atmosphere. Today it is a major boat and fishing centre at the mouth of the Swan River, but it also has the streetscape of a 19th-century port. It is a place to stay, unwind and watch the world go by. You can shop at the famous Fremantle Markets, or rest at a cafe on **South Terrace** and wait for the arrival of 'the Fremantle Doctor', the refreshing afternoon wind that blows in off the Indian Ocean.

European settlers arrived at Fremantle in 1829. The settlement developed gradually, its existence dependent on whaling and fishing. The population was boosted with the arrival in 1850 of British convicts, who constructed the forbidding Fremantle Prison (now open to the public) and the imposing lunatic asylum, now the Fremantle Arts Centre. Many heritage houses and terraces with cast-iron balconies from this period have survived.

Fremantle was at the centre of the world stage in 1987 when it hosted the America's Cup series of yacht races, following the win by Australia II – a Fremantle yacht – in 1983. Preparations for this huge event included the restoration of many old buildings in Fremantle and the boost to its tourist economy has lasted to the present day.

WESTERN AUSTRALIAN MARITIME MUSEUM

WESTERN AUSTRALIA → PERTH → **FREMANTLE**

VISITOR INFORMATION
Fremantle Visitor Centre
→ Town Hall, Kings Sq, High St
→ (08) 9431 7878
www.fremantlewa.com.au

Shipwreck Galleries

Part of the Western Australian Maritime Museum, the galleries are one of three sites showcasing Western Australia's maritime history. The state's treacherous coastline has doomed many ships to a watery grave. The Shipwreck Galleries, housed in the restored convict-built Commissariat building, document this chapter of maritime history. The most popular exhibit is the stern of the *Batavia*, wrecked in 1629, which has been reconstructed from recovered timbers. *Cliff St; www.museum.wa.gov.au/oursites/shipwreckgalleries; open 9.30am–5pm Thurs–Tues; admission by donation.*

Grand old buildings

Fremantle has a compact cluster of lovely old buildings, beginning with the Georgian-style **Elder's Building** at 11 Cliff Street. Made of brick and Donnybrook stone, it was once the hub of Fremantle's overseas trade. At 31–35 Cliff Street, the **Lionel Samson Building**'s rich facade epitomises the opulent style of gold-rush architecture. The **Esplanade Hotel**, on the corner of Marine Terrace and Essex Street, dates from the 1890s and its newer extension blends in seamlessly with the original facade. Now the Challenger TAFE e-Tech, the **Fremantle Technical College** displays Art Nouveau decorative touches and boasts Donnybrook stone facings and plinth. It's on the corner of South Terrace and Essex Street. On the corner of Ellen and Ord streets, the grand old **Samson House** dates from 1900 and was originally built for Michael Samson, who later became mayor of Fremantle. Finally, there's the stone bell-tower and large stained-glass window of **St John's Anglican Church**, on the corner of Adelaide and Queen streets, and Henderson Street's **Warders' Quarters**, a row of convict-built cottages built in 1851, and until recently used to house warders from Fremantle Prison. *(See also The Round House on this page and Fremantle Prison, p. 22)*

Fremantle Markets

One of the city's most popular attractions are these National Trust–classified markets, with their ornate gold-rush era architecture, which were opened in 1897. They offer a diversity of stalls: fresh produce, food, books, clothes, bric-a-brac, pottery and crafts. There is also a great tavern bar where buskers often perform. *Cnr South Tce and Henderson St; (08) 9335 2515; open 9am–8pm Fri, 9am–6pm Sat–Sun.*

The Round House

Its name a misnomer, the Round House is actually a dodecahedron, with its 12 sides erected around a central yard. Built in 1831 by the first settlers as a prison, it is the oldest public building in the state. At 1pm each day, the Round House's signal station fires a cannon – the time gun – and this activates a time ball (an instrument once used to give accurate time readings to vessels out at sea). The Whalers' Tunnel underneath the Round House was cut by a whaling company in 1837 for access to Bathers Bay. *10 Arthur Head; (08) 9336 6897; open 10.30am–3.30pm daily; admission by gold coin donation.*

Western Australian Maritime Museum

This stunning, nautically-inspired building perched on the waterfront has six galleries, each of which explores a different theme in the state's maritime history. Highlights of the collection of historic and significant boats include the yacht that won the America's Cup – *Australia II* – and the *Parry Endeavour*, in which Western Australian, Jon Sanders, circumnavigated the world three times. Outside the museum are the Welcome Walls, a series of engraved panels that list the names of thousands of migrants who arrived in Western Australia through the port of Fremantle, while next door to the museum is another of its prize exhibits, the submarine HMAS *Ovens*, which was in service during World War II. Take the tour to see what conditions are like inside a real submarine. *Victoria Quay; (08) 9431 8334; open 9.30am–5pm Thurs–Tues.*

Leeuwin Ocean Adventure

The *Leeuwin II* – a 55-metre, three-masted barquentine – is rated as the largest ocean-going tall ship in Australia. It is available for half-day or twilight sails and for longer voyages along the coast of Western Australia and the Northern Territory. When in Fremantle, it is open to the public. *B Berth, Victoria Quay; (08) 9430 4105.*

Fremantle Prison

The first convicts arrived in Fremantle in 1850. Built with their own hands, this complex of buildings was initially used as a barracks and became a prison in 1867. Huge, forbidding and full of history, it was in use until 1991. Now visitors can experience the atmosphere on a guided tour, running every half-hour and taking in the isolation chamber and the gallows. The entrance can be reached via steps and a walkway around Fremantle Oval from Parry Street. *1 The Terrace; (08) 9336 9200; open 10am–5pm daily; Tunnels Tours daily and Torchlight Tours Wed and Fri (bookings essential).*

Fremantle Arts Centre

This magnificent limestone building, with its steeply pitched roofs and Gothic arches, was also built by convicts. The colony's first lunatic asylum, it now offers an interesting display on the history of Fremantle, contemporary art exhibitions, a craft shop with a range of wares made by Western Australian artists, a ghost walk and a garden area with a cafe. *1 Finnerty St; (08) 9432 9555; open 10am–5pm daily; admission free.*

Fishing Boat Harbour

This popular restaurant strip for locals and tourists alike overlooks the boats of the local fishermen. Sample the fresh catch of the day at restaurants such as **Cicerello's**, famous for its fish and chips. On the footpath in front of Cicerello's is a statue of AC/DC's Bon Scott, unveiled in October 2008. Across the railway line is the **Esplanade Reserve**, an ideal spot to relax under the giant Norfolk Pines.

CITY ESSENTIALS
PERTH

Climate

Perth is Australia's sunniest capital, with an annual average of eight hours of sunshine per day. All this sunshine gives Perth a Mediterranean climate of hot, dry summers and mild, wet winters. The average maximum temperature in summer is 31°C; however, heat waves of temperatures in the high 30s and low 40s are not unusual. Fortunately, an afternoon sea breeze affectionately known as 'the Fremantle Doctor' eases the heat of summer.

	MAX °C	MIN °C	RAIN MM	RAIN DAYS
JANUARY	30	17	8	3
FEBRUARY	31	17	12	3
MARCH	29	16	19	4
APRIL	25	13	45	8
MAY	22	10	123	14
JUNE	19	8	184	17
JULY	18	7	173	18
AUGUST	18	8	136	17
SEPTEMBER	20	9	80	14
OCTOBER	22	11	54	11
NOVEMBER	26	14	21	6
DECEMBER	28	16	14	4

Getting around

The city is compact and easy to explore. A free bus service known as the CAT (Central Area Transit) System operates regular services, every five–ten minutes, around central Perth. The blue CAT runs in a north–south loop, the red CAT operates in an east–west loop, and the yellow CAT travels to the city centre from East Perth. (Note that a CAT bus also services Fremantle.) You can also travel free on Transperth buses or trains within the Free Transit Zone in the city centre, but only on trips that start and finish within the zone.

Trains run from the city out to the northern suburbs and down to Fremantle, while the Southern Suburbs Railway links Perth to Mandurah. Ferries and cruise boats depart regularly from Barrack Street Jetty to various destinations, including Fremantle, South Perth, Rottnest Island and the Swan Valley wine region. (Transperth runs the ferry to South Perth, while private operators travel further afield.) Perth, with its largely flat landscape, is also excellent for cycling; maps of the city's 700-kilometre bike network are available at bike shops or online at the Department of Transport website, www.transport.wa.gov.au.

Public transport Transperth (bus, train and ferry) 13 6213.

Airport shuttle bus Airport–city shuttle 1300 666 806.

Swan River and Rottnest ferries and cruises Captain Cook Cruises (08) 9325 3341; Oceanic Cruises (08) 9325 1191.

Motoring organisation RAC of WA (08) 9301 3113 or 13 1703.

Car rental Avis 13 6333; Budget 13 2727; Hertz 13 3039; Thrifty 13 6139.

Taxis Black and White Taxis 13 1008; Swan Taxis 13 1330.

Bicycle hire About Bike Hire (08) 9221 2665.

See also Getting around Fremantle, p. 28

Top events

Hopman Cup Prestigious international tennis event. JANUARY.

Perth Cup Western Australia's premier horseracing event. JANUARY.

Australia Day Skyworks A day-long party of events, culminating in a spectacular fireworks display. JANUARY.

Perth International Arts Festival Music, theatre, opera, dance, visual arts and film. FEBRUARY.

City of Perth Winter Arts Festival A three-month program of locally created arts and culture. JUNE–AUGUST.

Kings Park Wildflower Festival Australia's premier native plant and wildflower exhibition. SEPTEMBER.

Perth Royal Show Showcases the state's primary and secondary resources. SEPTEMBER–OCTOBER.

Red Bull Air Race A weekend of jaw-dropping, low-level aerial racing over the Swan River. NOVEMBER.

See also Top events in Fremantle, p. 28

 ## Shopping

London Court Mock-Tudor arcade with souvenir, jewellery and antique stores. See p. 8

Hay Street Mall, Murray Street Mall and Forrest Place The CBD's main shopping precinct with brand-name fashion outlets and major department stores Myer and David Jones. See p. 8

King Street High fashion, galleries and cafes with style. See p. 8

Rokeby Road, Subiaco Funky local designers sit alongside more established labels. 6 C3

Bay View Terrace, Claremont Perth's up-market fashion hot spot. 6 B4

Napoleon Street, Cottesloe Cafes, boutiques and designer homewares. 6 A4

 ## Markets

The Markets @ Perth Cultural Centre The only regular weekend market in the city with produce, flowers and arts and crafts. 8.30am–5pm Sat–Sun. See p. 8

Subiaco Pavilion Markets Art and craft stalls with large food hall in restored warehouse adjacent to station. Cnr Rokeby and Roberts rds, Subiaco; 10am–9pm Thurs–Fri, 10am–5pm Sat–Sun. 6 C3

Subiaco Station Street Markets A colourful outdoor and undercover market with an eclectic array of goods and live entertainment. 41 Station St, Subiaco; (08) 9382 2832; 9am–5.30pm Fri–Sun. 6 C3

Scarborough Fair Markets Specialty stalls and a food hall on Scarborough Beach. 9am–5.30pm Sat–Sun. 6 A2

Canning Vale Markets Huge undercover flea markets, and the primary fruit and vegetable wholesale market for the state. Cnr South St and Bannister Rd; 7am–1pm Sun. 254 B3, 257 B2

Wanneroo Markets Huge undercover markets with food court selling everything from locally grown fruit and vegetables to footwear and jewellery. 33 Prindiville Dr, Wangara; (08) 9409 8397; 9am–5pm Fri–Sun. 254 B2, 257 B2, 258 A3

See also Fremantle Markets, p. 21

 ## Grand old buildings

Government House Gothic arches and turrets reminiscent of the Tower of London. St Georges Tce (opposite Pier St).

His Majesty's Theatre 'The Maj', built in 1904, features an opulent Edwardian exterior. 825 Hay St; free foyer tours 10am–4pm Mon–Fri.

Kirkman House In front of this gracious edifice is an immense Moreton Bay fig tree, planted in the 1890s and now classified by the National Trust. 10 Murray St.

Old Court House Perth's oldest surviving building (1836), now home to the Francis Burt Law Museum. Cnr St Georges Tce and Barrack St.

Old Perth Boys' School Perth's first purpose-built school was made from sandstone ferried up the Swan River by convict labour. 139 St Georges Tce.

Perth Town Hall Built by convict labour (1867–70) in the style of an English Jacobean market hall. Cnr Hay and Barrack sts.

St George's Cathedral This 1879 Anglican church features an impressive jarrah ceiling. 38 St Georges Tce.

St Mary's Cathedral Grand Gothic-style cathedral, one end of which was built in 1865. Victoria Sq.

The Cloisters Check out the decorative brickwork of this 1858 building, originally a boys' school. The old banyan tree adjoining it is something special too. 200 St Georges Tce.

See also Fremantle's grand old buildings, p. 21

Entertainment

Cinema After once reigning supreme in town, Hoyts and Greater Union have moved out to the suburbs, leaving the city centre bereft of any major cinemas. There is, however, the Piccadilly Cinema in Piccadilly Arcade in the Hay Street Mall, which screens new-release films in Perth's only surviving grand old Art Deco cinema. The most easily accessible Hoyts cinemas are in Fremantle at the Queensgate on William Street and the Millennium on Collie Street. The closest Greater Union cinema to the city is in Innaloo. Subiaco has an independent cinema, the Ace, at 500 Hay Street on the corner of Alvan. There's also Cinema Paradiso in Northbridge, the Luna Palace in Leederville, the Windsor in Nedlands, the Cygnet in Como and, in Fremantle, Luna on SX (Essex Street). In summer, there are a number of outdoor cinemas that operate; favourites are the Moonlight Cinema in Kings Park and the Somerville Auditorium at the University of Western Australia. The latter, which screens films for the Perth International Arts Festival from December through March, is defined by a cathedral of Norfolk pine trees and patrons sit on deckchair-style seats under the stars. Programs and session times, including those for the open-air cinemas over summer, are listed daily in *The West Australian*.

Live music Northbridge, Leederville and Subiaco are the places to go for live music, as a healthy pub scene supports local musicians. In Northbridge popular venues include the Brass Monkey, the Mustang Bar, the Paramount, the Elephant & Wheelbarrow and Rosie O'Grady's. The Leederville Hotel on Oxford Street has a legendary Sunday afternoon session; the Ocean Beach Hotel in Cottesloe (known locally as the 'OBH') adds sunset views from the bar. In Fremantle, the premier live music venues are the Fly by Night Musicians Club on Parry Street, Kulcha on South Terrace and Mojos in North Freo. Pick up the free street publication *Xpress* for gig guides or visit www.xpressmag.com.au. Jazz venues include the Hyde Park Hotel in Bulwer Street, North Perth; the Navy Club in High Street, Fremantle; and the Ellington Jazz Club at 191 Beaufort Street, Perth. Aficionados should visit www.jazzwa.com or phone the recorded information Jazzline on (08) 9357 2807.

Classical music and performing arts
His Majesty's Theatre, Australia's only remaining Edwardian theatre, is Perth's premier venue for high-end theatre, opera and ballet. Black Swan State Theatre Company is Western Australia's flagship theatre company; there is also the Perth Theatre Company, based at the Playhouse Theatre in Pier Street. Other local productions can be seen at the Subiaco Arts Centre and the Regal Theatre, while Fremantle is home to Deckchair Theatre in High Street and Spare Parts Puppet Theatre in Short Street. The Perth Concert Hall in St Georges Terrace is the fine music venue for concerts by local and international musicians. The Burswood Entertainment Complex hosts touring shows and musicals; ME Bank Stadium in East Perth is the venue for big international acts. In the warmer months, outdoor concerts are held in the Supreme Court and Queens Gardens, and in Kings Park. Check *The West Australian* for details.

Walks & tours

Perth Walking Tours Take a free city orientation tour at 11am Monday to Saturday and noon on Sunday, or learn about Perth's history and culture on a free guided tour at 2pm weekdays. City of Perth Information Kiosk, Murray St Mall (near Forrest Pl).

Swan Brewery Tour This state-of-the-art brewery in Canning Vale is renowned for its Swan and Emu beers. 25 Baile Rd, Canning Vale; bookings (08) 9350 0222.

Swan Valley Wine Cruise Choose from full or half-day cruises up the Swan River to the Swan Valley, with wine-tastings included. Captain Cook Cruises, bookings (08) 9325 3341.

Kings Park Walks Free guided walks, including the Botanic Garden Discovery, Bushland Nature Trail and the Memorials Walk, among others. (08) 9480 3600; 10am and 2pm daily.

Kings Park Indigenous Heritage Tour Learn about bush medicines, bush tucker and Indigenous history in this 1.5-hour tour. (08) 9480 3600; 1.30pm daily.

Fremantle Prison Tours Choose from a range of tours including the fascinating 'Doing Time Tour', every 30 minutes between 10am and 5pm, and the spooky 'Torchlight Tour' on Wednesdays and Fridays at 7pm. 1 The Terrace, Fremantle; (08) 9336 9200.

Perth–Fremantle River Cruise Enjoy informative on-board commentary as you cruise from Perth to Fremantle and back again. Or take the Triple Tour, which adds an Open Top Bus Tour in Perth and a Tram Tour in Fremantle. (08) 9325 1191.

Pedal Oz City Discovery Tour Gentle bicycle tour from Perth to Fremantle, with coffee at Cottesloe Beach, lunch and beer tasting at Fremantle then river cruise back to Perth. 1300 784 864.

Sport

AFL (Australian Football League) is the most popular spectator sport in Perth, with crowds flocking to Subiaco Oval from April through September to support their local teams, the West Coast Eagles and the Fremantle Dockers. Subiaco Oval is also home to Western Australia's **Rugby Union** team, the Western Force, which plays in the Super 14 international rugby union competition.

The **cricket** season takes up where the footy leaves off, with the famous WACA hosting both interstate and international test matches over the summer months.

Perth's **soccer** club, the Perth Glory, play at nib Stadium (formerly Members Equity Stadium) in East Perth. **Basketball** fans can catch the popular Perth Wildcats from September to February at Challenge Stadium in Mount Claremont, while their female counterparts, the Perth Lynx, play nearby at the new $44 million WA Basketball Centre.

In January, Perth's Burswood Dome hosts the Hopman Cup, a prestigious international **tennis** event.

Horseracing is a year-round event, split between two venues: Ascot racecourse in summer and Belmont Park in winter. Events such as the Perth Cup (held on New Year's Day), the Easter Racing Carnival and the Opening Day at Ascot draw huge crowds. Night harness racing can be seen at Gloucester Park every Friday night.

Galleries

Aspects of Kings Park Contemporary Australian craft and design, with a focus on local artists. Fraser Ave, Kings Park and Botanic Garden, West Perth; (08) 9480 3900; open 9am–5pm daily.

Indigenart Mossenson Galleries
One of Australia's foremost Aboriginal art galleries. 115 Hay St, Subiaco; (08) 9388 2899; open 10am–5pm Mon–Fri, 11am–4pm Sat.

Greenhill Galleries New York–style gallery features works of leading Australian artists. 16 Gugeri St, Claremont; (08) 9383 4433; open 10am–5pm Tues–Fri, 10am–4pm Sat.

Holmes à Court Gallery Changing display of works from Australia's finest private art collection. Level 1, 11 Brown St, East Perth; (08) 9218 4540; open 12–5pm Wed–Sun; general admission free.

Kailis Australian Pearls Perfectly matched strands and handcrafted pieces made from exquisite cultured and seedless pearls. 29 King St; (08) 9422 3888; cnr Marine Tce and Collie St, Fremantle; (08) 9239 9330.

See also Art Gallery of Western Australia, p. 11, and Perth Institute of Contemporary Arts, p. 12

Museums

Fire and Emergency Services Education and Heritage Centre Refurbished in 2009, this limestone building dating from 1900 houses exhibitions on the history of the Perth fire brigade, including fire rescue and old Big Red engines. Cnr Murray and Irwin sts; (08) 9323 9353; 10am–4pm Tues–Thurs; admission free.

Francis Burt Law Museum The history of the state's legal system is housed in the Old Court House. Stirling Gardens, cnr St Georges Tce and Barrack St; (08) 9325 4787; open 10am–2.30pm Wed–Fri; admission free.

Museum of Performing Arts Entertainment history brought to life through exhibitions of costumes and memorabilia taken from backstage archives. His Majesty's Theatre, 825 Hay St; (08) 9265 0900; open 10am–4pm Mon–Fri; admission by gold coin donation.

WACA Museum Offers cricket memorabilia for fans of the sport. Gate 2, Nelson Cres, East Perth; (08) 9265 7222; open 10am–3pm Mon–Fri except match days; tours of ground and museum run at 10am and 1pm Mon–Thurs.

Army Museum of Western Australia Houses WA army memorabilia dating from colonial times to the present day. Artillery Barracks, Burt St, Fremantle; (08) 9430 2535; open 11am–4pm Wed–Sun.

See also The Perth Mint, p. 12, Western Australian Museum, p. 11, Western Australian Maritime Museum, p. 21, Shipwreck Galleries, p. 21, and Fremantle Arts Centre, p. 22

Day tours

Rottnest Island Just off the coast of Perth, the low-key island resort of Rottnest makes for a perfect day tour. Access is via ferry from Fremantle, Perth or Hillarys Boat Harbour. No private cars are permitted: island transport is by foot, bicycle or bus. Visitors to Rottnest can divide their time between the beach and the scenic and historic attractions of the island. *For more details see pp. 30–1*

Darling Range Follow the Great Eastern Highway for a tour of the Darling Range and its 80 000 hectares of escarpment and jarrah forest in the Hills Forest area. Highlights include a scenic drive through John Forrest National Park and a visit to the huge, forest-fringed Mundaring Weir. *For more details see pp. 32–3*

Swan Valley A premier winegrowing district, with vineyards along the scenic Swan River. Other attractions include the historic town of Guildford; Woodbridge House, a Victorian mansion in West Midland; Walyunga National Park; and Whiteman Park, a 2500-hectare area that includes Caversham Wildlife Park. *For more details see pp. 32–3*

Yanchep National Park On the coast north of Perth, Yanchep has long been one of the city's favourite recreation areas. Have your photo taken with a koala; see didgeridoo and dance performances; or take a guided tour of Crystal Cave, where stalactites hang above the inky waters of an underground pool.

FREMANTLE

Getting around

By car A drive of 20–30 minutes, either via Stirling Highway on the north bank of the Swan River or via Canning Highway on the south.

By train A 30-minute journey from Perth Railway Station, Wellington Street. Trains depart every 15 minutes on weekdays and less frequently on weekends.

By bus Many buses and routes link both cities. Timetables and route details from Transperth 13 6213.

By ferry Various ferry operators travel twice daily between Perth and Fremantle, departing Barrack Street Jetty, Perth. *See Getting around, p. 23*

Combined travel packages For combined ferry, train and 'tram' tours of Perth and Fremantle, contact either Fremantle Tram Tours (08) 9433 6674 or Perth Tram Company (08) 9322 2006.

Once you've arrived Look out for the free orange CAT bus, which runs regular services from Victoria Quay, through the city centre and down to South Fremantle. 'Tram' tours are another option, departing hourly between 10am and 5pm from the town hall.

Top events

St Patrick's Day Parade and Concert Celebrates the Irish national holiday with much gusto. MARCH.

Fremantle Street Arts Festival Local, national and international buskers perform on the streets. EASTER.

Freo's West Coast Blues 'n Roots Festival Day-long celebration of blues, roots, reggae and rock, with many big-name acts. APRIL.

Blessing of the Fleet Traditional Italian blessing of the fishing fleet. OCTOBER.

Fremantle Festival Performing arts and community activities culminating in a street parade and dance party. NOVEMBER.

CAPE LEVEQUE, KIMBERLEY

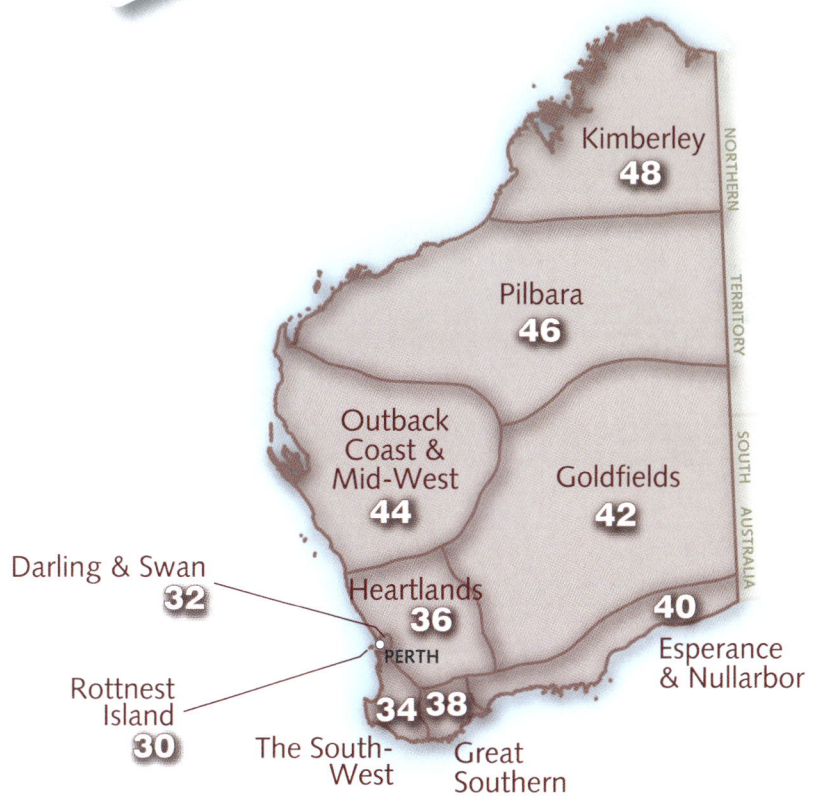

DOLPHIN FEEDING, MONKEY MIA, OUTBACK COAST & MID-WEST

REGIONS
western australia

- Kimberley **48**
- Pilbara **46**
- Outback Coast & Mid-West **44**
- Goldfields **42**
- Darling & Swan **32**
- Heartlands **36**
- PERTH
- Esperance & Nullarbor **40**
- Rottnest Island **30**
- The South-West **34**
- Great Southern **38**

WESTERN AUSTRALIA → REGIONS → ROTTNEST ISLAND

ROTTNEST ISLAND

In azure waters only 18 kilometres from Perth, Rottnest Island's white, sandy beaches are perfect for a range of aquatic pleasures. The island is also home to the famous quokka.

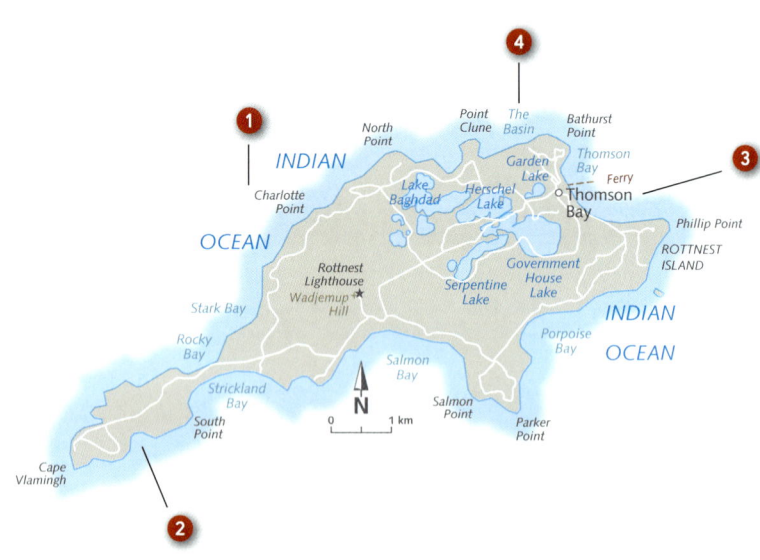

CLIMATE ROTTNEST ISLAND

MONTH	JAN	FEB	MAR	APR	MAY	JUN	JUL	AUG	SEP	OCT	NOV	DEC
MAXIMUM °C	26	27	25	23	20	18	17	17	18	20	22	24
MINIMUM °C	18	19	18	16	14	13	12	12	12	13	15	17
RAIN MM	7	13	14	37	106	156	149	104	61	39	17	10
RAIN DAYS	2	2	4	8	15	18	20	18	14	11	6	3

→ For more details see map 254. For descriptions of 🛈 towns see Towns A–Z (p. 50).

ROTTNEST ISLAND QUOKKA

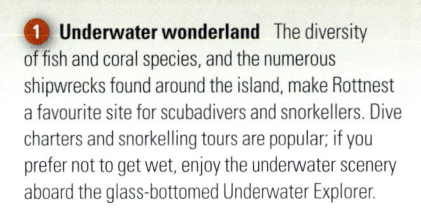

1 Underwater wonderland The diversity of fish and coral species, and the numerous shipwrecks found around the island, make Rottnest a favourite site for scubadivers and snorkellers. Dive charters and snorkelling tours are popular; if you prefer not to get wet, enjoy the underwater scenery aboard the glass-bottomed Underwater Explorer.

2 West End The 'West End' of Rottnest can be reached on an 11-kilometre bike ride along a sealed road, or on a bus tour. There are stunning ocean views from Cape Vlamingh (where you may also spot a humpback whale in winter) and a 1-kilometre heritage trail that affords sightings of wedge-tailed shearwaters, fairy terns, quokkas and bottlenose dolphins.

3 Quokka country The quokka is a native marsupial found primarily on Rottnest Island. It is semi-nocturnal and furry, and grows to the size of a hare. Find the interpretive signs about a kilometre south of Thomson Bay, just before Kingstown Barracks; if you don't see one of the 10 000 quokkas on the island here, then there are good viewing spots along the boardwalk at Garden Lake.

4 The Basin An outer reef surrounds Rottnest, protecting the clear waters and creating calm conditions for family swimming. The Basin is one of a number of beautiful sandy beaches on the eastern end of the island. It is within easy walking distance of Thomson Bay and has basic facilities.

TOP EVENTS

FEB	Rottnest Channel Swim
MAR	The Big Splash (watersports race, Fremantle–Rottnest Island)
JUNE	The State Open Surfing Series
OCT	Marathon and Fun Run
DEC	Rottnest Swim Thru

ISLAND HERITAGE

Known as Wadjemup to the Nyungar people, Rottnest Island was unoccupied when Europeans arrived, although there is evidence of Aboriginal occupation around 7000 years ago when the island was linked to the mainland. The island was given the unflattering name Rotte-nest, meaning 'rats' nest', in 1696 by explorer Willem de Vlamingh, who mistook the island's quokkas for large rats. Europeans settled on the island in 1831. From 1838 to 1903 it was used as a prison for Aboriginal people. During World War I it became an internment camp and in 1917 it was declared an A-class reserve. World War II saw it used as a military post. Many heritage sites can be found, including an original 1840s streetscape – Thomson Bay's Vincent Way. Other interesting sites are the Chapel (1858), the octagonal prison building known as the Quad (1864), the Oliver Hill Gun Battery (1930s) and Rottnest Lighthouse (1859) on Wadjemup Hill.

WESTERN AUSTRALIA → REGIONS → DARLING & SWAN

DARLING & SWAN

Barely half an hour from the centre of Perth are two distinct country landscapes perfect for picnicking, walking, sampling local produce and looking for wildflowers.

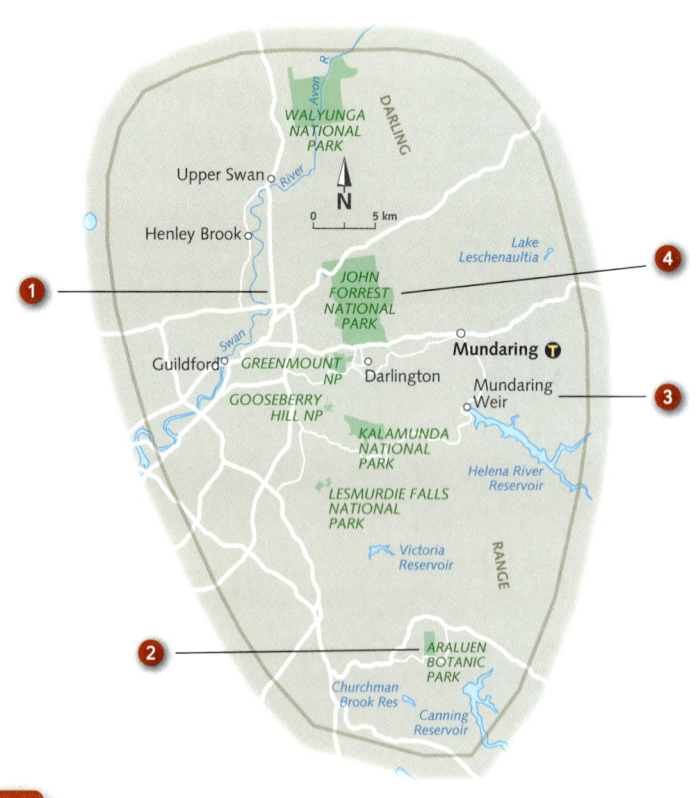

CLIMATE GUILDFORD

MONTH	JAN	FEB	MAR	APR	MAY	JUN	JUL	AUG	SEP	OCT	NOV	DEC
MAXIMUM °C	32	32	30	27	22	19	18	19	21	23	27	30
MINIMUM °C	17	17	15	13	10	8	7	8	9	10	13	15
RAIN MM	8	10	17	43	122	177	172	139	86	56	20	13
RAIN DAYS	2	2	4	7	14	17	19	17	14	11	6	4

→ For more details see map 254. For descriptions of ⓣ towns see Towns A–Z (p. 50).

① **Swan Valley wineries** The Swan Valley region is renowned for its chardonnay, shiraz, chenin blanc and verdelho. It boasts over 40 wineries; of these, Houghton and Sandalford are the best known. For a treat that offers scenery as well as wine-tasting, take a Swan River wineries cruise from Perth.

② **Araluen Botanic Park** Tall forest trees (jarrah, eucalypt and marri) frame the rockpools, cascades and European-style terraces of these beautiful 59-hectare gardens. Established in the 1930s by the Young Australia League, the gardens have picturesque walking trails, picnic and barbecue areas, and, in spring, magnificent tulip displays.

③ **Mundaring Weir** The rolling lawns and bush-clad surrounds of this weir reserve make it ideal for picnics. At the foot of the weir, the Number 1 Pump Station commemorates C. Y. O'Connor's extraordinary engineering feat in piping water to the goldfields some 600 kilometres east. Nearby, at the Hills Forest Discovery Centre, you can sign up for nature-based activities such as bushcraft.

④ **John Forrest National Park** Declared a national park in 1947, John Forrest is one of the oldest and best-loved picnic spots in the Perth Hills. A drive through the park has vantage points with superb views across Perth and the coastal plain. A popular walk is the Heritage Trail on the western edge, past waterfalls and an old rail tunnel.

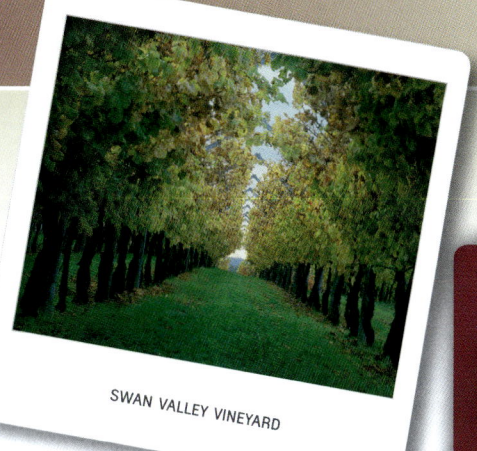

SWAN VALLEY VINEYARD

TOP EVENTS

MAR–APR	Taste of the Valley (food, wine and art festival, throughout Swan Valley)
AUG	Avon Descent (whitewater race down Avon and Swan rivers, from Northam to Perth)
OCT	Spring in the Valley (wine festival, throughout Swan Valley)
NOV	Darlington Arts Festival (Darlington)

HERITAGE SITES

In historic Guildford, roam among yesteryear's farm tools, fashions and household items at the Old Courthouse, Gaol and Museum. Then enjoy a drink at the nearby Rose and Crown Hotel (1841), the oldest trading hotel in the state. The faithfully restored Woodbridge House (1885), picturesquely located on the banks of the Swan River, is a fine example of late-Victorian architecture. And just south of Upper Swan, at Henley Brook on the western bank of the river, All Saints Church (1839–41) is the state's oldest church.

THE SOUTH-WEST

This region is renowned for its world-class wines, excellent surf breaks, towering old-growth forests and the 963-kilometre Bibbulmun Track.

CLIMATE BUSSELTON

MONTH	JAN	FEB	MAR	APR	MAY	JUN	JUL	AUG	SEP	OCT	NOV	DEC
MAXIMUM °C	29	28	26	23	19	17	16	17	18	20	24	27
MINIMUM °C	14	14	13	11	9	8	8	8	8	9	11	13
RAIN MM	10	11	22	42	118	175	167	117	75	52	24	13
RAIN DAYS	3	2	4	8	15	19	22	19	16	13	7	4

→ For more details see map 257. For descriptions of ⓣ towns see Towns A–Z (p. 50).

MEELUP BEACH, DUNSBOROUGH

① Swim with dolphins In Bunbury's Koombana Bay you can swim under ranger guidance with wild bottlenose dolphins. Learn about the dolphins and other marine life at the Dolphin Discovery Centre's interpretive museum and theatre.

② Busselton Jetty Stretching a graceful 2 kilometres into Geographe Bay, this wooden jetty is the longest in the Southern Hemisphere. Built in 1865, the jetty originally serviced American whaling ships. Today a small tourist train takes you from the Interpretive Centre at one end to the Underwater Observatory at the other.

③ Lake Cave One of hundreds of limestone caves in Leeuwin–Naturaliste National Park, magnificent Lake Cave is centred on the incredibly still, eerie waters of an underground lake, which reflects the cave's stunning crystal formations. Its other highlight is the Suspended Table, a huge column hanging precariously from the cave's ceiling.

④ Margaret River This beautiful area has long had a reputation as one of Australia's best wine-producing regions, a reputation that rests principally on its cabernet sauvignon and chardonnay grapes grown on grey-brown, gravelly sandy soils. Try the cabernet from Vasse Felix, Moss Wood and Cullen, and the chardonnay from Leeuwin, Voyager and Ashbrook.

⑤ Blackwood Valley The Blackwood River meanders for 500 kilometres through wheat-belt plains and forested valleys to its broad estuary at Augusta. Secluded spots along the river between Nannup and Alexandra Bridge offer tranquil camping, fishing, swimming and canoeing. The Sheoak Walk is a one-hour loop through the forest close to Nannup.

⑥ Valley of the Giants Gain a unique perspective on the majestic southern forests as you walk through the upper branches of giant tingle and karri trees. East of Walpole, this walkway, 38 metres above the forest floor, is one of the highest and longest of its kind in the world.

TOP EVENTS

FEB–MAR	Leeuwin Estate Concert (near Margaret River)
MAR–APR	Margaret River Pro (surfing competition)
MAY	Margaret River Wine Region Festival (Margaret River)
NOV	Blues at Bridgetown Festival (Bridgetown)
DEC	Ironman Western Australia Triathlon (Busselton)
DEC	Cherry Harmony Festival (Manjimup)

JARRAH, KARRI, TUART AND TINGLE

Western Australia's only forests are in the cool, well-watered South-West. The grey-barked tuart tree grows only on coastal limestone; just outside Busselton is the largest remaining pure tuart forest in the world. Jarrah, a beautifully grained, deep-red hardwood, flourishes between Dwellingup and Collie. The Forest Heritage Centre at Dwellingup has interpretive displays on forest management, and a treetop walk. Forests of karri – one of the world's tallest trees, that can reach 90 metres in 100 years – are found in the wetter areas, from Manjimup to Walpole. Near Pemberton, there are 4000 hectares of protected old-growth karri forest. In Gloucester National Park, is the 61-metre Gloucester Tree, with a spiral ladder to the top. The Valley of the Giants, east of Walpole, is home to towering red tingle trees. Nearby is the 25-metre-wide Giant Red Tingle, a huge fire-hollowed tree that is regarded as one of the ten largest living things on the planet.

HEARTLANDS

WESTERN AUSTRALIA → REGIONS → HEARTLANDS

Dominated by the wheat belt, this region features the Avon Valley, New Norcia and the extraordinary Pinnacles Desert.

CLIMATE NORTHAM

MONTH	JAN	FEB	MAR	APR	MAY	JUN	JUL	AUG	SEP	OCT	NOV	DEC
MAXIMUM °C	34	34	31	26	21	18	17	18	20	24	28	32
MINIMUM °C	17	17	15	12	9	7	5	6	7	9	12	15
RAIN MM	10	13	19	23	57	83	84	62	37	25	12	9
RAIN DAYS	2	2	3	6	11	15	16	14	11	7	4	2

→ For more details see maps 258–9. For descriptions of ⓣ towns see Towns A–Z (p. 50).

WESTERN AUSTRALIA → REGIONS → **HEARTLANDS**

① The Pinnacles Thousands of limestone pillars, the eroded remnants of what was once a thick bed of limestone, create a weirdly beautiful landscape in Nambung National Park. Other park attractions include a beautiful coastline with superb beaches where visitors can fish, swim, snorkel, walk or picnic.

② Avon Valley In the 1860s, bushranger Moondyne Joe hid in the forests, caves and wildflower fields of this lush valley. Now Avon Valley National Park preserves much of the landscape. In the valley's heart, and marking the start of the wheat belt, are the historic towns of Northam and York.

③ Wave Rock and Mulka's Cave Wave Rock, east of Hyden, is a 2.7-billion-year-old piece of granite, 15 metres high and 100 metres long. It looks like a giant wave frozen at the moment of breaking and has vertical bands of colour created by algal growth. To the north is Mulka's Cave, decorated with Aboriginal rock art.

④ New Norcia This town, with its Spanish Colonial architecture, was built in 1846 by Benedictine monks who established a mission for the local Indigenous population. It remains Australia's only monastic town. Visitors can tour the buildings and visit the fascinating museum and art gallery.

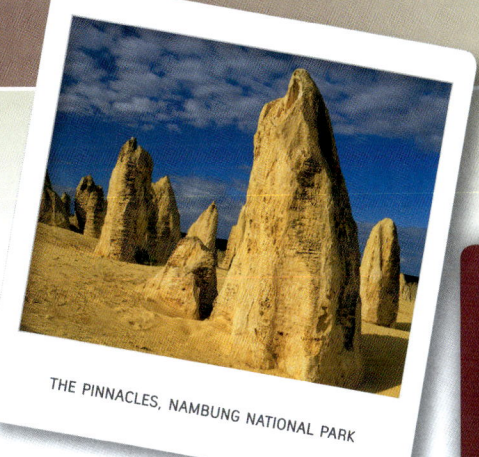

THE PINNACLES, NAMBUNG NATIONAL PARK

TOP EVENTS

JAN	Lancelin Ocean Classic (windsurfing competition)
MAY	Moondyne Festival (Toodyay)
AUG	Avon Descent (whitewater race down Avon and Swan rivers, from Northam to Perth)
SEPT–OCT	Jazz Festival (York)
OCT	Kulin Bush Races (Kulin)
NOV	Blessing of the Fleet (Jurien Bay)

WILDFLOWERS

Western Australia is home to some 12 500 kinds of wildflowers, and the Heartlands is one of the most accessible areas to see magnificent wildflower displays. Top spots include the Chittering Valley near Gingin, Lesueur and Badgingarra national parks near Jurien Bay, and the sand plains around Southern Cross. Up to 20 species of native orchids flourish around Hyden in spring; yellow wattles light up the countryside around Dalwallinu; and massed displays of white, pink and yellow everlastings line the road from Moora to Wubin.

WESTERN AUSTRALIA → REGIONS → GREAT SOUTHERN

GREAT SOUTHERN

This varied region encompasses sheep country, parts of the wheat belt, wineries, surf beaches and the historic town of Albany.

CLIMATE — ALBANY

MONTH	JAN	FEB	MAR	APR	MAY	JUN	JUL	AUG	SEP	OCT	NOV	DEC
MAXIMUM °C	25	25	24	22	19	17	16	16	17	19	21	24
MINIMUM °C	14	14	13	12	10	8	8	7	8	9	11	12
RAIN MM	27	24	28	63	102	103	124	106	82	78	48	25
RAIN DAYS	8	9	11	14	18	19	21	21	18	15	13	10

→ For more details see map 256. For descriptions of 🅣 towns see Towns A–Z (p. 50).

1 Stirling Range National Park The Stirling Range rises abruptly above the surrounding plains; its rock-faces are composed of the sands and silts laid down in the delta of an ancient river. The highest peaks can be veiled in swirling mists, which creates a cool and humid environment that supports a proliferation of flowering plants. Bluff Knoll, at 1073 metres, is one of the state's premier hiking challenges.

2 Great Southern wineries This region has over 40 wineries, extending from Frankland east through Mount Barker to Porongurup. Since the first plantings in 1967, the region has gained an international reputation for its aromatic rieslings. More recently, premium chardonnay, shiraz, cabernet sauvignon and pinot noir are also proving popular. Many of the wineries are open for tastings and sales.

3 Albany Whaleworld The bloody realities of whaling are displayed at the old Cheynes Beach Whaling Station on Frenchman Bay, 25 kilometres south-east of Albany. Visitors can explore *Cheynes IV*, a restored whalechaser, and relive the sights and sounds of the hunt. A 3D theatrette occupies one of the old whale-oil storage tanks.

4 Torndirrup National Park Located 15 minutes from Albany, this park features the Blowholes, the Gap and Natural Bridge, all sculpted into their current form by the treacherous Southern Ocean. Granite outcrops and cliffs alternate with dunes, and sandy heath supports peppermint, banksia and karri. Easy walking trails take in some of the spectacular sights.

5 The Old Farm at Strawberry Hill The Old Farm, near Albany, is a delightful stone cottage on Western Australia's oldest cultivated farm. Originally home to the first government resident in the state, the 1836 building at Strawberry Hill, as it was known, was the centre of Albany's social life in its day. These days the property welcomes swarms of visitors to its picturesque heritage buildings and stunning gardens.

LILY WINDMILL WITH VIEWS OF STIRLING RANGE, AMELUP

TOP EVENTS

JAN	Mount Barker D'Vine Wine Festival (Mount Barker)
JAN	Vintage Blues Festival (Albany)
MAR	Wine Summer Festival (Porongurup)
EASTER	Brave New Works (new performance art, Denmark)
SEPT	Wildflower Display (Cranbrook)
SEPT–OCT	Great Southern Wine Festival (Albany)

ALBANY HERITAGE

Albany, the oldest white settlement in Western Australia, was officially founded on 21 January 1827. The founders were a party of soldiers and convicts, under the command of Major Edmund Lockyer, who had arrived on the *Amity* a month earlier. Albany's magnificent harbour, once commanding the sea lanes running between Europe, Asia and eastern Australia, became a whaling station and later a coaling port for steamships. Museums now occupy several of the town's historic buildings, and a full-size replica of the *Amity* stands next to one of them, the Residency Museum. Stirling Terrace has some evocative Victorian shopfronts, while Princess Royal Fortress on Mount Adelaide has restored buildings and gun emplacements, and offers fine views.

ESPERANCE & NULLARBOR

Esperance's beaches are famed for their white sand and turquoise waters, while to the north-east lies the vast Nullarbor Plain.

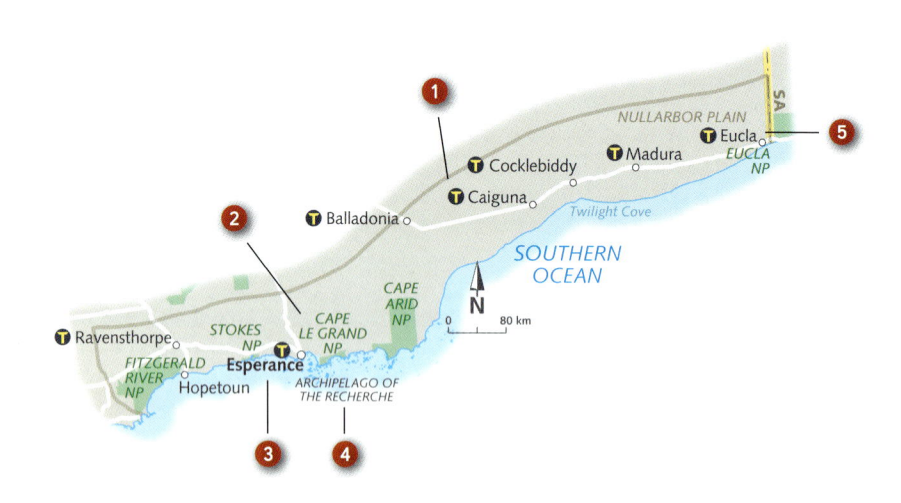

CLIMATE ESPERANCE

MONTH	JAN	FEB	MAR	APR	MAY	JUN	JUL	AUG	SEP	OCT	NOV	DEC
MAXIMUM °C	26	26	25	23	20	18	17	18	19	21	23	25
MINIMUM °C	16	16	15	13	11	9	8	9	10	11	13	14
RAIN MM	22	27	31	43	76	82	98	84	58	50	36	17
RAIN DAYS	6	6	8	11	14	16	17	17	14	12	10	7

→ For more details see maps 258–9. For descriptions of 🅣 towns see Towns A–Z (p. 50).

WESTERN AUSTRALIA → REGIONS → **ESPERANCE & NULLARBOR**

① 90-mile straight Four kilometres west of Caiguna, be sure to have your photo taken beside the signpost marking the eastern end of the longest straight stretch of road in Australia, which runs for 90 miles (146.6 kilometres) between Caiguna and a point east of Balladonia.

② Cape Le Grand National Park Swimming beaches, sheltered coves, heathlands, sand plains and the Whistling Rock are all features of this park, 56 kilometres east of Esperance. There are easy walking trails and two camping areas. Scenic spots include Thistle Cove, Hellfire Bay and Lucky Bay (where luck might have you spot a kangaroo on the beach).

③ Great Ocean Drive A 38-kilometre circuit drive explores the coast west of Esperance. Attractions include Australia's first wind farm, sheltered swimming at Twilight Cove, and Pink Lake, rendered lipstick-colour by algae. There are coastal lookouts, and sightings of southern right whales from June to October.

④ Archipelago of the Recherche This group of 105 granite islands and 1500 islets stretches for 250 kilometres along the Esperance coast. Boat tours, available from Esperance, may provide sightings of fur seals, sea lions, dolphins and, in season, southern right whales. Visitors can stay overnight in safari huts or camp on Woody Island.

⑤ Eucla This isolated outpost was established in 1877 as a telegraph station; today coastal dunes partially obscure the station's ruins. On the beach, a lonely jetty stretches out into startlingly blue waters, and in Eucla National Park you can wander among the rippling Delisser Sandhills.

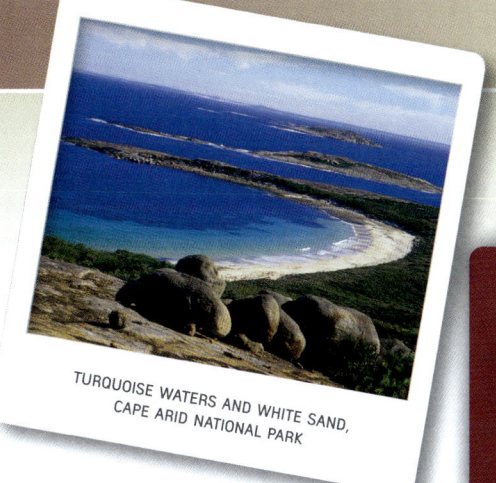

TURQUOISE WATERS AND WHITE SAND, CAPE ARID NATIONAL PARK

TOP EVENTS

JAN	Summer Festival (Hopetoun)
SEPT	Wildflower Show (Ravensthorpe)
SEPT	Wildflower Show (Esperance)
OCT	Agricultural Show (Esperance)

THE NULLARBOR

The Nullarbor is one of the country's essential touring experiences. This 250 000-square-kilometre treeless limestone slab was initially part of the seabed, and has been formed in part by deposits of marine fossils. The terrain is riddled with sinkholes, caverns and caves, only some of which are open to the public. Murrawijinie Caves include Koonalda Cave, which is open to the public and contains rock art that dates back 20 000 years. Although it can seem featureless, the country is far from monotonous, particularly where the highway veers to the coast for a view of dramatic cliffs and the wild Southern Ocean, and perhaps a lucky sighting of migrating southern right whales.

GOLDFIELDS

Gold continues to be mined in this region, while sheep stations the size of small nations produce fine wool. The area offers an excellent opportunity to delve into its fascinating heritage.

CLIMATE: KALGOORLIE–BOULDER

MONTH	JAN	FEB	MAR	APR	MAY	JUN	JUL	AUG	SEP	OCT	NOV	DEC
MAXIMUM °C	34	32	30	25	20	18	17	18	22	26	29	32
MINIMUM °C	18	18	16	12	8	6	5	5	8	11	14	17
RAIN MM	22	28	19	19	28	31	26	20	15	16	18	15
RAIN DAYS	3	4	4	5	7	8	9	7	5	4	4	3

→ For more details see maps 258–9. For descriptions of Ⓣ towns see Towns A–Z (p. 50).

GWALIA MINE SITE

1 North of Kalgoorlie The town of Menzies has 130 people and several intact old buildings, while Kookynie has retained its spacious 1894 Grand Hotel. Gwalia, almost a ghost town, has a museum, the restored State Hotel and tin houses preserved in their lived-in state. Laverton, 100 kilometres east, has historic buildings saved by the nickel industry.

2 Coolgardie The 100-plus street markers scattered through Coolgardie are a good introduction to this town, the first settlement in the eastern goldfields. Coolgardie's splendid historic buildings include the Marble Bar Hotel, now the RSL, and the 1898 Warden's Court. The latter is an architectural treasure and houses the comprehensive Goldfields Exhibition Museum and the visitor centre.

3 Peak Charles National Park In this park south-west of Norseman, granite mountains rise in wave-cut platforms to a height of 651 metres. Walking trails to the summit of Peak Charles and its twin, Peak Eleanora, should only be attempted in favourable weather, but at the top are fantastic views across saltpans, sand plains and dry woodlands.

4 Kalgoorlie–Boulder Kalgoorlie–Boulder produces half of Australia's gold. Take a circuit of the open-cut Superpit on the Loopline Railway, see the gold vault at the Museum of the Goldfields, and sample the rigours of 1890s mining at the Australian Prospectors and Miners Hall of Fame.

TOP EVENTS

FEB	Undies 500 Car Rally (Kalgoorlie–Boulder)
MAR	Norseman Cup (horseracing, Norseman)
MAY–JUNE	Leonora Golden Gift and Festival (Leonora)
SEPT	Race Round (horseracing, Kalgoorlie–Boulder)
SEPT–OCT	Metal Detecting Championships (Coolgardie, odd-numbered years)
OCT	Balzano Barrow Race (Kanowna to Kalgoorlie–Boulder)

GOLDFIELDS HISTORY

The discovery of gold in the region in 1892 secured the economic success of Western Australia. Since then, goldmines from Norseman to Laverton have yielded well over 1000 tonnes. A railway from Perth in 1896 and a water pipeline in 1903 helped Kalgoorlie and Boulder sustain a population of 30 000, the liquor requirements of which were met by 93 hotels. By 1900, surface gold was exhausted and big companies went underground. Exhausted mines have left a belt of ghost towns north of Kalgoorlie, while nickel mining since the 1960s has allowed towns such as Kambalda, Leonora and Laverton to survive.

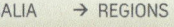

OUTBACK COAST & MID-WEST

This vast area is known for the richness and rarity of its natural features, from colourful Ningaloo Reef to the eroded cliffs and gorges of Kalbarri National Park.

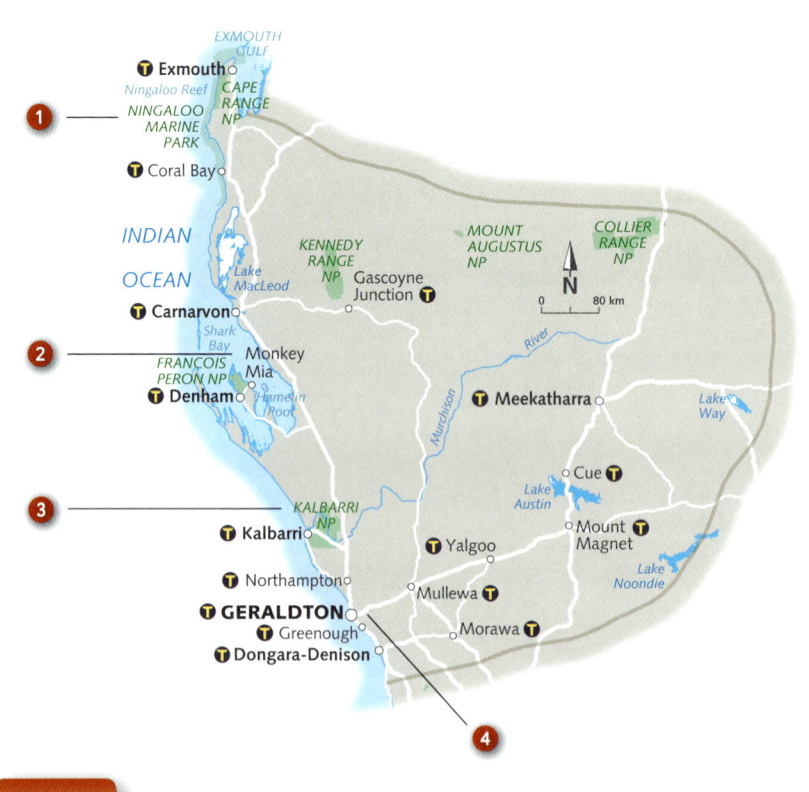

CLIMATE: CARNARVON

MONTH	JAN	FEB	MAR	APR	MAY	JUN	JUL	AUG	SEP	OCT	NOV	DEC
MAXIMUM °C	31	33	31	29	26	23	22	23	24	26	27	29
MINIMUM °C	22	23	22	19	15	12	11	12	14	16	19	21
RAIN MM	12	21	16	14	38	48	47	19	6	6	4	2
RAIN DAYS	2	3	2	3	5	7	7	5	3	2	1	1

→ For more details see maps 258 & 261. For descriptions of ⓣ towns see Towns A–Z (p. 50).

1 Ningaloo Reef Ningaloo Marine Park protects the state's largest reef, a stunning underwater landscape of fish and coral located directly off the beach. For a quintessential Ningaloo experience, take a swim with the whale sharks – this is one of the few places in the world where they come close to shore. These gentle giants migrate to the reef between March and June; tours can be arranged in Exmouth.

2 Monkey Mia The wild bottlenose dolphins of Monkey Mia are world famous for their daily morning ritual of swimming into the shallows to be handfed with fish. Under the guidance of rangers, visitors can wander into the water and witness this rare event. For a total marine encounter, dugong-watching cruises can also be arranged from here.

3 Kalbarri National Park This park is best known for its 80 kilometres of gorges carved out by the Murchison River. Watersports are popular on the river's lower reaches. The park is also one of the world's richest wildflower areas. Dolphins, whale sharks and whales frequent the coastal waters, and the fishing is excellent.

4 Geraldton Geralton is surrounded by superb swimming and surfing beaches, but if you prefer architecture to aquatics follow the Hawes Heritage Trail, which highlights the remarkable church buildings (1915–39) of architect-priest Monsignor John Cyril Hawes. In Geraldton, the Byzantine-styled St Francis Xavier Cathedral is considered to be one of Hawes' masterpieces.

AN UNDERWATER LANDSCAPE OF FISH AND CORAL, NINGALOO REEF

TOP EVENTS

MAR	Sport Fishing Classic (Kalbarri)
MAR	Gamex (gamefishing competition, Exmouth)
APR–MAY	Whale Shark Festival (Exmouth)
AUG–SEPT	Mullewa Wildflower Show (Mullewa)
OCT	Airing of the Quilts (Northampton)
OCT	Sunshine Festival (Geraldton)

SHARK BAY

World Heritage–listed Shark Bay is a sunny paradise of bays, inlets and shallow azure waters, blessed with a great number of unusual features. It boasts the world's most diverse and abundant examples of stromatolites – the world's oldest living fossils – which dot the shores of Hamelin Pool in rocky lumps. The bay region supports the largest number and greatest area of seagrass species in the world. Covering 4000 square kilometres, these vast underwater meadows are home to around 14 000 dugongs, 10 per cent of the world's total number. The bay's extraordinary marine population also includes humpback whales resting on their long migrations, manta rays, green and loggerhead turtles and, most famously, the dolphins that regularly visit Monkey Mia.

PILBARA

Home to the ochre-hued Hamersley Range, this region is characterised by rust-red landscapes and vast tidal flats broken by mangroves.

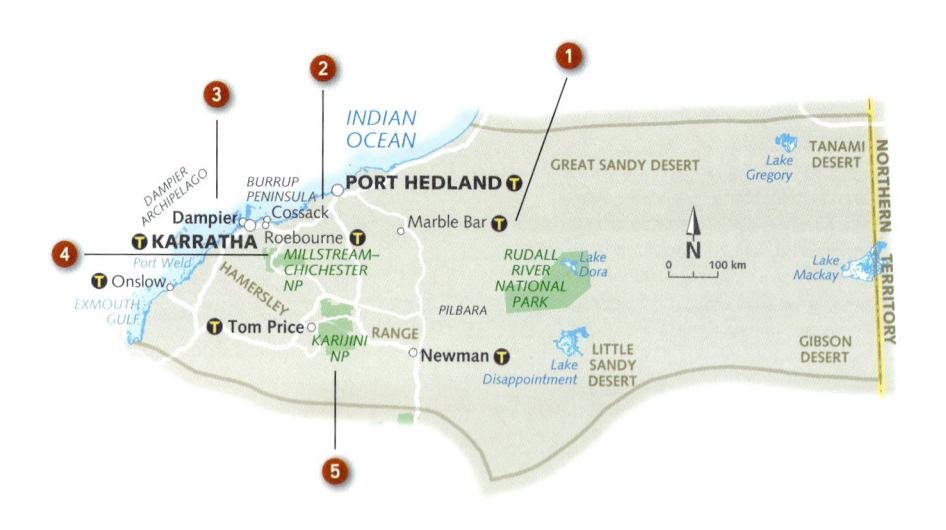

CLIMATE ROEBOURNE

MONTH	JAN	FEB	MAR	APR	MAY	JUN	JUL	AUG	SEP	OCT	NOV	DEC
MAXIMUM °C	39	38	38	35	30	27	27	29	32	35	38	39
MINIMUM °C	26	26	25	22	18	15	14	15	17	20	23	25
RAIN MM	59	67	63	30	29	30	14	5	1	1	1	10
RAIN DAYS	3	5	3	1	3	3	2	1	0	0	0	1

→ For more details see maps 262–3. For descriptions of ⊤ towns see Towns A–Z (p. 50).

MILLSTREAM–CHICHESTER NATIONAL PARK

1 Marble Bar The mining town of Marble Bar has gained the dubious reputation as the hottest town in Australia. For 161 consecutive days in 1923–24, the temperature in town did not drop below 37.8° Celsius. The heart of the town is the Ironclad Hotel, a classic outback pub where you can enjoy a counter meal and that cold beer you're going to need. You can also experience Marble Bar's goldmining past at Comet Gold Mine, a museum and tourist centre.

2 Cossack This first port in the north-west was built between 1870 and 1898, and is now a ghost town. Many buildings have been restored. The old post office houses a gallery and the courthouse has a museum, while the police barracks offer budget accommodation.

3 Pilbara islands The Dampier Archipelago and the Montebello and Mackerel islands seem a far-flung beach paradise from the industrial ports of the Pilbara. In reality, the nearest islands – those of the Dampier Archipelago – are just 20 minutes by boat from Dampier. These islands are a haven for marine life, including turtles, dolphins and migrating humpback whales, and are a renowned location for fishing.

4 Millstream–Chichester National Park
Located within the arid beauty of Millstream–Chichester National Park, spring-fed Chinderwarriner Pool has an almost mirage-like quality. Encircled by remnant rainforest, the oasis is a haven for a range of plants and animals, many of them rare. Visit historic Millstream homestead, and take a refreshing dip in the pool.

5 Karijini National Park Karijini was the name given to this area by the original inhabitants, the Banjima. It is renowned for extraordinary gorges, multicoloured walls, and hidden pools and waterfalls. Brilliant wildflowers carpet the rust-red hills in spring. Camping is available inside the park.

TOP EVENTS

MAR	Campdraft and Rodeo (Newman)
MAY	Welcome to Hedland Night (Port Hedland)
JULY	Roebourne Cup (horseracing, Roebourne)
AUG	FeNaCING Festival (Karratha)
SEPT	Pilbara Music Festival (Port Hedland)

HAMERSLEY RANGE RESOURCES

One of the world's richest deposits of iron ore was discovered in Hamersley Range in 1962, spearheading the Hamersley Iron Project. Towns with swimming pools, gardens and golf courses then sprang up in this landscape of mulga scrub, spinifex and red mountains. Visitors can inspect open-cut mines at Tom Price and Newman. At Dampier and Port Hedland there are iron-ore shipping ports; the latter boasts the largest iron-ore export centre in Australia. Offshore from Karratha is the massive North West Shelf Gas Project; a visitor centre at the processing plant on Burrup Peninsula explains its operations.

KIMBERLEY

Covering more than 420 000 square kilometres, this is an ancient landscape of mighty ranges, spectacular gorges and arid desert.

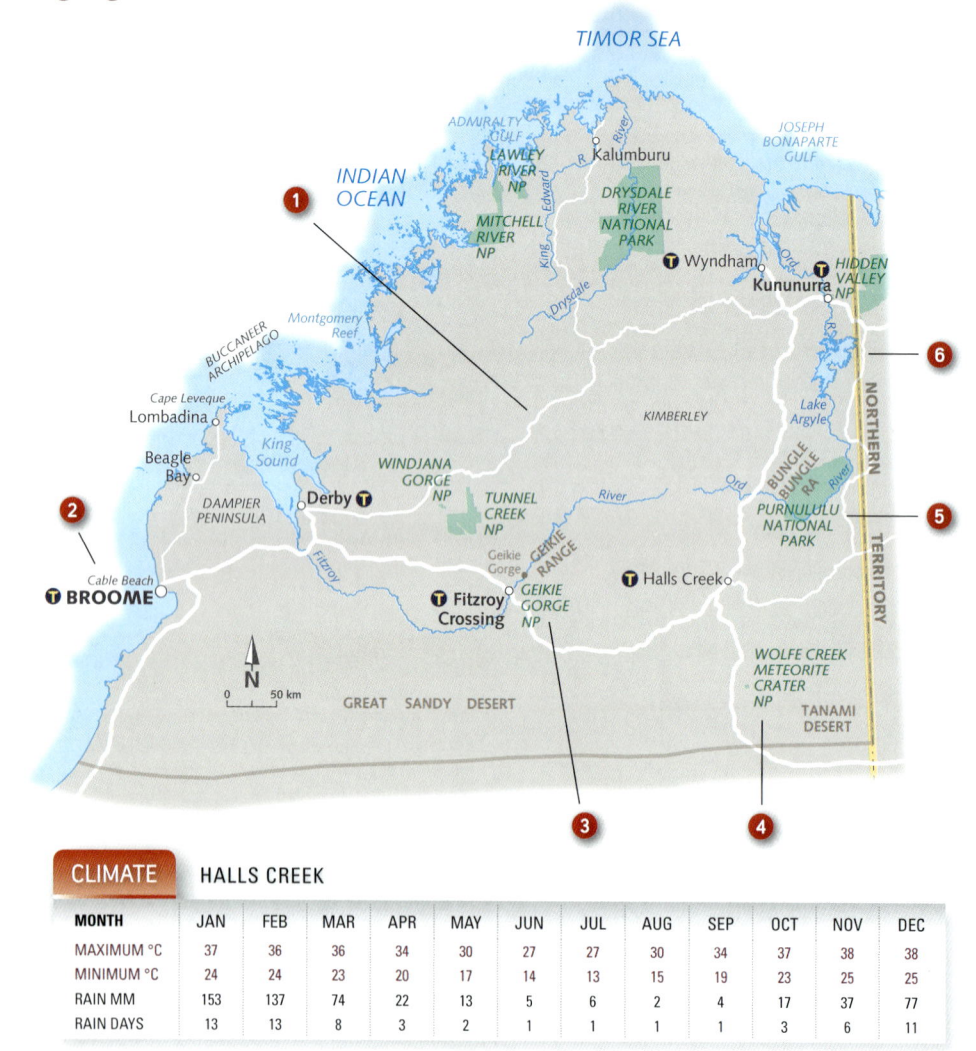

CLIMATE — HALLS CREEK

MONTH	JAN	FEB	MAR	APR	MAY	JUN	JUL	AUG	SEP	OCT	NOV	DEC
MAXIMUM °C	37	36	36	34	30	27	27	30	34	37	38	38
MINIMUM °C	24	24	23	20	17	14	13	15	19	23	25	25
RAIN MM	153	137	74	22	13	5	6	2	4	17	37	77
RAIN DAYS	13	13	8	3	2	1	1	1	1	3	6	11

→ For more details see maps 268–9. For descriptions of ⓣ towns see Towns A–Z (p. 50).

BUNGLE BUNGLE RANGE, PURNULULU NATIONAL PARK

1 Gibb River Road One of Australia's premier four-wheel-drive destinations, the Gibb River Road is a 649-kilometre outback adventure between Derby and Kununurra, traversing some of the most spectacular gorge country of the Kimberley. Highlights of the rugged and diverse landscape include the many gorges, where waterfalls and crystal-clear pools are fringed by palms and pandanus.

2 Port of pearls Broome's attractions include its tropical climate, cosmopolitan character and world-famous pearling industry. Enjoy a camel ride at sunset along Cable Beach, renowned as one of the most beautiful beaches in the world.

3 Geikie Gorge The Fitzroy River cuts through the Geikie Range to create a 7-kilometre gorge just north-east of Fitzroy Crossing. The riverbanks are inhabited by freshwater crocodiles, fruit bats and many bird species, and the only way to see the gorge is by boat – during the Dry.

4 Wolfe Creek Crater Two hours south of Halls Creek by unsealed road is the world's second largest meteorite crater. It is 850 metres across and was probably formed by a meteorite weighing at least several thousand tonnes crashing to earth a million years ago. It is most impressive from the air; scenic flights run from Halls Creek.

5 Purnululu National Park A rough track off the Great Northern Highway leads to the spectacular Bungle Bungle Range in Purnululu National Park, on the Ord River. A fantastic landscape of huge black-and-orange sandstone domes is intersected by narrow, palm-lined gorges where pools reflect sunlight off sheer walls.

6 Lake Argyle Lake Argyle was formed in the 1960s as part of the Ord River Scheme, the success of which is evident in the lush crops within its irrigation area. It has transformed a dusty, million-acre cattle station into a habitat for waterbirds, fish and crocodiles; the hills and ridges of the former station have become islands.

TOP EVENTS

APR–MAY	King Tide Day (celebrating Australia's highest tide, Derby)
MAY	Ord Valley Muster (Kununurra)
JULY	Boab Festival (mardi gras, mud football and Stockmen and Bushies weekend, Derby)
JULY	Rodeo (Fitzroy Crossing)
AUG	Opera Under the Stars (Broome)
AUG–SEPT	Shinju Matsuri (Festival of the Pearl, Broome)

ABORIGINAL ART

The Kimberley is one of Australia's most important regions for Aboriginal rock art. It is renowned for two styles – the Bradshaw and the Wandjina. The Bradshaw figures are painted in red ochre. One rock-face frieze shows figures dancing and swaying; another depicts figures elaborate with headdresses, tassels, skirts and epaulets. Significant Bradshaw sites have been found on the Drysdale River. The more recent Wandjina figures, depictions of ancestor spirits from the sky and sea who brought rain and fertility, are in solid red or black, outlined in red ochre, and sometimes on a white background. Wandjina figures are typically human-like, with pallid faces and wide, staring eyes, halos around their heads and, for reasons of religious belief, no mouths. Good examples of Wandjina art have been found near Kalumburu on the King Edward River and at the burial site known as Panda-Goornnya on the Drysdale River.

TOWNS A-Z
western australia

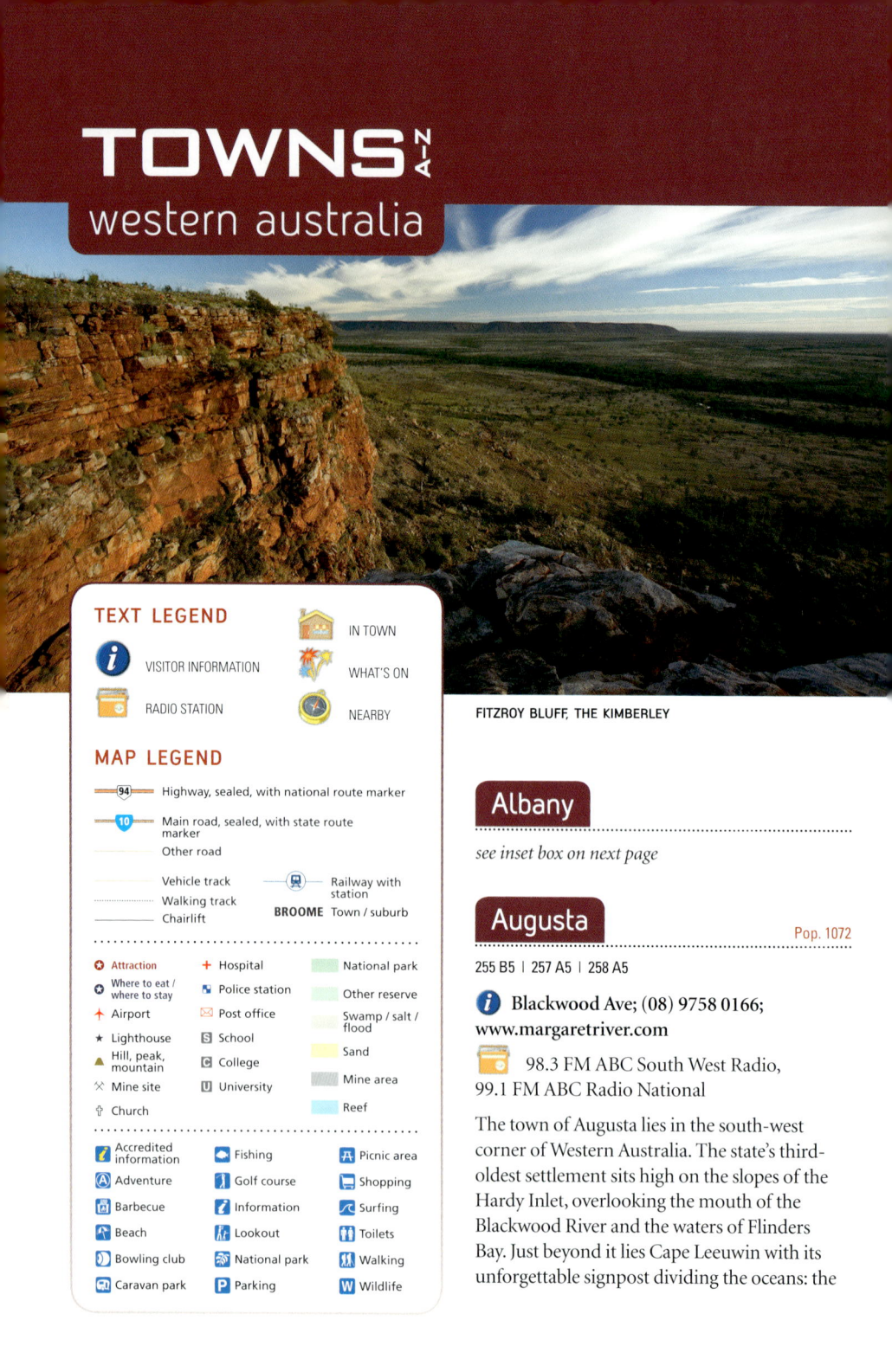

TEXT LEGEND

- VISITOR INFORMATION
- RADIO STATION
- IN TOWN
- WHAT'S ON
- NEARBY

FITZROY BLUFF, THE KIMBERLEY

MAP LEGEND

- **94** Highway, sealed, with national route marker
- **10** Main road, sealed, with state route marker
- Other road
- Vehicle track
- Walking track
- Chairlift
- Railway with station
- **BROOME** Town / suburb

- Attraction
- Where to eat / where to stay
- Airport
- Lighthouse
- Hill, peak, mountain
- Mine site
- Church
- Hospital
- Police station
- Post office
- School
- College
- University
- National park
- Other reserve
- Swamp / salt / flood
- Sand
- Mine area
- Reef

- Accredited information
- Adventure
- Barbecue
- Beach
- Bowling club
- Caravan park
- Fishing
- Golf course
- Information
- Lookout
- National park
- Parking
- Picnic area
- Shopping
- Surfing
- Toilets
- Walking
- Wildlife

Albany

see inset box on next page

Augusta
Pop. 1072

255 B5 | 257 A5 | 258 A5

Blackwood Ave; (08) 9758 0166; www.margaretriver.com

98.3 FM ABC South West Radio, 99.1 FM ABC Radio National

The town of Augusta lies in the south-west corner of Western Australia. The state's third-oldest settlement sits high on the slopes of the Hardy Inlet, overlooking the mouth of the Blackwood River and the waters of Flinders Bay. Just beyond it lies Cape Leeuwin with its unforgettable signpost dividing the oceans: the

Southern Ocean to the south and the Indian Ocean to the west.

Augusta Historical Museum Augusta's difficult beginning in 1830 is documented in this collection of artefacts and photographs. An exhibit details the 1986 rescue of whales that beached themselves near the town. Blackwood Ave; (08) 9758 0465.

Crafters Croft: locally made handcrafts, jams, emu-oil products; Ellis St.

Augusta River Festival: Mar. *Spring Flower Show:* Sept/Oct.

Leeuwin–Naturaliste National Park This park extends 120 km from Cape Naturaliste in the north to Cape Leeuwin in the south. Close to Augusta are three major attractions: Cape Leeuwin, Jewel Cave and Hamelin Bay. Cape Leeuwin (8 km sw) marks the most south-westerly point of Australia. Climb 176 steps to the top of the limestone lighthouse, mainland Australia's tallest. Nearby is the Old Water Wheel, built in 1895 from timber that has since calcified, giving it the appearance of stone. Jewel Cave (8 km NW on Caves Rd) is renowned for its limestone formations, including the longest straw stalactite found in any tourist cave. At Hamelin Bay (18 km NW) a windswept beach and the skeleton of an old jetty give little indication of the massive amounts of jarrah and karri that were once transported from here. In the heyday of the local timber industry, the port's exposure to the treacherous north-west winds resulted in 11 wrecks. These now form the state's most unusual Heritage Trail: the Hamelin Bay Wreck Trail, for experienced divers. *See also Margaret River and Dunsborough.*

The Landing Place: where the first European settlers landed in 1830; 3 km S. *Whale Rescue Memorial:* commemorates the 1986 rescue of beached pilot whales; 4 km S. *Matthew Flinders Memorial:* Flinders began mapping the Australian coastline from Cape Leeuwin in December 1801; 5 km S. *Alexandra Bridge:* picnic and camping spot with towering jarrah trees and beautiful wildflowers in season; 10 km N. *Boranup Maze and Lookout:* the maze offers a short walking track under trellis, while the lookout provides a picnic area with panoramic views towards the coast; 18 km N. *Augusta–Busselton Heritage Trail:* 100 km trail traces the history of the area through the pioneering Bussell and Molloy families, who settled in Augusta only to move further up the coast looking for suitable agricultural land; maps from visitor centre. *Cruises:* Blackwood River and Hardy Inlet. *Marron in season:* fishing licence required and available at the post office; Blackwood Ave. *Whale-watching:* charter boats and coastal vantage points offer sightings of migrating humpback whales (June–Aug) and southern right whales (June–Oct), plus pods of dolphins and fur seals; details from visitor centre.

See also THE SOUTH-WEST, pp. 34–5

Australind

Pop. 8716

255 C2 | 257 B4 | 258 B4

Henton Cottage, cnr Old Coast and Paris rds; (08) 9796 0122.

95.7 Hot FM, 1224 AM ABC Radio National

Lying on the Leschenault Estuary and bordered by the Collie River, Australind offers a multitude of aquatic pleasures including fishing, crabbing, prawning, swimming, boating, sailing and windsurfing. The town's unusual name is a contraction of Australia and India, coined by its founders in the hope of a prosperous trade in horses between the two countries.

St Nicholas Church: built in 1840, reputedly the smallest church in Australia;

continued on p. 55

RADIO STATION   IN TOWN   WHAT'S ON   NEARBY

ALBANY Pop. 25 197

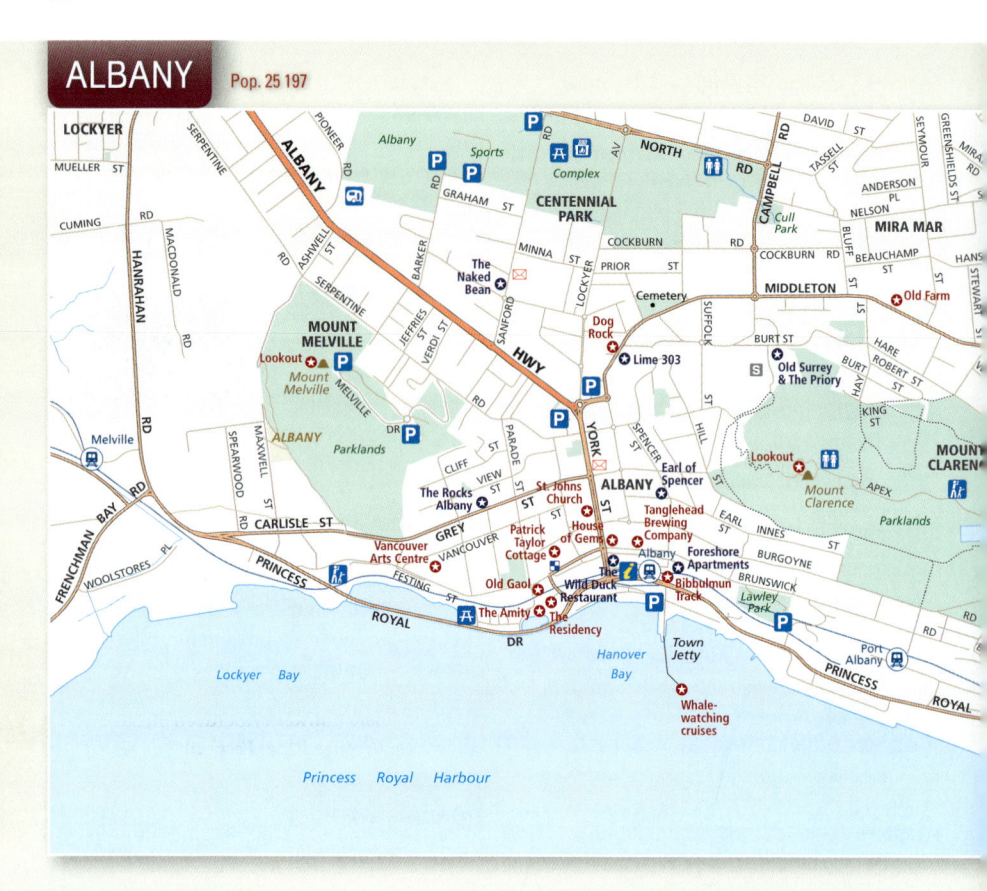

256 B6 | 257 D5 | 258 C5

ⓘ Old Railway Station, Proudlove Pde; (08) 9841 9290 or 1800 644 088; www.albanytourist.com.au

100.9 FM Albany Community Radio, 630 AM ABC Local Radio

Albany, a picturesque city on Western Australia's south coast, is the site of the state's first European settlement. On Boxing Day 1826, Major Edmund Lockyer, with a party of soldiers and convicts from New South Wales, came ashore to establish a military and penal outpost. Ninety years later, Albany was the embarkation point for Australian troops during World War I and, for many, their last view of the continent.

A whaling industry, which began in the 1940s, defined the town until the Cheynes Beach Whaling Company closed in 1978. Nowadays, whale-watching has taken its place. Lying within the protected shelter of the Princess Royal Harbour on the edge of King George Sound, Albany is one of the state's most popular tourist destinations.

Historic buildings Albany boasts more than 50 buildings of historical significance dating back to the early years of the settlement. Two of the oldest were built in the 1830s: Patrick Taylor Cottage on Duke St, which houses an extensive collection of period costumes and household goods, and the Old Farm at Strawberry Hill on Middleton Rd, site

of gemstones and jewellery; Cnr York St and Stirling Tce. **Dog Rock:** granite outcrop resembling the head of an enormous labrador is a photo opportunity not to be missed; Middleton Rd. **Princess Royal Fortress:** commissioned in 1893, Albany's first federal fortress was fully operational until the 1950s; off Forts Rd. **Tanglehead Brewing Company:** award-winning ales; Stirling Tce. **Spectacular views:** lookouts at the peaks of Mt Clarence and Mt Melville have 360-degree views. Near the top of Mt Clarence is the Desert Mounted Corps Memorial statue, a recast of the original statue erected at Suez in 1932; Apex Dr. John Barnesby Memorial Lookout at the top of Mt Melville is 23 m high, with observation decks; Melville Dr. **Bibbulmun Track:** 963 km walking track to Perth begins at Albany's Old Railway Station in Proudlove Pde; *see below*. **Whale-watching:** cruises daily from town jetty to see southern rights; June–Oct.

Farmers markets: Aberdeen St; Sat mornings. **Vintage Blues Festival:** Jan. **Great Southern Wine Festival:** Feb.

Bibbulmun Track At 963 km, this is WA's only long-distance walking trail and one of the longest continuously marked trails in Australia. It stretches from Kalamunda, a suburb on the outskirts of Perth, to Albany. On the way it passes through some of the state's most picturesque southern towns including Dwellingup, Collie, Balingup, Pemberton, Northcliffe, Walpole and Denmark. Named after a local Aboriginal language group, the track is marked by a stylised image of the 'Waugal' (rainbow serpent), a spirit being from the Aboriginal Dreaming. Whether taking a short walk or a 5-day hike, easy access points enable walkers of all ages and fitness levels to experience the Bibbulmun Track. Walk the track in springtime and see the bush at its best with

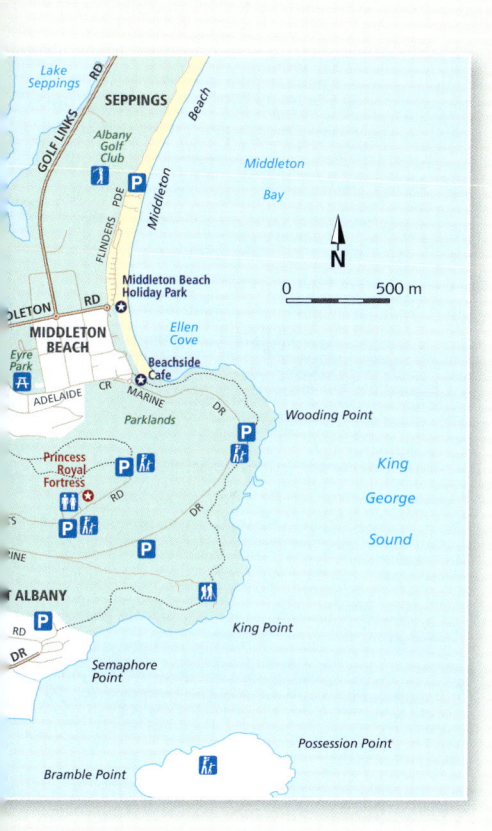

of the first government farm in WA. Other heritage buildings include the Old Gaol (1851), with its collection of social history artefacts, and The Residency (1850s), a showcase of historical and environmental exhibits, both in Residency Rd. There are self-guide walks available, including the Colonial Buildings Historical Walk; brochures from visitor centre.

The Amity: full-scale replica of the brig that brought Albany's first settlers from Sydney in 1826; Princess Royal Dr. **St. John's Church:** 1848 Anglican church is the oldest in the state; York St. **Vancouver Arts Centre:** gallery, craft shop, studio and workshop complex, originally the Albany Cottage Hospital (1887); Vancouver St. **House of Gems:** extensive range

continued overleaf

RADIO STATION   IN TOWN   WHAT'S ON   NEARBY

ALBANY continued

ALBANY'S TOWN HALL

WA's amazing array of wildflowers. Near Walpole you'll encounter the massive red tingle trees of the Valley of the Giants. Other well-known natural attractions on the track include Mt Cook, the highest point in the Darling Range, Beedelup Falls and the Gloucester Tree lookout. Details and maps from the Bibbulmun Track Office of DEC (08) 9334 0265 or visit www.bibbulmuntrack.org.au

Torndirrup National Park Torndirrup is one of the most visited parks in the state, featuring abundant wildflowers, wildlife and bushwalking trails. The park is renowned for its rugged coastal scenery, including such features as the Gap, a chasm with a 24 m drop to the sea, and the Natural Bridge, a span of granite eroded by huge seas to form a giant arch. Exercise extreme caution on this dangerous coastline; king waves can rush in unexpectedly. 17 km s.

Whale World Even before the Cheynes Beach Whaling Company closed in 1978, Albany's oldest industry was a major tourist attraction. In its heyday, the company's chasers took up to 850 whales a season. View the restored whale-chaser *Cheynes IV*, whale skeletons, the old processing factory, an aircraft display and the world's largest collection of marine mammal paintings. This is the only whaling museum in the world created from a working whaling station. Free guided tours are available on (08) 9844 4021. 25 km SE.

Albany Marron & Bird Park: tour the aquaculture production tanks full of marron, see over 250 native and exotic birds, and enjoy a meal at Nippers Cafe; 304 Two Peoples Bay Rd; 23 km E. *Deer-O-Dome:* showcases the Australian deer industry; 6 km N. *Mt Romance Sandalwood Factory:* skincare products, perfumes, therapeutics and free guided tours; (08) 9845 6888; 12 km N. *Albany Wind Farm:* 12 giant turbines, each 100 m high; 12 km SW. *Pt Possession Heritage Trail:* views and interpretive plaques; Vancouver Peninsula; 20 km SE. *Fishing:* Emu Pt (8 km NE), Oyster Harbour (15 km NE), Jimmy Newhill's Harbour (20 km s) and Frenchman Bay (25 km SE). *Diving:* former HMAS *Perth* was scuttled in 2001 as an artificial dive reef; Frenchman Bay; 25 km SE. *West Cape Howe National Park:* walking, fishing, swimming and hang-gliding; 30 km W. *Two Peoples Bay Nature Reserve:* sanctuary for the noisy scrub bird, thought to be extinct but rediscovered in 1961; 40 km E. *Tours:* include sailing, wineries, eco-tours, 4WD driving and national parks tours; details from visitor centre.

See also GREAT SOUTHERN, pp. 38–9

at only 3.6 m wide and 8.2 m long; Paris Rd. **Henton Cottage:** early 1840s heritage building now houses the visitor centre and an art and craft gallery; Cnr Old Coast and Paris rds. **Featured Wood Gallery:** fine furniture and craft made from the local timbers of jarrah, she-oak, marri, banksia and blackbutt. Also includes a museum of Australian and American West history; Piggott Dr; (08) 9797 2411. **Pioneer Memorial:** site of the first settlers' landing in 1840; Old Coast Rd. **Cathedral Ave:** scenic 2 km drive through arching paperbark trees with sightings of kangaroos and black swans, especially at sunset; off Old Coast Rd.

Carols in the Park: Dec.

Leschenault Inlet Offers recreational attractions from the simple pleasure of fishing from the Leschenault Inlet Fishing Groyne to picnicking, camping and bushwalking in the Peninsula Conservation Park. The park is a haven for native wildlife with over 60 species of birds recorded. Only walking or cycling is permitted in the park except for 4WD beach access from Buffalo Rd (1 km s). The Leschenault Waterway Discovery Centre has an interpretive gazebo with information on the estuary environment. Old Coast Rd; 2 km s.

Pioneer Cemetery: graves dating back to 1842 and beautiful wildflowers in season; Old Coast Rd; 2 km n. **Binningup and Myalup:** pleasant beach towns north of Leschenault. **Australind–Bunbury Tourist Drive:** coastal scenery, excellent crabbing and picnic spots; brochures from visitor centre.

See also THE SOUTH-WEST, pp. 34–5

Balingup

Pop. 443

255 D3 | 257 B4 | 258 B4

Brockman St; (08) 9764 1818; www.balinguptourism.com.au

93.3 ABC Classic FM, 1044 AM ABC Local Radio

This small town, nestled in the Blackwood River Valley, is surrounded by rolling hills, forests and orchards. Balingup is renowned for its glowing summer sunsets, amazing autumn colours and misty winter mornings.

Birdwood Park Fruit Winery: unique award-winning fruit wines, chutneys, jams and fruits; Brockman St; (08) 9764 1172. **Tinderbox:** herbal and natural products; South Western Hwy. **Old Cheese Factory Craft Centre:** the largest art and craft centre in WA, including pottery and timber products; Balingup–Nannup Rd; (08) 9764 1018.

Opera in the Valley: Jan. **Small Farm Field Day:** festival and roadside scarecrows; Apr. **Medieval Carnivale:** Aug. **Festival of Country Gardens:** Oct/Nov. **Balingup Jalbrook Concert:** Nov.

Golden Valley Tree Park This 60 ha arboretum boasts a superb collection of exotic and native trees. Other attractions include a tree information gazebo, walk trails, lookout and the historic Golden Valley Homestead. Old Padbury Rd; 2 km s.

Jalbrook Alpacas and Knitwear Gallery: alpacas to feed and alpaca knitwear; accommodation also available; (08) 9764 1190; 2 km E. **Lavender Farm:** oil-producing lavender farm with open gardens, picnic area, art gallery and giftshop. Take a distillation tour; open Sept–Apr, Balingup–Nannup Rd; (08) 9764 1436; 2.5 km w. **Balingup Heights Scenic Lookout:** stunning views of town and orchards; off Balingup–Nannup Rd; 2.5 km w. **Greenbushes:** boasts WA's first metal-producing mine (1888), still in production and now the world's largest tantalum producer. The Discovery Centre has interactive displays and walking trails, and there is an excellent lookout at the mine; 10 km w. **Heritage Country Cheese:** cheese-producing factory

RADIO STATION | IN TOWN | WHAT'S ON | NEARBY

with viewing window and tastings; 16 km w. **Wineries:** several in area; details from visitor centre. **Balingup–Nannup Rd:** enjoy wonderful scenery, interesting and historic landmarks and great marroning, fishing and picnic sites. **Bibbulmun Track:** sections of this trail pass through Balingup; see *Albany*.

See also THE SOUTH-WEST, pp. 34–5

Balladonia
Pop. 20

259 F3

ⓘ **Balladonia Roadhouse,** Eyre Hwy; (08) 9039 3453.

Balladonia lies on the Eyre Highway on the western edge of the Nullarbor Plain. Its closest towns are Norseman, 191 kilometres to the west, and Caiguna, 182 kilometres to the east. This arid desert shrubland is one of the world's oldest landscapes, containing seashells millions of years old from when the area was ocean floor. Balladonia made world headlines in 1979 when space debris from NASA's *Skylab* landed 40 kilometres east on Woorlba Station.

Cultural Heritage Museum Learn about the crash-landing of *Skylab*, local Indigenous culture, early explorers, Afghan cameleers and other chapters in the area's history. Balladonia Roadhouse, Eyre Hwy.

90-Mile Straight Have your photo taken beside the signpost marking the western end of the longest straight stretch of road in Australia, which runs for 90 miles (146.6 km) between Balladonia and Caiguna. Begins 35 km E.

Newman Rocks: superb views from rocky outcrop, with picnic and camping areas on-site; 50 km w. **Cape Arid National Park and Israelite Bay:** great birdwatching and fishing; access via 4WD track, south of town; check track conditions at roadhouse.

See also ESPERANCE & NULLARBOR, pp. 40–1

Beverley
Pop. 850

257 C2 | 258 B3

ⓘ **Aeronautical Museum,** 139 Vincent St; (08) 9646 1555; www.beverleywa.com

📻 99.7 FM ABC News Radio, 531 AM ABC Local Radio

Beverley is a small town set on the banks of the Avon River 130 kilometres east of Perth. Its main street boasts some beautifully preserved buildings, representing Federation to Art Deco architectural styles. This farming community, while having long been associated with wheat and wool, also produces grapes, olives, emus, deer and yabbies.

Aeronautical Museum This museum presents a comprehensive display of early aviation in WA. The museum's star attraction is the *Silver Centenary*, a biplane built between 1928 and 1930 by local man Selby Ford and his cousin Tom Shackles. Ford designed the plane in chalk on the floor where he worked. The plane first flew in July 1930, but was never licensed because of the lack of design blueprints. Vincent St.

Station Gallery: art exhibitions and sales in the Tudor-style (1889) railway station; Vincent St. **Dead Finish Museum:** the oldest building in town (1872) houses memorabilia and historic items from wooden cotton wheels to washing boards; open 11am–3pm Sun Mar–Nov or by appt through visitor centre; Hunt Rd.

Yabbie Races: Apr. **Annual Quick Shear:** Aug.

Avondale Discovery Farm Avondale is an agricultural research station with displays of historic farming machinery and tools. The 1850s homestead is furnished in period style and set in traditional gardens. There is also an animal nursery, Clydesdale horses and a picnic area with barbecues and a children's playground. A land-care education centre houses interactive displays. The farm hosts the Clydesdale and Vintage Day in June. Waterhatch Rd; (08) 9646 1004; 6 km w.

Brookton: attractions of this nearby town include the Old Police Station Museum and the Brookton Pioneer Heritage Trail, which highlights places significant to the local Aboriginal people; 32 km s. **County Peak Lookout:** spectacular views from the summit; 35 km SE. **The Avon Ascent:** take a self-drive tour of the Avon Valley; maps from visitor centre.

See also HEARTLANDS, pp. 36–7

Boyup Brook
Pop. 531

257 B4 | 258 B4

Cnr Bridge and Abel sts; (08) 9765 1444; www.bbvisitor.mysouthwest.com.au

100.5 Hot FM, 1044 AM ABC Local Radio

Boyup Brook is on the tranquil Blackwood River in the heart of Western Australia's grasstree country. The town's name is thought to derive from the Aboriginal word 'booyup', meaning 'place of big stones' or 'place of much smoke', which was given to the nearby Boyup Pool. Seasonal wildflowers are abundant during September and October.

Carnaby Beetle and Butterfly Collection
Keith Carnaby was such a leading light in the field of entomology that beetles have been named after him. His collection of Jewel beetles, part of which is on display at the Boyup Brook Tourist Information Centre, is regarded as the best outside the British Museum of Natural History. Cnr Bridge and Abel sts.

Pioneers' Museum: displays of historic agricultural, commercial and domestic equipment; open 2–5pm Mon, Wed, Fri or by appt; Jayes Rd. **Sandakan War Memorial:** honours 1500 Australian POWs sent to Sandakan to build an airfield for the Japanese; Sandakan Park. **The Flax Mill:** built during WW II for processing flax needed for war materials. At its peak it operated 24 hrs a day and employed over 400 people. A scale model of the mill can be viewed on-site, which is now the caravan park; off Barron St. **Heritage walk:** follows 23 plaques around town centre; self-guide pamphlet from visitor centre. **Bicentennial Walking Trail:** pleasant walk around town and beside the Blackwood River.

Country Music Festival and Ute Muster: Feb.
Blackwood Marathon: running, canoeing, horseriding, cycling and swimming a 58 km course to Bridgetown; Oct.

Harvey Dickson's Country Music Centre
This entertainment shed is decorated wall-to-wall and floor-to-rafter with music memorabilia spanning 100 years. The 'record room' containing hundreds of records also has Elvis memorabilia. There is a music show in Sept and a rodeo in Oct, with basic bush camping facilities. Open by appt; Arthur River Rd; (08) 9765 1125; 5 km N.

Roo Gully Wildlife Sanctuary: for injured and orphaned Australian wildlife, with a special focus on raising unfurred marsupial young; 1 km N. **Gregory Tree:** remaining stump of a tree blazed by explorer Augustus Gregory in 1845; Gibbs Rd; 15 km NE. **Norlup Homestead:** built in 1874, this is one of the district's first farms; to view contact (08) 9767 3034; off Norlup Rd; 27 km SE. **Wineries:** Scotts Brook Winery (20 km SE) and Blackwood Crest Winery (at Kilikup, 40 km E); both open daily. **Haddleton Flora Reserve:** displays of brown and pink boronia in season. Not suitable for campers or caravans; 50 km NE. **Boyup Brook flora drives:** self-guide maps from visitor centre.

See also THE SOUTH-WEST, pp. 34–5

BROOME Pop. 11 547

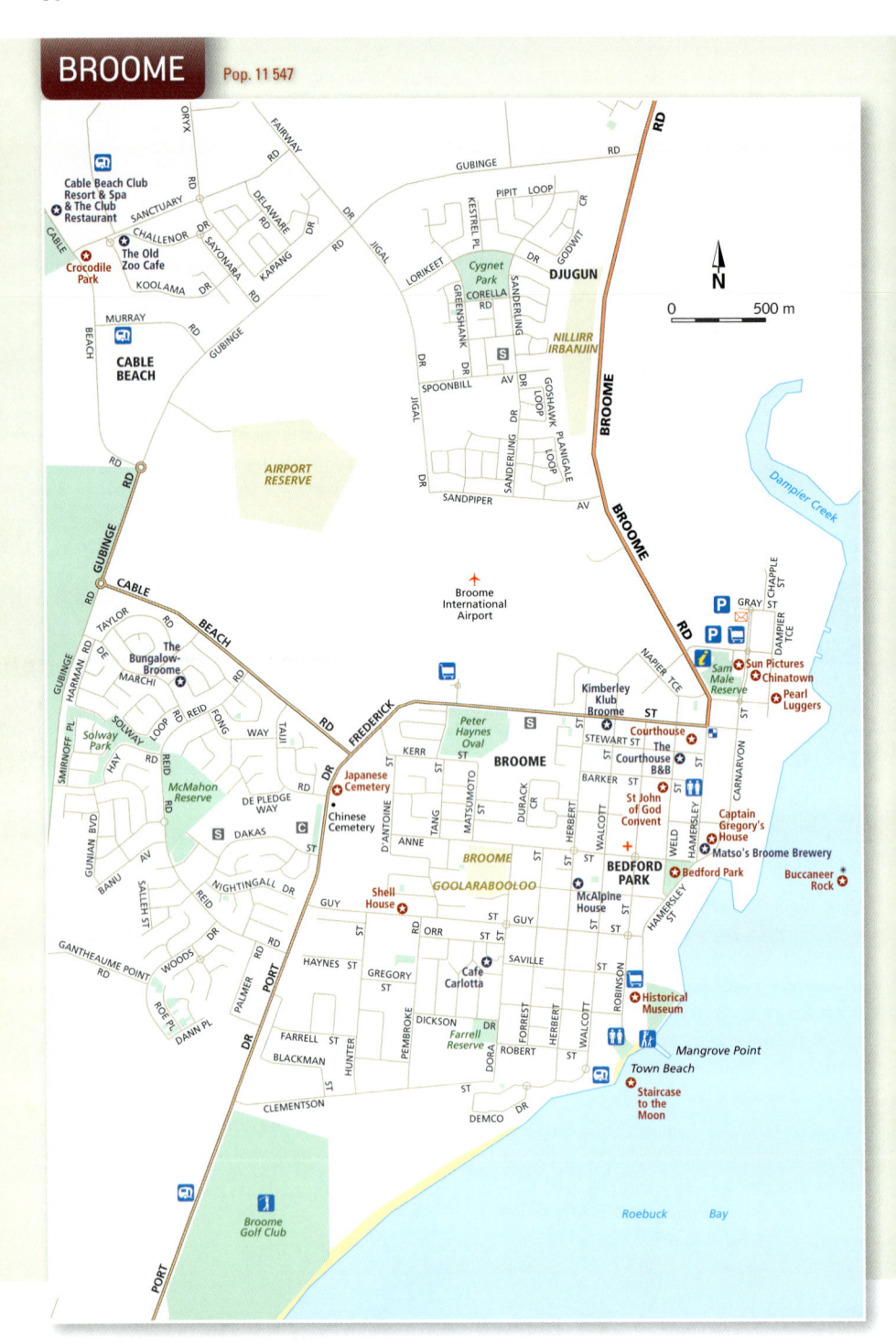

266 A5 | 268 D3

ℹ **Cnr Bagot St and Broome Rd; (08) 9192 2222; www.broomevisitorcentre.com.au**

📻 **100.3 WA FM, 675 AM ABC Local Radio**

Broome is distinguished by its pearling history, cosmopolitan character and startling natural assets: white sandy beaches, turquoise water and red soils. The discovery of pearling grounds off the coast in the 1880s led to the foundation of the Broome township in 1883. A melting pot of nationalities flocked to its shores in the hope of making a fortune. Japanese, Malays and Koepangers joined the Aboriginal pearl divers, while the Chinese became the shopkeepers in town. By 1910 Broome was the world's leading pearling centre. In those early, heady days, over 400 pearling luggers operated out of Broome. The industry suffered when world markets collapsed in 1914, but stabilised in the 1970s as cultured-pearl farming developed. Today remnants of Broome's exotic past are everywhere, with the town's multicultural society ensuring a dynamic array of cultural influences. Broome's beaches are ideal for swimming and there is good fishing year-round.

🏠 **Pearl Luggers** Experience Broome's pearling heritage by visiting two restored pearling luggers in Chinatown. Tours daily. Dampier Tce; (08) 9192 2059.

Japanese Cemetery The largest Japanese cemetery in Australia contains the graves of over 900 Japanese pearl divers, dating back to 1896. This is a sobering reminder of the perils of the early pearling days when the bends, cyclones and sharks claimed many lives. Cnr Port Dr and Savannah Way.

Staircase to the Moon This beautiful optical illusion is caused by a full moon reflecting off the exposed mudflats of Roebuck Bay at extremely low tides. Town Beach; 3 nights monthly from Mar–Oct; check dates and times at visitor centre.

Chinatown: an extraordinary mix of colonial and Asian influences, Chinatown was once the bustling hub of Broome where pearl sheds, billiard saloons and Chinese eateries flourished; now it is home to some of the world's finest pearl showrooms. *Buildings on Hamersley Street:* distinctive Broome-style architecture including the courthouse, made of teak inside and corrugated iron outside; Captain Gregory's House, a classic old pearling master's house, built in 1915, now an art gallery; and Matso's Broome Brewery, once the Union Bank Building. *Historical Museum:* pearling display and collection of photographs and literature on Broome's past; Robinson St. *Bedford Park:* war memorial, replica of explorer William Dampier's sea chest and an old train coach; Hamersley St. *Shell House:* one of the largest shell collections in Australia; Guy St. *Sun Pictures:* the world's oldest operating outdoor cinema, opened in 1916; Carnarvon St. *St John of God Convent:* built in 1926 by a Japanese shipbuilder using traditional methods that emphasise the external framing of the building; Cnr Barker and Weld sts. *Deep Water Jetty:* good for fishing; Port Dr. *Heritage trail:* 2 km walk introduces places of interest; self-guide pamphlet from visitor centre.

🎆 **Courthouse Markets:** Hamersley St; Sat and Sun mornings Apr–Oct. *Town Beach Markets:* Robinson St; 1st 2 nights of the Staircase to the Moon; check with visitor centre for dates and times. *Race Round:* horseracing; June–Aug. *Opera Under the Stars:* Aug. *Shinju Matsuri:* Festival of the Pearl, recalls Broome's heyday and includes Dragon Boat Regatta; Aug/Sept. *Mango Festival:* Nov.

🧭 **Cable Beach** With its 22 km of pristine white sands fringing the turquoise waters of

continued overleaf

BROOME continued

the Indian Ocean, Cable Beach is one of the most stunning beaches in the world. Every day the beach is washed clean by 10 m high tides. It takes its name from the telegraph cable laid between Broome and Java in 1889. While you are here, why not do that quintessential Broome activity and ride a camel along this famous beach. Details from visitor centre. 7 km NW.

Gantheaume Point Dinosaur footprints believed to be 130 million years old can be seen at very low tide. A plaster cast of the tracks has been embedded at the top of the cliff. Nearby, view the almost perfectly round Anastasia's Pool, built by a lighthouse keeper for his wife. 5 km NE.

Crocodile Park: home to some of Australia's biggest crocodiles; Cable Beach Rd; 7 km NW.
Riddell Beach: enjoy the dramatic sight of Broome's distinctive red soils, known as 'pindan', meeting white sands and brilliant blue water; 7 km SW. *Buccaneer Rock:* at entrance to Dampier Creek, this landmark commemorates Captain William Dampier and HMS *Roebuck*; 1 km SE. *Broome Bird Observatory:* see some of the 310 species of migratory wader birds that arrive each year from Siberia; 17 km E. *Willie Creek Pearl Farm:* the Kimberley's only pearl farm open to the public, with daily tours; (08) 9192 0000; 35 km N. *Dampier Peninsula:* this remote area north of Broome boasts unspoiled coastline (4WD access only). Record-breaking game fish have been caught in the surrounding waters, which may account for the fact that the coastal towns of the Pilbara boast the highest rate of private vessel ownership in the country. Charters and tours leave from Dampier. The Sacred Heart Church at Beagle Bay (118 km NE) was built by Pallotine monks in 1917 and boasts a magnificent pearl-shell altar. Lombadina (200 km NE) is a former mission now home to an Aboriginal community that offers sightseeing, fishing and mudcrabbing tours; contact (08) 9192 4936. Cape Leveque, at the north of the peninsula, is well known for its pristine beaches and rugged pindan cliffs; 220 km NE. *Buccaneer Archipelago:* in Broome you can arrange scenic flights over this

CAMEL RIDE ON CABLE BEACH

magnificent landscape that stretches north-east of the Dampier Peninsula. Also known as the Thousand Islands, this is a dramatic coastal area of rugged red cliffs, spectacular waterfalls and secluded white sandy beaches. Here you'll find whirlpools created by massive 11 m tides and the amazing horizontal two-way waterfall of Talbot Bay. **Hovercraft Spirit**

Bremer Bay
Pop. 239

258 D4

Community Resource Centre and Library, Mary St; (08) 9837 4171; www.bremerbay.com

103.5 WA FM, 531 AM ABC Local Radio

Bremer Bay on the south coast is a wide expanse of crystal-clear blue water and striking white sand. The main beach, only a ten-minute walk from the town, has a sheltered cove for swimming and fishing. Just north of Bremer Bay is the magnificent Fitzgerald River National Park with its four rivers, dramatic gorges, wide sand plains, rugged cliffs, pebbly beaches and spectacular displays of wildflowers between August and October.

Watersports: fishing, boating, swimming, surfing, waterskiing, scuba diving, bay cruises and seasonal whale-watching are the town's main attractions. *Rammed-earth buildings:* the Bremer Bay Hotel/Motel on Frantom Way and Catholic Church on Mary St are excellent examples of rammed-earth construction.

Fitzgerald River National Park This huge 242 739 ha park, lying between Bremer Bay and Hopetoun to the east, is renowned for its scenery and flora. A staggering 1800 species of flowering plants have been recorded. Royal hakea, endemic to this region, is one of the most striking. Quaalup Homestead (1858), restored as a museum, offers meals and accommodation in the park. Pt Ann has a

of Broome: tours of Roebuck Bay; details from visitor centre.

Travellers note: *Poisonous jellyfish frequent this stretch of coast, especially Nov–May. Pay attention to warning signs on the beaches and wear protective clothing if swimming.*

See also KIMBERLEY, pp. 48–9

viewing platform for whale-watching (southern rights, June–Oct). Campgrounds, barbecues and picnic areas available. 17 km N.

Wellstead Homestead Museum: the first residence in the area, now incorporating a gallery and museum with family heirlooms, historic farm equipment and vintage cars; Peppermint Grove, Wellstead Rd; (08) 9837 4448; 9 km SW. *Surfing:* nearby beaches include Native Dog Beach, Dillon Bay, Fosters Beach and Trigelow Beach; directions from visitor centre.

See also GREAT SOUTHERN, pp. 38–9

Bridgetown
Pop. 2321

255 D3 | 257 B4 | 258 B4

154 Hampton St; (08) 9761 1740 or 1800 777 140; www.bridgetown.com.au

100.5 Hot FM, 1044 AM ABC Local Radio

Bridgetown is a picturesque timber town nestled among rolling hills on the banks of the Blackwood River. Crossing the river, Bridgetown boasts the longest wooden bridge in the state, made of the area's famous jarrah. In addition to tourism, timber milling and mining (lithium, tantalum and tin) are now the largest industries in the area.

Brierley Jigsaw Gallery The only public jigsaw gallery in the Southern Hemisphere,

Brierley has over 170 jigsaws ranging from the world's smallest wooden puzzle to a huge 9000-piece jigsaw. A highlight is an 8000-piece jigsaw of the Sistine Chapel. Back of visitor centre, Hampton St.

Bridgedale: historic house owned by John Blechynden, one of the area's first European settlers, constructed in 1862 of local timber and bricks made from riverbank clay; South Western Hwy. *Memorial Park:* picnic area with a giant chessboard, 3 ft high pieces for hire from visitor centre; South Western Hwy.

Blackwood River Park Markets: Sun mornings each fortnight. *State Downriver Kayaking Championships:* Aug. *Blackwood Classic Powerboat Race:* Sept. *Blackwood Marathon:* between Boyup Brook and Bridgetown; Oct. *Blues at Bridgetown Festival:* Nov. *Festival of Country Gardens:* Nov.

The Cidery Discover the history of Bridgetown's apple industry and sample fresh juice, cider or award-winning beers. The orchard contains over 80 varieties of apples. Closed Tues; Cnr Forrest St and Gifford Rd; (08) 9761 2204; 2 km N.

Geegelup Heritage Trail: 52 km walk retraces history of agriculture, mining and timber in the region. It starts at Blackwood River Park. *Scenic drives:* choose from 8 scenic drives in the district through green hills, orchards and valleys into karri and jarrah timber country; self-guide maps from visitor centre. *Excellent views:* Sutton's Lookout, off Phillips St and Hester Hill, 5 km N. *Bridgetown Jarrah Park:* ideal place for a picnic or bushwalk. The Tree Fallers and Shield Tree trails commemorate the early timber history of the town; Brockman Hwy; 20 km w. *Karri Gully:* bushwalking and picnicking; 20 km w.

See also THE SOUTH-WEST, pp. 34–5

Broome

see inset box on previous page

Bunbury

see inset box on next page

Busselton

Pop. 15 385

255 B3 | 257 A4 | 258 A4

i 38 Peel Tce; (08) 9752 1288; www.geographebay.com

96.5 FM Western Tourist Radio, 684 AM ABC Local Radio

First settled by Europeans in 1834, Busselton is one of the oldest towns in Western Australia. It is situated on the shores of Geographe Bay and the picturesque Vasse River. Sheltered from most prevailing winds, the tranquil waters of the bay are an aquatic playground edged with 30 kilometres of white sand beaches. Over the past three decades, the traditional industries of timber, dairying, cattle and sheep have been joined by grape-growing and winemaking. Fishing is also important, particularly crayfish and salmon in season. In spring, the wildflowers are magnificent.

Busselton Jetty The longest timber jetty in the Southern Hemisphere was built over a 95-year period, beginning in 1865, principally for the export of timber. Over 5000 ships from all over the world docked here through the ages of sail, steam and diesel, before the port closed in 1972. The jetty stretches a graceful 1.8 km into Geographe Bay and has always been a popular spot for fishing, snorkelling and scuba diving because of the variety of marine life. An Interpretive Centre at the base of the jetty displays historical and environmental exhibits. At the seaward end is an Underwater Observatory featuring an observation chamber with viewing windows 8 m beneath the surface revealing vividly coloured corals, sponges and fish. Tours are available, bookings essential. End of Queen St.

WESTERN AUSTRALIA → TOWNS → **CAIGUNA** 63

Ballarat Engine: first steam locomotive in WA; Pries Ave. *St Mary's Anglican Church:* built in 1844 of limestone and jarrah, with a she-oak shingle roof. The churchyard has many pioneer graves, including John Garrett Bussell's, after whom Busselton was named; Peel Tce. *Nautical Lady Entertainment World:* family fun park with giant water slide, flying fox, minigolf, skate park, racing cars, lookout tower and nautical museum; on beachfront at end of Queen St; (08) 9752 3473. *Old Courthouse:* restored gaol cells and arts complex; Queen St. *Busselton Historical Museum:* originally a creamery, now houses historic domestic equipment; closed Tues; Peel Tce. *Vasse River Parkland:* barbecue facilities; Peel Tce.

Markets: Barnard Park, 1st and 3rd Sat each month; Railway Building Park, Causeway Rd, 2nd and 4th Sun each month. *Southbound:* music festival; Jan. *Festival of Busselton:* Jan. *Beach Festival:* Jan. *Busselton Jetty Swim:* Feb. *Geographe Bay Race Week:* yachting; Feb. *Bluewater Fishing Classic:* Mar. *Great Escapade:* cycling; Mar. *Busselton Agricultural Show:* one of the oldest and largest country shows in WA; Oct/Nov. *Smell the Roses, Taste the Wine:* Nov. *Ironman Western Australia Triathlon:* Dec.

Tuart Forest National Park The majestic tuart tree grows only on coastal limestone 200 km either side of Perth. Known locally as the Ludlow Tuart Forest, this 2049 ha park protects the largest natural tuart forest in the world. It also has the tallest and largest specimens of tuart trees on the Swan Coastal Plain, up to 33 m high and 10 m wide. Enjoy scenic drives, forest walks and picnics in a magnificent setting. 12 km SE.

Wonnerup House: built in 1859, now a National Trust museum and fine example of colonial architecture, furnished in period style; 10 km N. *Bunyip Craft Centre:* Ludlow; 15 km E. *Wineries:* numerous vineyards and wineries in the area. Many are open for cellar-door tastings; maps from visitor centre. *Augusta–Busselton Heritage Trail:* maps from visitor centre.

See also THE SOUTH-WEST, pp. 34–5

Caiguna
Pop. 10

259 G3

🛈 Caiguna Roadhouse; (08) 9039 3459.

The small community of Caiguna, on the Nullarbor Plain, consists of a 24-hour roadhouse, caravan park, motel, restaurant and service station. The nearest towns are Balladonia, 182 kilometres west, and Cocklebiddy, 65 kilometres east. To the south is the coastal wilderness of Nuytsland Nature Reserve. From immediately east of Caiguna until Border Village, locals operate on Central Western Time, 45 minutes ahead of the rest of Western Australia.

John Baxter Memorial In 1841, the explorer John Baxter, together with an Aboriginal guide known as Wylie and two other unnamed Aboriginal men, accompanied Edward John Eyre on his epic journey across the Nullarbor Plain. The party left Fowlers Bay in SA on 25 Feb and reached the site of modern-day Eucla on 12 Mar. Later, the two unnamed Aboriginal men killed Baxter and, taking most of the supplies, fled into the desert. Eyre and Wylie walked for another month and eventually reached Thistle Cove (near Esperance), where they were rescued by a French whaler. The Baxter memorial is on the Baxter Cliffs overlooking the Great Australian Bight; 4WD access only. 38 km s.

90-Mile Straight: have your photo taken beside the signpost marking the eastern end of the longest straight stretch of road in Australia, which runs for 90 miles (146.6 km) between Caiguna and a point east of Balladonia;

continued on p. 66

RADIO STATION   IN TOWN   WHAT'S ON   NEARBY

64 WESTERN AUSTRALIA → TOWNS → BUNBURY

BUNBURY Pop. 54 967

VIEW OF BUNBURY FROM LESCHENAULT INLET

255 B2 | 257 B4 | 258 A4

**Old Railway Station, Carmody Pl;
(08) 9792 7205 or 1800 286 287;
www.visitbunbury.com.au**

95.7 Hot FM, 684 AM ABC Local Radio

Bunbury is known as the 'city of three waters', surrounded by the Indian Ocean, Koombana Bay and the Leschenault Inlet. This is a water-lover's paradise with fishing, crabbing, diving, white sandy beaches, sailing and kayaking. Bunbury is also known for its wild dolphins that come close to the beach at Koombana Bay. Bunbury was settled by Europeans in 1838 and the Koombana Bay whalers were a source of initial prosperity. Today the port is the main outlet for the timber and mining industries.

Dolphin Discovery Centre Wild bottlenose dolphins regularly visit Koombana Bay. The centre has interpretive displays on dolphins and other marine life, and offers visitors the chance to swim with dolphins under ranger guidance. Dolphin visits usually occur in the mornings; however, times and days of visits are unpredictable. If you prefer not to get wet, take a dolphin-spotting cruise on the bay. Open daily 8am–5pm Sept–May, 9am–3pm June–Aug; Koombana Dr; (08) 9791 3088.

Historic buildings: many date back to the early decades of the settlement, including the 1865 Rose Hotel; Cnr Victoria and Wellington sts; details from visitor centre. *King Cottage:* this cottage was built in 1880 by Henry King using homemade bricks. It now displays items of domestic life from the early 20th century; open 2–4pm daily; Forrest Ave. *Sir John Forrest Monument:* born in Picton on the outskirts of Bunbury in 1847, Sir John Forrest was elected the first Premier of WA in 1890 and entered Federal Parliament in 1901; Cnr Victoria and Stephen sts. *Victoria Street:* a 'cappuccino strip' of sidewalk cafes and restaurants. *Bunbury Regional Art Galleries:* built in 1887, formerly a convent for the Sisters of Mercy and now the largest art gallery in the South-West; Wittenoom St. *Miniature Railway Track:* take a ride on this 800 m track through the trees at Forrest Park; 3rd Sun each month; Blair St. *Lookouts:* Boulter's Heights, Haig Cres and Marlston Hill; Apex Dr. *Lighthouse:* painted in black-and-white check, this striking landmark has a lookout at the base; end of Ocean Dr. *Basaltic rock:* formed by volcanic lava flow 150 million years ago; foreshore at end of Clifton St, off Ocean Dr.

continued overleaf

RADIO STATION   IN TOWN   WHAT'S ON   NEARBY

BUNBURY continued

Mangrove boardwalk: 200 m elevated boardwalk lets you view the southernmost mangrove colony in WA, estimated to be 20 000 years old; Koombana Dr. *Big Swamp Wildlife Park:* handfeed kangaroos, see bettongs, wombats, swamp wallabies and more, and enjoy the South-West's largest walk-through aviary; Prince Phillip Dr. *Heritage trail:* 12 km walk from the Old Railway Station; brochures from visitor centre.

Bunbury Carnaval: Mar. *Bunbury International Jazz Festival:* May. *Geographe Crush:* Food and Wine Festival; Nov.

St Marks Anglican Church: built in 1842, this is the second oldest church in WA. The churchyard contains the graves of many early Bunbury settlers; 5 km SE at Picton. *Lena Dive Wreck:* apprehended by the navy in 2002 for illegal fishing, the *Lena* was sunk three nautical miles from Bunbury as a dive wreck; suitable for snorkelling and diving for all levels of experience. *South West Gemstone Museum:* over 2000 gemstones; 12 km S. *Wineries:* at the heart of the Geographe Wine Region, many in the area offer cellar-door tastings, including Killerby Wines (10 km s) and Capel Vale Wines (27 km S); details from visitor centre. *Abseiling tours:* on the quarry face of the Wellington Dam; details from visitor centre. *Scenic flights:* over Bunbury and surrounds.

See also THE SOUTH-WEST, pp. 34–5

---

4 km w. *Caiguna Blowhole:* a hole in the flat limestone landscape where the earth seemingly breathes in and out; 5 km w.

See also ESPERANCE & NULLARBOR, pp. 40–1

Carnamah
Pop. 358

258 A2

ⓘ Council offices, Macpherson St; (08) 9951 7000; www.carnamah.wa.gov.au

📻 101.9 WA FM, 612 AM ABC Radio National

Carnamah is a typical wheat-belt town servicing the surrounding wheat and sheep properties. From late July through to December the shire of Carnamah and the rest of the wheat belt blossoms into a wildflower wonderland. This is one of Western Australia's richest areas of flowering plants, with more than 600 species.

Historical Society Museum: displays historic domestic equipment and old farm machinery; Macpherson St.

North Midlands Agricultural Show, Rodeo and Ute Parade: Sept.

Tathra National Park This park, with its diverse range of spring wildflowers, is named after the Nyungar word for 'beautiful place'. 25 km sw.

Macpherson's Homestead: an excellent example of pioneering architecture (1869), once the home of Duncan Macpherson, the first settler in the area; open by appt; Bunjil Rd; (08) 9951 1690; 1 km E. *Yarra Yarra Lake:* this salt lake changes from pink in summer to deep blue in winter. View it from the Lakes Lookout; 16 km s. *Eneabba:* spectacular wildflowers surround this mining town; 74 km w. *Lake Indoon:* a freshwater lake popular for sailing, boating, camping, picnics and barbecues (swimming is forbidden due to poor water quality); 85 km w.

See also HEARTLANDS, pp. 36–7

Carnarvon

see inset box on next page

Cervantes
Pop. 506

257 A1 | 258 A2

i Pinnacles Visitor Centre, Cadiz St; (08) 9652 7672 or 1800 610 660; www.visitpinnaclescountry.com.au

📻 99.9 WA FM, 612 AM ABC Radio National

This small but thriving fishing town was established in 1962 and named after the American whaling ship *Cervantes*, which sank off the coast in 1844. The town's fishing fleet nearly doubles in rock lobster season, and in spring the town is surrounded by spectacular displays of wildflowers with vistas of wattles stretching from horizon to horizon. Not far from Cervantes is one of Australia's best-known landscapes, the Pinnacles Desert, lying at the heart of Nambung National Park.

🏠 **Pinnacle Wildflowers:** displays of native WA flora, dried flower arrangements, souvenirs. Flowers are visible year-round, but at their peak in Aug and Sept; Bradley Loop. **Thirsty Pt:** lookout has superb views of the bay and Cervantes islands. A trail connects the lookouts between Thirsty Pt and Hansen Bay. Popular in wildflower season; off Seville St.

🧭 **Nambung National Park** In the Pinnacles Desert, thousands of limestone pillars rise out of a stark landscape of yellow sand, reaching over 3 m in places. They are the eroded remnants of a bed of limestone, created from sea-shells breaking down into lime-rich sands. See formations like the Indian Chief, Garden Wall and Milk Bottles. The loop drive is one-way and not suitable for caravans. The park allows day visits only; tours departing morning and sunset can be arranged at visitor centre. 17 km s.

Lake Thetis Stromatolites: one of WA's six known locations of stromatolites, the oldest living organism on earth; 5 km s. **Kangaroo Pt:** good picnic spot; 9 km s. **Hangover Bay:** a stunning white sandy beach ideal for swimming, snorkelling, windsurfing and surfing; 13 km s.

See also HEARTLANDS, pp. 36–7

Cocklebiddy
Pop. 75

259 G3

i Cocklebiddy Roadhouse; (08) 9039 3462.

📻 107.3 FM ABC Radio National, 648 AM ABC Local Radio

This tiny settlement, comprising a roadhouse with motel units, caravan sites and camping facilities, lies between Madura and Caiguna on the Nullarbor Plain. Nuytsland Nature Reserve extends southwards, a 400 000-hectare strip running along the Great Australian Bight. Locals operate on Central Western Time, 45 minutes ahead of the rest of the state.

🧭 **Eyre Bird Observatory** Housed in the fully restored 1897 Eyre Telegraph Station, Australia's first bird observatory offers birdwatching, bushwalking and beachcombing in Nuytsland Nature Reserve. Over 240 species of birds have been recorded at Eyre, including Major Mitchell cockatoos, brush bronzewings, honeyeaters and mallee fowl. It is near the site where Edward John Eyre found water and rested during his Nullarbor journey in February 1841. Courses, tours and whale-watching (June–Oct) as well as accommodation can be arranged on (08) 9039 3450. 4WD access only. 50 km SE.

continued on p. 70

📻 RADIO STATION   🏠 IN TOWN   🎆 WHAT'S ON   🧭 NEARBY

CARNARVON Pop. 5283

260 B1 | 261 A3

Civic Centre, 11 Robinson St;
(08) 9941 1146; www.carnarvon.org.au

99.7 Hot Hits FM, 846 AM ABC Local Radio

Carnarvon is a large coastal town at the mouth of the Gascoyne River. The river and the fertile red earth surrounding it are crucial to the town's thriving agricultural industry. Plantations stretching for 15 kilometres along the riverbanks draw water from the aquifer of the river basin to grow a host of tropical fruits such as bananas, mangoes, avocados, pineapples, pawpaws and melons. Carnarvon gained national prominence when a NASA tracking station operated nearby at Browns Range from 1964 to 1974.

Robinson Street In 1876 the region's founding fathers, Aubrey Brown, John Monger and C. S. Brockman, overlanded 4000 sheep from York. Carnarvon was gazetted in 1883 and developed into the centre of an efficient wool-producing area. Camel teams, driven by Afghan camel drivers, brought the wool to Carnarvon from the outlying sheep stations. This is the reason for the extraordinary width of the town's main street, which, at 40 m, gave the camel teams enough room to turn around.

Jubilee Hall: built in 1887 as the Roads Board building, now used as a craft market. In 1960 a cyclone blew the roof off and all the shire papers blew away; Francis St. *Pioneer Park:* good picnic spot; Olivia Tce. *Murals:* up to 15 buildings in the town, including the Civic Centre, are adorned with murals painted by local artists. *Heritage walking trail:* 20 historic landmarks around the town; maps from visitor centre.

Growers' market: Civic Centre; Sat mornings May–Nov. *Courtyard Markets:* Robinson St; every Sat May–Dec. *Fremantle–Carnarvon Yacht Race:* odd-numbered years, May. *Carnarfin:* fishing competition; June. *Carnarvon Festival:* Aug/Sept.

Carnarvon Heritage Precinct On Babbage Island and connected to the township by a causeway, this heritage precinct incorporates the

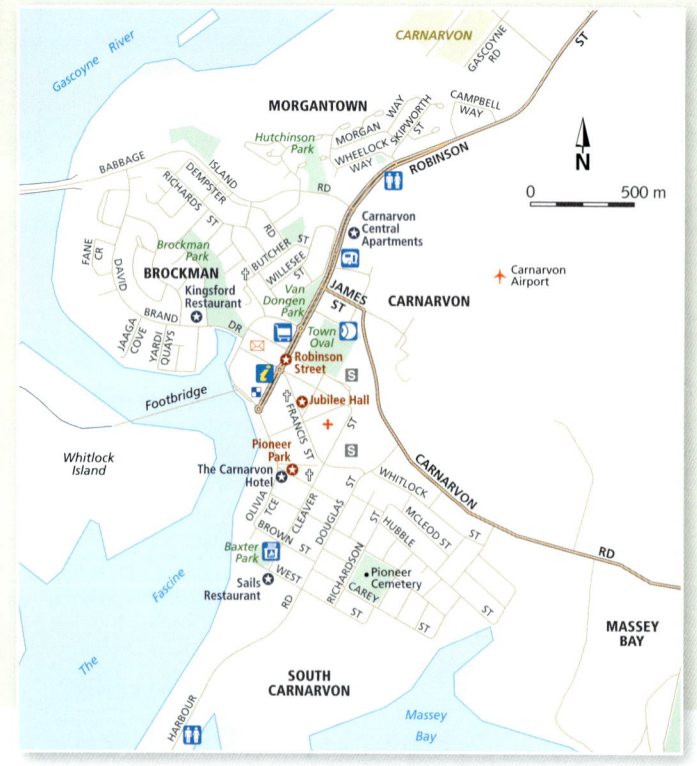

POINT QUOBBA

One Mile Jetty. Built in 1897, this is the longest jetty in WA's north, stretching for 1493 m into the Indian Ocean. It offers excellent fishing and a jetty train runs its length. Other attractions include the Lighthouse Keeper's Cottage museum, prawning factory at the old whaling station (tours in season, check times at visitor centre) and Pelican Pt, for picnics, swimming and fishing.

Blowholes Jets of water shoot up to 20 m in the air after being forced through holes in the coastal rock. When you arrive at the Blowholes, you are greeted by a huge sign declaring 'KING WAVES KILL' – a cautionary reminder that this picturesque coastline has claimed the lives of over 30 people in freak waves. 73 km N. Nearby, a sheltered lagoon provides good swimming and snorkelling (1 km s). A further 7 km north of the blowholes is a cairn commemorating the loss of HMAS *Sydney* in 1941.

'The Big Dish': a huge 29 m wide reflector, part of the old NASA station, with views of town and plantations from the base; 8 km E.
Bibbawarra Artesian Bore: hot water surfaces at 65° C and picnic area nearby; 16 km N.
Bibbawarra Trough: 180 m long, believed to be the longest in the Southern Hemisphere; adjacent to bore; 16 km N. **Miaboolya Beach:** good fishing, crabbing and swimming; 22 km N. **Rocky Pool:** picnic area and deep billabong ideal for swimming (after rains) and wildlife watching; Gascoyne Rd; 55 km E. **Red Bluff:** world-renowned surfing spot with waves 1–6 m, depending on the time of the year; 143 km N. **Mt Augustus:** considered the biggest rock in the world, twice the size of Uluṟu. It is known as Burringurrah to the local Aboriginal people. This 'monocline' is over 1750 million years old, cloaked in thick scrub, and offers many interesting rock formations, caves and Indigenous rock art. Camping and powered sites are available at Mt Augustus Outback Tourist Resort; (08) 9943 0527; road conditions vary; 450 km E; *see also Gascoyne Junction.* **Fishing:** excellent fishing for snapper or groper and game fishing for marlin or sailfish; charter boats available from Williams St. Also excellent fishing off One Mile Jetty.

See also **Outback Coast & Mid-West, pp. 44–5**

RADIO STATION   IN TOWN   WHAT'S ON   NEARBY

Chapel Rock: picnic area; 4 km E. *Twilight Cove:* fishing and whale-watching spot with views of 70 m high limestone cliffs overlooking the Great Australian Bight; 4WD access only; 32 km S.

See also ESPERANCE & NULLARBOR, pp. 40–1

Collie

Pop. 7084

255 D2 | 257 B4 | 258 B4

i Old Collie Post Office, 63 Throssell St; (08) 9734 2051; www.collierivervalley.org.au

95.7 Hot FM, 684 AM ABC Local Radio

Collie is Western Australia's only coalmining town. The surrounding area was first explored in 1829 when Captain James Stirling led a reconnaissance party to the land south of Perth. The region was originally considered ideal for timber production and as pasturelands. However, the discovery of coal along the Collie River in 1883 changed the region's fortunes. In dense jarrah forest, near the winding Collie River, the town has many parks and gardens. The drive into Collie on the Coalfields Highway along the top of the Darling Scarp offers spectacular views of the surrounding forests, rolling hills and farms.

Tourist Coal Mine Step back in time and gain an insight into the mining industry and the working conditions in underground mines. This replica mine was constructed in 1983 to commemorate the 100-year anniversary of coal discovery. Tours by appt only; details from visitor centre. Throssell St.

Coalfields Museum: displays of historic photographs, coalmining equipment, rocks and minerals, woodwork by local miner Fred Kohler, a doll house and art housed in the historic Roads Board building; Throssell St. *Collie Railway Station:* the rebuilt station houses railway memorabilia, a scale model of the Collie township with model trains, tearooms and a giftshop; Throssell St. *Soldiers' Park:* bordering the Collie River, features include a war memorial, rose garden, gazebo and childrens' playground; Steere St. *All Saints Anglican Church:* impressive Norman-style church distinctive for its unusual stained-glass windows, extensive use of jarrah timbers and elaborate mural, which in 1922 took renowned stage artist Philip Goatcher 8 months to complete. Tours by appt; contact visitor centre; Venn St. *Old Collie Goods Shed:* restoration of rolling stock; Forrest St. *Central Precinct Historic Walk:* self-guide walk of historic buildings; maps from visitor centre. *Collie River Walk:* pleasant walk along riverbank; maps from visitor centre.

Market: Old Goods Shed, Forrest St; 1st and 3rd Sun each month (except winter). *Collie Rock and Coal Music Festival:* Mar. *Collie–Donnybrook Cycle Race:* Aug. *Collie River Valley Marathon:* Sept. *Griffin Festival:* Sept.

Wellington National Park Covering 4000 ha, this park is characterised by jarrah forest. Picnic, swim, canoe or camp at Honeymoon Pool or Potters Gorge, or go rafting in winter on the rapids below the Wellington Dam wall (note that work is being carried out on the wall until 2010, when the Quarry picnic area will reopen). 18 km W.

Minninup Pool: where the Collie River is at its widest, ideal for swimming, canoeing or picnicking; off Mungalup Rd; 3 km S. *Stockton Lake:* camping and waterskiing; 8 km E. *Brew 42:* microbrewery producing 6 different beers, especially traditional Irish and English ales. Tastings and sales Thurs–Sun or by arrangement; Allanson; (08) 97344784; 8km W. *Harris Dam:* beautiful picnic area; 14 km N. *Collie River Scenic Drive:* views of jarrah forest and wildflowers in season; maps from visitor centre. *Munda Biddi Trail:* starting in the hills near Perth, this bike trail winds through scenic river valleys and forests south to Collie; details from visitor centre. *Bibbulmun Track:* sections of this trail pass through Collie; *see Albany.*

See also THE SOUTH-WEST, pp. 34–5

Coolgardie
Pop. 801

258 D2

Goldfields Exhibition Building, Bayley St; (08) 9026 6090; www.coolgardie.wa.gov.au

97.9 Hot FM, 648 AM ABC Local Radio

After alluvial gold was found in 1892, Coolgardie grew in ten years to a town of 15 000 people, 23 hotels, six banks and two stock exchanges. The main street, lined with some magnificent buildings, was made wide enough for camel trains to turn around in. As in many outback towns, the heat and the isolation led to innovation, in this case that of the Coolgardie safe, which used water and a breeze to keep food cool before the days of electricity.

Historic buildings There are 23 buildings in the town centre that have been listed on the National Estate register, many of them on the main street, Bayley St. Over 100 markers are positioned at buildings and historic sites across the town, using stories and photographs to recapture the gold-rush days. The index to markers is in Bayley St next to the visitor centre.

Goldfields Exhibition Museum Local photographs and displays inside the old Warden's Court including a display on the famous Varischetti mine rescue. In 1907 Modesto Varischetti was trapped underground in a flooded mine for 9 days. Varischetti survived in an air pocket until divers eventually found him. The dramatic rescue captured world attention. Bayley St.

Ben Prior's Open-Air Museum: unusual collection of machinery and memorabilia; Cnr Bayley and Hunt sts. *Warden Finnerty's House:* striking 1895 example of early Australian architecture and furnishings; open 11am–4pm daily except Wed; McKenzie St. *C. Y. O'Connor Dedication:* fountain and water course in memory of O'Connor, who masterminded the Goldfields Water Supply Scheme; McKenzie St. *Gaol tree:* used for prisoners in early gold-rush days, before a gaol was built; Hunt St. *Lindsay's Pit Lookout:* over open-cut goldmine; Ford St.

Coolgardie Day: Sept. *Metal Detecting Championships:* odd-numbered years, Sept/Oct.

Coolgardie Cemetery The town cemetery gives you an inkling of the harshness of the early gold-rush years. The register of burials records that of the first 32 burials, the names of 15 were unknown, and many entries for 'male child' and 'female child' note 'fever' as the cause of death. One of the most significant graves is that of Ernest Giles, an Englishman whose name is associated with the exploration of inland Australia. 1 km w.

Coolgardie Camel Farm: offers rides on the 'ships of the desert'; (08) 9026 6159; 4 km w. *Gnarlbine Rock:* originally an Aboriginal well, then one of the few water sources for the early prospectors; 30 km sw. *Kunanalling Hotel:* once a town of over 800 people, the ruins of the hotel are all that remain; 32 km n. *Victoria Rock:* camping, and spectacular views from the summit; 55 km sw. *Burra Rock:* popular camping and picnic area (55 km s). Cave Hill, a similar destination, lies a further 40 km s (4WD only). *Rowles Lagoon Conservation Park:* picnicking and camping spots available although recently there has been no water; 65 km n. *Wallaroo Rocks:* three dams with scenic views and good bushwalking; 90 km w. *Golden Quest Discovery Trail:* Coolgardie forms part of this 965 km self-guide drive trail of the goldfields; book, map and CD from visitor centre.

See also GOLDFIELDS, pp. 42–3

RADIO STATION   IN TOWN   WHAT'S ON   NEARBY

Coral Bay
Pop. 192

261 A2

ⓘ **Coastal Adventure Tours,** Coral Bay Arcade, Robinson St; (08) 9948 5190; www.coralbaytours.com.au

📻 91.7 FM ABC Radio National, 104.9 FM ABC Local Radio

Coral Bay is famous for one thing: its proximity to Ningaloo Marine Park. Ningaloo Reef boasts an incredible diversity of marine life and beautiful coral formations. At Coral Bay the coral gardens lie close to the shore, which makes access to the reef as easy as a gentle swim. Lying at the southern end of Ningaloo Marine Park, Coral Bay has pristine beaches and a near-perfect climate: it is warm and dry regardless of the season, and the water temperature only varies from 18°C to 28°C degrees. Swimming, snorkelling, scuba diving, and beach, reef and deep-sea fishing (outside sanctuary areas) are available year-round.

🧭 **Ningaloo Marine Park** This park protects the 260 km long Ningaloo Reef, the longest fringing coral reef in Australia. It is the only large reef in the world found so close to a continental land mass: about 100 m offshore at its nearest point and less than 7 km at its furthest. This means that even novice snorkellers and children can access the coral gardens. The reef is home to over 500 species of fish, 250 species of coral, manta rays, turtles and a variety of other marine creatures, with seasonal visits from humpback whales, dolphins and whale sharks. Ningaloo Reef is famous for the latter, and from Apr to June visitors from around the world visit the reef to swim with these gentle giants.

Pt Cloates: the wrecks of the *Zvir*, *Fin*, *Perth* and *Rapid* lie on the reef just off the point; 4WD access only; 8 km N. *Tours:* glass-bottomed boat cruises, snorkel and dive tours, kayak tours, fishing charters, scenic flights and marine wildlife-watching tours to see whale sharks (Apr–June), humpback whales (June–Nov) and manta rays (all year); details from visitor centre.

See also OUTBACK COAST & MID-WEST, pp. 44–5

Corrigin
Pop. 687

257 C2 | 258 C3

ⓘ **Corrigin Resource Centre,** Larke Cres; (08) 9063 2778; www.corrigin.wa.gov.au

📻 92.5 ABC Classic FM, 100.5 Hot FM

Corrigin was established in the early 1900s and was one of the last wheat-belt towns to be settled. Today the town has a healthy obsession with dogs, as demonstrated by its Dog Cemetery and its national record for lining up 1527 utes with dogs in the back.

🏠 **Corrigin Pioneer Museum** Superb collection of old agricultural equipment including an original Sunshine harvester and some early steam-driven farm machinery. A small working steam train carries passengers on a short circuit around the museum and local rest area. Open Sun and by appt; Kunjin St.

RSL Monument: a Turkish mountain gun from Gallipoli; McAndrew Ave.

🎆 *Dog in a Ute event:* held in varying years in Apr; dates from visitor centre.

🧭 **Dog Cemetery** Loving dog owners have gone to the considerable expense of having elaborate headstones placed over the remains of their faithful four-footed friends. There are over 80 dogs buried in the cemetery, with gravestones dedicated to Dusty, Rover, Spot et al. There is even one statue of a dog almost 2 m high. Brookton Hwy; 7 km W.

Wildflower scenic drive: signposted with lookout; 3 km W. *Gorge Rock:* large granite outcrop with picnic area; 20 km SE.

See also HEARTLANDS, pp. 36–7

Cranbrook
Pop. 279

257 C4 | 258 C4

ⓘ Council offices, Gathorne St; (08) 9826 1008; www.cranbrook.wa.gov.au

95.3 Hot FM, 630 AM ABC Local Radio

The small town of Cranbrook greets travellers with a large sign announcing that it is the 'Gateway to the Stirlings'. A mere 10 kilometres away is Stirling Range National Park, a mecca for bushwalkers and climbers. The nearby Frankland area has gained a national reputation for its premium-quality wines.

Station House Museum: restored and furnished 1930s-style; Gathorne St. **Wildflower walk:** 300 m walk to Stirling Gateway with displays of orchids in spring; Salt River Rd.

Cranbrook Shire on Show: Apr. **Wildflower Display:** Sept. **Art trail and Photographic Competition:** Oct.

Stirling Range National Park Surrounded by a flat, sandy plain, the Stirling Range rises abruptly to over 1000 m, its jagged peaks veiled in swirling mists. The cool, humid environment created by these low clouds supports 1500 flowering plant species, many unique to the area, earning the park recognition as one of the top-10 biodiversity hot spots in the world. This National Heritage–listed park is one of WA's premier destinations for bushwalking. Best time to visit is Oct–Dec. 10 km SE.

Sukey Hill Lookout: expansive views of farmland, salt lakes and Stirling Range; off Salt River Rd; 5 km E. **Lake Poorrarecup:** swimming and waterskiing; 40 km SW. **Wineries:** the nearby Frankland River region boasts several wineries, including Alkoomi, Frankland Estate and Ferngrove; 50 km W. **Wildflower drive and heritage trail:** brochures from visitor centre.

See also GREAT SOUTHERN, pp. 38–9

Cue
Pop. 273

261 D4 | 264 B5

ⓘ Golden Art Shop and Tourist Information Centre, Austin St; (08) 9963 1936; www.cue.wa.gov.au

102.9 WA FM, 106.1 FM ABC Local Radio

This town was once known as the 'Queen of the Murchison'. In 1891 Mick Fitzgerald and Ed Heffernan found large nuggets of gold not far from what was to become the main street. It was their prospecting mate, Tom Cue, who registered the claim on their behalf and when the town was officially proclaimed in 1894, it bore his name. Within ten years the population of this boom town had exploded to about 10 000 people. While Cue's population has dwindled, the legacy of those heady gold-rush days is evident in the town's remarkably grandiose buildings.

Heritage buildings Many early buildings still stand and are classified by the National Trust. A stroll up the main street takes in the elegant band rotunda, the former Gentleman's Club (now the shire offices, housing a photographic display of the region's history), the Old Gaol, the courthouse, the post office and the police station. One block west in Dowley St is the former Masonic Lodge built in 1899 and reputed to be the largest corrugated-iron structure in the Southern Hemisphere.

Walga Rock This monolith is 1.5 km long and 5 km around the base. It has several Aboriginal rock paintings. One of the most extraordinary paintings, considering that Cue is over 300 km from the sea, is of a white, square-rigged sailing ship. It is believed to depict one of the Dutch ships that visited WA's mid-west shores in the 17th century. 50 km W.

Day Dawn: once Cue's twin town, thanks to the fabulous wealth of the Great Fingall Mine.

RADIO STATION | IN TOWN | WHAT'S ON | NEARBY

The mine office, a magnificent century-old stone building now perched precariously on the edge of a new open-cut mine, is all that remains of the town; 5 km w. *Milly Soak:* popular picnic spot for early Cue residents. A tent hospital was set up nearby during the typhoid epidemic; three lone graves are the only reminder of the thousands who died; 16km N. *Heritage trail:* includes the abandoned towns Big Bell and Day Dawn; brochures from visitor centre. *Fossicking:* areas surrounding the town; details from visitor centre.

See also OUTBACK COAST & MID-WEST, pp. 44–5

Denham
Pop. 609

260 B3 | 261 A4

Knight Tce; (08) 9948 1590 or 1300 135 887; www.sharkbaywa.com.au

105.3 Hot Hits FM, 107.5 FM ABC Radio National

On the middle peninsula of Shark Bay, Denham is the most westerly town in Australia. Dirk Hartog, the Dutch navigator, landed on an island at the bay's entrance in 1616, the first known European to land on the continent. Centuries later, in 1858, Captain H. M. Denham surveyed the area and a town bearing his name was established. The Shark Bay region was once known for its pearling and fishing and the streets of Denham were literally paved with pearl shells. In the 1960s, however, the local roads board poured bitumen over the pearl shells, and so destroyed what could have been a unique tourist attraction. Fortunately, several buildings made from coquina shell block still stand in the town. Today Shark Bay is renowned for the wild dolphins that come inshore at Monkey Mia (pronounced 'my-a'). As a World Heritage area, it also protects dugongs, humpback whales, green and loggerhead turtles, important seagrass feeding grounds and a colony of stromatolites, the world's oldest living fossils.

Shell block buildings: St Andrews Anglican Church, cnr Hughes and Brockman sts, and the Old Pearlers Restaurant, cnr Knight Tce and Durlacher St, were both built from coquina shell block. *Town Bluff:* popular walk for beachcombers; from town along beach to bluff. *Pioneer Park:* contains the stone on which Captain Denham carved his name in 1858; Hughes St.

Monkey Mia The daily shore visits by the wild bottlenose dolphins at Monkey Mia are a world-famous phenomenon. The dolphins swim into the shallows, providing a unique opportunity for humans to make contact with them. It began in the 1960s when a local woman started feeding the dolphins that followed her husband's fishing boat to the shoreline. Feeding still occurs, although now it is carefully monitored by rangers to ensure that the dolphins maintain their hunting and survival skills. Visiting times, and the number of dolphins, vary. 26 km NE.

Dirk Hartog Island The state's largest and most historically significant island, named after Dutchman Dirk Hartog who landed here in 1616 – 154 years before Captain Cook. Hartog left behind an inscribed pewter plate, which was removed in 1697 by his countryman Willem de Vlamingh and replaced with another plate. The original was returned to Holland; Vlamingh's plate is now housed in the Maritime Museum in Fremantle. Flights and cruises depart daily; bookings at visitor centre. 30 km w.

Hamelin Pool stromatolites The shores of Hamelin Pool are dotted with stromatolites, the world's largest and oldest living fossils. These colonies of micro-organisms resemble the oldest and simplest forms of life on earth, dated at around 3.5 million years old. The Hamelin Pool stromatolites are relatively new colonies however, about 3000 years old. They thrive here because of the extreme salinity of the water, the occurrence of calcium bicarbonate and the limited water circulation. Visitors can view these extraordinary life forms from a boardwalk. Close by is the Flint Cliff Telegraph Station and Post Office Museum (1884) with a history of the region. 88 km SE.

Dugongs The Shark Bay World Heritage Area has the largest seagrass meadows in the world, covering about 4000 sq km. These meadows are home to around 10 000 dugongs, 10% of the world's remaining population. An endangered species, the dugong is nature's only vegetarian sea mammal. Also known as a sea cow, the dugong can live for up to 70 years and grow up to 3 m long. Tours are available offering visitors a unique opportunity to see dugongs in the wild. Details from visitor centre.

Little Lagoon: ideal fishing and picnic spot; 3 km N. *Francois Peron National Park:* Peron Homestead with its 'hot tub' of artesian water; 4WD access only; 7 km N. *Ocean Park:* marine park with aquarium and touch pool; 9 km s. *Eagle Bluff:* habitat of sea eagle and a good viewing spot for sharks and stingrays; 20 km s. *Blue Lagoon Pearl Farm:* working platform where black pearls are harvested; Monkey Mia; 26 km NE. *Shell Beach:* 120 km of unique coastline comprising countless tiny coquina shells; 45 km SE. *Steep Pt:* western-most point on mainland with spectacular scenery; 4WD access only; 260 km w. *Zuytdorp Cliffs:* extend from beneath Shark Bay region south to Kalbarri; 4WD access only. *Tours:* boat trips and charter flights to historic Dirk Hartog Island, catamaran cruises, safaris and coach tours; details from visitor centre.

See also OUTBACK COAST & MID-WEST, pp. 44–5

Denmark   Pop. 2735

256 A6 | 257 C5 | 258 C5

73 South Coast Hwy; (08) 9848 2055; www.denmark.com.au

92.1 FM ABC News Radio, 630 AM ABC Local Radio

Denmark lies at the foot of Mt Shadforth, overlooking the tranquil Denmark River and Wilson Inlet. It is surrounded by forests of towering karri trees that sweep down to meet the Southern Ocean. The Aboriginal name for the Denmark River is 'koorabup', meaning 'place of the black swan'. Originally a timber town, Denmark's economy is today sustained by a combination of dairying, beef cattle, fishing, timber and tourism. The town is close to some of the most beautiful coastline in the state.

Bert Bolle Barometer Huge water barometer that visitors can view by climbing the surrounding tower. Reputedly the world's largest, housed in the visitor centre.

Historical Museum: in old police station; Mitchell St. *Bandstand:* located on the riverbank with seating for the audience on the other side of the river; Holling Rd. *Arts and crafts:* galleries abound, including the Old Butter Factory in North St; details from visitor centre. *Mt Shadforth Lookout:* magnificent views; Mohr Dr. *Berridge and Thornton parks:* shaded picnic areas; along riverbank in Holling Rd.

Craft Market: Berridge Park; Jan, Easter and Dec. *Pantomime:* Civic Centre; Jan. *Brave New Works:* new performance art; Easter.

William Bay National Park This relatively small 1867 ha park protects stunning coastline and forest between Walpole and Denmark on WA's south coast. It is renowned for its primeval windswept granite tors. Green's Pool, a natural rockpool in the park, remains calm

and safe for swimming and snorkelling all year-round. Nearby are the Elephant Rocks, massive rounded boulders resembling elephants; Madfish Bay, a good fishing spot; and Waterfall Beach for swimming. 17 km sw.
Ocean Beach: one of the finest surfing beaches in WA; 8 km s. **Monkey Rock:** lookout with panoramic views; 10 km sw. **Bartholomew's Meadery:** honey, honey wines, gourmet honey ice-cream and other bee products, as well as a live beehive display; 20 km w. **Pentland Alpaca Stud and Tourist Farm:** diverse collection of animals, including alpacas, koalas, kangaroos, bison, water buffalo, llamas and many more; Cnr McLeod and Scotsdale rds; (08) 9840 9262; 20 km w. **Eden Gate Blueberry Farm:** spray-free fruit, a range of blueberry products and blueberry wines; open Thurs–Mon Dec–Apr; 25 km E. **Whale-watching:** viewing platform above Lowlands Beach (southern rights June–Oct); 28 km E. **Fishing:** at Wilson Inlet, Ocean Beach (8 km s) and Parry Beach (25 km w). **West Cape Howe National Park:** Torbay Head, WA's most southerly point, and Cosy Corner, a protected beach perfect for swimming; 30 km sw. **Wineries:** many wineries open for cellar-door tastings, including Howard Park Winery, West Cape Howe and Tinglewood Wines; maps from visitor centre. **Scenic drives:** the 25 km Mt Shadforth Scenic Drive and the 34 km Scotsdale Tourist Drive both feature lush forests, ocean views, wineries and galleries; maps from visitor centre. **Heritage trails:** 3 km Mokare trail, 5 km Karri Walk or 9 km Wilson Inlet trail; maps from visitor centre. **Bibbulmun Track:** a section of this world-class 963 km long-distance trail passes through Denmark; see Albany. **Valley of the Giants Tree Top Walk:** see Walpole; 65 km w.

See also GREAT SOUTHERN, pp. 38–9

Derby
Pop. 3091

266 B4 | 269 E3

i 2 Clarendon St; (08) 9191 1426 or 1800 621 426; www.derbytourism.com.au

102.7 WA FM, 873 AM ABC Local Radio

It is said that Derby, known as the 'Gateway to the Gorges', is where the real Kimberley region begins. The first town settled in the Kimberley, it features some spectacular natural attractions nearby: the Devonian Reef Gorges of Windjana and Tunnel Creek are only a few hours' drive along the Gibb River Road, and the magnificent islands of the Buccaneer Archipelago are just a short cruise away. Although King Sound was first explored in 1688, it wasn't until the early 1880s that the Port of Derby was established as a landing point for wool shipments and Derby was proclaimed a townsite. The first jetty was built in 1885, the same year that gold was discovered at Halls Creek. Miners and prospectors poured into the port on their way to the goldfields but by the 1890s, as gold fever died, the port was used almost exclusively for the export of live cattle and sheep. In 1951 iron-ore mining began at Cockatoo Island, which revitalised the town. Derby is now a service centre for the region's rich pastoral and mining industries. Rain closes some roads in the area from November to March, so check conditions before setting out on any excursion.

Old Derby Gaol: built in 1906, this is the oldest building in town; Loch St. **Wharfinger House Museum:** built in the 1920s for the local harbourmaster, the design is typical of the tropics. It now houses an extensive collection of historical memorabilia and Aboriginal artefacts. Key from visitor centre; Loch St. **Derby Jetty:** some of the highest tides in Australia, up to 12 m, can be seen from the jetty. It is now used to export ore from various local mines.

Market: Clarendon St; each Sat May–Sept. **King Tide Day:** festival celebrating highest tide in Australia; Apr/May. ***Moonrise Rock Festival:*** June. ***Derby Races:*** June/July. ***Mowanjum Festival:*** indigenous art and culture; July. ***Boab Festival:*** Mardi Gras, mud football, mud crab races and bush poets; July. ***Derby Rodeo:*** Aug. ***Boxing Day Sports:*** Dec.

Windjana Gorge National Park A 350-million-year-old Devonian reef rises majestically above the surrounding plains. An easy walking trail winds through the gorge, taking in primeval life forms fossilised within the gorge walls. 145 km E.

Tunnel Creek National Park Wear sandshoes, carry a torch and be prepared to get wet as you explore the 750 m long cave that runs through the Napier Range. Nearby Pigeon's Cave was the hideout of an 1890s Aboriginal outlaw, Jandamarra, also known as 'Pigeon'. Tour details from visitor centre. 184 km E.

Prison tree: 1000-year-old boab tree formerly used as a prison; 7 km S. ***Myall's Bore:*** beside the bore stands a 120 m long cattle trough reputed to be the longest in the Southern Hemisphere; 7 km S. ***Gorges:*** Lennard Gorge (190 km E), Bell Gorge (214 km E), Manning Gorge (306 km E), Barnett River Gorge (340 km NE) and Sir John Gorge (350 km E); 4WD access only. ***Mitchell Plateau:*** highlights include the Wandjina rock art and spectacular Mitchell Falls, King Edward River and Surveyor's Pool. In this remote region, visitors must be entirely self-sufficient; via Gibb River Rd and Kalumburu Rd; 580 km NE. Scenic flights can also be arranged from Drysdale River Station and Kununurra. ***Pigeon Heritage Trail:*** follow the story of the Aboriginal outlaw Jandamarra, nicknamed 'Pigeon', and his people, the Bunuba; maps from visitor centre. ***Gibb River Rd:*** 4WD road between Derby and Wyndham traverses some of the most spectacular gorge country of the Kimberley; guidebook and current road conditions from visitor centre. ***Buccaneer Archipelago:*** in Derby you can arrange a scenic flight or cruise around this archipelago which begins north of King Sound; *see Broome*.

See also KIMBERLEY, pp. 48–9

Dongara–Denison
Pop. 3052

258 A2

🛈 9 Waldeck St; (08) 9927 1404; www.irwin.wa.gov.au

📻 96.5 WA FM, 828 AM ABC Local Radio

Dongara and its nearby twin town of Port Denison lie on the coast 359 kilometres north of Perth. Dongara–Denison is the self-proclaimed 'Lobster Capital' of the state, with its offshore reefs supporting a profitable industry. Dongara's main street is lined with magnificent Moreton Bay fig trees while Port Denison provides local anglers with a large marina and harbour.

Irwin District Museum Housed in Dongara's Old Police Station, Courthouse and Gaol (1870), the museum features exhibits on the history of the buildings, the invasion of rabbits into WA and the Irwin Coast shipwrecks. Open 10am–4pm Mon–Fri; Waldeck St; (08) 9927 1323.

Russ Cottage: a beautifully restored farmworker's cottage (1870). The hard-packed material of the kitchen floor was made from scores of anthills, and the flood-level marker near the front door indicates how high the nearby Irwin River rose during the record flood of 1971; open 10am–12pm Sun or by appt; St Dominics Rd, Dongara. ***The Priory Hotel:*** this 1881 building has been an inn, a priory and a boarding college for girls and is now once again a hotel; St Dominics Rd, Dongara. ***Church of St John the Baptist:*** (1884) its pews were made from the driftwood of shipwrecks and its church bell is said to have come from Fremantle Gaol; Cnr Waldeck and Church sts, Dongara. ***The Royal Steam Flour Mill:*** (1894)

RADIO STATION   IN TOWN   WHAT'S ON   NEARBY

it served the local wheat-growing community until its closure in 1935; northern end of Waldeck St, Dongara. *Cemetery:* headstones dating from 1874 and a wall of remembrance to Dominican sisters; brochure from visitor centre; Dodd St, Dongara. *Town heritage trail:* 1.6 km walk that features 28 historic Dongara sites; maps from visitor centre. *Fisherman's Lookout:* 1 remaining of 2 obelisks built in 1869, with panoramic views of Port Denison; Pt Leander Dr, Port Denison.

Monthly Market: Priory Gardens; 1st Sat each month. *Craft Market:* old police station, Dongara; Easter and Christmas. *Dongara Races:* Easter. *Larry Lobster Community Festival and Blessing of the Fleet:* at the start of each rock lobster season; Nov.

Silverdale Olive Orchards: olive oil products and tastings; open Sat Apr–Nov or by appt; 10 km N. *Mingenew:* small town in agricultural surrounds. Nearby is Fossil Cliff, filled with marine fossils over 250 million years old; 47 km E.

See also OUTBACK COAST & MID-WEST, pp. 44–5

Donnybrook
Pop. 1932

255 C2 | 257 B4 | 258 B4

ⓘ Old Railway Station, South Western Hwy; (08) 9731 1720; www.donnybrook-balingup.wa.gov.au

95.7 Hot FM, 1224 AM ABC Radio National

Donnybrook is the centre of the oldest and largest apple-growing area in Western Australia. This is the home of the Granny Smith apple and where Lady William apples were developed. Gold was found here in 1897 but mined for only four years. Donnybrook is famous for its sandstone, which has been used in construction statewide since the early 1900s. In Perth, the GPO, St Mary's Cathedral and the University of Western Australia buildings have all been faced with Donnybrook stone. The quarry can be seen from the Upper Capel Road out of town.

Memorial Hall: built of Donnybrook stone; Bentley St. *Anchor and Hope Inn:* (1862) the oldest homestead in the district, now a private property; view outside from South Western Hwy. *Trigwell Place:* picnic and barbecue facilities, and canoeing on nearby Preston River; South Western Hwy.

Gourmet Wine and Food Fest: Feb. *Apple Festival Ball:* even-numbered years, Easter. *Marathon Relay:* Nov.

Old Goldfields Orchard and Cider Factory Combines goldfield history with a working orchard and restaurant. Climb the reconstructed poppet head over the mine, study the history of gold on the property and try your hand at gold prospecting. The orchard provides seasonal fruit for sale and you can enjoy tastings of cider, fruit juice and wines. Open 9.30am–4.30pm Wed–Sun and public/school holidays; Goldfields Rd; (08) 9731 0322; 6 km S.

Boyanup: features a transport museum; 12 km NW. *Ironstone Gully Falls:* barbecue area en route to Capel; 19 km W. *Gnomesville:* surprising roadside collection of garden gnomes; by the side of the Wellington Mills roundabout on the road between Dardanup and Lowden; 25 km SE.

See also THE SOUTH-WEST, pp. 34–5

Dunsborough
Pop. 3373

255 A3 | 257 A4 | 258 A4

ⓘ Seymour Blvd; (08) 9752 1288; www.geographebay.com

98.4 FM Western Tourist Radio, 1224 AM ABC Radio National

Dunsborough is a picturesque coastal town on the south-western tip of Geographe Bay. Just west of the town is Leeuwin–Naturaliste

National Park with its dramatic coastline and seasonal wildflower displays. Many of the wineries of the South-West region are only a short drive from the town.

Market: Dunsborough Hall, cnr Gibney St and Gifford Rd; 1st Sat each month. **Margaret River Wine Festival:** throughout region; Apr/May.

Leeuwin–Naturaliste National Park Close to Dunsborough at the northern end of the park is Cape Naturaliste, with its lighthouse, museum and whale-watching platform (humpback whales linger offshore Sept–Nov). Walking tracks offer spectacular views of the coastline. Sugarloaf Rock is a dramatic formation just south of the lighthouse – it is also a habitat of the endangered red-tailed tropic bird. 13 km NW. *See also Margaret River and Augusta.*

Country Life Farm: animals galore, plus merry-go-round, giant slide and bouncing castles; Caves Rd; (08) 9755 3707; 1 km w. **Simmo's Icecreamery:** 39 flavours of homemade ice-cream made fresh daily; Commonage Rd; 5 km SE. **Quindalup Fauna Park:** specialises in birds, fish, tropical butterflies and baby animals; (08) 9755 3933; 5 km E. **Wreck of HMAS Swan:** the largest accessible dive-wreck site in the Southern Hemisphere; tour bookings and permits at visitor centre; off Pt Picquet, just south of Eagle Bay; 8 km NW. **Beaches:** to the north-west, popular for fishing, swimming and snorkelling, include Meelup (5 km), Eagle Bay (8 km) and Bunker Bay (12 km). **Wineries:** as part of the Margaret River wine region, there are many wineries nearby; details from visitor centre. **Tours and activities:** whale-watching charters (Sept–Nov); deep-sea fishing charters; scuba diving, snorkelling and canoeing; wildflower displays in season.

See also THE SOUTH-WEST, pp. 34–5

Dwellingup

Pop. 344

254 C4 | 257 B3 | 258 B4

Marrinup St; (08) 9538 1108; www.murray.wa.gov.au

97.3 Coast FM, 684 AM ABC Local Radio

Set among pristine jarrah forest, this is a thriving timber town that was virtually destroyed in 1961 when lightning started a bushfire that lasted for five days, burnt 140 000 hectares of forest and destroyed several nearby towns. Dwellingup was the only town to be rebuilt, and is now a forest-management centre. The Hotham Valley Tourist Railway operates here.

Forest Heritage Centre This centre records WA's jarrah forest heritage and promotes fine wood design, training and education. The building is formed from rammed earth and designed to represent three jarrah leaves on a bough. It includes an Interpretive Centre, a School of Wood and a Forest Heritage Gallery. Learn about conservation and walk among the treetops on an 11 m high canopy walkway. Acacia Rd; (08) 9538 1395.

Historical Centre: includes a photographic display depicting early 1900s life in the mill towns. Also a 1939 Mack Fire Truck, the only one in WA; visitor centre, Marrinup St. *Community Hotel:* last community hotel in WA; Marrinup St. *Log Chop and Community Fair:* Feb. *Giant Pumpkin Competition:* Apr.

Lane–Poole Reserve Provides opportunities for picnicking, swimming, canoeing, rafting, fishing, camping and walking. Walk trails include sections of the Bibbulmun Track, the 18 km King Jarrah Track from Nanga Mill, the 17 km Nanga Circuit and a 1.5 km loop from Island Pool. 10 km s.

RADIO STATION   IN TOWN   WHAT'S ON   NEARBY

Marrinup Forest Tour: unique 16 km vehicle and walk tour that features many aspects of the Darling Scarp including the Marrinup POW camp and remnants of old mills and towns of days gone by; maps from visitor centre.
Hotham Valley Tourist Railway: travel from Perth via Pinjarra to Dwellingup by train, taking in lush green dairy country before climbing the Darling Range, WA's steepest and most spectacular section of railway, and finishing in the heart of the jarrah forest; steam-hauled May–Oct, diesel-hauled Nov–Apr; bookings (08) 9221 4444; Dwellingup Railway Station. *Etmilyn Forest Tramway:* takes visitors 8 km through farms and old-growth jarrah forest to the pioneer settlement of Etmilyn.
Bibbulmun Track: long-distance walk trail runs through the middle of the town; *see Albany.*
Munda Biddi Trail: WA's first long-distance off-road bike track begins in Mundaring near Perth and winds 182 km through native forest to Dwellingup. It will eventually be extended to Albany; details from visitor centre.

See also THE SOUTH-WEST, pp. 34–5

Esperance
Pop. 9536

259 E4

i Museum Village, Dempster St; (08) 9083 1555 or 1300 664 455; www.visitesperance.com

102.3 Hot FM, 837 AM ABC Local Radio

Esperance was a sleepy backwater until, in the 1950s, it was found that adding trace elements to the sandy soil made farming feasible. The town became a port and service centre for the agricultural and pastoral hinterland. However, it is the magnificent scenery, the pristine beaches and the proximity of many national parks that draw visitors to this town. Take the Great Ocean Drive, 38 kilometres of postcard-perfect scenery, and you will understand why Esperance is a popular holiday spot.

Municipal Museum Visit one of WA's outstanding regional museums. See exhibits about shipwrecks, including the famous *Sanko Harvest,* and learn of Australia's only recorded pirate, the bloodthirsty Black Jack Anderson, who roamed the Recherche Archipelago. There is also a comprehensive display about *Skylab,* which crashed and spread debris through the area in 1979. Open 1.30–4.30pm daily; James St; (08) 9071 1579.

Museum Village: collection of historic buildings housing craft shops, pottery shops, art gallery, cafe and visitor centre; Dempster St. *Cannery Arts Centre:* local exhibitions with wind garden and views behind; Norseman Rd. *Mermaid Leather:* unique range of leather products made from fish and shark skins; Wood St. *Aquarium:* 14 aquariums and touch pool; the Esplanade.

Market: Dempster St; Sun mornings. *Wildflower Show:* Sept. *Agricultural Show:* Oct.

Great Ocean Drive One of Australia's most spectacular scenic drives, this 38 km loop road passes wind farms, which supply 30% of the town's electricity and some of the region's best-known natural attractions. Maps from visitor centre.

Cape Le Grand National Park This spectacular coastline is lined with pristine beaches, including Hellfire Bay and Thistle Cove. At Lucky Bay, kangaroos can often be spotted lying on the beach. Visit Whistling Rock, which 'whistles' under certain wind conditions, and climb Frenchman's Peak for breathtaking views. There are magnificent displays of wildflowers in spring, and many bushwalks. Camping at Cape Le Grand and Lucky Bay. 56 km E.

Recherche Archipelago The Esperance region is known as the Bay of Isles because of this collection of 110 islands dotted along the coast that provide a haven for seals and sea lions. Cruises (3 hrs 30 min, subject to numbers and weather) take you around Cull, Button, Charlie, Woody and other islands; landing is permitted only on Woody Island. For an extraordinary camping experience, try a safari hut on Woody Island (open Sept–Apr). These canvas huts set high on timber decking overlook an idyllic turquoise bay framed by eucalyptus trees. Woody Island also has an interpretive centre to provide information to visitors.

Rotary Lookout: views of bay, town and archipelago; Wireless Hill; 2 km w. *Pink Lake:* a pink saltwater lake; 5 km w. *Twilight Cove:* sheltered swimming; 12 km w. *Observatory Pt and Lookout:* dramatic views of bay and islands; 17 km w. *Monjingup Lake Nature Reserve:* walk trails, birdwatching and wildflowers in spring; 20 km w. *Dalyup River Wines:* the most isolated winery in WA; open weekends in summer; (08) 9076 5027; 42 km w. *Stokes National Park:* beautiful coastal and inlet scenery; 80 km w. *Cape Arid National Park:* birdwatching, fishing, camping and 4WD routes; 120 km E. *Whale-watching:* southern right whales visit bays and protected waters to calve (June–Oct); along the Great Ocean Drive and at Cape Arid. *Great Country Drive:* takes visitors 92 km inland; maps from visitor centre.

See also ESPERANCE & NULLARBOR, pp. 40–1

Eucla
Pop. 50

259 H2

i Eucla Motel; (08) 9039 3468.

97.1 FM ABC Radio National, 531 AM ABC Local Radio

Eucla is the largest settlement on the Nullarbor Plain, located just near the South Australian border. The ruins of a telegraph station exist at the original townsite and beyond the ruins are the remains of a jetty, a reminder of pioneering days when supplies were transported by boat. Eucla is today located on the Hampton Tableland and operates on Central Western Time, 45 minutes ahead of the rest of Western Australia.

Telegraph station ruins Opened in 1877 (just 33 years after Samuel Morse invented the telegraph), the Eucla Telegraph Station helped link WA with the rest of Australia and the world, often sending over 20 000 messages a year. The first message, sent to Perth in December 1877, stated simply, 'Eucla line opened. Hurrah.' 4 km s.

Eucla Museum: local history, including exhibits of the telegraph station, told through newspaper clippings and old photographs; Eucla Motel. *Travellers' Cross:* dedicated to travellers and illuminated at night; on the escarpment, west of town. *Bureau of Meteorology:* visitors welcome; east of town; (08) 9039 3444. *9-hole golf course:* site of the Golf Classic in May; north of town.

Eucla National Park This small park extends between Eucla and Border Village. On the coast near the SA border is Wilsons Bluff Lookout, with views to the east following the Bunda Cliffs into the distance. Closer to Eucla are the enormous sculptural shapes of the Delisser Sandhills. Mark your footprints in the dunes.

Border Village: quarantine checkpoint for people entering WA (travellers should ensure they are not carrying fruit, vegetables, honey, used fruit and produce containers, plants or seeds). The Border Dash starts here every Oct; 13 km E.

See also ESPERANCE & NULLARBOR, pp. 40–1

Exmouth
Pop. 1845

261 A2

i Murat Rd; (08) 9949 1176 or 1800 287 328; www.exmouthwa.com.au

107.7 ABC Radio National, 1188 AM ABC Local Radio

RADIO STATION   IN TOWN   WHAT'S ON   NEARBY

One of the newest towns in Australia, Exmouth was founded in 1967 as a support town for the Harold E. Holt US Naval Communications Station, the main source of local employment. Excellent year-round fishing and proximity to Cape Range National Park and Ningaloo Reef have since made Exmouth a major tourist destination. The town is the nearest point in Australia to the continental shelf.

Mall Market: each Sun Apr–Sept. **Gamex:** world-class game-fishing competition; Mar. **Whale Shark Festival:** Apr/May. **Art Quest:** July. **Bill Fish Bonanza:** Oct/Nov.

Cape Range National Park This rugged landscape of arid rocky gorges is edged by the stunning coastline of Ningaloo Marine Park. Wildlife is abundant, with emus, euros, rock wallabies and red kangaroos often sighted. In late winter there is a beautiful array of wildflowers including the Sturt's desert pea and the superb bird flower. Attractions within the park include Shothole Canyon, an impressive gorge; Mangrove Bay, a sanctuary zone with a bird hide overlooking a lagoon; and Mandu Mandu Gorge where you can walk along an ancient river bed. Yardie Creek is the only gorge with permanent water. Turquoise Bay is a popular beach for swimming and snorkelling (watch for currents). The Milyering Visitor Centre (54 km sw), made of rammed earth and run by solar power, is 52 km from Exmouth on the western side of the park and offers information on both Cape Range and Ningaloo. Contact (08) 9949 2808.

Ningaloo Marine Park: see Coral Bay. **Naval Communication Station:** the centre tower in its antenna field, at 388 m, is one of the tallest structures in the Southern Hemisphere; not open to public; 5 km N. **Vlamingh Head Lighthouse and Lookout:** built in 1912, Australia's only kerosene-burning lighthouse served as a beacon to mariners until 1967. The lookout offers panoramic 360-degree views; 19 km N. **Learmonth Jetty:** popular fishing spot, rebuilt after Cyclone Vance; 33 km s.

Wildlife-watching: turtle-nesting (Nov–Jan); coral-spawning (Mar–Apr); boat cruises and air flights to see whale sharks (Mar–June); humpback whales (Aug–Nov) from lighthouse (17 km N) and from whale-watching boat tours. Snorkellers can swim with whale sharks and manta rays located by cruise boats. Coral-viewing boat cruises also available; details from visitor centre.

See also OUTBACK COAST & MID-WEST, pp. 44–5

Fitzroy Crossing
Pop. 925

266 D5 | 269 F3

i Cnr Great Northern Hwy and Flynn Dr; (08) 9191 5355.

102.9 WA FM, 106.1 FM ABC Local Radio

Fitzroy Crossing is in the heart of the Kimberley region. As its name suggests, the original townsite was chosen as the best place to ford the mighty Fitzroy River. In the wet season, the river can rise over 20 metres and spread out up to 15 kilometres from its banks. Fitzroy Crossing's main attraction is its proximity to the magnificent 30-metre-deep Geikie Gorge with its sheer yellow, orange and grey walls. Check road conditions before any excursions from December to March, as this area is prone to flooding.

Crossing Inn First established in the 1890s as a shanty inn and trade store for passing stockmen, prospectors and drovers, it has operated on the same site ever since and is one of the very few hotels in the state to retain a true outback atmosphere. A stop-off and drink are a must for all travellers passing by. Skuthorp Rd; (08) 9191 5080.

Rodeo: July. **Garnduwa Festival:** sporting events; Oct.

Geikie Gorge National Park Geikie Gorge has cliffs and sculptured rock formations carved by water through an ancient limestone reef. The Fitzroy River is home to sharks, sawfish and stingrays that have, over centuries, adapted to the fresh water. Freshwater crocodiles up to 3 m long and barramundi are plentiful, best seen on a guided boat tour. Aboriginal heritage and cultural tours are run by guides from the local Bunuba tribe; bookings essential. DEC rangers run tours on the geology, wildlife and history of the area. Entry to park is restricted during wet season (Dec–Mar). Details from visitor centre. 18 km NE.

Causeway Crossing: a concrete crossing that was the only way across the river until the new bridge was built in the 1970s; Geikie Gorge Rd; 4 km NE. **Tunnel Creek National Park:** unique formation created by waters from the creek cutting a 750 m tunnel through the ancient reef; 4WD access only; 110 km NW. **Windjana Gorge National Park:** 350-million-year-old Devonian reef rising majestically above the surrounding plains. An easy walking trail takes you past primeval life forms fossilised within the gorge walls; 4WD access only; 145 km NW. **4WD tours:** to Tunnel Creek and Windjana Gorge; bookings essential, details from visitor centre.

See also KIMBERLEY, pp. 48–9

Gascoyne Junction
Pop. 46

261 B3

i Shire offices, 4 Scott St; (08) 9943 0988; www.gascoyneonline.com.au

Lying at the junction of the Lyons and Gascoyne rivers, Gascoyne Junction is a small administration centre for the pastoral industry. Sheep stations in the area, ranging in size from around 36 000 to 400 000 hectares, produce a wool clip exceeding 1.5 million kilograms annually.

Junction Hotel: see the high-water mark from the 1982 floods on the wall of this Aussie pub; Carnarvon–Mullewa Rd. **Old Roads Board Museum:** memorabilia of the area; Scott St.

Bush Races: Sept/Oct. **Gascoyne Dash:** cross-country endurance; Oct.

Kennedy Range National Park Along with spectacular scenery, the park is home to fossils of the earliest known species of banksia in Australia and marine fossils that reflect the history of the region as an ocean bed. Ideal for sightseeing, hiking and bush camping, trails start from the camping area and pass through gorges where you can see honeycomb-like rock formations. 60 km N.

Mt Augustus National Park Mt Augustus is the world's largest monolith, twice the size of Uluṟu. It is also known as Burringurrah, named after a boy who, in Aboriginal legend, broke tribal law by running away from his initiation. On capture, he was speared in the upper right leg. The spear broke as the boy fell to the ground, leaving a section protruding from his leg. It is said that, as you look at Mt Augustus, you can see the shape of the boy's body with the stump of the spear being the small peak at the eastern end called Edney's Lookout. There are several walking and driving trails; maps from visitor centre. 294 km NE; see Carnarvon.

See also OUTBACK COAST & MID-WEST, pp. 44–5

Geraldton
Pop. 31 550

258 A1 | 261 B5

i Bill Sewell Complex, cnr Chapman Rd and Bayley St; (08) 9921 3999 or 1800 818 881; www.geraldtontourist.com.au

94.9 ABC Classic FM, 96.5 WA FM

Situated on the spectacular Batavia Coast, Geraldton is the largest town in the Mid-West region. As a port city, it is the major centre for the wheat belt and is renowned for its rock lobster industry. Geraldton is also regarded as one of the best windsurfing locations in the world. The nearby Houtman Abrolhos Islands are the site of 16 known shipwrecks. The most infamous is that of the Dutch ship *Batavia*, which foundered on a reef in 1629.

HMAS *Sydney* **Memorial** Built on Mt Scott overlooking the town to commemorate the loss of 645 men from HMAS *Sydney* on 19 November 1941. The ship sank after an encounter with the German raider HSK *Kormoran*. The wrecks of both ships were found in March 2008. Seven pillars representing the seven seas hold aloft a 9 m high domed roof formed of 645 interlocking figures of seagulls. At night an eternal flame lights the cupola. Near the memorial is the bronze sculpture of a woman looking out to sea, representing the women left behind waiting for those who would not return. Tours of the memorial site are conducted daily at 10.30am. Cnr George Rd and Brede St.

WA Museum Geraldton Exhibits focus on the cultural and natural heritage of the Geraldton region. Maritime displays include finds from Australia's oldest shipwrecks, notably the original stone portico destined to adorn the castle gateway in the city of Batavia and lost to the sea when the *Batavia* sank in 1629. Museum Pl, Batavia Coast Marina; (08) 9921 5080. Adjacent in the Geraldton Marina is a replica of the *Batavia* longboat.

Historic buildings: explore the town's historic architecture dating back to the mid-1800s, with works by noted architect Monsignor John Cyril Hawes a highlight. Many of the buildings have been restored and are open to the public, including the Old Geraldton Gaol (1858), which is now a craft centre and the Bill Sewell Complex (1884), which was built as a hospital and subsequently became a prison. In Cathedral Ave, St Francis Xavier Cathedral offers tours (10am Mon, Wed and Fri), and the Cathedral of the Holy Cross has one of the largest areas of stained glass in Australia. Self-guide walks are available, including the Heritage Trail; details from visitor centre. *Geraldton Regional Art Gallery:* the original Geraldton Town Hall (1907) converted to house art exhibitions and workshops; closed Mon; Chapman Rd. *Leon Baker Jewellers:* international jeweller works with Abrolhos pearls and Argyle diamonds. Workshop tours are available; Marine Tce Mall. *Rock Lobster Factory:* take a tour and follow the journey of Geraldton's most famous export, the western rock lobster, from processor to plate; covered shoes required; tours 9.30am Mon–Fri Nov–June; Willcock Dr, Fisherman's Wharf. *Pt Moore Lighthouse:* assembled in 1878 from steel sections prefabricated in England, and standing 34 m tall, this is the only lighthouse of its kind in Australia; Willcock Dr.

Sunshine Festival: Oct.

Houtman Abrolhos Islands These 122 reef islands with a fascinating history span 100 km of ocean and are the main source of rock lobster for the local lobster fishing industry. There are 16 known shipwrecks in the Abrolhos Islands, the most infamous of which is that of the Dutch ship *Batavia* from 1629. Captain Pelsaert and 47 of the survivors sailed north to Batavia (modern-day Jakarta) for help. When they returned three and a half months later, they discovered that a mutiny had taken place and 125 of the remaining survivors had been massacred. All of the mutineers were hanged, except for two who were marooned on the mainland, becoming Australia's first white inhabitants. There is no record of their subsequent fate. The wreck was discovered in 1963 and some skeletons of victims of the mutiny have been found on Beacon Island. The islands now offer diving, snorkelling, surfing, windsurfing, fishing and birdwatching. Access is via boat or plane; tours and charters are available. Details from and bookings at visitor centre. 65 km w.

Fishing: good fishing spots at Sunset Beach (6 km N) and Drummond Cove (10 km N). *Mill's Park Lookout:* excellent views over Moresby Range and coastal plain; 10 km NE. *Oakabella Homestead:* one of the region's oldest pioneering homesteads with a rare buttressed barn; tours available; 30 km N. *Chapman Valley:* an area of scenic drives and spectacular scenery, once home to the first coffee bean plantation in Australia. Also a huge diversity of wildflowers on display July–Oct. Wineries include Chapman Valley Wines, the northernmost winery in WA; enjoy free tastings; 35 km NE. *Scenic flights:* tours over nearby Abrolhos Islands, Murchison Gorges or the coastal cliffs of Kalbarri; details from visitor centre.

See also OUTBACK COAST & MID-WEST, pp. 44–5

Gingin
Pop. 527

254 B1 | 257 B2 | 258 A3

i Council offices, Brockman St; (08) 9575 2211; www.gingin.wa.gov.au

720 AM ABC Local Radio, 810 AM ABC Radio National

Gingin is one of the oldest towns in Western Australia, having been settled in 1832, only two years after the establishment of the Swan River Colony. For tourists, it has the charm of old original stone buildings within a picturesque natural setting. Situated 84 kilometres north of Perth, it is an ideal destination for a daytrip from the city.

Historic buildings Enjoy a pleasant self-guide stroll around the town on the Gingin Walkabout Trail, which features many fine examples of early architecture including Philbey's Cottage and St Luke's Anglican Church, both made from local stone. Maps from visitor centre.

Granville Park: in the heart of the town with free barbecue facilities, playground and picnic area. *Self-guide walks:* stroll along the Gingin Brook on the Jim Gordon VC Trail or try the Three Bridges Recreation Trail, rebuilt after being destroyed by fire in Dec 2002; maps from visitor centre.

Horticultural Expo: Apr. **British Car Club Day:** May. **Market Day Festival:** Sept.

Gravity Discovery Centre Opened in 2003, this $4 million centre offers hands-on and static scientific displays on gravity, magnetism and electricity. It includes the biggest public astronomy centre in the Southern Hemisphere and the largest telescope in WA. Visitors can take a high-tech look at heavenly bodies in an evening presentation (bookings essential) and see a number of WA inventions relating to physics. Military Rd; (08) 9575 7577; 15 km SW.

Cemetery: with a spectacular display of kangaroo paws in early spring; northern outskirts of town. *Jylland Winery:* open to public, wine-tastings and cellar-door sales; 2 km S. *West Coast Honey:* live bee display, honey extraction, tastings, sales of honey and bee products; open 9am–4pm Wed–Sun, or Mon and Tues by appt; Gingin Brook Rd; 3 km W. *Moore River National Park:* special area for conservation featuring banksia woodlands and wildflower displays in spring; 20 km NW.

See also HEARTLANDS, pp. 36–7

Greenough
Pop. 15 394

258 A2

i Cnr Chapman Rd and Bayly St, Geraldton; (08) 9921 3999 or 1800 818 881; www.cgg.wa.gov.au

96.5 WA FM, 99.7 FM ABC Radio National

RADIO STATION | IN TOWN | WHAT'S ON | NEARBY

Lying 24 kilometres south of Geraldton, the Greenough Flats form a flood plain close to the mouth of the Greenough River. At its peak in the 1860s and '70s, Greenough (pronounced 'Grennuff') was a highly successful wheat-growing area. However, the combined effects of drought, crop disease and floods led to the area's decline and from 1900 the population dropped dramatically. The historic hamlet that was once the centre of this farming community has been extensively restored and is classified by the National Trust.

Central Greenough Historic Settlement
Precinct of 11 restored stone buildings dating from the 1860s including a school, police station, courthouse, gaol and churches. Fully re-created interior furnishings. Self-guide maps are available, or tours by appt. Cnr Brand Hwy and McCartney Rd; (08) 9926 1084.

Pioneer Museum: folk display located in an original limestone cottage; tours available; Brand Hwy. *Leaning trees:* these trees are a unique sight, having grown sideways in response to the harsh salt-laden winds that blow from the Indian Ocean; seen from Brand Hwy on the Greenough Flats. *Hampton Arms Inn:* fully restored historic inn (1863); Company Rd.

Walkaway Railway Station: built in the style of a traditional British railway station, now housing a railway and heritage museum; closed Mon; Evans Rd; 10 km E. *Greenough River mouth:* ideal for swimming, canoeing, beach and rock fishing, birdwatching and photography; 14 km N. *Flat Rocks:* surfing, swimming and rock-fishing. A round of the State Surfing Championships is held here in June every year; 10 km S. *Ellendale Pool:* this deep, freshwater swimming hole beneath spectacular sandstone cliffs is an ideal picnic area; 23 km E. *Greenough River Nature Trail:* self-guide walk; brochures from visitor centre. *The Greenough/Walkaway Heritage Trail:* 57 km self-drive tour of the area; maps from visitor centre.

See also OUTBACK COAST & MID-WEST, pp. 44–5

Halls Creek

Pop. 1209

267 F5 | 269 G3

Hall St; (08) 9168 6262; www.hallscreek.wa.gov.au

102.9 WA FM, 106.1 FM ABC Local Radio

In the heart of the Kimberley region and on the edge of the Great Sandy Desert, Halls Creek is the site of the first payable gold discovery in Western Australia. In 1885 Jack Slattery and Charlie Hall (after whom the town is named) discovered gold, thereby sparking a gold rush that brought over 15 000 people to the area. In 1917 a seriously injured stockman named James 'Jimmy' Darcy was taken into Halls Creek. With neither doctor nor hospital in the town, the local postmaster carried out an emergency operation using a penknife as instructions were telegraphed by morse code from Perth. The Perth doctor then set out on the ten-day journey to Halls Creek via cattle boat, model-T Ford, horse-drawn sulky and finally, on foot, only to discover that the patient had died the day before his arrival. The event inspired Reverend John Flynn to establish the Royal Flying Doctor Service in 1928, a development that helped to encourage settlement throughout the outback.

Russian Jack Memorial: tribute to a prospector who pushed his sick friend in a wheelbarrow to Wyndham for medical help; Thomas St. *Trackers Hut:* restored original hut of Aboriginal trackers; Robert St, behind police station.

Rodeo: July. *Picnic Races:* Oct.

Wolfe Creek Crater National Park Wolfe Creek Crater is the second-largest meteorite crater in the world. Named after Robert Wolfe, a Halls Creek prospector, it is 870–950 m across and in Aboriginal legend, said to be the site of the emergence of a powerful rainbow serpent from the earth. Scenic flights afford magnificent views; details from visitor centre. 148 km S.

Purnululu National Park This World Heritage Area in the outback of the east Kimberley is home to the Bungle Bungle Range, a remarkable landscape of tiger-striped, beehive-shaped rock domes. A scenic flight is the best way to gain a perspective of the Bungle Bungles' massive size and spectacular scenery (details from visitor centre). The most visited site in Purnululu is Cathedral Gorge, a fairly easy walk. A couple of days and a backpack allow you to explore nearby Piccaninny Creek and Gorge, camping overnight. On the northern side of the park is Echidna Chasm, a narrow gorge totally different from those on the southern side. Purnululu is also rich in Aboriginal art, and there are many traditional burial sites within its boundaries. Purnululu is open to visitors (Apr–Dec) and is accessible by 4WD. There are few facilities and no accommodation; visitors must carry in all food and water and notify a ranger. 160 km E.

China Wall: white quartz formation said to resemble Great Wall of China; 6 km E. *Caroline's Pool:* deep pool ideal for swimming (in wet season) and picnicking; 15 km E. *Old Halls Creek:* remnants of original town including graveyard where James Darcy is buried; prospecting available; 16 km E. *Palm Springs:* fishing, swimming and picnicking; 45 km E. *Sawpit Gorge:* fishing, swimming, picnicking; 52 km E. *Billiluna Aboriginal Community:* fishing, swimming, camping, birdwatching and bushwalking, and bush tucker and cultural tours; 180 km s.

See also KIMBERLEY, pp. 48–9

Harvey

Pop. 2602

255 C1 | 257 B3 | 258 B4

James Stirling Pl; (08) 9729 1122; www.harveytourism.com

96.5 FM Harvey Community Radio, 810 AM ABC Radio National

On the Harvey River, 18 kilometres from the coast, the thriving town of Harvey is surrounded by fertile, irrigated plains. Beef production, citrus orchards and viticulture flourish in the region and intensive dairy farming provides the bulk of Western Australia's milk supply. Bordered by the Darling Range, Harvey offers a wealth of natural attractions, from the magnificent scenic drives through the escarpment to the pristine white beaches with excellent sunsets and fishing on the coast.

Tourist and Interpretive Centre: tourist information and display of local industries and May Gibbs characters; James Stirling Pl. *Big Orange:* lookout, one of Australia's big icons; Third St. *Harvey Museum:* memorabilia housed in renovated railway station; open 2–4pm Sun or by appt; Harper St. *Stirling Cottage:* replica of the home of Governor Stirling, which later became the home of May Gibbs, author of *Snugglepot and Cuddlepie*; James Stirling Pl tourist precinct. *Heritage Gardens:* picturesque country gardens on the banks of the Harvey River; James Stirling Pl tourist precinct. *Internment Camp Memorial Shrine:* the only roadside shrine of its type in the world, built by prisoners of war in the 1940s; collect key from visitor centre; South Western Hwy. *Heritage trail:* 6.2 km self-guide walk includes historic buildings and sights of town; maps from visitor centre. *Mosaics and murals:* unique collection throughout the region. See Uduc Rd, South Western Hwy, and entrances to Myalup and Binningup.

Summer Series Concerts: Jan–Mar. *Harvest Festival:* Mar. *Spring Fair:* Sept.

Harvey Dam: landscaped park with viewing platform, amphitheatre, barbecues and playground. Fishing is allowed in season with permit; 3 km E. *HaVe Cheese:* tours and

RADIO STATION | IN TOWN | WHAT'S ON | NEARBY

gourmet cheese tasting; (08) 9729 3949; 3 km s. **White Rocks Museum and Dairy:** founded in 1887. Compare current technology with display of machinery from the past; open 2–4pm or by appt for groups; 15 km s. **Beaches:** Myalup Beach provides good swimming, surfing and beach fishing; 21 km w. Binningup Beach is protected by a reef that runs parallel to shore and is ideal for sheltered swimming, snorkelling, beach fishing and boating; 25 km sw. **Wineries:** more than 10 wineries open to the public, only a short distance from town; details from visitor centre.

See also THE SOUTH-WEST, pp. 34–5

Hyden
Pop. 281

257 D2 | 258 C3

i Wave Rock; (08) 9880 5182; www.waverock.com.au

648 AM ABC Local Radio, 1296 AM ABC Radio National

The small wheat-belt town of Hyden is synonymous with its famous nearby attraction, Wave Rock, originally known as Hyde's Rock in honour of a sandalwood cutter who lived in the area. A typing error by the Lands Department made it Hyden Rock, and the emerging town soon became known as Hyden. The area around the town boasts beautiful wildflowers in spring, including a wide variety of native orchids.

Wave Rock Weekender: music festival; Sept/Oct.

Wave Rock Resembling a breaking wave, this 100 m long and 15 m high granite cliff owes its shape to wind action over the past 2.7 billion years. Vertical bands of colour are caused by streaks of algae and chemical staining from run-off waters (4 km E). At Wave Rock Visitor Centre see the largest lace collection in the Southern Hemisphere with fine examples of antique lace, including lace worn by Queen Victoria. There are local wildflower species on display, an Australiana collection at the Pioneer Town, fauna in a natural bush environment and a walking trail.

Hippo's Yawn: rock formation; 5 km E via Wave Rock. **The Humps and Mulka's Cave:** Aboriginal wall paintings; 22 km N via Wave Rock. **Rabbit-Proof Fence:** see the fence where it meets the road; 56 km E.

See also HEARTLANDS, pp. 36–7

Jurien Bay
Pop. 1175

257 A1 | 258 A2

i Council offices, 110 Bashford St; (08) 9652 1020; www.dandaragan.wa.gov.au

103.1 WA FM, 107.9 FM ABC Radio National

Jurien Bay, settled in the mid-1850s, is the centre of a lobster fishing industry. The jetty was constructed in 1885 to enable a more efficient route to markets for locally produced wool and hides. Located within a sheltered bay protected by reefs and islands, the town has wide beaches and sparkling waters ideal for swimming, waterskiing, windsurfing, snorkelling, diving and surfing. The Jurien Bay boat harbour services the fishing fleet and has facilities for holiday boating and fishing. Anglers can fish from boat, jetty and beach.

Jurien Bay Charters: boat and fishing charters, scuba diving, sea lion tours; bookings at dive shop; Carmella St. **Old jetty site:** plaque commemorates site of original jetty. Remains of the jetty's timber piles have been discovered 65 m inland from high-water mark, which indicates the gradual build-up of coastline over time; Hastings St.

Market: Bashford St; usually last Sat each month. **Blessing of the Fleet:** Nov.

Jurien Bay Marine Park Established in August 2003, this marine park extends from

Wedge Island to Green Head and encompasses major sea lion and seabird breeding areas. The reefs within the park are populated by a wide range of plants and animals including the rare Australian sea lion, and the seagrass meadows are a breeding ground for western rock lobsters.

Lions Lookout: spectacular views of town and surrounds; 5 km E. *Drovers Cave National Park:* rough limestone country with numerous caves, all of which have secured entrances limiting public access; 4WD access only; 7 km E. *Grigsons Lookout:* panoramic views of ocean and hinterland. Also wildflowers July–Nov; 15 km N. *Lesueur National Park:* with over 900 species of flora, representing 10% of the state's known flora, Lesueur is an important area for flora conservation. Enjoy coastal views from a lookout; 23 km E. *Stockyard Gully National Park:* walk through 300 m Stockyard Gully Tunnel along winding underground creek; 4WD access only; 50 km N.

See also HEARTLANDS, pp. 36–7

Kalbarri

Pop. 1329

261 B5

Grey St; (08) 9937 1104 or 1800 639 468; www.kalbarriwa.info

102.9 WA FM, 106.1 FM ABC Local Radio

Kalbarri lies at the mouth of the Murchison River, flanked by Kalbarri National Park. Established in 1951, the town is a popular holiday resort, famous for the magnificent gorges up to 130 metres deep along the river. Just south of the township a cairn marks the spot where in 1629 Captain Pelsaert of the Dutch East India Company marooned two crew members implicated in the *Batavia* shipwreck and massacre. These were the first, albeit unwilling, white inhabitants of Australia.

Oceanarium: large aquariums and touch pools; Grey St; (08) 9937 2027. *Pelican feeding:* daily feeding by volunteers on the river foreshore; starts 8.45am; off Grey St. *Family Entertainment Centre:* trampolines, minigolf, bicycle hire; Magee Cres; (08) 9937 1105.

Sport Fishing Classic: Mar. *Canoe and Cray Carnival:* June.

Kalbarri National Park Gazetted in 1963, this park has dramatic coastal cliffs along its western boundary, towering river gorges and seasonal wildflowers, many of which are unique to the park. The Murchison River has carved a gorge through sedimentary rock known as Tumblagooda sandstone, creating a striking contrast of brownish red and purple against white bands of stone. Embedded in these layers are some of the earliest signs of animal life on earth. There are many lookouts including Nature's Window at the Loop, which overlooks the Murchison Gorge, and the breathtaking scenery at Z Bend Lookout. Along the 20 km coastal section of the park, lookouts such as Mushroom Rock, Pot Alley and Eagle Gorge offer panoramic views and whale-watching sites. Bushwalking, rock climbing, abseiling, canoeing tours, rafting, cruises, camping safaris, coach and wilderness tours, and barbecue facilities are all available. Details from visitor centre. 57 km E.

Rainbow Jungle: breeding centre for rare and endangered species of parrots, cockatoos and exotic birds set in landscaped tropical gardens. Also here is the largest walk-in parrot free-flight area in Australia and an outdoor cinema featuring the latest movies; Red Bluff Rd; 3 km S. *Seahorse Sanctuary:* aquaculture centre focused on the conservation of seahorses and other tropical marine fish; Red Bluff Rd; 3 km S. *Wildflower Centre:* view over 200 species on display along a 1.8 km walking trail. Visit the plant nursery and herbarium, where you can purchase seeds and souvenirs; open July–Nov; Ajana–Kalbarri Rd; 3km E.

RADIO STATION | IN TOWN | WHAT'S ON | NEARBY

Murchison House Station: tours available of one of the oldest and largest stations in WA, which includes historic buildings and cemetery, display of local arts and crafts, and wildflowers; seasonal, check with visitor centre; Ajana–Kalbarri Rd; 4 km E. *Big River Ranch:* enjoy horseriding through the spectacular countryside; Ajana–Kalbarri Rd; 4 km E. *Wittecarra Creek:* cairn marking the site where 2 of the mutineers from the Dutch ship *Batavia* were left as punishment for their participation in the murders of 125 survivors of the wreck; 4 km S. *Hutt River Province:* independant sovereign state founded in 1970; 50 km SE; see *Northampton*.

See also OUTBACK COAST & MID-WEST, pp. 44–5

Kalgoorlie–Boulder

see inset box on next page

Karratha

Pop. 11 727

261 C1 | 262 B2 | 264 A1 | 268 A5

4548 Karratha Rd; (08) 9144 4600.

104.1 FM ABC News Radio, 106.5 WA FM

Karratha is the Aboriginal word for 'good country'. Founded in 1968 as a result of expansion of the iron-ore industry, Karratha was originally established for workers on the huge industrial projects nearby. For visitors, Karratha is an ideal centre from which to explore the fascinating Pilbara region.

TV Hill Lookout: excellent views over town centre and beyond; off Millstream Rd. *Jaburara Heritage Trail:* 3 hr walk features Aboriginal rock carvings; pamphlet from visitor centre.

FeNaClNG Festival: this celebration takes its name from the town's mining roots (Fe is the chemical symbol for iron ore, NaCl is the symbol for salt, and NG is an abbreviation for natural gas); Aug. *Gamefishing Classic:* Aug.

Millstream–Chichester National Park Rolling hills, spectacular escarpments and tree-lined watercourses with hidden rockpools characterise this park. The remarkable oasis of Millstream is an area of tropical palm-fringed freshwater springs, well known to the Afghan cameleers of Pilbara's past. Other notably scenic spots are Python, Deepreach and Circular pools, and Cliff Lookout. The Millstream Homestead Visitor Centre, housed in the Gordon family homestead (1919), has displays dedicated to the local Aboriginal people, early settlers and the natural environment. Popular activities include bushwalking, picnicking, camping, fishing, swimming and boating. Tours are available; details from visitor centre. 124 km S.

Salt Harvest Ponds: Australia's largest evaporative salt fields. Tours are available; details from visitor centre; 15 km N. *Dampier:* port facility servicing the iron-ore operations at Tom Price and Paraburdoo. Watersports and boat hire are available; 22 km N. *Hamersley Iron Port Facilities:* 3 hr tour and audiovisual presentation daily; bookings essential at visitor centre; 22 km N. *Cleaverville Beach:* scenic spot ideal for camping, boating, fishing and swimming; 26 km NE. *North-West Shelf Gas Project Visitor Centre:* displays on the history and technology of Australia's largest natural resource development, with panoramic views over the massive onshore gas plant; open 10am–4pm Mon–Fri Apr–Oct, 10am–1pm Mon–Fri Nov–Mar; Burrup Peninsula; 30 km N. *Aboriginal rock carvings:* there are more than 10 000 engravings on the Burrup Peninsula alone, including some of the earliest examples of art in Australia. A debate is currently raging over the damage being done to this magnificent outdoor gallery by the adjacent gas project; check with visitor centre for locations. *Dampier Archipelago:* 42 islands and islets ideal for swimming, snorkelling, boating, whale-watching and fishing; take a boat tour from

Dampier. ***Montebello Islands:*** site of Australia's first shipwreck, the *Tryal*, which ran aground and sank in 1622. It is now a good spot for snorkelling, beachcombing, fishing and diving; beyond Dampier Archipelago. ***Scenic flights:*** over the Pilbara outback; details from visitor centre.

See also PILBARA, pp. 46–7

Katanning
Pop. 3806

257 C4 | 258 C4

Old Mill, cnr Austral Tce and Clive St; (08) 9821 4390; www.katanningwa.com

94.9 Hot FM, 612 AM ABC Radio National

Katanning lies in the middle of a prosperous grain-growing and pastoral area. A significant development in the town's history was the 1889 completion of the Great Southern Railway, which linked Perth and Albany. Construction was undertaken at both ends, and a cairn north of town marks the spot where the lines were joined.

Old Mill Museum: built in 1889, it features an outstanding display of vintage roller flour-milling processes; Cnr Clive St and Austral Tce. ***All Ages Playground and Miniature Steam Railway:*** scenic grounds with playground equipment for all ages. Covered shoes required to ride the train, which runs on the 2nd and 4th Sun of each month; Cnr Great Southern Hwy and Clive St. ***Kobeelya:*** a majestic residence (1902) with seven bedrooms, ballroom, billiard room, tennis courts and croquet lawn, now a conference centre; Brownie St. ***Old Winery Ruins:*** inspect the ruins of the original turreted distillery and brick vats, with old ploughs and machinery on display; Andrews Rd. ***Historical Museum:*** the original school building has been converted into a museum of local memorabilia; open 2–4pm Sun, or by appt; Taylor St. ***Sale Yards:*** one of the biggest yards in Australia, sheep sales every Wed at 8am; viewing platform for visitors; Daping St. ***Heritage Rose Garden:*** with roses dating from 1830; Austral Tce. ***Piesse Memorial Statue:*** unveiled in 1916, this statue of Frederick H. Piesse, the founder of Katanning, was sculpted by P. C. Porcelli, a well-known artist in the early days of WA; Austral Tce. ***Art Gallery:*** a changing display and local collection; closed Sun; Austral Tce.

Farmers markets: Pemble St; 3rd Sat each month. ***Spring Lamb Festival:*** Oct.

Police Pools (Twonkwillingup): site of the original camp for the district's first police officers. Enjoy swimming, picnicking, birdwatching and bushwalking; 3 km s. ***Lake Ewlyamartup:*** picturesque freshwater lake ideal for picnicking, swimming, boating and waterskiing, particularly in early summer when the water level is high; 22 km E. ***Katanning-Piesse Heritage Trail:*** 20 km self-drive/walk trail; maps from visitor centre. ***Watersports:*** the lakes surrounding the town are excellent for recreational boating, waterskiing and swimming; details from visitor centre.

See also GREAT SOUTHERN, pp. 38–9

Kellerberrin
Pop. 868

257 C2 | 258 B3

Shire offices, 110 Massingham St; (08) 9045 4006; www.kellerberrin.wa.gov.au

107.3 FM ABC Radio National, 1215 AM ABC Local Radio

Centrally located in the wheat belt, Kellerberrin is 200 kilometres east of Perth. In springtime, magnificent displays of wildflowers adorn the roadsides, hills and plains around the town.

continued on p. 96

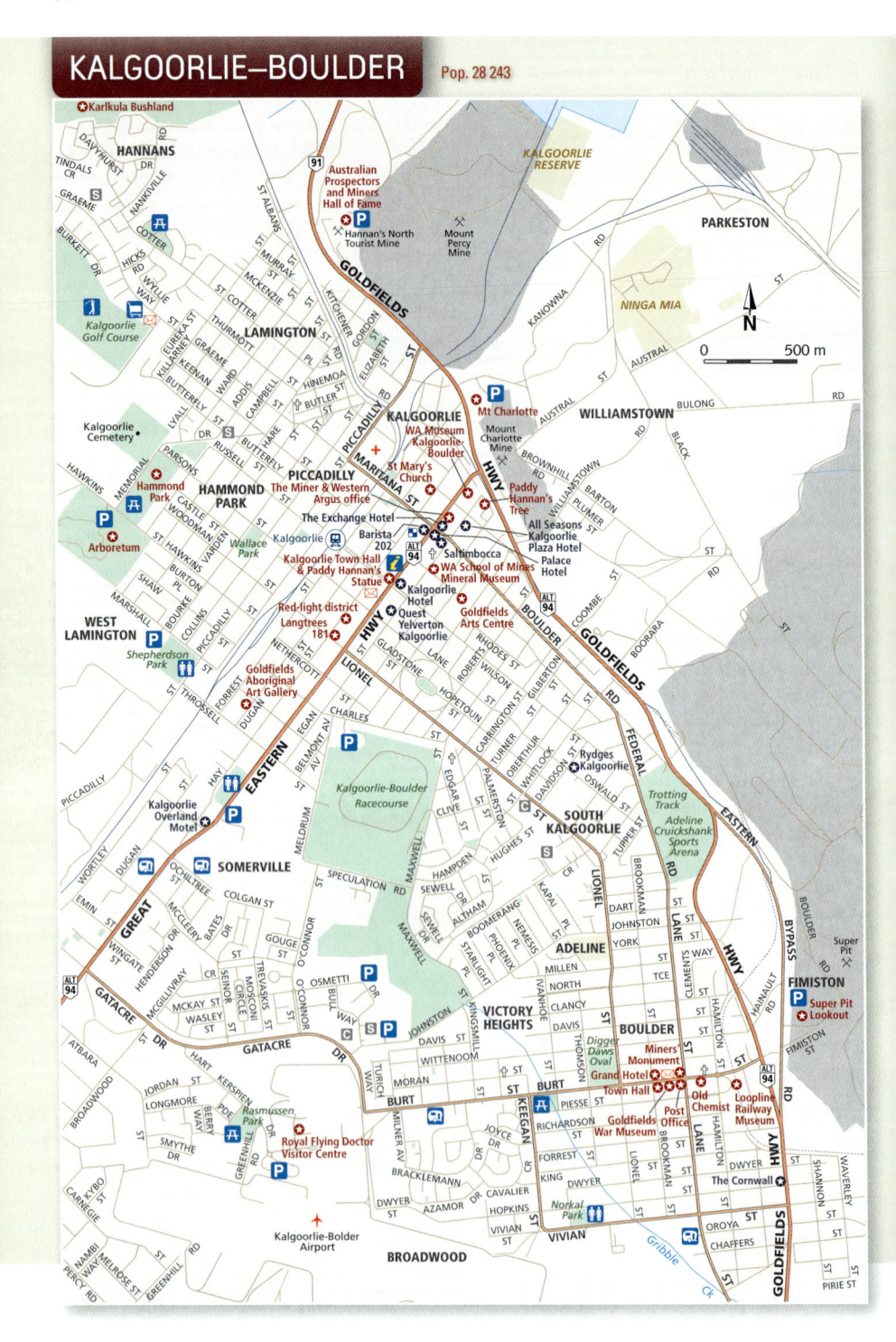

KALGOORLIE–BOULDER Pop. 28 243

258 D2

ℹ 250 Hannan St, (08) 9021 1966 or 1800 004 653; 106 Burt St, (08) 9093 1083; www.kalgoorlie.com

97.9 Hot FM, 648 AM ABC Local Radio

Kalgoorlie is the centre of Western Australia's goldmining industry. It was once known as Hannan's Find in honour of Paddy Hannan, the first prospector to discover gold in the area. In June 1893 Hannan was among a party of about 150 men who set out from Coolgardie to search for some lost prospectors. After a stop at Mount Charlotte, Hannan and two others were left behind, as one of their horses had lost a shoe. Here they stumbled on a rich goldfield – it soon grew to encompass the 'Golden Mile', which is reputedly the world's richest square mile of gold-bearing ore. Rapid development of Kalgoorlie and nearby Boulder followed, with thousands of men travelling to the field from all over the world. The shortage of water was always a problem, but in 1903 engineer C. Y. O'Connor opened a pipeline that pumped water 560 kilometres from Perth. In its heyday Kalgoorlie and Boulder boasted eight breweries and 93 hotels. The two towns amalgamated in 1989 to form Kalgoorlie–Boulder, and today the population is again close to peak levels due to the region's second gold boom. Unfortunatley, an earthquake in 2010 damaged many of the town's heritage buildings.

Historic buildings Although only a few kilometres apart, Kalgoorlie and Boulder developed independently for many years. The amalgamated towns now form a city with two main streets, each lined with impressive hotels and civic buildings. Built at the turn of the century, when people were flocking to the area, many of these buildings display ornamentation and fittings that reflect the confidence and wealth of the mining interests and are fine examples of early Australian architecture.

In Hannan St, Kalgoorlie, the Kalgoorlie Town Hall (1908) displays a collection of memorabilia including some impressive furniture. Dame Nellie Melba performed in this building on several occasions. The offices of newspapers the *Kalgoorlie Miner* and *Western Argus* was the first 3-storey building in town. Burt St in Boulder is regarded as one of the most significant streetscapes in WA. Buildings to see include the Grand Hotel (1897), the Old Chemist (1900), which now houses a pharmaceutical museum, and the post office (1899), which was once so busy it employed 49 staff. The Boulder Town Hall, built in 1908, is home to one of the world's last remaining Goatcher stage curtains, which elaborately depicts the Bay of Naples. Phillip Goatcher lived in Victorian times and was one of the greatest scenic painters of his era. His remarkable stage curtains could be found from London and Paris to New York. Public viewing of the curtain is on Tues, Wed and Thurs and Boulder Market Day (3rd Sun each month). Guided and self-guide heritage walks are available. Details from visitor centre.

Paddy Hannan's Statue: a monument to the first man to discover gold in Kalgoorlie; Hannan St. **St Mary's Church:** built in 1902 of Coolgardie pressed bricks, many of which are believed to contain gold; Cnr Brookman and Porter sts, Kalgoorlie. **WA School of Mines Mineral Museum:** displays include over 3000 mineral and ore specimens and many gold nuggets; open 8.30am–12.30pm Mon–Fri, closed on school holidays; Egan St, Kalgoorlie. **WA Museum Kalgoorlie–Boulder:** panoramic views of the city from the massive mining headframe at the entrance. Known locally as the Museum of the Goldfields, displays include a million-dollar gold collection, nuggets and jewellery. See the narrowest pub in the Southern Hemisphere, a re-created 1930s

continued overleaf

RADIO STATION   IN TOWN   WHAT'S ON   NEARBY

KALGOORLIE–BOULDER continued

AERIAL VIEW OF SALT LAKE NORTH-EAST OF KALGOORLIE

miner's cottage and other heritage buildings. Guided tours available; open 10am-4.30pm daily; 17 Hannan St, Kalgoorlie. *Goldfields Arts Centre:* art gallery and theatre; Cassidy St, Kalgoorlie. *Goldfields Aboriginal Art Gallery:* examples of local Aboriginal art and artefacts for sale; open 10.30am–4.30pm or by appt; Dugan St, Kalgoorlie. *Paddy Hannan's Tree:* a plaque marks the spot where Paddy Hannan first discovered gold; Brown Avenue, Kalgoorlie. *Red-light district:* view the few remaining 'starting stalls', in which women once posed as prospective clients walked by, and visit the only working brothel in the world that visitors can tour – Langtrees 181 (tours daily, bookings at visitor centre); Hay St, Kalgoorlie. *Super Pit Lookout:* underground mining on the Golden Mile became singly owned in the 1980s and '90s and was converted into an open-cut operation – what is now known as the Superpit. Peer into its depths from the lookout off Goldfields Hwy, Boulder (can coincide visit with blasting; check times at visitor centre); daily tours (free on market day) and scenic flights are also available. *Mt Charlotte:* the reservoir holds water pumped from the Mundaring Weir in Perth via the pipeline of C. Y. O'Connor. A lookout provides good views of the city; off Goldfields Hwy, Kalgoorlie. *Hammond Park:* miniature Bavarian castle made from thousands of local gemstones. There is also a sanctuary for kangaroos and emus, and aviaries for a variety of birdlife; Lyall St, Kalgoorlie. *Arboretum:* a living museum of species of the semi-arid zone and adjacent desert areas, this 26.5 ha parkland has interpretive walking trails and recreation facilities; Hawkins St, adjacent Hammond Park. *Miners' Monument:* tribute to mine workers; Burt St, Boulder. *Goldfields War Museum:* war memorabilia and armoured vehicles on display; 106 Burt St, Boulder. *WMC Nickel Pots:* massive nickel pots and interpretive panels describe the story of the development of the nickel industry in the region; Goldfields Hwy. *Loopline Railway Museum:* view the steam train that once carried hundreds of miners to the surrounds of the Golden Mile; Boulder Station. *Royal Flying Doctor Visitor Centre:* climb on board an authentic RFDS plane; tours available; open 10am–3pm Mon–Fri; Airport,

Hart Kerspien Dr. **Karlkurla Bushland:** pronounced 'gullgirla', this natural regrowth area of bushland offers a 4 km signposted walk trail, picnic areas and lookout over the city and nearby mining areas; Riverina Way. **Walks:** guided and self-guide heritage walks; details and maps from visitor centre.

Boulder Market Day: Burt St, Boulder; 3rd Sun each month. **Undies 500 Car Rally:** Feb. **Community Fair:** Mar/Apr. **Menzies to Kalgoorlie Cycle Race:** May. **Diggers and Dealers Mining Forum:** Aug. **Kalgoorlie and Boulder Cup:** Sept. **Back to Boulder Festival:** Oct. **Balzano Barrow Race:** Oct. **Art Prize Exhibition:** Dec. **St Barbara's Mining and Community Festival:** Dec.

Australian Prospectors and Miners Hall of Fame Tour a historic underground mine, watch a gold pour or visit the Exploration Zone, which is designed specifically for young people. You will find interactive exhibits on exploration, mineral discoveries and surface and underground mining, including panning for gold. The Environmental Garden details the stages and techniques involved in mine-site rehabilitation. At Hannan's North Tourist Mine, historic buildings re-create an early gold-rush town and visitors can take a first-hand look at the cramped and difficult working conditions of the miners. Goldfields Hwy, Kalgoorlie; (08) 9026 2700; 7 km N.

Bush 2-Up: visit the original corrugated-iron shack and bush ring where Australia's only legal bush 2-up school used to operate; off Goldfields Hwy; 8 km E. **Kanowna Belle Gold Mine lookouts:** wander the ghost town remains of Kanowna and see day-to-day mining activities from 2 lookouts over a previously mined open pit and processing plant; 20 km E. **Broad Arrow:** see the pub where scenes from the Googie Withers movie *Nickel Queen* were shot in the 1970s. Every wall is autographed by visitors; 38 km N. **Ora Banda:** recently restored inn; 54 km NW. **Kambalda:** nickel-mining town on Lake Lefroy (salt). Head to Red Hill Lookout for views across the expanse; 55 km S. **Prospecting:** visitors to the area may obtain a miner's right from the Dept of Mineral and Petroleum Resources in Brookman St, Kalgoorlie; strict conditions apply; details from the visitor centre. **Golden Quest Discovery Trail:** 965 km drive that traces the gold rushes of the 1890s through Coolgardie, Kalgoorlie–Boulder, Menzies, Kookynie, Gwalia, Leonora and Laverton; pick up the map, book and CD from visitor centre. **Golden Pipeline Heritage Trail:** follow the course of the pipeline from Mundaring Weir to Mt Charlotte. Finding a reliable water supply to support the eastern goldfields' booming population became imperative after the 1890s gold rush. C. Y. O'Connor's solution was radically brilliant: the construction of a reservoir at Mundaring in the hills outside Perth and a 556 km water pipeline to Kalgoorlie. His project was criticised relentlessly by the press and public, which affected O'Connor deeply. On 19 Mar 1902 he went for his usual morning ride along the beach in Fremantle. As he neared Robb Jetty, he rode his horse into the sea and shot himself. The pipeline was a success, delivering as promised 22 million litres of water a day to Kalgoorlie, and continues to operate today. On the coast just south of Fremantle, a half-submerged statue of a man on a horse is a poignant tribute to this man of genius; guidebook from visitor centre. **Tours:** self-drive or guided 4WD tours available to many attractions. Also fossicking, prospecting, camping and museum tours, and self-guide wildflower tours; details from visitor centre. **Scenic flights:** flights over Coolgardie, the Superpit, Lake Lefroy; details from visitor centre.

See also GOLDFIELDS, pp. 42–3

International Art Space Kellerberrin Australia This art gallery, built in 1998, is home to an ambitious art project. International artists are given the opportunity to live and work within the local community for a 3-month period. Workshops and mentoring programs provide collaboration between these established artists and emerging Australian talent. Many of the exhibitions created are then displayed in larger venues throughout Australia and the world. Massingham St; (08) 9045 4739.

Pioneer Park and Folk Museum: located in the old Agricultural Hall, displays include local artefacts, farming machinery and photographic records. Pick up the key from tourist information or Dryandra building next door; Cnr Leake and Bedford sts. *Centenary Park:* children's playground, in-line skate and BMX track, maze, heritage walkway and barbecue facilities all in the centre of town; Leake St. *Golden Pipeline Lookout:* interpretive information at viewing platform with views of the countryside and pipeline; via Moore St. *Heritage trail:* self-guide town walk that includes historic buildings and churches; brochures from visitor centre.

Keela Dreaming Cultural Festival: odd-numbered years, Mar. *Central Wheatbelt Harness Racing Cup:* May.

Durokoppin Reserve: take a self-guide scenic drive through this woodland area, which is beautiful in the wildflower season; maps from visitor centre; 27 km N. *Kokerbin Wave Rock:* the third largest monolith in WA. The Devil's Marbles and a historic well are also at the site. Restricted vehicle access to the summit, but the walk will reward with panoramic views; 30 km S. *Cunderdin:* museum housed in the No 3 pumping station has displays on the pipeline, wheat-belt farming and the Meckering earthquake; 45 km W. *Golden Pipeline Heritage Trail:* one of the main stops along the trail, which follows the water pipeline of C. Y. O'Connor from Mundaring Weir to the goldfields; guidebook from visitor centre. See Kalgoorlie–Boulder.

See also HEARTLANDS, pp. 36–7

Kojonup

Pop. 1124

257 C4 | 258 B4

i 143 Albany Hwy; (08) 9831 0500; www.kojonupvisitors.com

558 AM ABC Local Radio, 612 AM ABC Radio National

A freshwater spring first attracted white settlement of the town now known as Kojonup. In 1837 Alfred Hillman arrived in the area after being sent by Governor Stirling to survey a road between Albany and the Swan River Colony. He was guided to the freshwater spring by local Aboriginal people and his promising report back to Governor Stirling resulted in a military outpost being established. The Shire of Kojonup was the first shire in Western Australia to have a million sheep within its boundaries.

Kodja Place Visitor and Interpretative Centre: fascinating and fun displays about the land and its people, with stories of Aboriginal heritage and white settlement. It also includes the Australian Rose Maze, the only rose garden in the world growing exclusively Australian roses; 143 Albany Hwy. *Kojonup Museum:* in historic schoolhouse building with displays of local memorabilia; open by appt; Spring St. *A. W. Potts Kokoda Track Memorial:* a life-size statue of the brigadier facing towards his beloved farm 'Barrule'; Albany Hwy. *Centenary of Federation Wool Wagon:* commemorates the significance of the sheep industry to the Kojonup community; Albany Hwy. *Kojonup Spring:* grassy picnic area; Spring St. *Military Barracks:* built in 1845, this is one of the oldest surviving military buildings in WA and features historical information about the building; open by appt; Spring St. *Elverd's Cottage:* display of pioneer tools and farm machinery; open by appt; Soldier Rd. **Kodja Place Bush Tucker Walk:** follows the old railway line east where 3000 trees and shrubs indigenous to the area have been planted; maps from visitor centre. **Town walk trail:** self-guide signposted walk of historic sights; maps from visitor centre. **Wildflower Week:** Sept. **Kojonup Show:** Oct. **Myrtle Benn Memorial Flora and Fauna Sanctuary:** walk one of the numerous trails among local flora and fauna including many protected species; Tunney Rd; 1 km w. **Farrar Reserve:** scenic bushland and spectacular wildflower display in season; Blackwood Rd; 8 km w. **Australian Bush Heritage Block:** natural woodland featuring wandoo and species unique to the South-West; 16 km N. **Lake Towerinning:** boating, waterskiing, horseriding, camping; 40 km NW. **Aboriginal guided tours:** tours of Aboriginal heritage sites; details and bookings at visitor centre.

See also GREAT SOUTHERN, pp. 38–9

Kulin

Pop. 354

257 D3 | 258 C3

Resource Centre, Johnston St;
(08) 9880 1021; www.kulin.wa.gov.au

720 AM ABC Local Radio

The sheep- and grain-farming districts surrounding Kulin provide spectacular wildflower displays in season. The flowering gum, *Eucalyptus macrocarpa*, is the town's floral emblem. A stand of jarrah trees, not native to the area and not known to occur elsewhere in the wheat belt, grows near the town. According to Aboriginal legend, two tribal groups met at the site and, as a sign of friendship, drove their spears into the ground.

From these spears, the jarrah trees grew. The Kulin Bush Races event has expanded from horseracing to a major attraction including a weekend of live music, an art and craft show, foot races and Clydesdale horserides. In the months prior to the Kulin Races, tin horses appear in the paddocks lining the road on the way to the racetrack. These, along with the tin horses from past years, create an unusual spectacle.

Tin Horse Highway: starting in town and heading to the Jilakin racetrack, the highway is lined with horses made from a wide variety of materials. **Kulin Herbarium:** specialising in local flora; open by appt; Johnston St. **Butlers Garage:** built in the 1930s, this restored garage houses a museum of cars and machinery; open by appt; Cnr Johnston and Stewart sts. **Memorial Slide and Swimming Pool:** the longest water slide in regional WA; pool open 12–7pm Tues–Fri, 10am–7pm weekends/public holidays, summer months; check for opening hours of water slide; Holt Rock Rd; (08) 9880 1222. **Charity Car Rally:** Sept. **Kulin Bush Races:** Oct. **Longneck Roughneck Des Cook Memorial Quick Shears Shearing Competition:** Oct. **Macrocarpa Walk Trail:** 1 km self-guide signposted walk trail through natural bush; brochure from visitor centre; 1 km w. **Jilakin Rock and Lake:** granite monolith overlooking a 1214 ha lake; 16 km E. **Hopkins Nature Reserve:** important flora conservation area; 20 km E. **Buckley's Breakaways:** unusual pink and white rock formations; 70 km E. **Dragon Rocks Nature Reserve:** wildflower reserve with orchids and wildlife; 75 km E.

See also HEARTLANDS, pp. 36–7

RADIO STATION   IN TOWN   WHAT'S ON   NEARBY

Kununurra
Pop. 3745

267 G2 | 269 H2

ℹ 75 Coolibah Dr; (08) 9168 1177 or 1800 586 868; www.kununurratourism.com

📻 102.5 WA FM, 819 AM ABC Local Radio

Kununurra lies in the East Kimberley region not far from the Northern Territory border. It was established in the 1960s alongside Lake Kununurra on the Ord River at the centre of the massive Ord River Irrigation Scheme. Adjacent is the magnificent Mirima National Park. Lake Argyle to the south, in the Carr Boyd Range, was created by the damming of the Ord River and is the largest body of fresh water in Australia. Islands in the lake were once mountain peaks. The word 'Kununurra' means 'meeting of big waters' in the language of the local Aboriginal people. The climate in Kununurra and the East Kimberley is divided into two seasons, the Dry and the Wet. The Dry extends from April to October and is characterised by blue skies, clear days and cool nights. The Wet, from November to March, is a time of hot, humid days, when frequent thunderstorms deliver most of the annual rainfall to the region.

🏛 *Historical Society Museum:* artefacts and photos of the development of the town; Coolibah Dr. *Lovell Gallery:* art gallery exhibiting Kimberley artworks for sale; Konkerberry Dr. *Waringarri Aboriginal Arts:* large and varied display of Aboriginal art and artefacts for sale; open daily, weekends by appt; Speargrass Rd. *Red Rock Art:* a gallery and studio for Indigenous painters from across the Kimberley; open Mon–Fri; Coolibah Dr. *Kelly's Knob Lookout:* panoramic view of town and Ord Valley; off Speargrass Rd. *Celebrity Tree Park:* arboretum on the shore of Lake Kununurra where celebrities, including John Farnham, HRH Princess Anne, Harry Butler and Rolf Harris, have planted trees. Lily Creek Lagoon at the edge of the park is a good spot for birdwatching. The boat ramp was once part of the road to Darwin; off Victoria Hwy. *Historical Society walk trails:* choose between two trails of different lengths; maps from historical society.

🎉 *Ord Valley Muster:* May. *Kununurra Races:* Aug. *Rodeo and Campdraft:* Aug. *Night Rodeo:* Sept.

🧭 *Mirima National Park* Known by locals as the 'mini-Bungle Bungles', a striking feature of this park is the boab trees that grow on the rock faces, the seeds having been carried there by rock wallabies and left in their dung. There are walking trails within the park, and between May and Aug guided walks are available. Details from visitor centre; 2 km E.

Ivanhoe Farm: tastings and sales of melons and other local produce; open May–Sept; 1 km N. *Lake Kununurra:* formed after the completion of the Diversion Dam as part of the Ord River Scheme, the lake is home to a large variety of flora and fauna and is ideal for sailing, rowing, waterskiing and boat tours; details from visitor centre; 2 km S. *City of Ruins:* unusual sandstone formation of pinnacles and outcrops that resemble the ruins of an ancient city; off Weaber Plains Rd; 6 km N. *Ord River and Diversion Dam:* abundance of wildlife and spectacular scenery and a variety of watersports and cruises available; details from visitor centre; 7 km W. *Top Rockz Gallery:* exhibits gemstones and precious metals; open May–Sept; 10 km N. *Ivanhoe Crossing:* permanently flooded causeway is an ideal fishing spot; Ivanhoe Rd; 12 km N. *Hoochery Distillery:* visit a traditional old country and western saloon bar or take a tour of the only licensed distillery in WA; closed Sun; Weaber Plains Rd; 15 km N. *Zebra Rock Gallery:* view the amazing display of zebra rock, nearly 600 million years old and believed to be unique to the Kimberley, or feed fish from the lakeside jetty; Packsaddle Rd; 16 km S. *Middle Springs:* picturesque spot with diverse birdlife; 4WD access only; 30 km N. *Black Rock Falls:*

spectacular waterfall during the wet season that spills over rocks stained by the minerals in the water; 4WD access only; Apr–Oct (subject to road conditions); 32 km N. *Parry Lagoons Nature Reserve:* enjoy birdwatching from a shaded bird hide at Marlgu Billabong or scan the wide vistas of the flood plain and distant hills afforded from the lookout at Telegraph Hill; 65 km NW. *The Grotto:* ideal swimming hole (in the wet season) at the base of 140 stone steps; 70 km NW. *Argyle Downs Homestead Museum:* built in 1884 and relocated when the lake was formed, the building is a fine example of an early station homestead; open 7am–4pm dry season, wet season by appt; Parker Rd; 70 km S. *Lake Argyle:* the view of the hills that pop out of the main body of water is said to resemble a crocodile basking in the sun and is known locally as Crocodile Ridge. Fishing, birdwatching, camping, bushwalking, sailing, canoeing and lake cruises are all available; 72 km S. *Argyle Diamond Mine:* the largest producing diamond mine in the world. Access is via tour only; details from visitor centre; 120 km S. *Purnululu National Park:* scenic flights available in town; 375 km S; *see Halls Creek*. *Mitchell River National Park:* one of the Kimberley's newest national parks protects this scenic and biologically important area. Mitchell Falls and Surveyor's Pool are the two main attractions for visitors. The area is remote with 4WD access to the park only, and is about 16 hours' drive from Kununurra; 680 km NW. *Scenic flights:* flights from town take visitors over the remarkable Bungle Bungles, Argyle Diamond Mine, Mitchell Plateau or Kalumburu; details from and bookings at visitor centre. *Tours:* bushwalks, safaris, camping, canoeing, 4WD or coach; details from visitor centre.

See also KIMBERLEY, pp. 48–9

Lake Grace
Pop. 503

257 D3 | 258 C4

Stationmaster's house, Stubbs St; (08) 9865 2140; www.lakegrace.wa.gov.au

91.7 WA FM, 531 AM ABC Local Radio

The area around Lake Grace is a major grain-growing region for the state, producing wheat, canola, oats, barley, lupins and legumes. Sandy plains nearby are transformed into a sea of colour at the height of the wildflower season in September and October.

Inland Mission Hospital Museum: the only remaining inland mission hospital in WA, this fully restored building (est. 1926) is now a fascinating medical museum. Approach the building via Apex Park along the interpretive walkway; open daily by appt; Stubbs St. *Mural:* artwork depicting pioneering women was begun in 1912; Stubbs St. *Memorial Swimming Pool:* includes water playground for children; open 11am–6pm daily Oct–Apr; Bishop St.

Market: visitor centre; every Sat Oct–Mar. *Art Exhibition:* Oct.

Wildflower walk: easy walk through natural bushland with informative signage; details from visitor centre; 3 km E. *Lake Grace:* combination of two shallow salt lakes that gives the town its name; 9 km W. *Lake Grace Lookout:* ideal spot to view the north and south lakes system; 12 km W. *White Cliffs:* unusual rock formation and picnic spot on private property; details from visitor centre; 17 km S. *Holland Track:* in 1893 John Holland and his partners cut a track from Broomehill through bushland to Coolgardie in the goldfields. Hundreds of prospectors and their families trudged along this track in search of fortune, and cartwheel ruts are still evident today. A plaque marks the place where the track crosses the road; Newdegate Rd;

23 km E. *Dingo Rock:* now on private property, this reservoir for water run-off was built by labourers from Fremantle Gaol. Wildflowers are beautiful in season; details from visitor centre; 25 km NE. *Newdegate:* small town with a pioneer museum in the heritage-listed Hainsworth building. One of WA's major agricultural events, the Machinery Field Days, is held here in Sept each year; 52 km E.

See also HEARTLANDS, pp. 36–7

Lake King
Pop. 219

258 D4

ⓘ Lake's Breaks, Church Ave; (08) 9874 4007; www.lakeking.com.au

📻 92.5 WA FM, 531 AM ABC Local Radio

This small rural town lies on the fringe of sheep- and grain-farming country. With a tavern and several stores, Lake King is a stopping place for visitors travelling across the arid country around Frank Hann National Park to Norseman (adequate preparations must be made as there are no stops en route). Outstanding wildflowers in late spring include rare and endangered species.

🏠 *Self-guide walks:* signposted walk trails; maps from visitor centre.

🧭 *Lake King and Causeway:* 9 km road across the salt lake studded with native scrub and wildflowers. Lookout at eastern end; 5 km w. *Pallarup Reserve:* pioneer well and lake with abundant wildflowers in season; 15 km s. *Mt Madden:* cairn and lookout with picnic area that forms part of the Roe Heritage Trail; 25 km SE. *Frank Hann National Park:* good example of inland sand plain heath flora with seasonal wildflowers. The rabbit-proof fence forms a boundary to the park. Access is subject to weather conditions; 32 km E. *Roe Heritage Drive Trail:* begins south of Lake King and covers natural reserves and historic sites. It offers panoramic views from the Roe Hill lookout and retraces part of J. S. Roe's explorations in 1848; maps from visitor centre.

See also HEARTLANDS, pp. 36–7

Laverton
Pop. 314

259 E1 | 265 E5

ⓘ Great Beyond Explorers Hall of Fame, Augusta St; (08) 9031 1361; www.laverton.wa.gov.au

📻 102.1 WA FM, 106.1 FM ABC Local Radio

Surrounded by old mine workings and modern mines, Laverton is on the edge of the Great Victoria Desert. In 1900 Laverton was a booming district of gold strikes and mines, yet gold price fluctuations in the late 1950s made it almost a ghost town. In 1969 nickel was discovered at Mount Windarra, which sparked a nickel boom. Early in 1995 a cyclone blew through Laverton, leaving it flooded and isolated for three months. Mines closed down and supplies were brought in by air. During this time, locals held a 'wheelie bin' race from the pub to the sports club, which is now an annual event. Today the town has two major gold mines and one of the world's largest nickel-mining operations. Wildflowers are brilliant in season.

🏠 **Historic buildings** Restored buildings include the courthouse, the Old Police Station and Gaol, and the Mt Crawford Homestead. The original police sergeant's House is now the local museum with displays of local memorabilia. Details from visitor centre.

Great Beyond Explorers Hall of Fame: uses cutting-edge technology to bring to life the characters and stories of the early explorers of the region. It also houses the visitor centre; Augusta St. *Cross-Cultural Centre:* houses the Laverton Outback Gallery, a collection of art and artefacts made and sold by the local Wongi people; Augusta St.

🎉 **Race Day:** June. ***Laverton Day and Wheelie Bin Race:*** Nov.

🧭 **Giles Breakaway:** scenic area with interesting rock formation; 25 km E. ***Lake Carey:*** swimming and picnic spot exhibiting starkly contrasting scenery; 26 km w. ***Windarra Heritage Trail:*** walk includes rehabilitated mine site and interpretive plaques; Windarra Minesite Rd; 28 km NW. ***Empress Springs:*** discovered in 1896 by explorer David Carnegie and named after Queen Victoria. The spring is in limestone at the end of a tunnel that runs from the base of a 7 m deep cave. A chain ladder allows access to the cave. Enclosed shoes and torch required; 305 km NE. ***Warburton:*** the Tjulyuru Arts and Culture Regional Gallery showcases the art and culture of the Ngaanyatjarraku people; 565 km NE. ***Golden Quest Discovery Trail:*** Laverton forms part of the 965 km self-guide drive trail of the goldfields; book, map and CD available. ***Outback Highway:*** travel the 1200 km to Uluṟu from Laverton via the Great Central Rd. All roads are unsealed but regularly maintained.

Travellers note: *Permits are required to travel through Aboriginal reserves and communities – they can be obtained from the Dept of Indigenous Affairs in Perth, and the Central Lands Council in Alice Springs. Water is scarce. Fuel, supplies and accommodation are available at the Tjukayirla, Warburton and Warakurna roadhouses. Check road conditions before departure at the Laverton Police Station or Laverton Shire Offices; road can be closed due to heavy rain.*

See also GOLDFIELDS, pp. 42–3

Leonora
Pop. 400

258 D1

ℹ️ Rural Transaction Centre, cnr Tower and Trump sts; (08) 9037 7016; www.leonora.wa.gov.au

📻 102.5 WA FM, 105.7 FM ABC Local Radio

Leonora is the busy railhead for the north-eastern goldfields and the surrounding pastoral region. Mount Leonora was discovered in 1869 by John Forrest. Gold was later found in the area and, in 1896, the first claims were pegged. By 1908 Leonora boasted seven hotels and was the largest centre on the north-eastern goldfields. Many of the original buildings were constructed of corrugated iron and hessian, as these were versatile materials and light to transport. You can get a glimpse of these structures at nearby Gwalia, a town once linked to Leonora by tram.

🏠 **Historic buildings:** buildings from the turn of the century include the police station, courthouse, fire station and Masonic Lodge; details from visitor centre. ***Tank Hill:*** excellent view over town; Queen Victoria St. ***Miners Cottages:*** miners camps, auctioned and restored by locals; around town.

🎉 ***Leonora Golden Gift and Festival:*** May/June.

🧭 **Gwalia** Gwalia is a mining ghost town that has been restored to show visitors what life was like in the pioneering gold-rush days. The original mine manager's office now houses the Gwalia Historical Museum with displays of memorabilia that include the largest steam winding engine in the world and a headframe designed by Herbert Hoover, the first mine manager of the Sons of Gwalia mine and eventually the 31st President of the United States. Self-guide heritage walk available. 4 km S.

Mt Leonora: sweeping views of the surrounding plains and mining operations; 4 km s. *Malcolm Dam:* picnic spot at the dam, which was built in 1902 to provide water for the railway; 15 km E. *Kookynie:* tiny township with restored shopfronts, and historic memorabilia on display at the Grand Hotel. The nearby Niagara Dam was built in 1897 with cement carried by camel from Coolgardie; 92 km SE. *Menzies:* small goldmining town with an interesting historic cemetery. View 'stick figure' sculptures, for which locals posed, about 55 km west of town on bed of Lake Ballard; 110 km s. *Golden Quest Discovery Trail:* self-guide drive trail of 965 km takes in many of the towns of the northern goldfields; maps, book and CD from visitor centre, or visit www.goldenquesttrail.com

See also GOLDFIELDS, pp. 42–3

Madura

Pop. 9

259 G3

i Madura Pass Oasis Motel and Roadhouse; (08) 9039 3464.

Madura, comprising a roadhouse, motel and caravan park on the Eyre Highway, lies midway between Adelaide and Perth on the Nullarbor Plain. It is remarkable, given the isolation of the area, that Madura Station was settled in 1876 to breed horses, which were then shipped across to India for use by the British Army. Now Madura is surrounded by private sheep stations. Locals operate on Central Western Time, 45 minutes ahead of the rest of Western Australia.

Blowholes: smaller versions of the one found at Caiguna. Look for the red marker beside the track; 1 km N. *Madura Pass Lookout:* spectacular views of the Roe Plains and Southern Ocean; 1 km w on highway.

See also ESPERANCE & NULLARBOR, pp. 40–1

Mandurah

Pop. 67 783

254 B4 | 257 B3 | 258 A4

i 75 Mandurah Tce; (08) 9550 3999; www.visitmandurah.com

97.3 Coast FM, 810 AM ABC Radio National

Mandurah has long been a popular holiday destination for Perth residents. The Murray, Serpentine and Harvey rivers meet at the town to form the vast inland waterway of Peel Inlet and the Harvey Estuary. This river junction was once a meeting site for Aboriginal groups who travelled here to barter. The town's name is derived from the Aboriginal word 'mandjar', meaning trading place. The river and the Indian Ocean offer a variety of watersports and excellent fishing and prawning. But, the aquatic activity for which Mandurah is perhaps best known is crabbing. It brings thousands during summer weekends, wading the shallows with scoop nets and stout shoes.

Christ's Church Built in 1870, this Anglican church has hand-worked pews believed to be the work of early settler Joseph Cooper. Many of the district's pioneers are buried in the churchyard, including Thomas Peel, the founder of Mandurah. In 1994 the church was extended and a bell-tower added to house eight bells from England. Cnr Pinjarra Rd and Sholl St.

Australian Sailing Museum: displays and models of vessels from the 1860s to Olympic yachts; Ormsby Tce. *Hall's Cottage:* (1832) restored home of one of the original settlers, Henry Hall; Leighton Rd. *Museum:* (1898) originally a school then a police station, now houses displays on Mandurah's social, fishing and canning histories; open Tues–Sun; Pinjarra Rd. *King Carnival Amusement Park:* funfair attractions including giant water slide, Ferris wheel and more; Leighton Rd. *Estuary Drive:* scenic drive along Peel Inlet and Harvey Estuary.

WESTERN AUSTRALIA → TOWNS → **MANJIMUP** 103

Smart Street Markets: off Mandurah Tce; each Sat. ***Crab Fest:*** Mar. ***Boat and Fishing Show:*** Oct.

Coopers Mill: the first flour mill in the Murray region, located on Cooleenup Island near the mouth of the Serpentine River. Joseph Cooper built it by collecting limestone rocks and every morning, sailing them across to the island. Accessible only by water; details from visitor centre. ***Abingdon Miniature Village:*** display of miniature heritage buildings and gardens from UK and Australia with maze, picnic area and children's playground; Husband Rd; 3 km E. ***Marapana Wildlife Park:*** handfeed and touch native and exotic animals; 14 km N at Karnup. ***Yalgorup National Park:*** swamps, woodlands and coastal lakes abounding with birdlife. Lake Clifton is one of only three places in Australia where the living fossils called thrombolites survive. A boardwalk allows close-up viewing; 45 km s. ***Wineries:*** several in the area; details from visitor centre. ***Tours:*** including estuary cruises and dolphin interaction tours; details from visitor centre.

See also THE SOUTH-WEST, pp. 34–5

Manjimup

Pop. 4236

255 D4 | 256 A1 | 257 B4 | 258 B5

80 Giblett St; (08) 9771 1831; www.manjimupwa.com

100.5 Hot FM, 738 AM ABC Local Radio

Manjimup is the gateway to the South-West region's tall-timber country. Magnificent karri forests and rich farmlands surround the town. While timber is the town's main industry, Manjimup is also the centre of a thriving fruit and vegetable industry that supplies both local and Asian markets. The area is well known for its apples and is the birthplace of the delicious Pink Lady apple.

Timber and Heritage Park A must-see for any visitor to Manjimup, this 10 ha park includes the state's only timber museum, an exhibition of old steam engines, an 18 m climbable fire-lookout tower and a historic village with an early settler's cottage, blacksmith's shop, old police station and lock-up, one-teacher school and early mill house. Set in natural bush and parkland, there are many delightful spots for picnics or barbecues. Cnr Rose and Edwards sts.

Manjimup Motocross 15000: June. ***Festival of Country Gardens:*** Oct/Nov. ***Cherry Harmony Festival:*** Dec.

One Tree Bridge In 1904 a single enormous karri tree was felled so that it dropped across the 25 m wide Donnelly River, forming the basis of a bridge. Winter floods in 1966 swept most of the bridge away; the 17 m piece salvaged is displayed near the original site with information boards. Nearby is Glenoran Pool, a scenic spot for catching rainbow trout and marron in season, with walking trails and picnic areas. Graphite Rd; 21 km W.

King Jarrah: estimated to be 600 years old, this massive tree is the centrepiece for several forest walks; Perup Rd; 3 km E. ***Wine and Truffle Company:*** tastings and information about truffle farming and dog training; (08) 9777 2474; 7 km SW. ***Fonty's Pool:*** dammed in 1925 by Archie Fontanini for the irrigation of vegetables, it is now a popular swimming pool and picnic area in landscaped grounds; Seven Day Rd; 7 km S. ***Dingup Church:*** built in 1896 by the pioneer Giblett family and doubling as the school, this church is one of the few remaining local soapstone buildings; Balbarrup Rd; 8 km E. ***Pioneer Cemetery:*** poignant descriptions on headstones testify to the hardships faced by first settlers; Perup Rd; 8 km E. ***Diamond Tree Lookout:*** one of

RADIO STATION | IN TOWN | WHAT'S ON | NEARBY

8 tree towers constructed from the late 1930s as fire lookouts. Climb to the wooden cabin atop this 51 m karri, used as a fire lookout from 1941 to 1947; 9 km s. *Fontanini's Nut Farm:* gather chestnuts, walnuts, hazelnuts and fruit in season; open Apr–June; Seven Day Rd; 10 km s. *Nyamup:* old mill town redeveloped as a tourist village; 20 km SE. *Four Aces:* four giant karri trees 220–250 years old and 67–79 m high stand in Indian file; Graphite Rd; 23 km w. *Great Forest Trees Drive:* self-guide drive through Shannon National Park; maps from visitor centre; 45 km s. *Perup Forest Ecology Centre:* night spotlight walks to see rare, endangered and common native animals; contact DEC on (08) 9771 7988 for details; 50 km E. *Lake Muir Lookout/Bird Observatory:* boardwalk over salt lake to bird hide; 55 km E. *Wineries:* several in area; maps from visitor centre.

See also THE SOUTH-WEST, pp. 34–5

Marble Bar
Pop. 194

263 F2 | 264 C1 | 268 C5

🅘 11 Francis St; (08) 9176 1375.

📻 102.7 WA FM, 107.5 FM ABC Radio National

Marble Bar has gained a dubious reputation as the hottest town in Australia. For 161 consecutive days in 1923–24 the temperature in Marble Bar did not drop below 37.8°C (100°F). This mining town was named after a bar of mineral deposit that crosses the nearby Coongan River and was originally mistaken for marble. It proved to be jasper, a coloured variety of quartz.

🏠 *Government buildings:* built of local stone in 1895, now National Trust listed; General St.

🎆 *Marble Bar Races:* July.

🧭 **Comet Gold Mine** This mine operated from 1936 to 1955. The Comet is now a museum and tourist centre with displays of gemstones, rocks, minerals and local history. Also here is a 75 m high smoke stack, reputed to be the tallest in the Southern Hemisphere. Underground mine tours occur twice daily. (08) 9176 1015; 10 km s.

Marble Bar Pool: site of the famous jasper bar (splash water on it to reveal its colours) and a popular swimming spot; 4 km w. *Corunna Downs RAAF Base:* built in 1943 as a base for long-range attacks on the Japanese-occupied islands of the Indonesian archipelago; 40 km SE. *Doolena Gorge:* watch the cliff-face glow bright red as the sun sets; 45 km NW.

See also PILBARA, pp. 46–7

Margaret River

see inset box on next page

Meekatharra
Pop. 799

261 D4 | 264 B4

🅘 Shire offices, 54 Main St; (08) 9981 1002; www.meekashire.wa.gov.au

📻 103.1 WA FM, 106.3 FM ABC Local Radio

The name Meekatharra is believed to be an Aboriginal word meaning 'place of little water' – an apt description for a town sitting on the edge of a desert. Meekatharra is now the centre of a vast mining and pastoral area. It came into existence in the 1880s when gold was discovered in the area. However, the gold rush was short-lived and it was only the arrival of the railway in 1910 that ensured its survival. The town became the railhead at the end of the Canning Stock Route, a series of 54 wells stretching from the East Kimberleys to the Murchison. The railway was closed in 1978, but the town continues to provide necessary links to remote outback areas through its Royal Flying Doctor Service.

🏠 ***Royal Flying Doctor Service:*** operates an important base in Meekatharra; open to public 9am–2pm daily; Main St. ***Old Courthouse:*** National Trust building; Darlot St. ***Meekatharra Museum:*** photographic display and items of memorabilia from Meekatharra's past; open 8am–4.30pm Mon–Fri; shire offices, Main St. ***State Battery:*** relocated to the town centre in recognition of the early prospectors and miners; Main St. ***Meeka Rangelands Discovery Trail:*** walk or drive this trail for insight into the town's mining past, Aboriginal heritage and landscapes; maps from visitor centre.

🧭 ***Peace Gorge:*** this area of granite formations is an ideal picnic spot; 5 km N. ***Meteorological Office:*** watch the launching of weather balloons twice daily at the airport; tours available on (08) 9981 1191; 5 km SE. ***Bilyuin Pool:*** swimming (but check water level in summer); 88 km NW. ***Old Police Station:*** remains of the first police station in the Murchison; Mt Gould; 156 km NW.

See also OUTBACK COAST & MID-WEST, pp. 44–5

Merredin
Pop. 2556

257 D2 | 258 C3

ℹ️ Barrack St; (08) 9041 1666; www.wheatbelttourism.com

📻 105.1 Hot FM, 107.3 FM ABC Radio National

Merredin started as a shanty town where miners stopped on their way to the goldfields. In 1893 the railway reached the town and a water catchment was established on Merredin Peak, guaranteeing the town's importance to the surrounding region. An incredible 40 per cent of the state's wheat is grown within a 100-kilometre radius of the town.

🏠 **Cummins Theatre** Heritage-listed theatre that was totally recycled from Coolgardie in 1928. Used regularly for local productions, events and visiting artists. Open 9am–3pm Mon–Fri; Bates St. ***Military Museum:*** significant collection of restored military vehicles and equipment; closed Sat; Great Eastern Hwy. ***Old Railway Station Museum:*** prize exhibits are the 1897 locomotive that once hauled the *Kalgoorlie Express* and the old signal box with 95 switching and signal levers; open 9am–3pm daily; Great Eastern Hwy. ***Pioneer Park:*** picnic area adjacent to the highway including a historic water tower that once supplied the steam trains; Great Eastern Hwy. ***Merredin Peak Heritage Walk:*** self-guide walk that retraces the early history of Merredin and its links with the goldfields and the railway; maps from visitor centre. ***Merredin Peak Heritage Trail:*** leads to great views of the countryside, and a rock catchment channel and dam from the 1890s. Adjacent to the peak is the interpretation site of a WW II field hospital that had over 600 patients in 1942; off Benson Rd. ***Tamma Parkland Trail:*** a 1.2 km walk around this 23 ha of bushland will give an insight into the flora and fauna of the area. Wildflowers in spring; South Ave.

🎆 **Community Show:** Oct.

🧭 **Pumping Station No 4:** built in 1902 but closed in 1960 to make way for electrically driven stations, this fine example of early industrial architecture was designed by C. Y. O'Connor; 3 km w. ***Hunt's Dam:*** one of several wells sunk by convicts under the direction of Charles Hunt in 1866. It is now a good spot for picnics and bushwalking; 5 km N. ***Totadgin Conservation Park:*** interpretive walk, Hunt's Well and mini rock formation similar to Wave Rock. Picnic tables and wildflowers in spring; 16 km SW. ***Rabbit-Proof Fence:*** roadside display gives an insight into the history of this feature; 25 km E. ***Mangowine Homestead:*** now a restored National Trust property, in the

continued on p. 108

📻 RADIO STATION 🏠 IN TOWN 🎆 WHAT'S ON 🧭 NEARBY

MARGARET RIVER Pop. 4413

255 A4 | 257 A4 | 258 A4

Cnr Tunbridge St and Bussell Hwy;
(08) 9780 5911; www.margaretriver.com

100.3 Hot FM, 1224 AM ABC Radio National

One of the best-known towns in Western Australia, Margaret River is synonymous with world-class wines, magnificent coastal scenery, excellent surfing beaches and spectacular cave formations. A pretty township, it lies on the Margaret River near the coast, 280 kilometres south-west of Perth.

Wine Tourism Showroom Although the first grapevines were only planted in the area in 1967, Margaret River is now considered to be one of the top wine-producing regions in Australia. A huge 20% of Australia's premium wines are made here. The 'terroir' is perfect for grape-growing: cool frost-free winters, good moisture-retaining soils and low summer rainfall provide a long, slow ripening period. These conditions produce greater intensity of fruit flavour, the starting point for all great wines. There are now more than 100 wine producers in the region, many of which are open to the public for tastings and cellar-door sales. Others have restaurants and tours of their premises. A good place to start a wine tour is the Margaret River Wine Tourism Showroom at the visitor centre. It provides information about the regional wineries and vineyards, an interactive wineries screen, videos, a sensory display and wine-making paraphernalia. Bussell Hwy.

Rotary Park: picnic area on the riverbank with a display steam engine; Bussell Hwy. *St Thomas More Catholic Church:* one of the first modern buildings built of rammed earth; Wallcliffe Rd. *Fudge Factory:* fudge and chocolate made before your eyes; Bussell Hwy; (08) 9758 8881. *Arts and crafts:* many in town, including Margaret River Gallery on Bussell Hwy; details from visitor centre.

Town Square Markets: 11am–1pm Sun in summer, 2nd Sun each month rest of year. *Margaret River Pro:* surfing competition; Mar/Apr. *Great Escapade:* cycling; Mar/Apr.

CAPE MENTELLE VINEYARD

Margaret River Wine Region Festival: May. *Margaret River Classic:* surfing competition; Oct/Nov.

Mammoth and Lake caves, Leeuwin–Naturaliste National Park Lying beneath the Leeuwin–Naturaliste Ridge that separates the hinterland from the coast is one of the world's most extensive and beautiful limestone cave systems. Mammoth Cave is home to the fossil remains of prehistoric animals. An audio self-guide tour lets you travel through the cave at your own pace (21 km sw). Only a few kilometres away is the beautiful Lake Cave with its delicate formations and famous reflective lake. The adjacent interpretive centre, CaveWorks, features a walk-through cave model, interactive displays and a boardwalk with spectacular views of a collapsed cavern (25 km sw). Further south, also in the national park, are Jewel and Moondyne caves; *see Augusta and Dunsborough.*

Eagles Heritage: the largest collection of birds of prey in Australia, with free-flight displays at 11am and 1.30pm daily; Boodjidup Rd; (08) 9757 2960; 5 km sw. *Surfer's Pt:* the centre of surfing in Margaret River and home to the Margaret River Pro; 8 km w, just north of Prevelley. *Leeuwin Estate Winery:* the picturesque venue for the world-renowned open-air Leeuwin Estate Concert, held each Feb/Mar; 8 km s. *Cape Mentelle:* excellent cellar-door tastings; 331 Wallcliffe Rd; (08) 9757 0888; 5 km sw. *Prevelly Park:* huge waves attract surfers from around the world; detailed maps with surf spots from visitor centre; 12 km w. *Margaret River Regional Wine Centre:* a one-stop centre for tastings and sales, offering in-depth information on local wines and wineries; Cowaramup; (08) 9755 5501; 13 km N. *Candy Cow:* free tastings of fudge, nougat and honeycomb, with demonstrations at 11am daily; Cowaramup; (08) 9755 9155; 13 km N. *Gnarabup Beach:* safe swimming beach for all the family; 13 km w. *Cheese outlet:* Margaret River Cheese Factory; Bussell Hwy; 15 km N. *The Berry Farm:* jams, pickles, naturally fermented vinegars, fruit and berry wines; Bessell Rd; 15 km SE. *Ellensbrook Homestead:* this wattle-and-daub homestead (1857) was once the home

continued overleaf

RADIO STATION   IN TOWN   WHAT'S ON   NEARBY

MARGARET RIVER continued

of Alfred and Ellen Bussell, the district's first pioneers; open weekends; (08) 9755 5173. Nearby is the beautiful Meekadarribee Waterfall, a place steeped in Aboriginal legend; 15 km NW. **Olio Bello:** boutique, handmade olive oil, with tastings available; Cowaramup; (08) 9755 9771; 17 km NW. **Grove Vineyard:** learn about and make your own sparkling wine. It also includes Yahava KoffeeWorks with coffee-appreciation sessions; Willyabrup; 20 km N. **Arts and crafts:** many in area, including Boranup Galleries, 20 km S on Caves Rd; details from visitor centre. **Margaret River Chocolate Company:** free chocolate tastings, interactive displays and viewing windows to watch the chocolate products being made; Cnr Harmans Mill and Harmans South rds, Metricup; (08) 9755 6555; 30 km NW. **Bootleg Brewery:** enjoy naturally brewed boutique beers in a picturesque setting; Puzey Rd, Willyabrup; (08) 9755 6300; 45 km NW. **Bushtucker River and Winery Tours:** experience the Margaret River region through its wine, wilderness and food; open 12–5pm daily; bookings essential (08) 9757 9084. **Land-based activities:** abseiling, caving, canoeing, coastal treks, horseriding and hiking; details from visitor centre. **Heritage trails:** including the Rails-to-Trails and Margaret River heritage trails; maps from visitor centre.

See also THE SOUTH-WEST, pp. 34–5

1880s this was a wayside stop en route to the Yilgam goldfields. Nearby is the Billyacatting Conservation Park with interpretative signage; open 1–4pm Mon–Sat, 10am–4pm Sun (closed Jan); Nungarin; 40 km NW. **Shackelton:** Australia's smallest bank; 85 km SW. **Kokerbin Rock:** superb views from summit; 90 km SW. **Koorda:** museum and several wildlife reserves in area; 140 km NW.

See also HEARTLANDS, pp. 36–7

Moora

Pop. 1606

257 B1 | 258 A2

 34 Padbury St; (08) 9651 1401; www.moora.wa.gov.au

 90.9 WA FM, 612 AM ABC Radio National

On the banks of the Moore River, Moora is the largest town between Perth and Geraldton. The area in its virgin state was a large salmon gum forest. Many of these attractive trees can still be seen.

Historical Society Genealogical Records and Photo Display: open by appt; Clinch St. **Painted Roads Initiative:** murals by community artists on and in town buildings.

Moora Races: Oct.

The Berkshire Valley Folk Museum James Clinch, who came from England in 1839, created a village in the dry countryside of WA based on his home town in Berkshire. Over a 25-year period from 1847, Clinch built a homestead, barn, manager's cottage, stables, shearing shed and bridge. The elaborate buildings were made from adobe, pise, handmade bricks and unworked stone. Open by appt; 19 km E.

Western Wildflower Farm: one of the largest exporters of dried wildflowers in WA, with dried flowers, seeds and souvenirs for sale and an interpretive education centre; open 9am–5pm daily Easter–Christmas; Midlands Rd, Coomberdale; (08) 9651 8010; 19 km N. **Watheroo National Park:** site of Jingamia Cave; 50 km N. **Moora Wildflower Drive:** from Moora to Watheroo National Park, identifying flowers on the way; maps from visitor centre.

See also HEARTLANDS, pp. 36–7

Morawa
Pop. 594

258 A2

ℹ️ Winfield St (May–Oct), (08) 9971 1421; or council offices, cnr Dreghorn and Prater sts, (08) 9971 1204; www.morawa.wa.gov.au

📻 103.1 WA FM, 531 AM ABC Local Radio

Morawa, a small wheat-belt town, has the distinction of being home to the first commercial iron ore to be exported from Australia. In springtime the area around Morawa is ablaze with wildflowers.

🏠 **Church of the Holy Cross and Old Presbytery** From 1915 to 1939, the famous WA architect-priest Monsignor John C. Hawes designed a large number of churches and church buildings in WA's mid-west region. Morawa boasts 2 of them: the Church of the Holy Cross and an unusually small stone hermitage known as the Old Presbytery. The latter, which Hawes used when visiting the town, is reputed to be the smallest presbytery in the world with only enough room for a bed, table and chair. Both buildings are part of the Monsignor Hawes Heritage Trail. Church is usually open; if not, contact council offices; Davis St.

Historical Museum: housed in the old police station and gaol with displays of farm machinery, household items and a collection of windmills; open by appt; Cnr Prater and Gill sts.

🧭 *Koolanooka Mine Site and Lookout:* scenic views and a delightful wildflower walk in season; 9 km E. *Perenjori:* nearby town has historic St Joseph's Church, designed by Monsignor Hawes, and the Perenjori–Rothsay Heritage Trail, a 180 km self-drive tour taking in Rothsay, a goldmining ghost town; 18 km SE. *Bilya Rock Reserve:* with a large cairn, reportedly placed there by John Forrest in the 1870s as a trigonometrical survey point; 20 km N. *Koolanooka Springs Reserve:* ideal for picnics; 26 km E.

See also OUTBACK COAST & MID-WEST, pp. 44–5

Mount Barker
Pop. 1760

256 B5 | 257 D5 | 258 C5

ℹ️ Old Railway Station, Albany Hwy; (08) 9851 1163; www.mountbarkertourismwa.com.au

📻 92.1 FM ABC News Radio, 95.3 Hot FM

Mount Barker lies in the Great Southern region of Western Australia, with the Stirling Range to the north and the Porongurups to the east. The area was settled by Europeans in the 1830s. Vineyards were first established here in the late 1960s. Today, Mount Barker is a major wine-producing area.

🏠 **Old Police Station and Gaol:** built by convicts in 1867–68, it is now a museum of memorabilia; open 10am–4pm Sat and Sun, daily during school holidays, or by appt; Albany Hwy, north of town. *Banksia Farm:* complete collection of banksia and dryandra species; guided tours daily, closed July; Pearce Rd; (08) 9851 1770.

🎆 *Mount Barker D'Vine Wine Festival:* Jan. *Mount Barker Wildflower Festival:* Sept/Oct.

🧭 **Porongurup National Park** This is a park of dramatic contrasts, from stark granite outcrops and peaks to lush forests of magnificent karri trees. Many unusual rock formations, such as Castle Rock and Balancing Rock, make the range a fascinating place for bush rambles. The Tree in the Rock, a mature

karri, extends its roots down through a crevice in a granite boulder. 24 km E.
Lookout and TV tower: easily pinpointed on the summit of Mt Barker by 168 m high television tower, it offers panoramic views of the area from the Stirling Ranges to Albany; 5 km sw. **St Werburgh's Chapel:** small mud-walled chapel (1872) overlooking Hay River Valley; 12 km sw. **Kendenup:** historic town, location of WA's first gold find; 16 km E. **Porongurup:** hosts Wine Summer Festival each Mar and boasts many small wineries; 24 km E. **Wineries:** several in the area, including Goundrey, Marribrook and Plantagenet; maps from visitor centre. **Mt Barker Heritage Trail:** 30 km drive tracing the development of the Mt Barker farming district; maps from visitor centre. **Stirling Range National Park:** 80 km NE; see Cranbrook.

See also GREAT SOUTHERN, pp. 38–9

Mount Magnet
Pop. 422

258 B1 | 261 D5 | 264 B5

ⓘ Hepburn St; (08) 9963 4172; www.mtmagnet.wa.gov.au

102.5 WA FM, 105.7 FM ABC Local Radio

In 1854 the hill that rises above this Murchison goldmining town was named West Mount Magnet by surveyor Robert Austin after he noticed that its magnetic ironstone was playing havoc with his compass. Now known by its Aboriginal name, Warramboo Hill, it affords a remarkable view over the town and mines. Located 562 kilometres north-east of Perth on the Great Northern Highway, Mount Magnet offers visitors a rich mining history, rugged granite breakaway countryside and breathtaking wildflowers in season.

Mining and Pastoral Museum: collection of mining and pioneering artefacts includes a Crossley engine from the original State Battery;

Hepburn St. **Heritage trail:** see the surviving historic buildings and sites of the gold-rush era on this 1.4 km walk; maps from visitor centre.
The Granites: rocky outcrop with picnic area and Aboriginal rock paintings; 7 km N. **Heritage drive:** 37 km drive of local historic and natural sights, including views of old open-cut goldmine. Also takes in the Granites and various ghost towns; maps from visitor centre. **Fossicking for gemstones:** take care as there are dangerous old mine shafts in the area.

See also OUTBACK COAST & MID-WEST, pp. 44–5

Mullewa
Pop. 419

258 A1 | 261 C5

ⓘ Jose St; (08) 9961 1500; www.mullewatourism.com.au

107.5 FM ABC Radio National, 828 AM ABC Local Radio

Mullewa, 100 kilometres north-east of Geraldton, is in the heart of wildflower country. In spring, the countryside surrounding the town bursts forth with one of the finest displays of wildflowers in Western Australia. The wreath flower is the star attraction of the annual Mullewa Wildflower Show.

Our Lady of Mt Carmel Church This small church is widely considered to be the crowning achievement of noted priest-architect Monsignor John C. Hawes. Built of local stone, this gem of Romanesque design took seven years to build with Hawes as architect, stonemason, carpenter, modeller and moulder. The adjoining Priest House is now a museum in honour of Hawes, housing his personal belongings, books, furniture and drawings (Cnr Doney and Bowes sts). Both of these buildings are part of the Monsignor Hawes Heritage Trail, which also features the Pioneer Cemetery (Mullewa–Carnarvon Rd; 1 km N) and a site at the old showground just outside town, where a rock carved by Monsignor Hawes was once a simple altar where he held mass for the local Aboriginal people (Mt Magnet Rd; 1.5 km E). Details and maps from visitor centre.

Mullewa Wildflower Show: Aug/Sept.

Butterabby Gravesite This gravesite is a grim reminder of the harsh pioneering days. A stone monument recalls the spearing to death in 1864 of a convict labourer and the hanging in 1865 of five Aboriginal people accused of the crime. Mullewa–Mingenew Rd; 18 km s.

Tenindewa Pioneer Well: example of the art of stone pitching that was common at the time of construction, reputedly built by Chinese labourers en route to the Murchison goldfields. Also walking trails; 18 km w. **Bindoo Hill:** glacial moraine where ice-smoothed rocks dropped as the face of the glacier melted around 225 million years ago; 40 km NW. **Coalseam Conservation Park:** remnants of the state's first coal shafts, now a picnic ground; 45 km sw. **Tallering Peak and Gorges:** ideal picnic spot; Mullewa–Carnarvon Rd; check accessibility at visitor centre; 59 km N. **Wooleen Homestead:** stay on a working sheep and cattle station in the central Murchison district. Visit Boodra Rock and Aboriginal sites, and experience station life; (08) 9963 7973; 194 km N.

See also OUTBACK COAST & MID-WEST, pp. 44–5

Mundaring
Pop. 3004

254 C2 | 257 B2 | 258 B3

The Old School, 7225 Great Eastern Hwy; (08) 9295 0202; www.mundaringtourism.com.au

94.5 Mix FM, 720 AM ABC Local Radio

Mundaring is virtually an outer suburb of Perth, being only 34 kilometres east. Nearby, the picturesque Mundaring Weir is the water source for the goldfields 500 kilometres further east. The original dam opened in 1903. The hilly bush setting makes the weir a popular picnic spot.

Mundaring Arts Centre: contemporary WA fine art and design with comprehensive exhibition program; Great Eastern Hwy; (08) 9295 3991. **Mundaring District Museum:** displays on the diverse history of the shire; Great Eastern Hwy. **Mundaring Sculpture Park:** collection of sculptures by WA artists, set in natural bush park with grassed areas for picnics and children's playground; Jacoby St.

Market: Nichol St, 2nd Sun each month. **Truffle Festival:** Aug. **Perth Hills Wine Show:** Aug. **Trek the Trail:** Sept. **Darlington Arts Festival:** Nov.

Mundaring Weir The Number 1 Pump Station, formerly known as the C. Y. O'Connor Museum, houses an exhibition on the mammoth project of connecting the weir to the goldfields (open 10am–4pm Mon–Sun and public holidays; Mundaring Weir Rd; 8 km s). This is also the starting point of the 560 km Golden Pipeline Heritage Trail to Kalgoorlie, which follows the route of O'Connor's water pipeline, taking in towns and heritage sites. Nearby, the Perth Hills National Park Centre includes Nearer to Nature who provide hands-on activities including bush craft, animal encounters, bush walks and information about Aboriginal culture; contact (08) 9295 2244. The Mundaring Weir Gallery, built in 1908 as a Mechanics Institute Hall, showcases the work of local craftspeople; open 10am–4pm Thurs, Sat, Sun and public holidays; Cnr Hall and Weir Village rds.

John Forrest National Park: on a high point of the Darling Range with sensational views and a lovely picnic spot beside a natural pool at Rocky Pool; 6 km w. **Karakamia Sanctuary:** native wildlife sanctuary with guided dusk walks; bookings essential (08) 9572 3169; Lilydale Rd, Chidlow; 8 km NE. *Calamunnda Camel Farm:* camel rides; open Thurs–Sun; 361 Paulls Valley Rd; (08) 9293 1156; 10 km s. *Lake Leschenaultia:* swimming, canoeing, bushwalks and camping with picnic/barbecue facilities; 12 km NW. *Kalamunda National Park:* walking trails through jarrah forest, including the first section of the 963 km Bibbulmun Track; 23 km s; *see Albany*. *Kalamunda History Village:* collection of historic buildings; open Sat–Thurs; 23 km s. *Lesmurdie Falls National Park:* good views of Perth and Rottnest Island near spectacular falls over the Darling Escarpment; 29 km s. *Walyunga National Park:* beautiful bushland and wildflowers and venue for the Avon Descent, a major whitewater canoeing event held each Aug; 30 km NW. *Wineries:* several in the area; *Heart of the Hills Wine Trail* map from visitor centre. *Munda Biddi Bike Trail:* passes through Mundaring; maps from visitor centre.

See also DARLING & SWAN, pp. 32–3

Nannup
Pop. 503

255 C4 | 257 B4 | 258 B4

 4 Brockman St; (08) 9756 1211; www.nannupwa.com

 98.9 FM ABC Radio National, 684 AM ABC Local Radio

Nannup is a historic mill town in the Blackwood Valley south of Perth. Known as 'The Garden Village', it has beautiful private and public gardens, tulip farms, daffodils and wildflowers. The countryside is a series of lush, rolling pastures alongside jarrah forests and pine plantations.

 Old Police Station: now a visitor centre, original cell block open for viewing; Brockman St. *Town Arboretum:* fine collection of old trees planted in 1926; Brockman St.

Kealley's Gemstone Museum: displays of rocks, shells, gemstones, bottles and stamps; closed Wed; Warren Rd. *Marinko Tomas Memorial:* memorial to the local boy who was the first serviceman from WA killed in the Vietnam War; Warren Rd. *Blackwood Wines:* beautiful winery and restaurant overlooking an artificial lake; closed Wed; Kearney St; (08) 9756 0077. *Arts, crafts and antiques:* many in town, including Crafty Creations for quality timber goods on Warren Rd (closed June). *Heritage trail:* in 2 sections, with a 2.5 km town walk highlighting historic buildings, and a 9 km scenic drive; maps from visitor centre.

 Market: Warren Rd; 2nd Sat each month. *Art and Photography Exhibition:* Jan. *Music Festival:* Feb/Mar. *Forest Car Rally:* Mar. *Nannup Cup Boat Race:* June. *Flower and Garden Festival:* tulips; Aug. *Rose Festival:* Nov.

 Kondil Park: bushwalks and wildflowers in season; 3 km w. *Barrabup Pool:* largest of several pools, ideal for swimming, fishing and camping. Also has barbecue facilities; 10 km w. *Cambray Sheep Cheese:* award-winning cheeses, visitors can watch the milking and cheese-making; samples available. There are also guest cottages; 12 km N. *Carlotta Crustaceans:* marron farm; 14 km s off Vasse Hwy. *Tathra:* fruit winery and restaurant; open 11am–4.30pm daily; 14 km NE. *Mythic Mazes:* mazes including sculptures of myths from around the world; 20 km N. *Donnelly River Wines:* open daily for cellar-door tastings; (08) 9301 5555; 45 km s. *Blackwood River:* camping, swimming, canoeing and trout fishing. *Self-guide walks:* wildflower (in spring), waterfall (in winter) and forest walks; maps from visitor centre. *Scenic drives:* through jarrah forest and pine plantations, including 40 km Blackwood Scenic Drive; maps from visitor centre.

See also THE SOUTH-WEST, pp. 34–5

Narrogin
Pop. 4240

257 C3 | 258 B4

ℹ️ **Dryandra Country Visitor Centre,** cnr Park and Fairway sts; (08) 9881 2064; www.dryandratourism.org.au

📻 100.5 Hot FM, 918 AM Radio West

Narrogin, 192 kilometres south-east of Perth on the Great Southern Highway, is the commercial hub of a prosperous agricultural area. Sheep, pigs and cereal farms are the major industries. First settled in the 1870s, the town's name is derived from an Aboriginal word 'gnarojin', meaning waterhole.

🏠 **Gnarojin Park** This park is a national award winner for its original designs and artworks portraying local history and culture, which include the Centenary Pathway, marked with 100 locally designed commemorative tiles, Newton House Barbecue and Noongar Cultural Sites. Gordon St.

History Hall: local history collection; Egerton St. *Old Courthouse Museum:* built in 1894 as a school, it later became the district courthouse; open Mon–Sat; Egerton St. *Narrogin Art Gallery:* exhibitions; open 10am–4pm Tues–Fri, 10am–12pm Sat; Federal St. *Lions Lookout:* excellent views; Kipling St. *Heritage trail:* self-guide walk around the town's historic buildings; maps from visitor centre.

🎆 *State Gliding Championships:* Jan. *Spring Festival:* Oct. *Rev Heads:* car rally; Nov/Dec.

🧭 **Dryandra Woodland** One of the few remaining areas of virgin forest in the wheat belt, Dryandra is a paradise for birdwatchers and bushwalkers. The open, graceful eucalypt woodlands of white-barked wandoo, powderbark and thickets of rock she-oak support many species of flora and fauna including numbats (the state's animal emblem), woylies, tammar wallabies, brush-tailed possums and many others. Over 100 species of birds have been identified, including the mound-building mallee fowl. Tune your radio to 100FM for 'Sounds of Dryandra', a 25 km radio drive trail with 6 stops featuring tales of the local Nyungar people, early forestry days, bush railways and Dryandra's unique wildlife. There are day-visitor facilities and accommodation, walk trails, a weekend Ecology Course (runs in autumn and spring; try your hand at radio-tracking, trapping and spotlighting) and school holiday programs. 22 km NW.

Barna Mia Animal Sanctuary The sanctuary, within the Dryandra Woodland, has guided spotlight walks at night that reveal threatened marsupials, including the bilby and boodie. Bookings essential; contact DEC on (08) 9881 9200 or visitor centre which also has maps; Narrogin–Wandering Rd; 26 km NW.

Foxes Lair Nature Reserve: 60 ha of bushland with good walking trails, wildflowers in spring and 40 species of birds; maps and brochures from visitor centre; Williams Rd; 1 km SW. *Yilliminning and Birdwhistle Rocks:* unusual rock formations; 11 km E. *District heritage trail:* maps from visitor centre.

See also HEARTLANDS, pp. 36–7

New Norcia
Pop. 70

257 B1 | 258 B3

ℹ️ **Museum and art gallery,** Great Northern Hwy; (08) 9654 8056; www.newnorcia.wa.edu.au

📻 612 AM ABC Radio National, 720 AM ABC Local Radio

In 1846 Spanish Benedictine monks established a mission 132 kilometres north of Perth in the secluded Moore Valley in an attempt to help the local Aboriginal population. They named their mission after the Italian town of Norcia, the birthplace of the order's founder, St Benedict. The imposing Spanish-inspired buildings of New Norcia, surrounded by the gum trees and dry grasses of the wheat belt, provide a most unexpected vista. The town still operates as a monastery and is Australia's only monastic town. Visitors may join the monks at daily prayers.

Abbey Church This fine example of bush architecture was built using a combination of stones, mud plaster, rough-hewn trees and wooden shingles. It is the oldest Catholic church still in use in WA and contains the tomb of Dom Rosendo Salvado, the founder of New Norcia and its first Abbot. Hanging on a wall is the painting of Our Lady of Good Counsel, given to Salvado before he left for Australia in 1845 by Bishop (later Saint) Vincent Palotti. One of New Norcia's most famous stories relates how, in 1847, Salvado placed this revered painting in the path of a bushfire threatening the mission's crops. The wind suddenly changed direction and drove the flames back to the part already burnt, and the danger was averted.

Museum and art gallery: the museum tells the story of New Norcia's history as an Aboriginal mission, while the art gallery houses priceless religious art from Australia and Europe as well as Spanish artefacts, many of which were gifts from Queen Isabella of Spain. The Museum Gift Shop features New Norcia's own produce including bread, nutcake, pan chocolatti, biscotti, wine, honey and olive oil. *Monastery:* daily tours of the interior. A guesthouse allows visitors to experience the monastic life for a few days. *New Norcia Hotel:* this magnificent building, featuring a massive divided central staircase and high, moulded pressed-metal ceilings, was opened in 1927 as a hostel to accommodate parents of the children who were boarding at the town's colleges. *Old Flour Mill:* the oldest surviving building in New Norcia dates from the 1850s. *Heritage trail:* 2 km self-guide walk highlights New Norcia's historic and cultural significance and the role of the Benedictine monks in colonial history; maps from visitor centre. *Guided tour:* 2 hr tour of the town with an experienced guide takes you inside buildings not otherwise open to the public; 11am and 1.30pm daily from museum.

Mogumber: town with one of the state's highest timber-and-concrete bridges; 24 km sw. *Piawaning:* magnificent stand of eucalypts north of town; 31 km NE. *Bolgart:* site of historic hotel; 49 km SE. *Wyening Mission:* former mission, now a historic site; open by appt; 50 km SE.

See also HEARTLANDS, pp. 36–7

Newman
Pop. 4247

263 F5 | 264 C2

Cnr Fortescue Ave and Newman Dr; (08) 9175 2888; www.newman-wa.org

88.9 Red FM, 567 AM ABC Local Radio

Located in the heart of the Pilbara, Newman was built in the late 1960s by the Mount Newman Mining Company to house the workforce required at nearby Mount Whaleback, the largest open-cut iron-ore mine in the world. At the same time a 426-kilometre railway was constructed between Newman and Port Hedland to transport the ore for export to Japan.

Mt Whaleback Mine Tours: the mine produces over 100 million tonnes of iron ore every year. Tours (minimum 4 people) run Mon–Sat Apr–Sept, Tues and Thurs Oct–Mar; bookings at visitor centre. *Mining and Pastoral Museum:* interesting display of relics from the town's short history, including the first Haulpak (giant iron-ore truck) used at Mt Whaleback and outback station life; located at visitor centre. *Radio Hill Lookout:* panoramic view of town and surrounding area; off Newman Dr.

Campdraft and Rodeo: Mar. ***Fortescue Festival:*** Aug.

Ophthalmia Dam: swimming, sailing, barbecues and picnics (no camping); 20 km E. ***Mt Newman:*** excellent views; 25 km NW. ***Eagle Rock Falls:*** permanent pools and picnic spots nearby; 4WD access only; 80 km NW. ***Wanna Munna:*** site of Aboriginal rock carvings; 74 km W. ***Rockpools and waterholes:*** at Kalgans Pool (65 km NE), Three Pools (75 km N) and Weeli Wolli (99 km W). ***Newman Waterholes and Art Sites Tour:*** maps from visitor centre. ***Karijini National Park:*** 196 km N; *see Tom Price.*

See also PILBARA, pp. 46–7

Norseman
Pop. 861

259 E3

68 Roberts St; (08) 9039 1071; www.norseman.info

105.7 FM ABC Goldfields, 107.3 FM ABC Radio National

Norseman is the last large town on the Eyre Highway for travellers heading east towards South Australia. Gold put Norseman on the map in the 1890s with one of the richest quartz reefs in Australia. The town is steeped in goldmining history, reflected in its colossal tailings dump. If visitors could stand atop this dump they could have up to $50 million in gold underfoot (although the rock has been processed, much residual gold remains). The story behind the town's name has become folklore. The settlement sprang up in 1894 when a horse owned by prospector Laurie Sinclair pawed the ground and unearthed a nugget of gold; the site proved to be a substantial reef. The horse's name was Norseman.

Historical Collection: mining tools and household items; open 10am–1pm Mon–Sat; Battery Rd. ***Phoenix Park:*** open-plan park with displays, stream and picnic facilities; Prinsep St. ***Statue of Norseman:*** bronze statue by Robert Hitchcock commemorates Norseman, the horse; Cnr Roberts and Ramsay sts. ***Camel Train:*** corrugated-iron sculptures represent the camel trains of the pioneer days; Prinsep St. ***Gem fossicking:*** gemstone permits from visitor centre.

Norseman Cup: Mar.

Beacon Hill Lookout: spectacular at sunrise and sunset, this lookout offers an outstanding 360-degree panorama of the salt lakes, Mt Jimberlana, the township, tailings dump and surrounding hills and valleys; Mines Rd; 2 km E. ***Mt Jimberlana:*** reputed to be one of the oldest geological areas in the world. Take the walking trail to the summit for great views; 5 km E. ***Dundas Rocks:*** barbecue and picnic area amid granite outcrops near old Dundas townsite, where the lonely grave of a seven-month-old child is one of the only signs that the area was once inhabited. Travel here via the highway (22 km S) or along the 33 km heritage trail that follows an original Cobb & Co route (maps from visitor centre). ***Buldania Rocks:*** picnic area with beautiful spring wildflowers; 28 km E. ***Bromus Dam:*** freshwater dam with picnic area; 32 km S. ***Peak Charles National Park:*** good-weather track for experienced walkers and climbers to Peak Eleanora, with a magnificent view from top; 50 km S, then 40 km W off hwy. ***Cave Hill Nature Reserve:*** a granite outcrop with a cave set in its side and a dam nearby. Popular spot for camping, picnicking and rock climbing; 4WD access only; 55 km N, then 50 km W. ***Fraser Range Station:*** working pastoral property that specialises in Damara sheep. The station has a range of available accommodation and opportunities to experience a remote working pastoral property; (08) 9039 3210; 100 km E.

See also GOLDFIELDS, pp. 42–3

Northam
Pop. 6007

254 D1 | 257 B2 | 258 B3

ℹ️ Avon Valley Visitor Centre, 2 Grey St; (08) 9622 2100; www.visitnorthamwa.com.au

📻 96.5 Hot FM, 1215 AM ABC Local Radio

Northam lies in the heart of the fertile Avon Valley. The Avon River winds its way through the town and on its waters you'll find white swans, a most unusual sight in a state where the emblem is a black swan. White swans were brought to Northam from England in the 1900s and have flourished here. Northam is also synonymous with hot-air ballooning as it is one of the few areas in Western Australia ideally suited to this pastime. Northam is home to the famous Avon Descent, a 133-kilometre whitewater race down the Avon and Swan rivers to Perth.

🏛️ **Historic buildings** Of the many historic buildings in Northam, two are particularly noteworthy: Morby Cottage (1836) on Avon Dr, the home of Northam's first settler, John Morrell, now a museum and open 10.30am–4pm Sun or by appt; and the National Trust–classified Sir James Mitchell House (1905), cnr Duke and Hawes sts, with its elaborate Italianate architecture. Take the 90 min self-guide walk for the full tour of the town. Maps from visitor centre.

Old Railway Station Museum: displays include a steam engine and renovated carriages, plus numerous artefacts from the early 1900s; open 10am–4pm Sun or by appt; Fitzgerald St West. *Visitor centre:* exhibition showcasing the area's significant postwar migrant history; Grey St. *Suspension bridge:* the longest pedestrian suspension bridge in Australia crosses the Avon River adjacent to the visitor centre.

🎉 **Vintage Car Swap Meet:** Feb. *Avon Descent:* Aug. ***Northam Cup:*** Oct. *Motorcycle Festival:* Nov. ***Wheatbelt Cultural Festival:*** Dec.

🧭 *Mt Ommanney Lookout:* excellent views of the township and agricultural areas beyond; 1.5 km w. ***Hot-air ballooning:*** Northam Airfield; Mar–Nov; bookings essential; 2 km NE. *Meckering:* small town made famous in 1968 when an earthquake left a huge fault line in its wake; 35 km E. ***Cunderlin Museum:*** The museum housed in the No 3 pumping station has displays on the pipeline, wheat-belt farming and the Meckering earthquake; 50 km E.

See also HEARTLANDS, pp. 36–7

Northampton
Pop. 814

261 B5

ℹ️ Old police station, Hampton Rd; (08) 9934 1488; www.northamptonwa.com.au

📻 96.5 WA FM

Northampton, nestled in the valley of Nokarena Brook, 51 kilometres north of Geraldton, was awarded Historic Town status by the National Trust in 1993. It was declared a townsite in 1864 and is one of the oldest settlements in Western Australia. A former lead-mining centre, its prosperity is now based on sheep and wheat-farming.

🏛️ *Chiverton House Historical Museum:* unusual memorabilia housed in what was originally the home of Captain Samuel Mitchell, mine manager and geologist. Surrounding gardens include herbarium and restored farm machinery; open 10am–12pm and 2–4pm Fri–Mon; Hampton Rd. ***Mary Street Railway Precinct:*** railway memorabilia at the site of the town's 2nd railway station, built 1913; Eastern end. ***Church of Our Lady in Ara Coeli:*** designed in 1936 by Monsignor John Hawes, WA's famous architect-priest; Hampton Rd. ***Gwalla Church and Cemetery:*** ruins of town's first church (1864); Gwalla St. ***Hampton Road Heritage Walk:*** 2 km walk includes 37 buildings of historical interest including the

WESTERN AUSTRALIA → TOWNS → **NORTHCLIFFE** 117

Miners Arms Hotel (1868) and the Old Railway Station (1879); maps from visitor centre.

Market: Kings Park, cnr Essex St and Hampton Rd; 1st Sat each month. *Airing of the Quilts:* quilts hung in main street; Oct.

Alma School House: built in 1916 as a one-teacher school; 12 km N. *Aboriginal cave paintings:* at the mouth of the Bowes River; 17 km W. *Oakabella Homestead:* one of the first farms in WA to plant canola, or rapeseed as it was then known. Take a guided tour of the historic homestead and outbuildings; open daily Mar–Nov; 18 km S. *Horrocks Beach:* beautiful bays, sandy beaches, good swimming, fishing and surfing; 20 km W. *Lynton Station:* ruins of labour-hiring depot for convicts, used in 1853–56; 35 km NW. *Lynton House:* squat building with slits for windows, probably designed as protection from hostile Aboriginal people; 35 km NW. *Principality of Hutt River:* visitors are given a tour by the royals of this 75 sq km principality. With their own government, money and postage stamps, Hutt River exists as an independent sovereign state, seceded from Australia in 1970; 35 km NW. *Hutt Lagoon:* appears pink in midday sun; 45 km NW. *Port Gregory:* beach settlement, ideal for swimming, fishing and windsurfing; 47 km NW. *Warribano Chimney:* Australia's first lead smelter; 60 km N.

See also OUTBACK COAST & MID-WEST, pp. 44–5

Northcliffe
Pop. 299

255 D5 | 256 B2 | 257 B5 | 258 B5

Muirillup Rd; (08) 9776 7203; www.northcliffe.org.au

102.7 WA FM, 105.9 FM ABC Local Radio

Magnificent virgin karri forests surround the township of Northcliffe, 31 kilometres south of Pemberton in the state's South-West. Just a kilometre from the town centre is Northcliffe Forest Park, where you can see purple-crowned lorikeets, scarlet robins and in spring, a profusion of wildflowers. Not far away is the coastal settlement of Windy Harbour, a popular swimming beach.

Pioneer Museum Northcliffe came into existence as a result of the Group Settlement Scheme, a WA government plan to resettle returned WW I soldiers and immigrants by offering them rural land to farm. The scheme was enthusiastically backed by English newspaper magnate Lord Northcliffe (hence the town's name). Unfortunately, by the 1920s, when the scheme began, all the good land in the state had already been settled. The group settlers were left to contend with inhospitable country and with only crosscut saws and axes, they were faced with the daunting task of clearing some of the world's biggest trees from their land. It is not surprising that by the mid-1930s all of the Group Settlement projects in the South-West timber country had failed. A visit to the Pioneer Museum with its excellent displays is the best way to understand the hardships the group settlers experienced. Open 10am–2pm daily Sept–May, 10am–2pm Sat, Sun and school holidays June–Aug; Wheatley Coast Rd; (08) 9775 1022.

Canoe and mountain-bike hire: details from visitor centre.

Great Karri Ride: Mar. *Mountain Bike Championship:* May/June. *Night-time Mountain Bike Race:* Nov.

Northcliffe Forest Park: follow the Hollow Butt Karri and Twin Karri walking trails or enjoy a picnic; Wheatley Coast Rd. *Warren River:* trout fishing and sandy beaches; 8 km N. *Mt Chudalup:* spectacular views of the

RADIO STATION | IN TOWN | WHAT'S ON | NEARBY

surrounding D'Entrecasteaux National Park and coastline from the summit of this giant granite outcrop; 10 km s. *Moon's Crossing:* delightful picnic spot; 13 km NW. *Lane Poole Falls and Boorara Tree:* 3 km walking trail leads to the falls, passing the Boorara Tree with 50 m high fire-lookout cabin; 18 km SE. *Pt D'Entrecasteaux:* limestone cliffs, popular with rock climbers, rise 150 m above the sea where 4 viewing platforms provide superb views; 27 km s. *Windy Harbour:* swimming, snorkelling, fishing, camping and whale-watching (from platform, best times Sept–Nov); 27 km s. *Cathedral Rocks:* watch seals and dolphins; 27 km s. *Salmon Beach:* surf beach offers salmon fishing Apr–June; 27 km s. *The Great Forest Trees Drive:* 48 km self-guide scenic drive takes in the karri giants at Snake Gully Lookout, the Boardwalk and Big Tree Grove; maps from visitor centre. *Bibbulmun Track:* section of this long-distance walking trail links the 3 national parks around Northcliffe: D'Entrecasteaux (5 km s), Warren (20 km NW) and Shannon (30 km E); *see Albany.* *Mountain-bike trails:* 4 permanent trails have been established around Northcliffe; details from visitor centre.

See also THE SOUTH-WEST, pp. 34–5

Onslow
Pop. 574

261 B1 | 262 A4

ⓘ Second Ave (May–Oct), (08) 9184 6644; or council offices, Second Ave, (08) 9184 6001; www.ashburton.wa.gov.au

📻 106.7 WA FM, 107.5 FM ABC Radio National

Onslow, on the north-west coast between Exmouth and Karratha, is the supply base for offshore gas and oil fields. This part of the coast is among the north's most cyclone-prone and Onslow has often suffered severe damage. The town was originally at the Ashburton River mouth and a bustling pearling centre. In the 1890s gold was discovered nearby. In 1925 the townsite was moved to Beadon Bay after cyclones caused the river to silt up. During World War II, submarines refuelled here and the town was bombed twice. In the 1950s it was the mainland base for Britain's nuclear experiments at Montebello Islands. In 1963 Onslow was almost completely destroyed by a cyclone. It is now an attractive tree-shaded town.

Goods Shed Museum: memorabilia from the town's long history and collections of old bottles, shells and rocks; in visitor centre; Second Ave. *Beadon Creek and Groyne:* popular fishing spot. *Ian Blair Memorial Walkway:* 1 km scenic walk; starts at Beadon Pt and finishes at Sunset Beach. *Heritage trail:* covers sites of interest in town; maps from visitor centre.

Termite mounds: with interpretive display; 10 km s. *Mackerel Islands:* excellent fishing destination. Charter boats are available for daytrips or extended fishing safaris; details from visitor centre; 22 km off the coast. *Ashburton River:* swimming, camping and picnicking; 45 km sw. *Old townsite heritage trail:* self-guide walk around original townsite including old gaol; maps from visitor centre; 45 km sw.

See also PILBARA, pp. 46–7

Pemberton
Pop. 757

255 D5 | 256 A2 | 257 B5 | 258 B5

ⓘ Brockman St; (08) 9776 1133 or 1800 671 133; www.pembertontourist.com.au

📻 97.3 WA FM, 558 AM ABC Local Radio

Pemberton sits in a quiet valley surrounded by some of the tallest trees in the world and, in spring, brilliant wildflowers. This is the heart of karri country, with 4000 hectares of protected virgin karri forest in the nearby Warren and

Beedelup national parks. Pemberton is a centre for high-quality woodcraft and is renowned for its excellent rainbow trout and marron fishing.

Karri Forest Discovery Centre: interpretive centre includes museum with collection of historic photographs and forestry equipment; at visitor centre. ***Pioneer Museum:*** utensils, tools and other memorabilia from pioneer days plus a full-scale settler's hut; at visitor centre. ***Craft galleries:*** many in town, including the Fine Woodcraft Gallery in Dickinson St and the Peter Kovacsy Studio in Jamieson St.

Mill Hall Markets: Brockman St; 2nd Sat each month and public holidays. ***CWA Markets:*** Brockman St; 4th Sat each month. ***Autumn Festival:*** May.

Gloucester National Park In this park is the town's most popular tourist attraction, the Gloucester Tree. With its fire lookout teetering 61 m above the ground and a spine-tingling 153 rungs spiralling upwards, this is not a climb for the faint-hearted. The Gloucester Tree is one of eight tree towers constructed from the late 1930s as fire lookouts. As the extremely tall trees in the southern forests offered few vantage points for fire-lookout towers, it was decided to simply build a cabin high enough in one of the taller trees to serve the purpose. Also within the park are the Cascades, a scenic spot for picnicking, bushwalking and fishing. 1 km s.

Warren National Park This park boasts some of the most easily accessible virgin karri forest. The Dave Evans Bicentennial Tree has another fire lookout with picnic facilities and walking tracks nearby. 9 km sw.

Beedelup National Park Here you'll find the Walk Through Tree, a 75 m, 400-year-old karri with a hole cut in it big enough for people to walk through. The Beedelup Falls, a total drop of 106 m, are rocky cascades best seen after heavy rain. Nearby are walk trails and a suspension bridge. 18 km w.

Lavender & Berry Farm: enjoy berry scones, lavender biscuits and other unusual produce; Browns Rd; 4 km N. ***Big Brook Dam:*** the dam has its own beach, picnic and barbecue facilities, trout and marron fishing in season, and walking trails; 7 km N. ***Big Brook Arboretum:*** established in 1928 to study the growth of imported trees from around the world; 7 km N. ***King Trout Restaurant and Marron Farm:*** catch and cook your own trout; closed Thurs; 8 km sw. ***Founder's Forest:*** part of the 100-Year-Old Forest, with karri regrowth trees over 120 years old; 10 km N. ***Wineries:*** more than 28 wineries in the area, many offering tours, tastings and sales; details from visitor centre. ***Pemberton Tramway:*** tramcars based on 1907 Fremantle trams operate daily through tall-forest country to the Warren River Bridge; (08) 9776 1322. ***Fishing:*** in rivers, inland fishing licence is required for trout and marron; contact post office for details and permits. ***Tours:*** river tours, scenic bus tours, 4WD adventure tours, self-guide forest drives, walking trails and eco-tours; details from visitor centre. ***Drive trails:*** include the Heartbreak Trail, a one-way drive through the karri forest of Warren National Park; maps from visitor centre. ***Walk trails:*** include the 1 hr return Rainbow Trail; maps from visitor centre. ***Bibbulmun Track:*** walking trail passes through Pemberton; *see Albany.*

See also THE SOUTH-WEST, pp. 34–5

Pingelly Pop. 817

257 C3 | 258 B3

Council offices, 17 Queen St; (08) 9887 1066; www.pingelly.wa.gov.au

99.7 FM ABC News Radio, 612 AM ABC Radio National

Located 158 kilometres south-east of Perth on the Great Southern Highway, Pingelly is part of the central-southern farming district. Sandalwood was once a local industry, but today sheep and wheat are the major produce.

Courthouse Museum: built in 1907, now houses historic memorabilia and photographs; Parade St. *Apex Lookout:* fine views of town and surrounding countryside; Stone St.

Autumn Country Show and Ute Muster: Mar.

Pingelly Heights Observatory: audio tour and telescope viewing of the stars and constellations; bookings essential (08) 9887 0088; 5 km NE. *Moorumbine Heritage Trail:* walk or drive through this old townsite featuring early settlers' cottages and St Patrick's Church, built in 1873; maps from council office; 8 km E. *Tutanning Flora and Fauna Reserve:* botanist Guy Shorteridge collected over 400 species of plants from here for the British Museum between 1903 and 1906; 22 km E. *Boyagin Nature Reserve:* widely recognised as one of the few areas of original fauna and flora left in the wheat belt, this picnic reserve has important stands of powderbark, jarrah and marri trees and is home to numbats and tammar wallabies; 26 km NW.

See also HEARTLANDS, pp. 36–7

Pinjarra

Pop. 3295

254 B4 | 257 B3 | 258 B4

Pinjarra Heritage Train Station, Fimmel La; (08) 9531 1438; www.pinjarravisitorcentre.com.au

97.3 Coast FM, 585 AM ABC News Radio

A pleasant 84-kilometre drive south of Perth along the shaded South Western Highway brings you to Pinjarra, picturesquely set on the Murray River. Predominantly a dairying, cattle-farming and timber-producing area, Pinjarra was also once known as the horse capital of Western Australia when horses were bred for the British Army in India. Today horseracing, pacing and equestrian events are a major part of Pinjarra culture. The Alcoa Refinery north-east of town is the largest alumina refinery in Australia.

Edenvale Complex Built in 1888 with locally fired clay bricks, Edenvale was the home of Edward McLarty, member of the state's Legislative Council for 22 years. Nearby is Liveringa (1874), the original residence of the McLarty family, now an art gallery. There is a Heritage Rose Garden featuring 364 varieties of old-fashioned roses, a quilters' display in the Old School House, and a machinery museum. Cnr George and Henry sts.

Suspension bridge: across the Murray River, with picnic areas at both ends; George St. *Heritage trail:* 30 min river walk follows series of tiles explaining the heritage of the area; maps from visitor centre.

Railway Markets: Lions Park; 2nd Sun morning each month Sept–June. *Community Markets:* Fimmel La; 4th Sat morning each month Sept–May. *Pinjarra Cup:* Mar. *Pinjarra Festival:* June. *Murray Arts and Craft Open Day:* Nov.

Fairbridge Established by Kingsley Fairbridge in 1912 as a farm school for British children, many of them orphans. Over the years more than 8000 English children were educated here. The boarding houses, which are today used as holiday cottages, have famous British names such as Clive, Shakespeare, Nightingale, Exeter, Evelyn and Raleigh. South Western Hwy; 1800 440 770; 6 km N.

Peel Zoo: set in lush native flora, includes opportunities to feed and interact with the animals and has picnic area and barbecues; (08) 9531 4322; 2 km N. *Old Blythewood:* beautiful National Trust property built in 1859 by John McLarty, who arrived in Australia in 1839; open Sat 10.30am–3.30pm, Sun 12.30pm–3.30pm, or by appt; 4 km s. *Alcoa Mine and Refinery Tours:* includes the mining process, and the world's biggest bulldozer. Tours are free Wed and the last Fri of each month (except during the summer school holidays); bookings essential (08) 9531 6752; 6km NE. **Alcoa Scarp Lookout:** good views of coastal plain, surrounding farming area and Alcoa Refinery; 14 km E. **North Dandalup Dam:** recreation lake, picnic area and coastal views from lookout; 22 km NE. **South Dandalup Dam:** barbecues and picnic areas; 30 km E. **Lake Navarino:** formerly known as Waroona Dam, it is good for watersports, fishing, walking and horseriding; 33 km s. **Coopers Mill:** first flour mill in the Murray region, located on Cooleenup Island near the mouth of the Serpentine River. It is accessible only by water; details from visitor centre. **Hotham Valley Tourist Railway:** travel from Pinjarra to Dwellingup by train, taking in lush green dairy country before climbing the steep and spectacular Darling Range and finishing in the heart of the jarrah forest. The train is steam-hauled May–Oct and diesel-hauled Nov–Apr; check times with visitor centre. **Ravenswood Adventures:** explore the Murray River by kayak, dinghy, canoe or pedal boat; Ravenswood; (08) 9537 7173.

See also THE SOUTH-WEST, pp. 34–5

Port Hedland

Pop. 11 557

262 D2 | 264 B1 | 268 B5

🛈 13 Wedge St; (08) 9173 1711.

📻 91.7 WA FM, 94.9 WA ABC News Radio

Port Hedland was named after Captain Peter Hedland, who reached this deep-water harbour in 1863. An iron-ore boom that began in the early 1960s saw the town grow at a remarkable rate. Today, Port Hedland handles the largest iron-ore export tonnage of any Australian port. Iron ore is loaded onto huge ore carriers; the 2.6-kilometre trains operated by BHP Iron Ore are hard to miss. Salt production is another major industry with about 2 million tonnes exported per annum.

Don Rhodes Mining Museum: open-air museum with displays of historic railway and mining machinery; Wilson St. **Pioneer and Pearlers Cemetery:** used between 1912 and 1968, it has graves of early gold prospectors and Japanese pearl divers; off Stevens St. **Town tour:** visit the town's many attractions; 11am Mon, Wed and Fri June–Oct; bookings at visitor centre. **BHP Iron Ore Tour:** see the enormous machinery required to run this industrial giant; departs 9.30am Mon–Fri from visitor centre. **Heritage trail:** 1.8 km self-guide walk around the town; maps from visitor centre.

Australia Day Festival: Jan. **Port Hedland Cup:** Aug. **Pilbara Music Festival:** Sept. **Welcome to Hedland Night:** every few months.

Stairway to the Moon Like the Broome version, this beautiful illusion is created when a full moon rises over the ocean at low tide. The moon's rays hit pools of water left by the receding tide, creating the image of a stairway leading up to the moon. It lasts for about 15 minutes. Check with visitor centre for dates and times. Coastal side of Goode St; 7 km E.

Pretty Pool: picnic, fish and swim at this scenic tidal pool; 8 km NE. **Dampier Salt:** see giant cone-shaped mounds of salt awaiting export; 8 km s. **Royal Flying Doctor Service:** operates an important base in Port Hedland at the airport; open to public 8–11am Mon–Fri; closed public holidays, school holidays and weekends; 15 km s. **School of the Air:** experience schooling outback-style at the airport; open to public 8–11am Mon–Fri; closed public and school holidays; 15 km s. **Turtle-watching:** flatback turtles nest in the

RADIO STATION | IN TOWN | WHAT'S ON | NEARBY

area Oct–Mar at Pretty Pool, Cooke Pt and Cemetery Beach. **Cruises:** scenic harbour and sunset cruises; details from visitor centre.

Travellers note: *Poisonous stonefish frequent this stretch of coast, especially Nov–Mar, so wear strong shoes when walking on rocky reef areas and make local inquiries before swimming in the sea.*

See also PILBARA, pp. 46–7

Ravensthorpe
Pop. 438

258 D4

ⓘ Morgans St; (08) 9838 1277; www.ravensthorpe.wa.gov.au

📻 101.9 WA FM, 105.9 FM ABC Local Radio

Ravensthorpe is encircled by the Ravensthorpe Range. This unspoiled bushland is home to many plants unique to the area such as the Qualup bell, warted yate and Ravensthorpe bottlebrush. Gold was discovered here in 1898 and by 1909 the population had increased to around 3000. Coppermining reached a peak in the late 1960s; the last coppermine closed in 1972. Many old mine shafts can be seen around the district and fossicking is a favourite pastime. **Historical Society Museum:** local history memorabilia; in Dance Cottage near visitor centre, Morgans St. **Historic buildings:** many in town including the impressive Palace Hotel (1907) and the restored Commercial Hotel (now a community centre); both in Morgans St. **Rangeview Park:** local plant species, picnic and barbecue facilities; Morgans St. **Wildflower Show:** Sept. **WA Time Meridian:** plaque on a boulder marks the WA time meridian; at First Rest Bay west of town. **Eremia Camel Treks:** offers rides along the beach; open by appt Dec–Apr; Hopetoun Rd; (08) 9838 1092; 2 km SE. **Old Copper Smelter:** in operation 1906–18, now site of tailings dumps and old equipment;

2 km SE. **Archer Drive Lookout:** extensive views over farms and hills; 3 km N in Ravensthorpe Range. **Mt Desmond Lookout:** magnificent views in all directions; Ethel Daw Dr; 17 km SE in Ravensthorpe Range. **Hopetown:** seaside village with pristine beaches ideal for swimming, surfing, windsurfing, fishing and boating. Summer Festival each June. Walk on the Hopetoun Trail Head Loop (part of the Hopetoun–Ravensthorpe Heritage Walk) or visit Fitzgerald River National Park to the west; *see* Bremer Bay; 49 km s. **Scenic drives:** include the 170 km circular Hamersley Drive Heritage Trail; maps from visitor centre. **Rock-collecting:** check locally to avoid trespass.

See also ESPERANCE & NULLARBOR, pp. 40–1

Rockingham
Pop. 67 521

254 B3 | 257 B3 | 258 A3

ⓘ 43 Kent St; (08) 9592 3464; www.rockinghamvisitorcentre.com.au

📻 97.7 FM ABC Classic Radio, 720 AM ABC Local Radio

Lying on the edge of Cockburn Sound just 47 kilometres south of Perth, the coastal city of Rockingham offers sheltered waters ideal for swimming, snorkelling, sailing, windsurfing, fishing and crabbing. Established in 1872 to ship timber from Jarrahdale to England, Rockingham was the busiest port in Western Australia until the end of the 19th century, after which all port activities were shifted north to Fremantle. It was only because of the industrial area nearby at Kwinana in the 1950s and the development of the HMAS *Stirling* Naval Base on Garden Island in the 1970s that the town was revitalised. Today, its magnificent beaches and proximity to Perth are Rockingham's main attractions.

Rockingham Museum: folk museum featuring local history exhibits including displays on the Group Settlement farms, the timber industry, domestic items and antique photographic equipment; open 1–4pm Tues, Wed, Thurs and Sat, 10am–4pm Sun; Cnr Flinders La and Kent St; (08) 9592 3455. **Art Gallery and Craft Centre:** features local artists, with market every 3rd Sun; Civic Blvd. **The Granary:** museum of artefacts celebrating the history of WA's grain industry; open for tours (minimum group size 4) by appt; northern end of Rockingham Rd; (08) 9599 6333. **Mersey Pt Jetty:** departure point for cruises and island tours; Shoalwater. **Kwinana Beach:** hull of wrecked SS *Kwinana*. **Cape Peron:** the lookout was once the main observation post for a WW II coastal battery; Pt Peron Rd. **Bell and Churchill Park:** family picnics and barbecues in shaded grounds; Rockingham Rd.

Swap Mart: opposite Churchill Park; each Sun. **Sunset Jazz Festival:** Mar. **Musslefest:** Oct. **Spring Festival:** Nov.

Penguin Island Take a trip to this offshore island, which is home to a colony of little penguins. The Discovery Centre allows you to see the penguins up close in an environment similar to their natural habitat and to learn about them through daily feedings, commentaries and displays. The island also provides picnic areas, lookouts and a network of boardwalks, and you can swim, snorkel or scuba dive at any of the pristine beaches. The island is open to the public in daylight hours Sept–June. Ferries to the island leave regularly from Mersey Pt, south of Rockingham. The ferry also provides bay cruises and snorkelling tours.

Sloan's Cottage: restored pioneer cottage; open Mon–Fri; Leda; 2 km w. **Lake Richmond:** walks, flora and fauna, and thrombolites (domed rock-like structures like the famous stromatolites of Hamelin Pool near Denham, built by ancient micro-organisms); 4 km sw. **Marapana Wildlife Park:** handfeed and touch native and exotic animals; Karnup; 15 km se. **Wineries:** in the area include Baldivis Estate (15 km se) and Peel Estate (17 km se).

details from visitor centre. **Secret Harbour:** surfing, snorkelling and windsurfing; 20 km s. **Serpentine Dam:** major water storage with brilliant wildflowers in spring, bushland and the nearby Serpentine Falls; 48 km se. **Garden Island:** home to HMAS *Stirling* Naval Base, two-thirds of the island is open to the public but is accessible only by private boat during daylight hours. **Shoalwater Bay Islands Marine Park:** extends from just south of Garden Island to Becher Pt. Cruises of the park are available; details from visitor centre. **Dolphin Watch Cruises:** swim with dolphins between Pt Peron and Garden Island; daily Sept–May; details from visitor centre. **Scenic drives:** including Old Rockingham Heritage Trail, a 30 km drive that takes in 23 points of interest in the Rockingham–Kwinana area, and Rockingham–Jarrahdale Timber Heritage Trail, a 36 km drive retracing the route of the 1872 timber railway; maps from visitor centre.

See also THE SOUTH-WEST, pp. 34–5

Roebourne
Pop. 853

261 C1 | 262 C2 | 264 A1 | 268 A5

Old Gaol, Queens St; (08) 9182 1060; www.roebourne.wa.gov.au

107.5 FM ABC Radio National, 702 AM ABC Local Radio

Named after John Septimus Roe, Western Australia's first surveyor-general, Roebourne was established in 1866 and is the oldest town on the north-west coast. As the centre for early mining and pastoral industries in the Pilbara, it was connected by tramway to the pearling port of Cossack and later to Point Samson. Now Cossack is a ghost town and Point Samson is known for its beachside pleasures.

Historic buildings: some original stone buildings remain, many of which have been classified by the National Trust. The Old Gaol, designed by the well-known colonial architect George Temple Poole, now operates as the visitor centre and museum; Queen St. **Mt Welcome:** offers views of the coastal plains and rugged hills surrounding town. Spot the railroad from Cape Lambert to Pannawonica, and the pipeline carrying water from Millstream to Wickham and Cape Lambert; Fisher Dr.

Roebourne Cup: July.

Cossack Originally named Tien Tsin after the boat that brought the first settlers there in 1863, Cossack was the first port in the north-west region. During its days as a pearling centre in the late 1800s the population increased dramatically. Although now a ghost town, the beautiful stone buildings have been restored and nine are classified by the National Trust. Cruises are available from the wharf. 14 km N.

Wickham: the company town for Robe River Iron Ore offers a spectacular view from Tank Hill lookout; tours available; 12 km N. **Pt Samson:** good fishing, swimming, snorkelling and diving. Boat hire, whale-watching and fishing charters are available; 19 km N. **Cleaverville:** camping and fishing; 25 km N. **Harding Dam:** ideal picnic spot; 27 km S. **Millstream–Chichester National Park:** 150 km S; *see Karratha*. **Emma Withnell Heritage Trail:** 52 km historic self-drive trail, named after the first European woman in the north-west, takes in Roebourne, Cossack, Wickham and Pt Samson; maps from visitor centre. **Tours:** include historic Pearls and Past tour and trips to Jarman Island; details from visitor centre.

See also PILBARA, pp. 46–7

Southern Cross
Pop. 709

258 C3

Council offices, Antares St; (08) 9049 1001; www.yilgarn.wa.gov.au

100.7 WA FM, 106.3 FM ABC Local Radio

A small, flourishing town on the Great Eastern Highway, Southern Cross is the centre of a prosperous agricultural and pastoral region. Its claim to fame is as the site of the first major gold discovery in the huge eastern goldfields. Although it never matched the fever pitch of Kalgoorlie and Coolgardie, Southern Cross remains the centre for a significant gold-producing area. The town's wide streets, like the town itself, were named after stars and constellations.

Yilgarn History Museum: originally the town courthouse and mining registrar's office, it now houses displays on mining, agriculture, water supply and military involvement; Antares St. **Historic buildings:** including the post office in Antares St, the Railway Tavern in Spica St and the restored Palace Hotel in Orion St.

King of the Cross: 2 days of motorcycle races; Aug.

Hunt's Soak: once an important water source, now a picnic area; 7 km N. **Frog Rock:** large rock with wave-like formations. Popular picnic spot; 34 km S. **Baladjie Rock:** granite outcrop with spectacular views; 50 km NW. **Karalee Rock and Dam:** this dam was built to provide water for steam trains and is now popular for swimming and picnics; 52 km E.

See also HEARTLANDS, pp. 36–7

Tom Price
Pop. 2721

261 D2 | 262 D4 | 264 B2

Central Rd; (08) 9188 1112; www.tompricewa.com.au

103.3 WA FM, 567 AM ABC Local Radio

The huge iron-ore deposit now known as Mount Tom Price was discovered in 1962 in the heart of the Pilbara, after which the Hamersley

Iron Project was established. A mine, two towns (Dampier and Tom Price) and a railway line between them all followed. Today, the town is an oasis in a dry countryside. On the edge of the Hamersley Range at an altitude of 747 metres, this is the state's highest town, hence its nickname of 'Top Town in WA'.

Karijini National Park The second largest national park in Western Australia, this park features ochre-coloured rock faces with bright-white snappy gums, bundles of spinifex dotting the red earth and chasms up to 100 m deep. The waterfalls and rockpools of Karijini offer some of the best swimming in the state. The park protects the many different wildlife habitats, plants and animals of the Pilbara. The landscape is dotted with huge termite mounds and the rock piles of the rare pebble mouse; other species include red kangaroos and rock wallabies, and reptiles from legless lizards to pythons. Kalamina Gorge and Pool is the most accessible gorge, while at Hamersley Gorge a wave of tectonic rock acts as a backdrop to a swimming hole and natural spa. Oxer Lookout reveals where the Joffre, Hancock, Weano and Red gorges meet. Mt Bruce, the second-tallest peak in the state, offers spectacular views and interpretive signs along the trail to the top. The Karijini Visitor Centre is located off the road to Dales Gorge and has information on camping. 50 km E.

Kings Lake: constructed lake with nearby park offering picnic and barbecue facilities (no swimming); 2 km w. **Mt Nameless Lookout:** stunning views of district around Tom Price; 6 km w via walking trail or 4WD track. **Aboriginal carvings:** thought to be 35 000 years old; 10 km s. **Mine tours:** marvel at the sheer enormity of Hamersley Iron's open-cut iron-ore mine; bookings essential at visitor centre. **Hamersley Iron Access Road:** this private road is the most direct route between Tom Price and Karratha via Karijini and Millstream national parks. It requires a permit to travel along it; available from visitor centre.

Travellers note: *To the north-east is Wittenoom, an old asbestos-mining town. Although the mine was closed in 1966, there is still a health risk from microscopic asbestos fibres present in the abandoned mine tailings in and around Wittenoom. If disturbed and inhaled, blue asbestos dust may cause cancer. The Ashburton Shire Council advocates avoidance of the Wittenoom area.*

See also PILBARA, pp. 46–7

Toodyay
Pop. 1068

254 C1 | 257 B2 | 258 B3

🛈 **7 Piesse St; (08) 9574 2435; www.toodyay.com**

📻 558 AM ABC Local Radio, 612 AM ABC Radio National

This National Trust–classified town is nestled in the Avon Valley surrounded by picturesque farming country and bushland. The name originates from 'Duidgee', which means the 'place of plenty'. Founded in 1836, Toodyay was one of the first inland towns to be established in the colony. It was a favourite haunt of Western Australia's most famous bushranger, Joseph Bolitho Johns, who was more commonly known as 'Moondyne Joe'.

Historic buildings Some original buildings from the early settlement of Toodyay still stand, including Stirling House (1908), Connor's Mill (1870s) with displays of working flour-milling equipment, the Old Newcastle Gaol (1865) built by convict labour and where Moondyne Joe was imprisoned, and the Police Stables (1870) built by convict labour from random rubblestone. Self-guide walk available; pamphlet from visitor centre.

Duidgee Park: popular picnic spot on the banks of the river has a miniature railway and a walking track; check at visitor centre for running times; Harper Rd. *Newcastle Park:* contains a unique stone monument of Charlotte Davies, the first white female to set foot on the soil of the Swan River Colony. Also has a children's playground; Stirling Tce. *Pelham Reserve and Lookout:* nature walks, a lookout with views over the town and a memorial to James Drummond, the town's first resident botanist; Duke St.

Moondyne Festival: May. *Avon Descent:* whitewater rafting; Aug. *Kombi Konnection:* Sept. *Music Festival:* Sept.

Avon Valley National Park The park offers spectacular scenery with abundant wildflowers in season. Being at the northern limit of the jarrah forests, the jarrah and marri trees mingle with wandoo woodland. This mix of trees creates diverse habitats for fauna, including a wide variety of birdlife. The Avon River, which in summer and autumn is a series of pools, swells to become impressive rapids during winter and spring. These rapids provide the backdrop for the Avon Descent, a well-known annual whitewater race held every Aug, which begins in Northam and passes through the park. The park is ideal for camping, bushwalking, canoeing and picnicking, although all roads are unsealed. Whitewater rafting tours are available. 25 km sw.

Pecan Hill Tearoom Museum: tearoom and museum set in a pecan nut orchard with a lookout offering spectacular views over the Avon Valley; Julimar Rd; 4 km NW. *Coorinja Winery:* dating from the 1870s; open for tastings and sales; closed Sun; 4 km sw. *Ringa Railway Bridge:* constructed in 1888, this timber bridge has 18 spans, but is not readily accessible; details from visitor centre; 6 km sw. *Windmill Hill Cutting:* the deepest railway cutting in Australia; 6 km SE. *Avonlea Park Alpaca Farm:* alpacas and other farm animals, and sales of alpaca wool products; 12 km SE.

Emu Farm: one of the oldest in Australia. Birds range free in natural bushland. Also crafts and emu products for sale; 15 km sw. *Cartref Park Country Garden:* 2 ha park of English-style landscaped gardens and native plants, with prolific birdlife; 16 km NW. *Oliomio Farm:* olive and lavendar farm offering tastings and sales; Parkland Dr; 20 km NW. *Wyening Mission:* this Benedictine farm and winery runs tours of their mission, cellars and grounds; by appt; (08) 9364 6463; 38 km N. *Toodyay Pioneer Heritage Trail:* honouring the pioneering spirit in the Avon Valley, this 20 km self-drive trail retraces the route of the first settlers; maps from visitor centre. *Avon Valley Tourist Drive:* 95 km scenic drive includes Toodyay, Northam, York and Beverley; maps from visitor centre. *Hotham Valley Steam Railway:* the famous steam-train service runs special trips including a monthly 'murder-mystery' night; details from visitor centre.

See also HEARTLANDS, pp. 36–7

Wagin
Pop. 1424

257 C3 | 258 B4

Historical Village, Kitchener St; (08) 9861 1232; www.wagintouristinfo.com.au

96.3 FM ABC News Radio, 558 AM ABC Local Radio

Wagin, 177 kilometres east of Bunbury, is the sheep capital of Western Australia. The importance of the wool industry to the district is celebrated in its annual Wagin Woolorama, one of the largest rural shows in the state, and its Giant Ram, an enormous structure that visitors from around the country come to photograph.

Wagin Historical Village Explore 24 relocated or re-created historic buildings and machinery providing a glimpse of pioneering rural life. The buildings are furnished with

WESTERN AUSTRALIA → TOWNS → **WALPOLE** 127

original pieces, and audio commentaries are available. Open 10am–4pm; Kitchener St.

Giant Ram and Ram Park: 9 m high statue provides a photo opportunity not to miss; Arthur River Rd. ***Wagin Heritage Trail:*** self-guide walk around the town; maps from visitor centre.

Wagin Woolorama: Mar. ***Foundation Day:*** June.

Puntapin Rock: spectacular views over the town and surrounding farmlands from the top of the rock. Enjoy the picnic and barbecue facilities nearby; Bullock Hill Rd; 4 km SE. ***Mt Latham:*** interesting rock formation with walk trails, a lookout and abundant wildflowers in season; Arthur River Rd; 8 km W. ***Lake Norring:*** swimming, sailing and waterskiing; picnic and barbecue facilities; water levels vary considerably; check conditions at visitor centre; 17 km SW. ***Lake Dumbleyung:*** where Donald Campbell established a world water-speed record in 1964. Swimming, boating and birdwatching are subject to water levels that vary considerably; check conditions at visitor centre; 18 km E. ***Wait-jen Trail:*** self-guide 10.5 km signposted walk that follows ancient Aboriginal Dreaming. The word 'wait-jen' means 'emu footprint' in the language of the local Aboriginal people; maps from visitor centre. ***Wheat Belt Wildflower Drive:*** self-guide drive that includes the Tarin Rock Nature Reserve; maps from visitor centre.

See also **HEARTLANDS**, pp. 36–7

Walpole
Pop. 322

256 C3 | 257 C5 | 258 B5

Pioneer Cottage, South Coast Hwy; (08) 9840 1111; www.walpole.com.au

102.9 WA FM, 106.1 FM ABC Local Radio

Walpole is entirely surrounded by national park and is the only place in the South-West where the forest meets the sea. The area is renowned for its striking ocean and forest scenery, which provides an idyllic setting for outdoor activities. The town of Walpole was established in 1930 through the Nornalup Land Settlement Scheme for city families hit by the Great Depression.

Pioneer Cottage: re-creation of a historic cottage to commemorate the district's pioneer settlers; South Coast Hwy.

Easter Markets: Apr.

Walpole–Nornalup National Park The many forest attractions include the Valley of the Giants, the Hilltop Drive and Lookout, Circular Pool and the Knoll. The park is probably best known for its huge, buttressed red tingle trees, some more than 400 years old, which are unique to the Walpole area. The world-class Bibbulmun Track, between Perth and Albany, passes through the park. *See Albany*; 4 km SE.

Valley of the Giants Here visitors can wander over a walkway suspended 38 m above the forest floor, the highest and longest tree-top walkway of its kind in the world. The Ancient Empire interpretive boardwalk weaves its way through the veteran tingle trees. Twilight walks are available in holiday season. Contact (08) 9840 8263; 16 km E.

Giant Red Tingle: a 25 m circumference defines this tree as one of the 10 largest living things on the planet; 2 km E. ***Hilltop Lookout:*** views over the Frankland River out to the Southern Ocean; 2 km W. ***John Rate Lookout:*** panoramic views over the mouth of the Deep River and of the nearby coastline and forests; 4 km W. ***Thurlby Herb Farm:*** herb garden display with sales of herbal products; Gardiner Rd; 13 km N. ***Mandalay Beach:*** site of the 1911 shipwreck of the Norwegian *Mandalay*. A boardwalk has descriptive notes about the wreck. Also popular for fishing;

TOWNS

RADIO STATION | IN TOWN | WHAT'S ON | NEARBY

20 km w. ***Dinosaur World:*** a collection of native birds and reptiles, and exotic birds; 25 km E. ***Mt Frankland National Park:*** noted for its exceptional variety of birdlife, it also offers breathtaking views from the top of Mt Frankland, known as 'Caldyanup' to the local Aboriginal people; 29 km N. ***Peaceful Bay:*** small fishing village with an excellent beach for swimming; 35 km E. ***Fernhook Falls:*** ideal picnic spot with boardwalk, at its best in winter when it is popular for canoeing and kayaking; 36 km NW. ***Walk trails:*** many trails in the area, including self-guide Horseyard Hill Walk Trail through the karri forest and the signposted Coalmine Beach Heritage Trail from the coastal heathland to the inlets; maps from visitor centre. ***Tours:*** take a guided cruise through the inlets and rivers, hire a boat or canoe, or go on a forest tour or wilderness eco-cruise; details from visitor centre.

See also THE SOUTH-WEST, pp. 34–5

Wickepin
Pop. 245

257 C3 | 258 B4

District Resource and Telecentre, 24 Wogolin Rd; (08) 9888 1500; www.wickepin.wa.au

100.5 Hot FM, 612 AM ABC Radio National

The first settlers arrived in the Wickepin area in the 1890s. Albert Facey's internationally acclaimed autobiography, *A Fortunate Life*, details these pioneering times. However, Facey is not the only major literary figure to feature in Wickepin's history. The poet and playwright, Dorothy Hewett, was born in Wickepin in 1923, and much of her work deals with life in the area.

Historic buildings in Wogolin Road: excellent examples of Edwardian architecture. ***Facey Homestead:*** the home of author Albert Facey has been relocated and restored with its original furniture; open 10am–4pm daily Mar–Nov, 10am–4pm Fri–Sun and public holidays Dec–Feb.

Tarling Well: the circular stone well marks the original intended site for the town; 8 km w. ***Malyalling Rock:*** unusual rock formation; 15 km NE. ***Toolibin Lake Reserve:*** see a wide variety of waterfowl while you enjoy a barbecue; 20 km s. ***Yealering and Yealering Lake:*** historic photographs on display in town, and swimming, boating, windsurfing and birdwatching at lake; 30 km NE. ***Harrismith Walk Path:*** self-guide trail through wildflowers in season, including orchids and some species unique to the area; brochures from visitor centre. ***Albert Facey Heritage Trail:*** 86 km self-drive trail brings to life the story of Albert Facey and the harshness of life in the early pioneering days of the wheat belt; maps from visitor centre.

See also HEARTLANDS, pp. 36–7

Wyndham
Pop. 672

267 F2 | 269 H2

Kimberley Motors, Great Northern Hwy; (08) 9161 1281; www.wyndham.wa.au

102.9 WA FM, 1017 AM ABC Local Radio

Wyndham, in the Kimberley region, is the most northerly town and safe port in Western Australia. The entrance to the town is guarded by the 'Big Croc', a 20-metre-long concrete crocodile.

Historical Society Museum: in the old courthouse building, its displays include a photographic record of the town's history, artefacts and machinery; open Apr–Oct; O'Donnell St. ***Warriu Dreamtime Park:*** bronze statues representing the Aboriginal heritage of the area; Koolama St. ***Zoological Gardens and Crocodile Park:*** daily feeding of crocodiles and alligators; Barytes Rd; (08) 9161 1124. ***Durack's Old Store:*** has an informative plaque with details of its history; O'Donnell St. ***Pioneer Cemetery:*** gravestones of some of the area's original settlers; Great Northern Hwy. ***Boat charters:*** scenic, fishing and camping cruises; details from visitor centre.

Races: Aug. ***Art and Craft Show:*** Aug/Sept.

Three Mile Valley On offer is spectacular scenery typical of the Kimberley region, with rough red gorges and pools of clear, cold water during the wet season. Walk trails lead the visitor through the brilliant displays of wildflowers in season. Three Mile Valley is the home of the 'Trial Tree', a sacred Aboriginal site into which, when a person died of unnatural causes, the body was placed. Rocks were placed around the base of the tree, each rock representing a relative of the deceased. When the body started to decompose, the first rock to be marked by the decomposition indicated the name of the person responsible for the death. This person was then banished from the tribe. 3 km N.

Afghan Cemetery: containing the graves of Afghan camel drivers who carried supplies throughout the Kimberley region. All the gravestones face towards Mecca; 1 km E. ***Koolama Wreck Site:*** the *Koolama* was hit by Japanese bombs near Darwin in 1942. After limping along the coast to Wyndham, it sank just 40 m from the jetty. The spot is marked by unusual swirling in the water; 5 km NW. ***Five Rivers Lookout:*** spectacular views of the Kimberley landscape from the highest point of the Bastion Range, particularly good for viewing the striking sunsets. Also a good picnic area with barbecue facilities; 5 km N. ***Moochalabra Dam:*** completed in 1971, the dam was constructed to provide an assured water supply to the Wyndham area. The construction is unique in Australia, designed to allow overflow to pass through the rock on the crest of the hill. 4WD access only; King River Rd; 18 km sw. ***Aboriginal rock paintings:*** 4WD access only; well signposted off the King River Rd; 18 km sw. ***Parry Lagoons Nature Reserve:*** visitors can enjoy birdwatching from a shaded bird hide at Marlgu Billabong or scan the wide vistas of the flood plain and distant hills afforded from the lookout at Telegraph Hill; 20 km SE. ***Prison Tree:*** 2000–4000-year-old boab tree once used by local police as a lock-up; King River Rd; 22 km sw. ***The Grotto:*** this rock-edged waterhole, estimated to be 100 m deep, is a cool, shaded oasis offering year-round swimming; 36 km E.

See also **KIMBERLEY**, pp. 48–9

Yalgoo
Pop. 164

258 B1 | 261 C5 | 264 B5

Old Railway Station, Geraldton–Mt Magnet Rd; (08) 9962 8157; www.yalgoo.wa.gov.au

104.5 WA FM, 106.1 FM ABC Local Radio

Alluvial gold was discovered in the 1890s in Yalgoo, which lies 216 kilometres east of Geraldton. Today, gold is still found in the district and visitors are encouraged to try their luck fossicking in the area. The name Yalgoo is from the Aboriginal word meaning 'blood', a rather odd fact given that in 1993 a Yalgoo resident was the first person in Australia to be the victim of a parcel bomb.

Courthouse Museum: exhibits of local artefacts; Gibbons St. ***Gaol:*** built in 1896 and recently relocated to the museum precinct, it has photographs illustrating the town's history; Gibbons St. ***Chapel of St Hyacinth:*** designed by Monsignor Hawes and built in 1919 for the Dominican Sisters who lived in a wooden convent school near the chapel; Henty St. ***Heritage walk:*** self-guide town walk; pamphlet from visitor centre.

RADIO STATION | IN TOWN | WHAT'S ON | NEARBY

Cemetery: the history of Yalgoo as told through headstones; 5 km w. *Joker's Tunnel:* a tunnel carved through solid rock by early prospectors and named after the Joker's mining syndicate, it has panoramic views near the entrance; 10 km SE. *Meteorite crater:* discovered in 1961, a portion of the meteorite is held at the WA Museum in Perth; 100 km N. *Gascoyne Murchison Outback Pathways:* three self-drive trips exploring outback history: the Wool Wagon Pathway, the Kingsford Smith Mail Run and the Miners Pathway; maps from visitor centre or downloadable from website.

See also OUTBACK COAST & MID-WEST, pp. 44–5

Yallingup
Pop. 300

255 A3 | 257 A4 | 258 A4

Seymour Blvd, Dunsborough; (08) 9752 1288; www.geographebay.com

98.4 FM Western Tourist Radio, 684 AM ABC Local Radio

Yallingup, known for its limestone caves and world-class surf breaks, is also an ideal location for swimming, fishing and beachcombing. Nearby Leeuwin–Naturaliste National Park offers spectacular scenery, interesting bushwalks and beautiful wildflowers in season. Art and craft galleries abound and many of the wineries of the South-West region are only a short drive from the town. Yallingup continues to live up to its Aboriginal meaning of 'place of love', with nearby Caves House Hotel being a favourite destination for generations of honeymooners and holiday-makers.

Caves House Hotel: originally built in 1903 as a holiday hotel, the building was damaged by fire in 1938 and rebuilt; off Caves Rd; (08) 9755 2131. *Yallingup Beach:* surfing, scuba diving, whale-watching and salmon fishing in season.

Amberley Estate Seafood and Semillon Weekend: Feb. *Yallingup Malibu Surfing Classic:* Dec.

Leeuwin–Naturaliste National Park: stretches north and south of town; see *Dunsborough, Margaret River and Augusta*. *Ngilgi Cave:* (pronounced 'Nillgee') semi-guided adventure tours are available for this stunning display of stalactite, stalagmite and shawl rock formations. An interpretive area details the history of the cave; 2 km E. *Canal Rocks and Smith's Beach:* interesting rock formation plus fishing, surfing, swimming, snorkelling and diving; 5 km sw. *Gunyulgup Gallery:* over 120 artists and craftspeople are represented, with paintings, prints, ceramics and sculpture on display and for sale; (08) 9755 2177; 9 km sw. *Yallingup Gallery:* specialises in custom-built furniture; 9 km sw. *Quinninup Falls:* falls that are particularly attractive in winter and can be reached only by 4WD or on foot; 10 km s. *Shearing Shed:* sales of wool products, and shearing demonstrations at 11am; closed Fri; Wildwood Rd; (08) 9755 2309; 10 km E. *Wineries and breweries:* many award-winning wineries and boutique breweries in the area offer tastings and sales; details from visitor centre.

See also THE SOUTH-WEST, pp. 34–5

Yanchep
Pop. 2481

254 A1 | 257 A2 | 258 A3

Information office, Yanchep National Park; (08) 9561 1004

94.5 Mix FM, 720 AM ABC Local Radio

Only 58 kilometres north of Perth, Yanchep is a rapidly developing recreational area and popular tourist destination. It provides safe, sandy beaches and good fishing areas, as well as natural attractions such as the series of caves found within Yanchep National Park. The town derives its name from the Aboriginal word 'yanjet', which means bullrushes, a feature of the area.

Yanchep Lagoon: good swimming and fishing beach; off Lagoon Dr.

Yanchep National Park On a belt of coastal limestone, this 2842 ha park has forests of massive tuart trees, underground caves and spring wildflowers. Within the park, attractions include the historic Tudor-style Yanchep Inn; the Crystal Cave featuring magnificent limestone formations (daily tours available); a koala boardwalk; rowing-boat hire on freshwater Loch McNess; self-guide walk trails; and Aboriginal cultural tours (available on weekends and public holidays). Boomerang Gorge follows an ancient collapsed cave system and has an interpretive nature trail with access for people with disabilities. Grassy areas with barbecues and picnic tables provide a perfect setting for a family outing. 5 km E.

Marina: charter fishing boat hire; 6 km NW at Two Rocks. **Guilderton:** peaceful town at the mouth of the Moore River. Estuary provides safe swimming, and upper reaches of the river can be explored by boat or canoe (hire on river foreshore). Also good fishing; 37 km N. **Ledge Pt:** great destination for diving, with dive trail to 14 shipwrecks. Also the starting point for Lancelin Ocean Classic, a major windsurfing race each Jan; 62 km N. **Lancelin:** great base for fishing and boating because of a natural breakwater offshore. White sandy beaches provide safe swimming, and sand dunes at the edge of town have designated areas for off-road vehicles and sand-boarding; 71 km N.

See also HEARTLANDS, pp. 36–7

York
Pop. 2091

254 D2 | 257 B2 | 258 B3

Town Hall, 81 Avon Tce; (08) 9641 1301; www.yorkwa.org

101.3 York FM, 612 AM ABC Radio National

On the banks of the Avon River in the fertile Avon Valley, York is one of the best preserved and restored 19th-century towns in Australia. It is now classified by the National Trust as 'York Historic Town'. Settled in 1831, only two years after the establishment of the Swan River Colony, York was the first inland European settlement in Western Australia.

Historic buildings There are a significant number of carefully preserved historic buildings in York. The three remaining hotels are fine examples of early coaching inns. The Romanesque-style Town Hall (1911) reflects gold-rush wealth. Details from visitor centre.

Avon Park: on the banks of the river with playground and barbecue facilities; Low St. **York Motor Museum:** vehicles on display represent the development of motor transport; Avon Tce. **Mill Gallery:** display and sales of unique and award-winning recycled jarrah furniture and craft; Broome St. **Residency Museum:** personal possessions, ceramics and silverware reflect aspects of civic and religious life in early York; open 1–3pm Tues–Thurs, 11am–3.30pm Sat, Sun and public holidays; Brook St. **Suspension bridge and walk trail:** built in 1906, the bridge crosses the Avon River at Avon Park. A 1.5 km nature and heritage walk starts at the bridge; Low St.

Antique Fair: Apr. **York Society Photographic Awards:** Apr. **Olive Festival:** June. **Jazz Festival:** Sept/Oct. **Spring Garden Festival:** Oct.

Mt Brown Lookout: provides 360-degree views over town; 3 km SE. **Gwambygine Park:** overlooking the river with boardwalk and viewing platform; 10 km S. **Skydive Express:** award-winning centre; (08) 9641 2905; 10 km N. **Toapin Weir and Mt Stirling:** panoramic views; 64 km E. **Self-drive trails:** eight different routes including the Avon Ascent through Perth's scenic hinterland to a series of special places in the Avon Valley; maps from visitor centre.

See also HEARTLANDS, pp. 36–7

RADIO STATION | IN TOWN | WHAT'S ON | NEARBY

WHERE TO EAT A–Z

western australia

PRIVATE DINING ROOM, 1907 RESTAURANT AND COCKTAIL BAR, PERTH

Town entries are ordered alphabetically, with places nearby listed at the end.

LEGEND
- $ = under $15
- $$ = $15–$25
- $$$ = $25–$35
- $$$$ = $35–$45
- $$$$$ = over $45

For the average price of a main meal

- BYO AVAILABLE
- CREDIT CARDS ACCEPTED
- DISABLED ACCESS
- DRESS CODE APPLIES
- FAMILY FRIENDLY
- LICENSED
- OUTDOOR DINING
- VEGETARIAN OPTIONS

Perth

1907 RESTAURANT AND COCKTAIL BAR $$$$$
MODERN AUSTRALIAN
Map ref. p. 8

Situated within a heritage building and opulently decked out, innovative 1907 is helmed by world-class chef, Graeme Shapiro. The aim here is to achieve a unique dining experience and many dishes incorporate imported delicacies paired with fresh local produce. Manjimup marron and mussels in an Asian broth is a signature dish and the abalone is a rare surprise. The wine list is extensive and features many classics along with some boutique gems. The element of surprise is what sets 1907 apart, something that becomes clear as soon as you wander down one of the CBD's lesser-known alleys, step through the oversized doors and are greeted by a life-size horse lit up by the lampshade hovering above its head.

Alleyway, 26 Queen St; (08) 9436 0233; open Tues–Fri for lunch and Tues–Sat for dinner; www.1907.com.au

ANNALAKSHMI ON THE SWAN $
VEGETARIAN
Map ref. p. 8

Annalakshmi means the Hindu Goddess of Food, which perfectly defines the concept at this vegetarian Indian restaurant. All the food is selflessly prepared by volunteers, who consist predominantly of mothers and grandmothers working from recipes handed down through the generations. There are no set prices, as diners donate whatever they feel their dining experience was worth. Contributions go towards serving the underprivileged in India. Cooking courses and performances by one of India's greatest sitar players, Pandit Baluji Shrivatsav, are also available. Strictly no alcohol.

Jetty 4, Barrack St; (08) 9221 3003; open Tues–Sun for lunch and dinner; www.annalakshmi.com.au

AQUARIUM $$$
SEAFOOD

Located a few minutes out of the city on a busy highway, this surprisingly up-market Chinese restaurant has an emphasis on seafood. Many of the dishes are plucked straight from the tank, soon to be delivered to eagerly awaiting diners. Don't fret if you can't get a table at this very busy restaurant, you can always take your food away and picnic by the river a few metres away.

202 Great Eastern Hwy, Ascot; (08) 9478 1868; open Tues–Sat for lunch and dinner

BALTHAZAR $$$$
ITALIAN
Map ref. p. 8

Balthazar is like a private club in its tucked-away location. Once inside, its cool Art Deco interior does nothing to dispel this exclusive vibe. The Italian-style food is hearty and although the dish prices are heading towards the high end of the market, the serve sizes are generous. Beneath the seductive lighting, swift waiters share their knowledge of the menu and the extensive wine room in a cacophony of exotic accents.

6 The Esplanade; (08) 9421 1206; open Mon–Sat for lunch and dinner

BLUE DUCK $$$
CAFE
Map ref. p. 6 A4

This beachfront cafe attracts an eclectic crowd, from surfers to starlets. Although low-key inside, it's the endless ocean views that have been the drawcard since it opened in 1988. Gorgeous year-round and busy anytime of the day or night, the international menu caters to all tastes. Being a seaside cafe, seafood features prominently, and Asian and European influences appear throughout the menu. The drinks list is generous, and vegetarian and gluten-free options are available.

151 Marine Pde, Cottesloe; (08) 9385 2499; open daily for breakfast, lunch and dinner; www.blueduck.com.au

C RESTAURANT $$$$$
MODERN AUSTRALIAN
Map ref. p. 8

Experience never-ending views of the CBD, metropolitan area and Perth hills in Western Australia's only revolving restaurant. The contemporary menu includes dishes such as lime scallop ceviche, tea-smoked salmon and Margaret River wagyu beef. Also on offer are private champagne breakfasts, high tea, long lunches or luxuriating with a cocktail in the swanky lounge as the city lights twinkle below.

Level 33, 44 St Georges Tce; (08) 9220 8333; open Sun–Fri for lunch and daily for dinner; www.crestaurant.com.au

CANTINA 663 $$$$
ITALIAN
Map ref. p. 6 D2

As you enter the doors of Cantina 663 you are transported to an Italian village trattoria. Although the food is rustic, the vibe is hip and the staff are upbeat. But it's the food that leaves first-timers wondering why they had waited so long to visit. This is earthy Italian fare at its best, with velvety gnocchi and moist White Rocks veal to give you a taste teaser. If you don't want to choose, a selection of antipasti provides a wider scope to sample more from the menu, and you'll probably still have room for a decadent finale.

663 Beaufort St, Mount Lawley; (08) 9370 4883; open daily for breakfast, lunch and dinner; www.cantina663.com

CREAM
$$$$
MODERN AUSTRALIAN
Map ref. p. 12

Think luxuriant decor and decadent food and you've got chef-owner, John Mead's, culinary vision. Bring your appetite as you start with homemade cognac pâté, followed by twice-baked lemon and goat's cheese soufflé with grilled scallops and finish with orange and almond pudding. Surrounded by walls lined with shagpile and groovy hanging red lanterns, you wouldn't be surprised if Austin Powers took your order at this cosy retro-styled restaurant.

Suite 2, 11 Regal St, East Perth; (08) 9221 0404; open Tues–Sat for dinner

DECO RESTAURANT
$$$$
MODERN AUSTRALIAN
Map ref. p. 6 D5

The restored Art Deco Raffles Hotel oozes cool sophistication synonymous with the building's era. The Deco Restaurant serves a modern Australian menu as sensational as the river and city views, with favourites including slow-roasted duck with pappardelle pasta, classic squid ink risotto, and chargrilled veal.

67 Canning Beach Rd; (08) 9314 9000; open Sun–Fri for lunch and daily for dinner

FRASER'S RESTAURANT
$$$$$
MODERN AUSTRALIAN
Map ref. p. 6 C3

Featuring a showcase of Perth's local produce within stunning Kings Park, Fraser's walls of windows frame beautiful views of the Swan River and the city skyline. The broad menu is crafted by celebrity chef, Chris Taylor, and the 500+ wine list has been selected by French sommelier, Patrick Salord. Several functions and culinary events are held throughout the year, with the more casual Botanical Cafe just next door.

Fraser Ave, West Perth; (08) 9481 7100; open daily for lunch and dinner, and weekends for breakfast; www.frasersrestaurant.com.au

HA-LU
$$$
JAPANESE
Map ref. p. 6 C2

Ha-Lu was a finalist in the Restaurant & Catering Australia awards within its first year of trading. Offering Japanese cuisine in the Izakaya style, where unstructured meals are served on an 'as they come' basis to accompany drinks, the dining experience becomes a social event here. The menu includes many familiar favourites as well as interesting choices like Patagonian toothfish. The wine list includes Australian drops, some Japanese wines and a good selection of sake. A takeaway menu is also available.

Shop 4, 401 Oxford St, Mt Hawthorn; (08) 9444 0577; open daily for dinner; www.halu.net.au

INDIANA COTTESLOE BEACH
$$$$
MODERN AUSTRALIAN
Map ref. p. 6 A4

The iconic Indiana Cottesloe Beach, formerly known as the Indiana Tea Rooms, has been a landmark on Cottesloe Beach since colonial times. The modern Australian cuisine is served in surroundings synonymous with a Victorian conservatory and menu favourites include tempura soft shell crab with Asian coleslaw and confit of duck. The drinks list is as extensive as the ocean views.

91 Marine Pde; (08) 9385 5005; open daily for lunch and dinner; www.indiana.com.au

JACKSON'S RESTAURANT
$$$$$
MODERN AUSTRALIAN
Map ref. p. 6 D2

This award-winning, innovative restaurant continues to vie for the position of the state's top restaurant. The à la carte menu is broad, but if you'd like to do a little judging yourself, the degustation menu allows a sampling of seven courses, which can be enjoyed with or without wine. Neal Jackson is considered a pioneer in

BYO AVAILABLE   CREDIT CARDS ACCEPTED   DISABLED ACCESS   DRESS CODE APPLIES

the Western Australian eating scene, blending flavours to provide a fresh approach to the classics.

483 Beaufort St, Highgate; (08) 9328 1177; open Mon–Sat for dinner; www.jacksonsrestaurant.com.au

JUST WINE AND TAPAS BAR $$$
SPANISH
Map ref. p. 6 D4

Just Wine and Tapas Bar is so much more than 'just' wine and tapas. Paying homage to Spanish restaurant elBulli's notoriety, the dishes are adventurous, with smatterings of foamed milk and iced jelly of blood orange, presented by waiters who are entrusted with making all the ordering decisions for you. Surrender yourself to their expertise, specialty coffees and an endless list of international wines while you graze the day or night away.

20 Preston St, Como (08) 9474 1977; open Fri–Wed for breakfast, lunch and dinner

MISS SANDALFORD $$$$$
VINEYARD RESTAURANT
Map ref. p. 8

Cruise down the Swan River in style aboard the Miss Sandalford as you lounge in plush surroundings while nibbling on petits fours, cheese and Sandalford's award-winning wines. Once you arrive at Sandalford, one of Australia's oldest vineyards, enjoy a three-course lunch and wine beneath grapevines creeping over the pergola or within the rustic dining room in front of the huge fireplace. The international menu is seasonal and draws upon much of the locally grown produce. The tour includes information about the winemaking process, samples of aged and fortified wine straight from the barrel, and the opportunity to purchase some of the famous wines.

Barrack St Jetty; (08) 9374 9397; open daily for lunch

MUST WINEBAR $$$$
FRENCH
Map ref. p. 6 D2

With a suspended wine rack separating the bar from the bistro, owner, Russell Blaikie, serves food to rival any French Provincial kitchen. Wooden floors, white tablecloths and red walls set the scene and the bistro-style menu offers a signature charcuterie plate, rotisserie and pâtés, terrines and sausages crafted by head chef Andre Mahe. With 40 wines by the glass and 500 selections on the wine list, it's just as well there are sommeliers on hand to help. Champagne and sparkling wine lovers have not been forgotten: upstairs is an elite champagne lounge boasting a long list of bubblies. Blaikie has indulged in his South-West heritage with the opening of a Margaret River branch.

519 Beaufort St, Highgate; (08) 9328 8255; open daily for lunch and dinner; www.must.com.au

NEW NORCIA BAKERY $
BAKERY
Map ref. p. 6 C2

Working with the Benedictine community in New Norcia, this Mount Hawthorn bakery produces natural sourdough breads and yeasted breads baked in a wood-fired oven. The aroma of baked goods wafting out to the pavement will draw you inside, so join one of the communal tables and forget about the diet. Many of the goodies are available to take home and some of the products like the nut cake and biscotti are sold in outlets all over Australia.

163 Scarborough Beach Rd, Mt Hawthorn; (08) 9443 4114; open daily for breakfast and lunch; www.newnorciabaker.com.au

FAMILY FRIENDLY   LICENSED   OUTDOOR DINING   VEGETARIAN OPTIONS

OPUS RESTAURANT $$$$
MODERN AUSTRALIAN
Map ref. p. 6 C3

Timeless style in a contemporary setting is the best way to describe the Opus Restaurant, situated in the swanky Richardson hotel and with a smart casual dress code. Vanilla seared scallops, foie gras and Tasmanian ocean trout are just some of the dishes on offer. Diners can also order from the grill or linger into the evening with a degustation menu.

The Richardson, 32 Richardson St, West Perth; (08) 9217 8880; open daily for dinner

RED CABBAGE $$$$
MODERN AUSTRALIAN
Map ref. p. 6 D4

In an unobtrusive location in an office building overlooking a freeway ramp, the Red Cabbage is just a few minutes from the CBD. Offering one of the most innovative menus in town, chef, Adam Sayles, uses his expertise gained from working under the direction of Gordon Ramsay. The menu includes game, succulent oysters, seafood and imported cheeses. The complimentary appetite-whetting amuse-bouche and palate cleanser have diners vowing to return.

Lot 49, 15 Labouchere Rd; (08) 9367 5744; open Wed–Fri for lunch and Tues–Sat for dinner; www.redcabbagefoodandwine.com.au

RESTAURANT AMUSÉ $$$$$
FRENCH
Map ref. p. 12

Restaurant Amusé is a relatively recent addition to the Perth dining scene, but its reputation has already spread nationally with its 2007 Restaurant & Catering Australia Award for Best New Restaurant. Owner and chef, Hadleigh Troy's, Michelin-star training has paid off and this up and coming talent is one to watch.

With only a degustation menu available, diners are delighted to be left in the hands of a professional and the seamless service and innovative dishes are sublime. A vegetarian degustation is always available and the wines, although optional, are perfectly selected by Hadleigh's wife, Carolynne, whose wine expertise is indisputable.

64 Bronte St, East Perth; (08) 9325 4900; open Tues–Sat for dinner; www.restaurantamuse.com.au

SHUN FUNG ON THE RIVER $$$
CHINESE
Map ref. p. 8

Situated next to one of Perth's most popular tourist attractions, the Bell Tower and Perth-Eye Ferris wheel on the shores of the Swan River, Shun Fung specialises in live seafood, both local and in some instances imported. Master chef Lin uses Chinese techniques to create the ideal accompaniments to enhance the freshness of the seafood, chosen by diners directly from the tank.

Old Perth Port, Barrack St Jetty; (08) 9221 1868; open daily for lunch and dinner; www.shunfung.com.au

SOTO ESPRESSO $
CAFE
Map ref. p. 6 D2

Situated in the heart of Mount Lawley, an area that boasts many gourmet delights, funky shops and a lively evening vibe, Soto Espresso's central location is perfect for keeping an eye on all the passing action while tucking into hearty cafe fare like soups, chunky sandwiches and pies. Although many a local has spent an afternoon just mulling over bottomless coffees. Cash only.

507 Beaufort St, Mt Lawley; (08) 6460 7336; open daily for breakfast, lunch and dinner; www.sotoespresso.com

BYO AVAILABLE   CREDIT CARDS ACCEPTED   DISABLED ACCESS   DRESS CODE APPLIES

STAR ANISE RESTAURANT $$$$$

MODERN AUSTRALIAN
Map ref. p. 6 B3

Vibrant Star Anise is situated on a leafy street in one of Perth's well-to-do suburbs, where chef, David Coomer, sources ingredients locally from a long list of suppliers. Inspired by cuisines from Europe and Asia, his five-spice pigeon, three textures of wagyu beef, suckling pig and duck crackling are sure to cause a heart-stopping response in any foodie.

225 Onslow Rd, Shenton Park; (08) 9381 9811; open Tues–Sat for dinner; www.staranisrestaurant.com.au

Fremantle

BLUEWATER GRILL $$$$

MODERN AUSTRALIAN
Map ref. p. 6 C4

Housed in a heritage-listed building just metres away from the Swan River, the Bluewater Grill has uninterrupted city views and is a favourite spot for weddings, private and corporate functions. The simply prepared, well-cooked food has an emphasis on seafood. Whether you're nestled away in one of the nooks or soaking up the view in a group, you'll agree that this is one of Perth's best dining establishments.

Heathcote Crt, 56 Duncraig St; (08) 9315 7700; open daily for breakfast, lunch and dinner; www.bluewatergrill.com.au

CAPRI $$

ITALIAN
Map ref. p. 20

The Capri may have been around for decades, but this is comfort food at its best, with the same rustic favourites appearing on the menu for an eternity. Normally this isn't something to boast about, but in this instance it's the consistently outstanding Italian food, lovingly prepared under Mama's guidance in the kitchen that keeps locals coming back time and time again. The osso bucco and pastas are deliciously moreish, and the free soup and bread has become a tradition. Cash only.

21 South Tce; (08) 9335 1399; open daily for lunch and dinner

CICERELLO'S $$

SEAFOOD
Map ref. p. 20

Cicerello's is the epitome of fish and chip dining. Perched on Fremantle's Fishing Boat Harbour, diners dream of owning one of the luxury vessels floating by while soaking up the lively atmosphere. Your seafood can be deep-fried, chargrilled as in the famous Fremantle sardines, or if you prefer, the ginger and soy steamed fish is outstanding. If you want to get closer to the source of your meal, there is the option of dining aboard a prawn trawler, the Miss Cicerello.

44 Mews Rd; (08) 9335 1911; open daily for lunch and dinner; www.cicerellos.com.au

LITTLE CREATURES $$

BREWERY RESTAURANT
Map ref. p. 20

Right on the Fremantle Fishing Boat Harbour Little Creatures is a brewery, bar and restaurant situated in a converted boatshed, where the beer is poured directly from the conditional tanks. The beer is award-winning but the quality of the food isn't secondary, with marinated kangaroo, tasty sharing plates, wood-fired pizza and slow-roasted lamb featuring on the menu. If you want to get away from the throbbing crowd, upstairs is a lounge

THE CONVERTED BOATSHED EXTERIOR OF LITTLE CREATURES, FREMANTLE

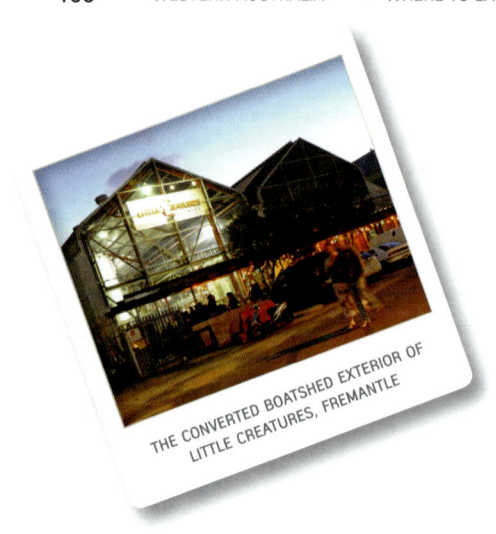

bar with cosy seating, performance space and a tasty supper menu.

40 Mews Rd; (08) 9430 5555; open daily for lunch and dinner, and weekends for breakfast; www.littlecreatures.com.au

MAYA $$$
INDIAN
Map ref. p. 20

Established in 1992 and right in the centre of town, Maya serves authentic Indian cuisine. Traditional favourites are chicken mumtaz (butter chicken), lamb rogan josh, Goan fish curry and a good selection of vegetarian options. If you're after some intimacy, one of the dining rooms may appeal to your senses with lounge-style seating and warm decor.

75–77 Market St; (08) 9335 2796; open Fri for lunch and Tues–Sun for dinner; www.mayarestaurant.com.au

RUOCCO'S $$
ITALIAN
Map ref. p. 20

Ruocco's has been around so long it's now run by the second generation of the Ruocco family. It's an ode to family tradition, not just by its owners, but also by its clientele that consists mainly of large family groups. The wood-fired oven is at the heart of this pizzeria and the calzone has become a household name, with other rustic delights including the handmade pasta. The smell of the baking dough floating along the stone floors and throughout the labyrinth of rooms painted with murals will stay with you long after you've feasted.

217 South Tce; (08) 9335 6939; open Tues–Sun for lunch and dinner

SALA THAI $$$
THAI
Map ref. p. 20

For over ten years, Sala Thai has been serving authentic, classic Thai cuisine. Set within a converted old cottage, with three intimate dining rooms, tables here are usually booked in advance. Long-time favourite dishes include steamed whole fish, the jungle curry and spicy salads. Banquets can be arranged in advance and the wine list includes a good selection of mainly West Australian classics.

22 Norfolk St; (08) 9335 7749; open daily for dinner; www.salathai.com.au

THE RED HERRING $$$$
SEAFOOD

With a rich history dating back to 1921 and with links to the oyster industry and the Greek community, The Red Herring deserves its wonderful riverside location. Specialising in seafood, the live oysters are shucked on-site, demonstrating the Auguste family's dedication to serving fresh cuisine. The wine cellar holds an extensive range of rare and vintage bottles.

26 Riverside Rd, East Fremantle; (08) 9339 1611; open daily for lunch and dinner, and Sunday for breakfast; www.redherring.com.au

BYO AVAILABLE   CREDIT CARDS ACCEPTED   DISABLED ACCESS   DRESS CODE APPLIES

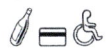

CLARKE'S OF NORTH BEACH $$$$
MODERN AUSTRALIAN

Owner and chef, Stephen Clarke, has cooked for English royalty, so it's only natural the atmosphere appears formal as you enter this intimate restaurant, 25 minutes north of the CBD. However, diners immediately relax as the first morsel of food passes their lips in anticipation of the evening's delights. The ingredients are sourced locally and prepared meticulously, with the menu including slow-cooked lamb shanks, game, seafood and house-baked bread. Clarke's of North Beach was the deserving winner of the 2008 BYO Restaurant Category in the Restaurant and Catering Australia Awards.

97A Flora Tce, North Beach; (08) 9246 7621; open Tues–Sat for dinner; www.clarkesofnorthbeach.com.au

Albany

BEACHSIDE CAFE $$
CAFE
Map ref. p. 53

What a fabulous location to kick back and relax, with the waves of Middleton Beach practically lapping at your feet. The contemporary cafe menu features seafood among other low-key delights and is popular with beachgoers.

Middleton Beach, 2 Flinders Pde; (08) 9841 7733; open daily for breakfast and lunch

EARL OF SPENCER $$$
INTERNATIONAL
Map ref. p. 52

Established in 1874, the Earl of Spencer is one of the oldest taverns in the state. The open fireplaces, friendly beer garden and historic charm have made it a popular restaurant and watering hole for many years. The hearty menu includes typical pub fare, burgers, fish and chips, steak, homemade pies and ribs.

Cnr Earl and Spencer sts; (08) 9841 1322; open daily for lunch and dinner; www.earlofspencer.com.au

LIME 303 $$$
MODERN AUSTRALIAN

Situated in the heart of the township at the unassuming Dog Rock Motel, Lime 303 is a contemporary restaurant headed by celebrated local chef, Greg Pepall, who brings his creative touch to the menu. Ingredients such as quail, crocodile, duck and venison are served among old favourites like steak and seafood. If you've forgotten to book and need to wait for an available table, you won't mind biding your time at the funky bar. Dress code here is smart casual.

The Dog Rock Motel, 303 Middleton Rd; (08) 9841 1400; open daily for breakfast and dinner; www.dogrockmotel.com.au/lime303.php

THE NAKED BEAN $
CAFE
Map ref. p. 52

You'll be drawn in off the street by the aroma of coffee if your caffeine addiction hasn't already beckoned you to the Naked Bean. Thankfully, the owners of this smart hang-out haven't left their beans naked and have applied advanced roasting techniques to beans imported from PNG, East Timor, Africa and South America. Light meals and pastries are swiftly served. Don't forget to take home a sample or order your beans online.

21 Sanford Rd; (08) 9841 4225; open Mon–Sun for breakfast, lunch and coffee; www.thenakedbean.com.au

FAMILY FRIENDLY   LICENSED   OUTDOOR DINING   VEGETARIAN OPTIONS

THE WILD DUCK RESTAURANT $$$$
MODERN AUSTRALIAN
Map ref. p. 52

Seductive lighting, filmy curtains and private nooks make for a romantic dining experience at the Wild Duck. Naturally, duck appears on the menu in duck liver parfait on pepper tuille, smoked breast salad and confit leg with pearl barley and puy lentils. Rabbit ravioli, marron, pigeon, confit of fish and liquorice ice-cream all star in the seductive menu.

112 York St; (08) 9842 2554; open Wed–Sun for dinner; yourrestaurants.com.au

THE LILY RAILWAY STATION RESTAURANT $$
EUROPEAN

With views of the Stirling Ranges from the Lily Railway Station Restaurant, you'll enjoy the European-influenced menu here. The wholemeal spelt bread is grown, stone-ground, milled and baked at The Lily. The bread accompanies most of the dishes, which include meat and cheese platters and the plates for two of beef croquettes and herring fillets. Delicious desserts, local wines, imported beers and liqueurs are also available. A candlelit dinner can be arranged if booked in advance.

9793 Chester Pass Rd, Amelup; (08) 9827 9205 or 1800 980 002; open for lunch and dinner by reservation; www.thelily.com.au

Augusta

THE COLOURPATCH CAFE $$
CAFE

Serving home-style food sourced locally, this riverside cafe claims to be 'the last eating-house before the Antarctic'. Although it's debatable whether the cafe is en-route to an Antarctic adventure, you can dream of intrepid travels from the balcony nonetheless as you watch the lazy river drift by. The signature dish is the battered Blackwood River whiting and calamari rings.

98 Albany Tce; (08) 9758 1295; open daily for breakfast and lunch, and Wed–Mon for dinner

Balingup

BALINGUP BRONZE CAFE $$$
CAFE

Coeliac sufferers, vegans and vegetarians will be thrilled to dine at the Balingup Bronze Cafe, an eatery committed to catering for people with allergies and intolerances. Such a claim might fill the average diner with trepidation, but the delicious seafood, curries and house-baked breads on the menu give patrons no reason to panic. Since they pride themselves on sourcing their produce locally or from certified organic growers, the menu regularly changes to suit the seasons. Also available is organic coffee, more

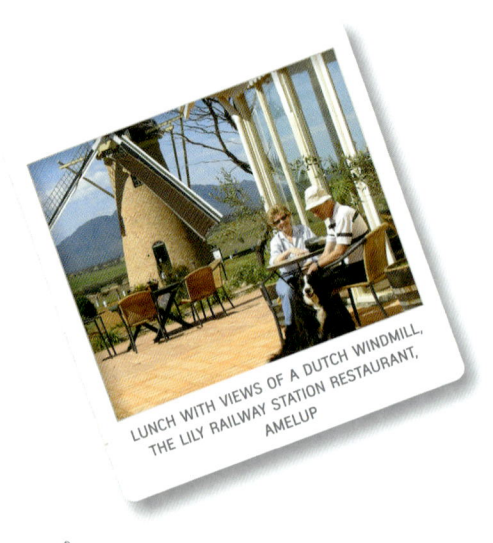

LUNCH WITH VIEWS OF A DUTCH WINDMILL, THE LILY RAILWAY STATION RESTAURANT, AMELUP

BYO AVAILABLE   CREDIT CARDS ACCEPTED   DISABLED ACCESS   DRESS CODE APPLIES

than 30 varieties of exotic teas and a wide range of gluten-free products to stock your pantry.

Balingup Bronze Gallery, South Western Hwy; (08) 9764 1843; open daily for breakfast and lunch, and Fri for dinner; www.balingupbronzegallery.com.au

BLACKWOOD BISTRO $$
VINEYARD RESTAURANT

Overlooking a scenic lake, diners will enjoy the modern Australian fare served here after tasting a local drop or two. The wine label includes a tiger print, because legend has it that the Nannup Tiger has been sighted on occasion in the region. Surrounded by landscaped gardens and wildlife, the Blackwood Winery and Restaurant is in the centre of town and also features the work of local artists.

Blackwood Wines, Kearney St; (08) 9756 0077; open Thurs–Sun for brunch and lunch; www.blackwoodwines.com.au

FRE-JAC FRENCH RESTAURANT $$$
FRENCH

The Parisian owners of Fre-Jac have lovingly brought a slice of France to Balingup. The menu changes monthly with the seasons, and favourites include duck confit, escargots from Bourgogne and crème brûlée. The dress code here is smart casual, with diners enjoying the gardens in summer and snuggling up around the fire during the cooler months. It's best to make a booking at this popular restaurant, otherwise you'll be fighting off the locals for a table. Also on-site is the Fre-Jac Balingup Bakery and cafe, where all the ingredients for the pastries and breads are imported from France.

Forrest St; (08) 9764 1883; open Thurs–Mon for dinner; www.balinguprestaurant.com.au

THE 1896 CAFE $$
CAFE

The friendly atmosphere at the 1896 Cafe is what draws in locals and tourists alike. Supporting the local community, the owners provide a venue for live music and wall space for artists. The menu is seasonal and best described as wholesome. Located in a heritage building on the main street, it is a relaxed place to drop in for a coffee during the day or for a more substantial meal at lunch or dinner time.

145–151 Hampton St; (08) 9761 1699; open daily for lunch and dinner

Balladonia

BALLADONIA ROADHOUSE $$
CAFE

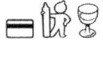

On the long journey across the Nullarbor Plain, the Balladonia Roadhouse is a welcome sight. Serving light meals or hearty fare, depending on your hunger levels, the food is substantial with meals like hamburgers, lasagne and roast of the day. The decor is modern and within the roadhouse is a bar and accommodation.

Eyre Hwy; (08) 9039 3453; open daily for breakfast, lunch and dinner

Beverley

FREEMASONS HOTEL $
INTERNATIONAL

The Freemasons Hotel is a classic Australian pub serving counter meals and à la carte in the Gallery Restaurant. The town of Beverley is one of the oldest settlements in Western Australia,

FAMILY FRIENDLY   LICENSED   OUTDOOR DINING   VEGETARIAN OPTIONS

and the Freemasons Hotel, built in 1886, is one of the town's original buildings.

104 Vincent St; (08) 9646 1094; open daily for lunch and dinner

Boyup Brook

CHUDACUD ESTATE $$
VINEYARD RESTAURANT

Known as the smallest winery in the Blackwood Valley wine region, Chudacud Estate offers more than just a lovely drop. The property also has a shop selling bric-a-brac, beauty products, chocolate and other gourmet delights. The restaurant offers versatile dining options with a cook-your-own barbecue, an à la carte menu, Devonshire teas or just a simple cheese platter to nibble on.

Lot 22, Wade Rd; (08) 9764 4053; open Wed–Sun for lunch and Fri–Sat for dinner; www.chudacud.mysouthwest.com.au

Bremer Bay

MOUNT BARREN RESTAURANT $$
INTERNATIONAL

Overlooking natural bushland and the Bremer River, patrons dine beneath high exposed ceilings here. Located within the Bremer Bay Resort, the Mount Barren Restaurant sources its produce locally wherever possible. Serving a good range of seafood and meat dishes, both the menu and wine list are very well priced.

Bremer Bay Resort, 1 Frantom Way; (08) 9837 4133; open daily for breakfast, lunch and dinner; www.bremerbayresort.com.au

Bridgetown

BRIDGETOWN POTTERY TEAROOMS & GALLERY $
CAFE

Priding themselves on their home-style cooking, the Bridgetown Pottery Tearooms and Gallery has been run by the same family for the past 21 years, and is housed in one of the oldest buildings in Bridgetown. Featuring a collection of memorabilia reflecting the town's history, the pottery workshop sells artworks by local and visiting artists. Renowned for their pumpkin soup, Devonshire teas, sticky puddings and milkshakes.

81 Hampton St; (08) 9761 1038; open daily for breakfast and lunch

NELSON'S OF BRIDGETOWN $$
INTERNATIONAL

Snuggle up by the cosy fire during the cooler months at Nelson's and savour the country charm and hospitality. The à la carte menu draws upon local and regional produce to create hearty fare. Those seeking a little afternoon delight can be found relaxing in the lounge bar with coffee and cake. The great service ensures Nelson's is popular with the locals and tourists passing through the pretty town of Bridgetown.

38 Hampton St; (08) 9761 1641 or 1800 635 565; open daily for breakfast, lunch and dinner; www.nelsonsofbridgetown.com.au

THE BRIDGETOWN HOTEL $$$
INTERNATIONAL

Housed in a restored 1920s boutique hotel, the Bridgetown Hotel restaurant serves simple pub fare. Favourites include sirloin steak, rack of lamb and pasta. Blackwood Valley wines accompany your meal, after which you may choose to curl up by the fire with a glass of port.

BYO AVAILABLE   CREDIT CARDS ACCEPTED   DISABLED ACCESS   DRESS CODE APPLIES

157 Hampton St; (08) 9761 1034; open daily for lunch and dinner, and weekends for breakfast; www.bridgetownhotel.com.au

Broome

CAFE CARLOTTA
$$
ITALIAN
Map ref. p. 58

Cafe Carlotta's popularity derives mainly from its delicious pastas and thin-crust wood-fired pizzas. Typically Italian fare, the menu is rustically simple and what could be better than dining under the stars with such appetising delights?

Jones Pl; (08) 9192 7606; open Tues–Sat for dinner; www.cafecarlotta.com.au

MATSO'S BROOME BREWERY
$$$
BREWERY RESTAURANT
Map ref. p. 58

Matso's is practically an institution in Broome, with its corrugated walls and languid fans. The building was erected in 1900, originally as a bank, and operated among opium dens and brothels, until a fire destroyed the street of ill-repute and the building was relocated to its current location. Today, award-winning beer is crafted at Matso's microbrewery, and patrons linger around the bar, lounges and garden. The menu includes seafood, rib-eye steak and hearty breakfasts and is well matched to the beer and laid-back Broome lifestyle.

60 Hammersley St; (08) 9193 5811; open daily for breakfast, lunch and dinner; www.matsosbroomebrewery.com.au

THE CLUB RESTAURANT
$$$$
MODERN AUSTRALIAN
Map ref. p. 58

The Club at Cable Beach Club Resort is Broome's premier restaurant, with a smart dress code. It is simply a must, if only to try pearl meat prepared as a ceviche and the fresh seafood. The barramundi, in particular, is hard to pass up. If seafood isn't your thing, stock standards like lamb, beef fillet and chicken are served with flair. For dessert, the chocolate fondant is a decadent finale. The wine list is extensive, featuring a predominantly Australian selection as well as a cigar menu. The lovely teak pitched ceiling and walls are adorned with original artworks and as the breeze sweeps through the palm trees, you'll find yourself taken back to colonial times.

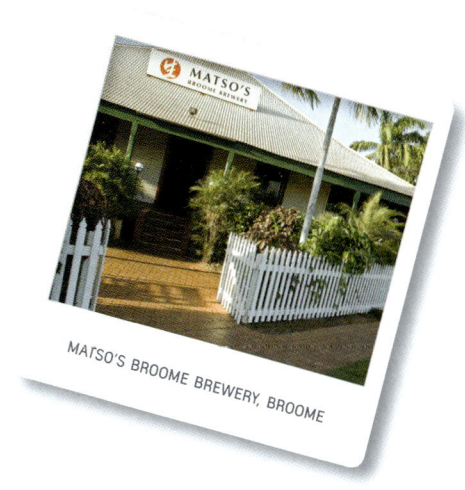

Cable Beach Club Resort & Spa, Cable Beach Rd; 1800 199 099; open daily for lunch and dinner; www.cablebeachclub.com

THE OLD ZOO CAFE
$$$
CAFE
Map ref. 58

Although housed in the original feeding house of the Pearl Coast Zoological Gardens, you won't find animal feed on the menu here. Instead, you'll enjoy well-prepared tasty dishes to accompany the alfresco setting. Very popular with locals and tourists alike, especially for

MATSO'S BROOME BREWERY, BROOME

FAMILY FRIENDLY   LICENSED   OUTDOOR DINING   VEGETARIAN OPTIONS

breakfast and romantic dinners, so it's advisable to book ahead.

2 Challenor Dr; (08) 9193 6200; open daily for breakfast, lunch and dinner; www.zoocafe.com.au

THE WHARF RESTAURANT $$
SEAFOOD

The Asian-inspired seafood menu is the perfect accompaniment to the azure sea you'll be dining beside. Fans claim The Wharf serves the best seafood in town, and the chilli mud crab is a local favourite. Dine overlooking the Port of Broome or take your meal away along with cooking instructions.

On the Wharf, Port Dr; (08) 9192 5700; open daily for lunch and dinner

Bunbury

ALEXANDERS RESTAURANT $$$
MEDITERRANEAN
Map ref. p. 64

Located within the Lord Forrest Hotel, Alexanders Restaurant offers some of the finest food in town. Produce from the region features on the extremely well-priced menu, with a good mix of vegetarian, seafood and meat dishes. Naturally, the food is complemented by the South-West's outstanding wines.

20 Symmons St; (08) 9726 5777; open daily for breakfast, lunch and dinner; www.lordforresthotel.com.au

ARISTOS WATERFRONT $
SEAFOOD
Map ref. p. 64

Known as the Surprise Chef from his own cooking show, Aristos Papandroulakis returned to his home town of Bunbury in 1992 to open Aristos Waterfront. An up-market fish and chippery, the product is so fresh and delicious that patrons travel from all over the South-West to either dine in overlooking the harbour, order takeaway or buy seafood to prepare at home.

2/15 Bonnefoi Blvd; (08) 9791 6477; open Tues–Sun for lunch and Wed–Sat for dinner; www.aristos.com.au

BOARDWALK BAR & BISTRO $$$
INTERNATIONAL
Map ref. p. 64

Within the Parade Hotel, on the banks of the Leschenault Inlet, a cool breeze accompanies the sunset as you feast on local seafood or sample the region's wines or beers. Also on the menu is standard bistro fare and a complimentary salad bar.

The Parade Hotel, 1 Austral Pde; (08) 9721 2933; open daily for breakfast, lunch and dinner; www.paradehotel.com.au/Bars

MOJO'S RESTAURANT $$$$
MODERN AUSTRALIAN
Map ref. p. 64

Mojo's is a cosy establishment that has captured Bunbury's progressive vibe. The menu features fresh and innovative selections such as sautéed Capel marron with spicy lemon garlic sauce, exotic mushrooms and asparagus. Diners with dietary requirements will be relieved to find an eatery that offers gluten-free and vegetarian options. The wine and cocktail lounge is a place to relax with a tipple and some tapas. There are functions throughout the year including a degustation and meet the winemaker evenings.

Grand Cinema Complex, Victoria St; (08) 9792 5900; open daily for breakfast, lunch and dinner

VAT 2 $$$
MODERN AUSTRALIAN
Map ref. p. 64

What a superb place to kick back with harbour views and delicious fare. The seasonal menu will appease most patrons and the oysters are exceptionally good. Vat 2's rising reputation reflects the same quality as its flagship Margaret River restaurant, Vat 107. The contemporary mocha interior is lovely day or night and there are several areas to relax with a cocktail or a selection from the extensive wine room.

2 Jetty Rd; (08) 9791 8833; open daily for breakfast, lunch and dinner; www.vat2.com.au

CARLAMINDA WINES BISTRO $$$
VINEYARD RESTAURANT

In the midst of the green pastures of the Ferguson Valley, Carlaminda serves up traditional French cuisine. Locals and tourists alike venture from Bunbury and Perth for the delicious country cooking, with traditional favourites including escargots French onion soup, duck leg confit, coq au vin and a Moroccan-inspired lamb tagine. The mousse au chocolat and cheese platter finish off the meal nicely, and Carlaminda wines accompany the meal superbly.

Carlaminda Wines, Richards Rd, Ferguson Valley; (08) 9728 3002; open Wed–Sun for lunch; www.carlaminda.com

NICOLA'S RISTORANTE $$$
ITALIAN

Authentic Italian food is only a meal away in Bunbury, with this warm and friendly restaurant turning out wonderful Italian classics. Pasta dishes are guaranteed to please, with interesting combinations like gnocchi filled with veal, Italian sausage and spinach, dressed in a grappa cream sauce. Mains cover the basics such as vitello tonnato, but also venture into more exotic territory with a pork rack in Moroccan spices. Service is good, so you can sit back and enjoy a three-course meal. After all, when in Rome …

62–64 Victoria St; (08) 9791 3926; open Mon–Sat for lunch (12pm–2pm) and daily for dinner (6pm–late); www.nicolaristorante.com

HACKERSLEY $$$
VINEYARD RESTAURANT

Relax over a long lunch at Hackersley in the beautiful Ferguson Valley. The seasonal menu suits the winery's produce well, with offerings such as charred salmon with wild lime, orange and rosemary sauce and a delicious liquorice panna cotta. The owners love the good life, and their joie de vive is carried through in the jovial atmosphere, especially during the Sunday-night jazz sessions.

Ferguson Rd, Ferguson Valley; (08) 9728 3033; open Thurs–Sun for lunch and once a month for dinner; www.hackersley.com.au

Busselton

NEWTOWN HOUSE RESTAURANT $$$$
MODERN AUSTRALIAN

Established in 1851, this original homestead is now the cosy Newtown House. Surrounded by country gardens, the restaurant has been a success since its opening in 1991 and has won countless awards. Chef, Steve Reagan, draws on the many local flavours of the region to produce consistently tasty morsels, including Margaret River venison, asparagus and local marron. Being a BYO venue, patrons won't be short of finding a drop to bring along in

FAMILY FRIENDLY   LICENSED   OUTDOOR DINING   VEGETARIAN OPTIONS

the renowned wine region. Newtown House also produces a range of preserves and has a guesthouse.

737 Bussell Hwy; (08) 9755 4485; open Tues–Sat for lunch and dinner; www.newtownhouse.com.au

THE EQUINOX $$$
INTERNATIONAL

With sensational views of iconic Busselton Jetty and the foreshore, The Equinox's casual menu includes traditional breakfasts, seafood chowder and steak sandwiches for lunch and more sophisticated dishes for the evening, such as roast duck breast on vanilla bean mash, barramundi or venison sausages. The day-long tapas menu is a recent addition and the kiosk gives diners the option to stroll the few feet to the beach to eat their fish and chips. Gluten-free and vegetarian options are also available.

343 Queen St; (08) 9752 4641; open daily for breakfast, lunch and dinner; www.theequinox.com.au

THE GOOSE $$$
INTERNATIONAL

Located directly on the Geographe Bay foreshore, The Goose has been operational since 1998 and was originally located in the town centre. The longevity of this dining establishment is evidence of its consistent performance. The familiar menu is sure to suit most palates and the tapas selections tempt those seeking a nibble. The wooden floors, outdoor balcony, nautical decor and beach just a few metres away create the laid-back seaside feel that's synonymous with the region.

Geographe Bay Rd; (08) 9754 7700; open Wed–Sun for breakfast, lunch and dinner; www.thegoose.com.au

VASSE BAR CAFE $$
CAFE

It's refreshing to find such a slick place as this in a small country town. The contemporary cafe serves up unpretentious food such as steak sandwiches, pasta, pizzas and a good selection of vegetarian and gluten-free dishes. All-day dining and drinking provide a distinct Mediterranean feel and patrons can often be seen relaxing at a sidewalk table. The owners of Vasse pride themselves on their wide range of beers and for having one of the best cocktail bars in the region.

44 Queen St; (08) 9754 8560; open daily for breakfast, lunch and dinner; www.vassebarcafe.com.au

Carnarvon

KINGSFORD STEAK HOUSE $$
STEAKHOUSE
Map ref. p. 68

Just a short stroll to the centre of town is the Fascine Lodge, where you will find accommodation, the Pure Steel Bar and the Kingsford Steak House. The popular steakhouse caters well to carnivores longing for something other than seafood.

Fascine Lodge, 34 David Brand Dr; (08) 9941 2411; open daily for breakfast and dinner

SAILS RESTAURANT $$$
INTERNATIONAL
Map ref. p. 68

Located within Carnarvon's Best Western Hospitality Inn, Sails Restaurant showcases superb regional ingredients on its à la carte menu. With a choice of seafood, Mediterranean and vegetarian options available, the whole family are catered for. The alfresco dining area is covered and offers a casual dining experience.

BYO AVAILABLE   CREDIT CARDS ACCEPTED   DISABLED ACCESS   DRESS CODE APPLIES

6 West St; (08) 9941 1600; open daily for breakfast and dinner; www.carnarvon.wa.hospitalityinns.com.au

SCHNAPPERS $$
INTERNATIONAL

With an international menu, Schnappers is a popular spot with locals and guests of the Gateway Motel. Several dining options are offered, including a buffet with a variety of culinary themes served nightly. The cosy restaurant is air-conditioned, providing relief from the heat, so after your meal why not relax with a cold drink at the bar?

Gateway Motel, 379 Robinson St; (08) 9941 1532; open daily for breakfast and dinner

Cervantes

RONSARD BAY TAVERN $$$
SEAFOOD

Experience authentic Australian outback charm at the Ronsard Bay Tavern. Located at the gateway to Pinnacles, the rammed-earth tavern serves fresh food in friendly surroundings. It's known for serving excellent crayfish (when in season), while the dhufish can be enjoyed year-round.

219 Cadiz St; (08) 9652 7009; open daily for lunch and dinner

THE EUROPA ANCHOR RESTAURANT $$
SEAFOOD

Housed within the Cervantes Pinnacles Motel, the Europa Anchor Restaurant specialises in local seafood, especially rock lobster and dhufish. The restaurant is fully licensed with a range of Western Australian wines, and guests are treated to a barbecue on Sundays.

Cervantes Pinnacles Motel, 7 Aragon St; (08) 9652 7145; open daily for breakfast, lunch and dinner

Collie

THE RIDGE $$$$
INTERNATIONAL

Situated in the Collie Ridge Motel, The Ridge restaurant serves a contemporary menu based on the region's produce. The menu is hearty, with local Mediterranean and Asian flavours like steak, seafood, pizza, curry and an Asian tasting plate. The children's menu should keep everyone happy and although the wine list is compact, the selection is worthy of any wine lover.

Collie Ridge Motel, 185–195 Throssell St; (08) 9734 6666; open daily for breakfast, Fri–Sat for lunch and Mon–Sat for dinner; www.collieridgemotel.com.au

Coral Bay

FIN'S CAFE $$
INTERNATIONAL

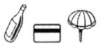

Casual beachside cafe by day and oozing romance by night, Fin's is quite the chameleon considering its shopping village location. The international menu features influences from Creole and Mexico, brought to the table by Melbourne chef, Paul Minnear. Other menu stars are the smoked kangaroo, paella, and scallop and prawn risotto.

People's Park Shopping Village; (08) 9942 5900; open daily for breakfast, lunch and dinner

FAMILY FRIENDLY   LICENSED   OUTDOOR DINING   VEGETARIAN OPTIONS

SHADES $$
INTERNATIONAL

Situated in the Ningaloo Reef Resort, the recently refurbished Shades cafe serves a selection of international dishes. The fresh seafood caught daily in the bay is always a popular choice. The atmosphere is laid-back and ideal for enjoying the sunset or your cocktail of choice at the end of another peaceful day.

Ningaloo Reef Resort, 1 Robinson St; (08) 9942 5934 or 1800 795 522; open daily for breakfast, lunch and dinner; www.ningalooreefresort.com.au

THE REEF CAFE $$
SEAFOOD

This local favourite features the standard Italian and seafood fare that's popular in the region. The seafood on the menu was probably pulled from the same ocean you were enjoying right before dinner and the atmosphere here is relaxed. The specials board includes snapper, prawns and Morton Bay bugs, and the house-made pizza is a family favourite.

Robinson St; (08) 9942 5882; open daily for dinner

Denham

OLD PEARLER RESTAURANT $$
SEAFOOD

Made almost entirely of shells and with walls decorated with maritime relics, The Old Pearler Restaurant captures the nautical theme in a charming way. As you would expect, when dining only a few metres away from the ocean, fresh seafood is the order of the day. The abundant seafood platter is the specialty and rumour has it that room should be left to sample the puddings that owner-chef, Wayne Viney, has mastered. If you've forgotten to make a booking and can't score a table at this popular eatery, takeaway is available.

71 Knight Tce; (08) 9948 1373; open daily for dinner

THE BOUGHSHED RESTAURANT $$$
INTERNATIONAL

Overlooking Dolphin Bay, diners are in for a treat at the Boughshed Restaurant as they sample the menu's fresh seafood, beef and vegetarian options. Wherever possible, local produce is sourced and the wholesome meals are the perfect accompaniment to the pristine surroundings. Keep an eye out for visiting dolphins while you dine.

Monkey Mia Dolphin Resort, Monkey Mia; (08) 9948 1320 or 1800 653 611; open daily for breakfast, lunch and dinner; www.monkeymia.com.au

Denmark

CHE SERA SERA $$
MODERN AUSTRALIAN

Simple food in cosy surroundings is typical of the pretty town of Denmark. At Che Sera Sera patrons are treated to water views through gum trees while they enjoy steak or Mount Barker free-range chicken from the compact menu. Variations on dishes include Italian nights, live entertainment and a seasonal menu on weekends.

The Denmark Waterfront, 63 Inlet Dr; (08) 9848 3314; open daily for dinner; www.denmarkwaterfront.com.au

BYO AVAILABLE   CREDIT CARDS ACCEPTED   DISABLED ACCESS   DRESS CODE APPLIES

GREENPOOL RESTAURANT $$$
VINEYARD RESTAURANT

Wood, stone and glass encapsulate the lovely views of green pastures from the Greenpool restaurant. The slick dining room reflects the quality of the constantly evolving menu. Drawing on local produce, constant favourites include freshly caught seafood, the regional tasting plate, dry-aged Scotch fillet and cheese platters. Part of the boutique Forest Hill Winery, whose wines have been voted as some of the best in the state, it's no wonder this restaurant is so popular.

Forest Hill Winery, cnr Myers Rd and South Coast Hwy; (08) 9848 0091; open daily for lunch and Fri for dinner; www.foresthillwines.com.au

THE SOUTHERN END RESTAURANT $$$
MODERN AUSTRALIAN

Pair spectacular views of the Wilson Inlet with lovely food and you have the Southern End Restaurant. The lush landscape accompanies local fare and the wood-fired pizzas are popular, especially by the log fire during the cooler season. The walk-in cellar is a nice touch, where patrons can learn about their wine selections. Families will appreciate the children's menu and playground.

Denmark Observatory Resort, 427 Mt Shadforth Rd; (08) 9848 2600; open daily for lunch and dinner, and weekends for breakfast; www.southernend.com.au

Derby

DERBY BOAB INN $$
INTERNATIONAL

Derby's premier restaurant is situated in the Derby Boab Inn. Steak and barramundi are a menu favourite and the airy dining room can seat up to 120 patrons. The Derby Boab Inn is an oasis in the harsh Kimberly landscape, making it a regular local and tourist haunt.

100 Loch St; (08) 9191 1044; open daily for breakfast, lunch and dinner

OASIS BISTRO $$
INTERNATIONAL

Derby is known as the home of the barramundi, so you can be sure this fishy favourite features on the menu at the Oasis Bistro. Situated in the King Sound Resort Hotel, it is conveniently located close to the town centre. The dining room is casual, ensuring a relaxing wind down from the day's adventures.

King Sound Resort Hotel, 112 Loch St; (08) 9193 1044; open daily for dinner

THE POINT RESTAURANT $$
SEAFOOD

Much like its namesake in Broome, fresh seafood is served with spectacular ocean views. Situated on the edge of the King Sound, the specialty here is the Barra Wings, which is an unusual cut from local barramundi. There is a takeaway section and fresh seafood is sold with cooking instructions.

1 Jetty Rd; (08) 9191 1195; open daily for lunch and dinner

FAMILY FRIENDLY   LICENSED   OUTDOOR DINING   VEGETARIAN OPTIONS

Dongara–Denison

THE SEASON TREE $
CAFE

In the historic town of Dongara, the lovely Season Tree is known for its traditional homemade English breakfasts, lunches and coffee. Locals and tourists alike can be found relaxing underneath the shade of a Moreton Bay fig tree here.

8 Moreton Tce; (08) 9927 1400; open daily for breakfast and lunch

Donnybrook

OLD GOLDFIELDS ORCHARD & CIDER FACTORY $$
INTERNATIONAL

With dam views and lovely grounds, the Old Goldfields Orchard & Cider Factory oozes country cosiness. Fresh produce features on the menu in the rammed-earth restaurant and wine-tastings are offered, although it's the award-winning ciders that draw the crowds. After lunch, take a stroll through the gardens or visit the gallery featuring the work of local artists.

75 Goldfields Rd; (08) 9731 0311; open Wed–Sun for lunch; www.oldgoldfields.com.au

Dunsborough

DUNSBOROUGH BAKERY $
BAKERY CAFE

Established in 1942 and reputedly one of the best bakeries in Australia, the Dunsborough Bakery is famous for its pies and sourdough loaves. Constantly packed with locals, tourists and surfers, this cash-only bakery is one of the oldest businesses in the region. Drop in anytime of the day for a treat at this traditional Australian eatery.

243 Naturaliste Tce; (08) 9755 3137; open daily for breakfast and lunch; www.dunsboroughbakery.net.au

OTHER SIDE OF THE MOON RESTAURANT $$$$
MODERN AUSTRALIAN

With Bunker Bay at your feet and the Indian Ocean beyond, you could imagine you have visited somewhere as special as the moon. Inside, the swanky decor does little to persuade you otherwise, as does the innovative menu. Fresh oysters, tempura soft-shell crab, braised pork belly and kangaroo are just a few of the temptations that accompany the local wine list. During the warmer months diners relax on the outdoor terrace, although the contemporary interior is just as appealing.

Quay West Resort, Bunker Bay Rd, Bunker Bay; (08) 9756 9159; open daily for breakfast, lunch and dinner

WISE VINEYARD RESTAURANT $$$
VINEYARD RESTAURANT

A short drive from the town of Dunsborough and perched high on a hill, Wise Vineyard's restaurant is run by chef, Heath Townsend. The seasonal menu draws on regional delights such as venison, lamb and seafood, and the wine list includes Wise Wines as well as other labels, beers and spirits. A tasting at the cellar door while looking out to Geographe Bay leaves little question as to why this boutique winery and restaurant is an award-winning enterprise.

80 Eagle Bay Rd; (08) 9755 3331; open daily for breakfast and lunch, and Fri–Sat for dinner; www.wisewine.com.au

Dwellingup

DWELLINGUP COMMUNITY HOTEL MOTEL $

INTERNATIONAL

One of the few buildings in town that survived the massive bushfires of 1961, the Dwellingup Community Hotel Motel has been operating since the 1900s. Serving typical counter meals with old-fashioned charm, the hotel's live music on weekends is popular with the locals.

Marrinup St; (08) 9538 1056; open daily for lunch and dinner

DWELLINGUP MILLHOUSE RESTAURANT $$

CAFE

Although delicious wood-fired pizzas and excellent wines are on the menu, it's the glass cabinet containing chocolates that is the real attraction at the Millhouse Cafe and Chocolate Company. The cafe is especially popular at weekends, when patrons linger for the all-day dining.

41 McLarty St; (08) 9538 1122; open Thurs for lunch and Fri–Sun for breakfast, lunch and dinner

LAKE NAVARINO RESTAURANT $$

INTERNATIONAL

Situated in the Lake Navarino Forest Resort, this licensed restaurant seats up to 60 people. Featuring slate and timber throughout, it has a cosy feeling and diners may be treated to wildlife sightings since the restaurant is located within state forest.

Lake Navarino Forest Resort, 147 Invarell Rd, Waroona; (08) 9733 3000 or 1800 650 626; open Sat for lunch and Fri–Sat for dinner; www.navarino.com.au

NEWBLISS VINEYARD CAFE $$

VINEYARD RESTAURANT

Nestled among jarrah forest in the pretty township of Dwellingup, the Newbliss Winery and Cafe serves rustic, home-style light lunches such as quiche, lasagne, pizzas and platters. The service is friendly and the views over the Mandurah Estuary inspire relaxation, especially after a tasting at the cellar door.

Newbliss Winery, Lot 20, Irwin Rd; (08) 9538 1665; open Fri–Sun for lunch; www.newblisswinery.com

Esperance

BONAPARTE SEAFOOD RESTAURANT $$

INTERNATIONAL

Considered to be the finest restaurant in Esperance, this understated dining establishment provides swift service. Although the menu is a little dated, dishes are delivered with old-fashioned charm and the portions are generous. Located on the first floor, tables with water views are always the first to be booked out. Downstairs is the more casual Ollie's Licensed Cafe, serving a basic cafe menu.

51 The Esplanade; (08) 9071 7727; open Tues–Sat for dinner

LOOSE GOOSE $$$

MODERN AUSTRALIAN

The catchy name suits the vibrant mood at the Loose Goose. The open kitchen opens onto the modern interior manned by enthusiastic staff. The menu includes interesting dish combinations like pork mignon with beetroot risotto. The flavours blend well together as the

FAMILY FRIENDLY   LICENSED   OUTDOOR DINING   VEGETARIAN OPTIONS

room fills with the aromas of many equally enticing dishes.

9A Andrews St; (08) 9071 2320; open Tues–Sat for dinner

OCEAN BLUES RESTAURANT $$
INTERNATIONAL

Overlooking the sea, the Ocean Blues Restaurant serves simple food that's enjoyed by a clientele of all ages. The service is as bright as the decor and the restaurant is well situated near the centre of town.

19 The Esplanade; (08) 9071 7107; open Tues–Sun for breakfast, lunch and dinner

TAYLOR STREET CAFE $$
CAFE

This beachfront cafe is a year-round favourite as customers cosy up by the open fires in winter and relish the warmth on the terrace or grassed area during summer. The food is consistent and those in the know order salt-and-pepper squid. Upstairs is another dining area featuring high ceilings and artworks.

Taylor St Jetty; (08) 9071 4317; open daily for breakfast, lunch and dinner

THE DECK $
CAFE

Situated between Esperance and Albany in a region renowned as the gateway for the Fitzgerald River National Park, The Deck is a tourist drop-in centre for information, national park passes, the Southern Ocean and Discovery Centre and a giftshop. The cafe not only serves up light food and fruit smoothies but has also become renowned for its gourmet ice-creams and sorbets. The building was originally the town's post office and today retains much of its charm.

Cnr Clarke and Veal sts, Hopetoun; (08) 9838 3303; open daily for lunch Sept–May; www.gotothedeck.com.au

Exmouth

MANTARAY'S RESTAURANT $$$$
INTERNATIONAL

Situated in the Novotel Ningaloo Resort on Sunrise Beach is the modern, brasserie-style Mantaray's Restaurant. Naturally, seafood is on the menu, but there are other options for those seeking an alternative, such as duck risotto or lamb rump. If you're visiting during August and November you might catch a glimpse of a humpback whale and the full moon rising from the sea is always a magnificent sight.

Novotel Ningaloo Resort, Madaffari Dr; (08) 9949 0000; open daily for breakfast, lunch and dinner; www.novotelningaloo.com.au

POTSHOT RESORT RESTAURANT $$
INTERNATIONAL

For laid-back dining in a casual atmosphere, try the Potshot Inn for bistro-style food. Whether seated indoors or by the pool, diners can enjoy fresh seafood including red emperor, crabs and prawns. Kick back later on with a few drinks at the bar, which is also one of the town's main watering holes.

Potshot Resort, Murat Rd; (08) 9949 1200; open daily for lunch and dinner; www.potshotresort.com

SAILFISH BAR AND RESTAURANT $$
SEAFOOD

Located a few kilometres from Exmouth, the Seabreeze Resort is where you'll find the

BYO AVAILABLE   CREDIT CARDS ACCEPTED   DISABLED ACCESS   DRESS CODE APPLIES

Sailfish Bar and Restaurant. Although out of town, transportation can be arranged back to your accommodation. Boasting a large beer garden and a palm-filled alfresco dining area, the restaurant's tropical ambience suits the predominantly seafood menu. The playground is a hit with parents and the little ones.

Seabreeze Resort, 116 North C St; (08) 9949 1800; open daily for lunch and dinner; www.seabreezeresort.com.au

WHALER'S RESTAURANT $$
INTERNATIONAL

Like every place in town, the Whaler's Restaurant exudes a laid-back holiday atmosphere despite being known as the fanciest place in town. The menu caters to most tastes and includes locally caught seafood, as well as Italian and Asian dishes.

5 Kennedy St; (08) 9949 2416; open daily for lunch and Tues–Sun for dinner

Fitzroy Crossing

RIVERSIDE RESTAURANT $$
TRADITIONAL AUSTRALIAN

Catering to guests of the Fitzroy River Lodge, you can be guaranteed that the atmosphere will be friendly at the Riverside Restaurant, a travellers' hub in the middle of the bush. The casual dining room serves traditional Australian fare and the lounge bar is a great place to continue your night – if you're lucky you might catch one of the local gigs regularly held at the lodge.

Fitzroy River Lodge, Great Northern Hwy; (08) 9191 5141; open daily for dinner; www.fitzroyriverlodge.com.au

Gascoyne Junction

THE JUNCTION HOTEL $$
INTERNATIONAL

Gascoyne Junction is the gateway to Mount Augustus National Park, which is twice the size of Uluru and estimated to be 1750 million years old. The Junction Hotel isn't quite as old, but has been standing and operating since 1906, when it began as a general store. These days it is the town pub serving counter meals and cold beer and since the town is remote, you will probably be rubbing shoulders with one of the town's resident locals, of whom there are less than 50.

Lot 27, Carnarvon Meekatharra Rd; (08) 9943 0504; open daily for dinner

Geraldton

BOATSHED RESTAURANT $$$
INTERNATIONAL

Considered to be one of Geraldton's finest eating establishments, the charming Boatshed Restaurant is housed in a 1940s building with boating memorabilia adorning the walls. The balcony is very popular during the warmer months and you will be fighting for a spot around the fire when it's cooler.

359 Marine Tce; (08) 9921 5500; open Mon–Sat for dinner; boatshedgeraldton.com.au

THE FREEMASON'S HOTEL $$$
INTERNATIONAL

The Freemason's Hotel is one of the town's most popular haunts. Serving brasserie-style food, the menu features Asian flavours as well as steaks and local seafood. Stone grill dining

FAMILY FRIENDLY   LICENSED   OUTDOOR DINING   VEGETARIAN OPTIONS

is the latest offering, where your meal is cooked on a heated stone at your table. Famous for its iconic spire, the surroundings are elegant whether dining inside or alfresco, where you are perfectly situated to watch the passing crowd.

Cnr Durlacher St and Marine Terrace Mall; (08) 9964 3457; open daily for lunch and dinner; www.freemasonshotel.com.au

TIDES OF GERALDTON $$$
SEAFOOD

Contemporary decor overlooking harbour views and a vista of the Moresby Ranges greets diners at Tides. A seafood-dominated menu suits the restaurant's waterfront location; however, special dietary requirements can be met, and both vegetarians and meat lovers won't be disappointed. The menu is accompanied by an extensive range of beer, as well as high-end wines, some available by the glass.

103 Marine Tce; (08) 9965 4999; open daily for lunch and dinner; www.tidesofgeraldton.com.au

CHAPMAN VALLEY WINES RESTAURANT $$
VINEYARD RESTAURANT

Approximately 30 kilometres north-east of Geraldton is Western Australia's most northern vineyard. After sampling Chapman Valley Wines', patrons can enjoy a lunch platter, grab a barbecue pack or, if they're lucky, feast on local yabbies when in season. Overlooking the vineyard, the winery is an unexpected oasis in a somewhat harsh landscape.

Chapman Valley Wines, Lot 14 Howatharra Rd, Nanson; (08) 9920 5148; open Wed–Sun for lunch and night functions upon request; www.chapmanvalleywines.com.au

Gingin

AMIRAGE RESTAURANT $$$
EUROPEAN

Situated in magnificent gardens, the Amirage Restaurant prides itself on using local produce wherever possible. In particular, the steak, olive oil and olives are sourced from within the valley. The menu has European influences as a result of owner, June Reith, spending many years in Europe. Ruth has created a friendly community atmosphere by hosting many functions and charity events throughout the years. With picturesque gardens, a billabong with a fountain and abundant wildlife, it's an ideal spot for the whole family to enjoy.

1654 Gingin Brook Rd; (08) 9575 7646; open Thurs–Sun for lunch and dinner; www.amiragerestaurantbb.com.au

GINGIN HOTEL $$$
EUROPEAN

The Gingin Hotel is yet another example of the rewards of saving our heritage. Originally built in 1902, the hotel has undergone extensive renovations and now up to 100 patrons can dine in country elegance while overlooking the Gingin Brook. The menu includes prime examples of comfort food such as steak and seafood, plus a light lunch menu and a hot wok menu offering a range of Eastern-flavoured delights. The wine list has many state favourites, as well as samples of wineries closer to home.

5 Jones St; (08) 9575 2214; open Thurs–Sun for lunch and dinner; www.ginginhotel.com.au

KYOTMUNGA ESTATE $
VINEYARD RESTAURANT

Kyotmunga offers laid-back dining overlooking the spectacular Avon Valley National Park.

BYO AVAILABLE   CREDIT CARDS ACCEPTED   DISABLED ACCESS   DRESS CODE APPLIES

Platters include dolmades, cheese, olives, fresh bread, extra-virgin olive oil and dukkah spice mixture. The olive oil and dukkah are made on the premises and are available for tasting. Wine tasting is also a must and a lovely accompaniment to savour with your platter. Devonshire teas are also available on this historic estate, which is the first recorded place in the Chittering area.

287 Chittering Valley Rd, Lower Chittering; (08) 9571 8001; open weekends for lunch; www.kyotmunga.com.au

STRINGYBARK WINERY & RESTAURANT $$$

VINEYARD RESTAURANT

Serving hearty traditional favourites, the rustic Stringybark Winery and Restaurant is a lovely country escape only an hour from Perth. One of the oldest vineyards in the Chittering Valley, a limited quantity of wines are produced here yearly and can be enjoyed with your meal or bought from the cellar door. Whether you choose the rack of lamb, bangers and mash, Atlantic salmon or the roast of the day from the menu, a wine suggestion will be made to best suit your meal.

2060 Chittering Rd; Chittering; (08) 9571 8069; open Wed–Sun for lunch and dinner; www.stringybarkwinery.com.au

WILLOWBROOK FARM TEAROOMS $

CAFE

Overlooking a picturesque property under the pergola of an old homestead built in 1874, the Willowbrook Farm Tearooms is approximately 20 kilometres from Gingin and oozes country charm. Come here for home-cooked breakfasts, lunches, and morning and afternoon teas. The property includes a caravan park, pioneer cemetery (where the original owners are buried), shady trees, wildflowers in spring and roaming farm animals. Payment in cash only.

1679 Gingin Brook Rd, West Gingin; (08) 9575 7566; open Thurs–Sun for breakfast and lunch

Greenough

ABROLHOS RESTAURANT $$

SEAFOOD

Just a few kilometres from Geraldton and a plane ride away from the stunning Abrolhos Islands, is the Abrolhos Restaurant. Being so close to the sea, a selection of fresh seafood is popular and can be enjoyed within the nine hectares of the Greenough River Resort.

Greenough River Resort, Greenough River Rd; (08) 9921 5888; open daily for dinner

Halls Creek

RUSSIAN JACK'S RESTAURANT $$

INTERNATIONAL

Russian Jack's Restaurant, located in the Best Western Halls Creek Motel, serves hearty fare in the midst of the spectacular Kimberley region and the motel's landscaped gardens. The bar is a great way to meet the locals. Perhaps you'll hear the tale about Russian Jack, a pioneer from the 1885 gold rush who pushed his ill friend 300 kilometres to safety in a wheelbarrow. A memorial was erected in his honour and to symbolise the many pioneers of this striking, yet brutal landscape.

Best Western Halls Creek Motel, 194 Great Northern Hwy; (08) 9168 9600; open daily for dinner; hallscreek.bestwestern.com.au

FAMILY FRIENDLY   LICENSED   OUTDOOR DINING   VEGETARIAN OPTIONS

Harvey

OLD COAST ROAD BREWERY $$
BREWERY RESTAURANT

The Old Coast Road Brewery encapsulates all there is to love about Australian hospitality: boutique beer on tap, a playground for the kids to run amok and tasty food in a rural setting. Postcards are made of in this 24-hectare property complete with an olive grove. The menu includes tasting plates to share, typical pub fare, a kid's menu and Simmo's gourmet ice-cream to finish.

West Break Rd, Myalup; 1300 792 106; open weekends and public holidays for lunch; www.ocrb.com.au

Hyden

WAVE ROCK MOTEL HOMESTEAD $
INTERNATIONAL

The Wave Rock Motel Homestead has three restaurants to choose from. The Bush Bistro is open year-round, serving food fresh from the grill. The Gimlet, open on selected nights, offers an à la carte menu. The Sandalwood Restaurant caters well to large groups with a buffet.

2 Lynch St; (08) 9880 5052; open daily for dinner; www.waverock.com.au

Jurien Bay

LEUSEURS GALLERY CAFE $
CAFE

This cafe is known for its monster burgers, but Turkish bread rolls, souvlaki and fish and chips are also menu favourites. Whether you're dining inside surrounded by artworks or outside, the atmosphere here is suitably relaxed.

36 Bashford St; (08) 9652 2113; open daily for breakfast and lunch

SANDPIPER BAR & GRILL $$
INTERNATIONAL

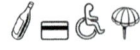

Patrons would agree that the Sandpiper Bar & Grill serves more than your standard pub meals. The menu includes not only fresh seafood plucked from the bay, but also Asian flavours, which can be enjoyed either inside the dining room or outside in the beer garden.

Cnr Roberts and Sandpiper sts; (08) 9652 1229; open daily for lunch and dinner

Kalbarri

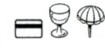

BLACK ROCK CAFE $$$
MODERN AUSTRALIAN

With an emphasis on freshness, since the seafood comes from the Indian Ocean, it's no wonder the Black Rock Cafe is so popular with locals and tourists. Established in 1999 and overlooking the Murchison River, the tasty menu is affordable and the drinks list features many of Australia's outstanding wines and a selection of imported beers. The cafe's name comes from a large, pointed black rock used as a navigational guide to mark the channel entrance.

80 Grey St; (08) 9937 1062; open daily for breakfast, lunch and dinner; www.blackrockcafe.com.au

THE GRASS TREE CAFE & RESTAURANT $$$
SEAFOOD

Catering well to the passing tourist trade, the Grass Tree Cafe & Restaurant sources many of its fresh ingredients locally. The menu has an

BYO AVAILABLE CREDIT CARDS ACCEPTED DISABLED ACCESS DRESS CODE APPLIES

emphasis on seafood with an Asian twist and diners might be lucky enough to be visiting during the crayfish season. Whether patrons dine inside the cosy restaurant or alfresco while savouring the sunset, a relaxed experience is guaranteed at this laid-back restaurant.

94–96 Grey St; (08) 9937 2288; open daily for breakfast, lunch and dinner

THE JETTY SEAFOOD SHACK $
SEAFOOD

Enjoy spectacular marina views and Kalbarri sunsets while savouring the fresh seafood at The Jetty Seafood Shack. This fish and chippery cooks fresh to order, with the option of having your fish battered, crumbed or grilled. The seafood is caught locally where possible and includes fish, prawns, seasonal crayfish, oysters, squid and mussels. In the cooler months, the seafood soup is a favourite. Also on the menu are burgers and vegetarian options and patrons can dine alfresco or order takeaway.

Shop 1, Marina Shopping Centre, 365 Grey St; (08) 9937 1067; open Sun–Fri for lunch and daily for dinner

ZUYTDORP RESTAURANT $$$
INTERNATIONAL

Situated in the Kalbarri Beach Resort, the Zuytdorp serves international cuisine catering well to many of the region's visitors. Also on-site is Jake's Bistro, offering a blackboard menu, buffet and takeaway.

Kalbarri Beach Resort, Clotworthy St; (08) 9937 1061 or 1800 096 002; open Mon–Sat for dinner; www.kalbarribeachresort.com

Kalgoorlie–Boulder

BARISTA 202 $$
CAFE
Map ref. p. 92

Run by the owners of Saltimbocca, Barista 202 is the place to go for coffee and a light breakfast or lunch. This funky little place offers sidewalk dining on a laneway between buildings and attracts commuters on their way to work for a caffeine fix, delicious breakfasts or Italian-style panini at lunch.

202 Hannan St, Kalgoorlie; (08) 9022 2228; open Mon–Sat for breakfast and lunch

KALGOORLIE HOTEL $$
INTERNATIONAL
Map ref. p. 92

The Kalgoorlie Hotel contains two dining options. Judd's Balcony Restaurant is where diners come to indulge in the Australian tradition of hearty pub fare enjoyed in relaxed surroundings. This popular spot has patrons people-watching from the balcony and in the cooler months the dining room is a cosy option. Downstairs, the ZeZe Pizza Bar serves gourmet pizzas, with jumbo prawns a local favourite.

Cnr Hannan and Wilson sts, Kalgoorlie; (08) 9021 3046; open daily for lunch and dinner

SALTIMBOCCA $$$
ITALIAN
Map ref. p. 92

This Italian restaurant is undoubtedly one of the best eateries in town. 'Saltimbocca' means 'jumps in the mouth' and the menu doesn't disappoint. Naturally, veal saltimbocca is the signature dish, cooked traditionally, as is most of the menu. Situated in a historic building, the restaurant retains its charm with polished floorboards, high pressed-tin ceilings, crisp white tablecloths and bistro-style wooden chairs. The wine list features many excellent Australian drops and there is also a takeaway menu.

90 Egan St, Kalgoorlie; (08) 9022 8028; open Mon–Sat for dinner

THE CORNWALL $$$
INTERNATIONAL
Map ref. p. 92

A fairly recent addition to the eating scene in town, The Cornwall brings a touch of sophistication to an eager crowd. Located in Boulder in a heritage-listed hotel there are three main dining areas: downstairs is the casual bar offering tapas, the beer-garden serves pizzas and jazz on Sundays and upstairs the bistro-style food is hearty.

25 Hopkins St, Boulder; (08) 9093 0911; open Tues–Sat for lunch and dinner

THE EXCHANGE HOTEL $$
TRADITIONAL AUSTRALIAN
Map ref. p. 92

Established in 1896, The Exchange Hotel is one of the oldest hotels in town and was the original miners' pub back in the gold-rush days. After having undergone extensive renovations, today it still functions as a hotel and includes Paddy's Ale House and the Wild West Saloon. Serving traditional Irish and Australian food, the kitchen in Paddy's Ale House is open from 11am until closing time. The Ale House boasts of serving over 20 brands of beer on tap, provides live music and hosts the viewing of many sporting events.

135 Hannan St, Kalgoorlie; (08) 9021 2833; open daily for lunch and dinner; www.exchangehotelkalgoorlie.com

Karratha

ETCETERA BRASSERIE $$
INTERNATIONAL

Rumoured to offer the finest dining in the Pilbara, Etcetera Brasserie is set within a pavilion-style restaurant overlooking the hotel's pool and tropical gardens. The menu of delicious brasserie fare impresses and the alfresco dining area and excellent service are also noteworthy. Afterwards, kick back in Etcetera Bar and enjoy the enormous skies above. For a more low-key experience, try Montebello's Poolside Bar and Cafe, also part of the hotel complex.

Karratha International Hotel, cnr Hillview and Millstream rds; (08) 9187 3333; open daily for breakfast and lunch, and Mon–Sat for dinner; www.karrathainternational.com.au

HEARSON'S BISTRO $$
INTERNATIONAL

Hearson's Bistro at the All Seasons Karratha serves a seasonal menu alfresco style by the pool. Located within walking distance to the town's facilities, the hotel and bistro are well placed for visitors to enjoy the region's attractions. Poolside dining definitely sets the scene for a relaxed Pilbara stay.

All Seasons Karratha, Lot 1079, Searipple Rd; 9185 1155; open daily for breakfast, lunch and dinner; www.accorhotels.com

WHIM CREEK PUB $
INTERNATIONAL

It's not hard to miss this pink-painted pub on the rugged horizon halfway between Karratha and Port Hedland. Serving counter meals and recounting the legend of a camel with a taste for beer is all part of the quirkiness at the Whim Creek Pub.

North West Coastal Hwy, Whim Creek; (08) 9176 4914; open daily for dinner

Katanning

KIMBERLEY RESTAURANT $$$
INTERNATIONAL

Situated in the grounds of The White House, established in 1913, and in the centre of town, the Kimberley Restaurant is part of the New Lodge Motel. The high ceilings, bay windows and soft decor create an intimate atmosphere for dining.

New Lodge Motel, 170 Clive St; (08) 9821 1788; open Mon–Thurs for dinner; www.newlodge.com.au

LORETTA @ FEDDY $
INTERNATIONAL

Serving fresh salads and other tasty treats, the seasonal menu makes Loretta @ Feddy at the Federal Hotel a popular lunchtime spot. Also open for dinner, the menu features local produce, bringing out the gourmets in this historic town.

Federal Hotel, 111 Clive St; (08) 9821 7128; open daily for lunch and dinner

Kellerberrin

KELLERBERRIN MOTOR HOTEL $
INTERNATIONAL

Situated in the centre of town, the Kellerberrin Motor Hotel serves hearty counter meals and being a country pub, a fair share of local yarns are shared over a pint or two. Although known for its wheat, Kellerberrin showcases the work of local and international artists at the International Art Space Kellerberrin Australia, with the aim of using the outback as inspiration without outside contemporary influences.

108 Massingham St; (08) 9045 5000; open daily for dinner

Kojonup

COMMERCIAL HOTEL $
INTERNATIONAL

Established in 1867, the Commercial Hotel is the oldest currently licensed hotel in the state. Hearty food is served in the cosy dining room or in the contemporary alfresco area and there is a country-style pub. While in town, check out the military barracks, built in 1845 and converted into a museum and Elverd's Cottage housing pieces of local memorabilia.

118 Albany Hwy; (08) 9831 1044; open daily for dinner; www.kojonupcomhotel.com

Kulin

KULIN HOTEL & MOTEL $
INTERNATIONAL

The steady agricultural trade has ensured the farming community of Kulin is one of the largest grain receiving points in the area. Although Kulin isn't exactly on the tourist trail, the Kulin Hotel and Motel is a low-key place to grab a bite to eat or a drink and rest your head. If you time your visit during the Kulin Bush Races, however, you might need to book. In the lead up to the races, the Tin Horse

FAMILY FRIENDLY   LICENSED   OUTDOOR DINING   VEGETARIAN OPTIONS

Highway showcases the quirkier side of the town, displaying horses made of tin and other materials on the roadside.

Johnston St; (08) 9880 1201; open daily for dinner

Kununurra

GULLIVER'S TAVERN $
INTERNATIONAL

With a reputation for being the place where you can let your hair down, Gulliver's Tavern has been host to many travellers over several years and continues to ensure a lively night out. The menu is typical pub fare and a prelude to festivities in this rugged region of extremes.

186 Cottontree Ave; (08) 9168 1666; open daily for dinner

IVANHOES GALLERY RESTAURANT $$
INTERNATIONAL

Serving an à la carte menu or buffet, Ivanhoes inspires relaxation as you dine in air-conditioned comfort inside or out beside the pool. In case you haven't chilled out enough, the cocktail bar is a popular spot to unwind.

All Seasons Kununurra, Messmate Way; (08) 9168 4000; open daily for breakfast and dinner; www.accorhotels.com

KELLY'S BAR & GRILL $$
INTERNATIONAL

Chill out with the locals or the other hotel guests at popular Kelly's, where the tempting menu includes many specialities of the region. The contemporary restaurant is part of the Best Western Country Club Hotel Kununurra in the heart of town. Also on-site is the pool bar serving light meals.

Kununurra Country Club Resort, 47 Coolibah Dr; (08) 9168 1024 or 1800 808 999; open daily for breakfast, lunch and dinner; www.kununurracountryclub.com.au

Lake Grace

LAKE GRACE HOTEL $
INTERNATIONAL

For a counter meal, refreshing drink and a yarn from a local, head to the Lake Grace Hotel. Attractions in the area include Mount Madden, a granite outcrop, and Lake Grace, which was originally part of an ancient river system from 20 million years ago.

Stubbs St; (08) 9865 1219

Lake King

LAKE KING TAVERN & MOTEL $
INTERNATIONAL

Close to the attractions of Lake Grace, the township of Lake King's rammed-earth tavern

KELLY'S BAR & GRILL, KUNUNURRA

BYO AVAILABLE   CREDIT CARDS ACCEPTED   DISABLED ACCESS   DRESS CODE APPLIES

is popular with those passing through on their way from Frank Hann National Park to Norseman.

165 Varley Rd; (08) 9874 4048; lakekingtavernmotel.com.au

Laverton

THE DESERT INN HOTEL $
INTERNATIONAL

A 12-hour drive north-east of Perth and a starting point to the Great Victoria Desert, Laverton has ghost-town status from its former gold-rush heydays. More recently known for its nickel, the area is being rehabilitated to establish the Windarra Heritage Trail. In this inhospitable region of the wild, wild west, it's worth a stop at the Desert Inn Hotel to learn about the town's chequered past and help blow away the tumbleweeds.

2 Laver St; (08) 9031 1188; open daily for dinner

Leonora

WHITE HOUSE HOTEL $
INTERNATIONAL

The heritage-listed White House Hotel is a prime example of the architecture from the gold-rush days, and so well preserved that you can imagine miners sharing tall tales from the bar. Although these days you will find it bustling with a tamer form of locals, and tourists fascinated by the town's rich mining past.

120 Tower St; (08) 9037 6030; open daily for dinner

Mandurah

CAFE PRONTO $$$
INTERNATIONAL

Located in one of Mandurah's oldest buildings, Eureka Cottage (c. 1915), Cafe Pronto has had a recent revamp to bring it up to date while remaining sympathetic to its heritage. Winner of countless hospitality awards and most recently the Peel's Barista of the Year, its extensive menu caters to all tastes, with influences from the Mediterranean and Asia. The desserts are deservedly decadent and breakfasts are guaranteed to get the heart started. This funky cafe also promises a brisk lunchtime service by having your meal served within 15 minutes.

Cnr Pinjarra Rd and Mandurah Tce; (08) 9535 1004; open daily for breakfast, lunch and dinner; www.cafepronto.au.com

RED MANNA WATERFRONT RESTAURANT $$$$
SEAFOOD

Situated on the waterfront with views of the Peel Estuary and the Indian Ocean through the glass walls, Red Manna is one of Mandurah's premier locations. As the name suggests, seafood is the speciality and in particular the crabs, barramundi and local crayfish. Meat eaters haven't been forgotten, as veal, lamb and wagyu sirloin are available, as are vegetarian and gluten-free options. The wine list is well matched to the menu and includes some premium selections like the South Australian Henschke.

Upstairs, 5/9 Mandurah Tce; (08) 9581 1248; open daily for lunch and dinner; www.redmanna.com.au

FAMILY FRIENDLY   LICENSED   OUTDOOR DINING   VEGETARIAN OPTIONS

SCUSI
$$$
ITALIAN

Drawing on some of the finest ingredients available, including local seafood and prime beef, Scusi is one of Mandurah's premier dining establishments. The Mediterranean-inspired menu features many local favourites, such as grilled crayfish, osso bucco, pasta and made-to-order pizza. Chef-owner, Ashley Parnham, brings his experience of working in some of Perth's finest restaurants and his passion is evident in the menu. Gluten-free, vegetarian and lactose-free options are available on request.

Shop 6, Lot 4, Old Coast Rd, Halls Head; (08) 9586 3479; open Wed–Sun for lunch and daily for dinner; www.scusi.com.au

THE MEDITERRANEAN
$$$
INTERNATIONAL

The stylish Mediterranean overlooks the outstanding Cut Golf Course and embraces the laid-back lifestyle synonymous with Western Australia. Both golfers and non-golfers will delight in the menu which draws on local ingredients well matched to a wine list typical of the region. The Sprig Bar adjoins the restaurant and offers lighter meals, and opens out onto the golf course.

The Cut Golf Course, Country Club Dr, Dawesville; (08) 9582 4444; open daily for lunch and dinner; www.the-cut.com.au

THE MIAMI BAKEHOUSE
$
BAKERY CAFE

Although located within a low-key shopping centre, the Miami Bakehouse is the winner of countless awards. The privately owned bakery bakes numerous gourmet pies, specialty breads and other naughty delights to either take away or enjoy in-house with a coffee. Light lunches are also served in the alfresco area.

Falcon Grove Shopping Centre, Old Coast Rd; (08) 9534 2705; open daily for lunch; www.miamibakehouse.com.au

CAFE ON THE DAM
$$$
CAFE

Overlooking one of Western Australia's largest dams, Serpentine Cafe on the Dam inspires a relaxed outing, whether it is for lunch or a coffee. The menu is seasonal and includes country favourites such as burgers and fish and chips, along with dishes with a gourmet touch using interesting ingredients such as lemon myrtle and wattleseed-infused beef. Lighter snacks and afternoon and morning tea are available and special dietary requirements are also catered for. Young children will love the playground and the cafe also caters for functions.

Serpentine Dam, Kingsbury Dr, Jarrahdale; (08) 9525 9920; open daily for breakfast and lunch; www.cafeonthedam.com

MILLBROOK WINERY RESTAURANT
$$$$
VINEYARD RESTAURANT

Located at Chestnut Farm among rolling hills, glittering lakes and vineyards, freshness is guaranteed at the Millbrook Winery Restaurant with marron and fruit sourced from the farm itself. Although compact, the menu includes refreshing choices such as local seafood in a bag and orange and fennel cured salmon. Picnic baskets are also available and the Millbrook Wines make a lovely Mediterranean drop suited to the Perth Hills region.

Millbrook Winery, Old Chestnut La, Jarrahdale; (08) 9525 5796; open Wed–Sun for lunch; www.millbrookwinery.com.au

---

BYO AVAILABLE   CREDIT CARDS ACCEPTED   DISABLED ACCESS   DRESS CODE APPLIES

Manjimup

CABERNET RESTAURANT $$$
INTERNATIONAL

Cabernet is situated in the heart of the state's southern forest region at the Kingsley Motel. Whether you choose to dine inside the elegant dining room or alfresco, the broad-ranging menu is sure to appeal.

Kingsley Motel, 74 Chopping St; (08) 9771 1177 or 1800 359 177; open daily for dinner; www.kingsleymotel.com.au

DÉJÀ VU CAFE $$
CAFE

Situated in the centre of town, Déjà vu Cafe encourages patrons to relax and take their time with their meal or coffee. The food consists of light meals, a deluxe breakfast and popular pancakes. Coffee and cake can be enjoyed while you browse the internet and little ones are well catered for with their own special menu and designated play area.

43A Giblett St; (08) 9771 2978; open daily for breakfast and lunch, and Thurs–Sat for dinner

SLICE OF HEAVEN CAFE $
CAFE

Rumour has it that the coffee at Slice of Heaven has other-worldly qualities since it is roasted at Mojo's in Bunbury. The food is prepared in-house and served in warm surroundings situated in the centre of town. Light meals include standard lunchtime fare such as salads, rolls and blackboard specials.

31B Rose St; (08) 9777 1331; open Mon–Sat for lunch

Marble Bar

MARBLE BAR TRAVELLERS STOP $
SEAFOOD

The Marble Bar Travellers Stop is famous for its seafood and also for dishing out tourist information on the area. Despite having a reputation as being the hottest town in Australia, Marble Bar is also one of the most ruggedly beautiful and historic places to explore in the country. The very naming of the town gives some insight into those crazy gold-rush days, as one day a pioneer mistook a slab of jasper for a bar of marble.

Halse Rd; (08) 9176 1166; open daily for dinner

Margaret River

BROOKWOOD ESTATE $$
VINEYARD RESTAURANT

Famous for their platters, Brookwood Estate offers casual dining in the typical laid-back manner of the region. Grab a group of friends and graze on tasty morsels as you unwind on the verandah, sampling a drop of the estate's award-winning wines.

Treeton Rd, Cowaramup; (08) 9755 5604; open daily for lunch; www.brookwood.com.au

LEEUWIN RESTAURANT $$$$$
VINEYARD RESTAURANT

The Leeuwin Estate winery restaurant serves a seasonal menu using the plentiful local produce like marron, venison, berries and cheese to create a fine-dining experience. An entrée of seared Abrolhos Island scallops with shredded duck, pineapple and chilli mint could be

FAMILY FRIENDLY   LICENSED   OUTDOOR DINING   VEGETARIAN OPTIONS

followed by black Angus 30-day aged, grain-fed scotch fillet with chargrilled asparagus and superbly finished off with a chocolate fondant or cheese platter. Many of the acclaimed Leeuwin Estate wines are available by the glass to be savoured with your meal surrounded by majestic karri trees. Leeuwin Estate also offers a range of attractions. including concerts and art events.

Leeuwin Estate Winery, Stevens Rd; (08) 9759 0000; open daily for lunch and Sat for dinner; www.leeuwinestate.com.au

MUST MARGARET RIVER $$$$

MODERN AUSTRALIAN
Map ref. p. 106

Must creates dishes designed for savouring. The menu includes the signature angel hair pasta with blue manna crab, Plantagenet pork and dry-aged Butterfield beef, where cuts are aged for 30 days or more. In keeping with the Must spirit, sommeliers are on hand to assist with selections from a wine list that includes varieties from the region, Australia and internationally. Although new to the Margaret River dining scene, if this version of Must follows the same formula as its Highgate branch in Perth, it is sure to become a permanent fixture. Also worth mentioning are the comfortably appointed Must Margaret River Suites located in the heart of the Margaret River township.

107 Bussell Hwy; (08) 9758 8877; open daily for lunch and dinner; www.must.com.au

THE BERRY FARM COTTAGE CAFE $$

CAFE

Oozing country charm, the Cottage Cafe serves homemade pies, platters and their famous scones with Berry Farm jam and cream for morning or afternoon tea. Tiny birds flit about the cottage gardens and inside the cafe the timber floors creak with character. The menu is ever-changing and caters well to vegetarians and kids. Next door is an extensive range of gourmet delights and the cellar door has an abundance of fruity wines, ports and liqueurs.

43 Bessell Rd; (08) 9757 5054; open daily for lunch; www.berryfarm.com.au

THE MARGARET RIVER CHOCOLATE FACTORY $

CAFE

Although light lunches are available, decadent chocolate delights are the star attraction at this rural ode to pleasure. Chocolate fondues, naughty cakes and desserts, including their famous chocolate brownies. Chocolate-inspired drinks are also there to break the diet. The chocolate products encourage take-home indulgences, which overflow into books, merchandise and pampering body products. After the kids have overdosed, this bustling tourist attraction has thoughtfully provided a lawn for them to burn off their cocoa high.

Cnr Harmans Mill Rd and Harmans South Rd; (08) 9755 6555; open daily for lunch; www.chocolatefactory.com.au

VOYAGER ESTATE RESTAURANT $$$$

VINEYARD RESTAURANT

Situated in a Cape Dutch–style building nestled in formal gardens, the opulent dining room of Voyager Estate showcases the delights of the region. Dine on the likes of grilled Pemberton marron, venison chorizo and lamb loin, or opt for the degustation menu as an opportunity to taste as many dishes as possible. Also available are innovative vegetarian and gluten-free menus and the dishes are teamed with Voyager Estate wines.

Lot 1, Stevens Rd; (08) 9757 6354; open daily for lunch; www.voyagerestate.com.au

---

BYO AVAILABLE   CREDIT CARDS ACCEPTED   DISABLED ACCESS   DRESS CODE APPLIES

WINO'S MARGARET RIVER $$
MODERN AUSTRALIAN
Map ref. p. 106

Boasting 700 wine selections on its menu, Wino's couldn't be a more fitting name for this casual eatery. The food is also sensational and seasonal, with many hearty classics to choose from. Tapas-style 'Bar Grits' are available between 3pm and 6pm, ideal to snack on after perusing the many gorgeous shops located in the town centre.

85 Bussell Hwy; (08) 9758 7155; open daily for dinner; www.winos.com.au

XANADU RESTAURANT $$$
VINEYARD RESTAURANT

With distinctive Asian influences appearing on the menu, Xanadu makes for a refreshing lunch choice. Using many local ingredients, this award-winning restaurant takes an innovative approach to its dishes such as ox cheek and sweet potato rendang curry, confit corn-fed pork with seared Abrolhos Island scallops and its delicious vegetarian plate. The stunning double-sided stone fireplace makes a statement, and many an hour has been spent lingering over lunch in the lovely alfresco area with a drop of Xanadu wine.

Boodjidup Rd; (08) 9758 9531; open daily for lunch; www.xanaduwines.com

CULLEN RESTAURANT $$$
VINEYARD RESTAURANT

Cullen's must have one of the prettiest outlooks in the region, where undulating acres of vineyards are framed by rolling hills. In keeping with the natural environment, the stone and timber building blends beautifully with the surroundings. The politically correct menu has vegetarian, gluten-free, biodynamic, vegan and free-range options, and only the freshest ingredients are used, ensuring the menu remains seasonal. Although compact, the choice is tempting and platters cater to the indecisive. Naturally, Cullen's wines accompany the meal well and a tasting is essential before, during and after your lunchtime feast.

Cullen Wines, Caves Rd, Cowaramup; (08) 9755 5656; open daily for lunch; www.cullenwines.com.au

CLAIRAULT $$$
VINEYARD RESTAURANT

Down a windy track and nestled within marri trees, you will find some of the best food served in Western Australia's most renowned wine region. Clairault's superb wines are the perfect complement to the modern Australian menu of dishes such as wagyu beef, pork belly and local marron. The degustation menu will appeal to the indecisive. The architecturally designed restaurant features natural building materials such as wood and stone, and the glass doors open onto a grassed area which overlooks the vineyard.

Caves Rd, Willyabrup; (08) 9755 6655; open daily for lunch; www.clairaultwines.com.au

A DELIGHTFUL DISH AT CLAIRAULT, WILLYABRUP

FAMILY FRIENDLY   LICENSED   OUTDOOR DINING   VEGETARIAN OPTIONS

GNARABAR RESTAURANT $$$
MODERN AUSTRALIAN

Conveniently located in Gnarabar Beach at the Margaret's Beach Resort, the relaxed Gnarabar Restaurant & Bistro has two dining options. The Gnarabar Restaurant offers terrace dining and modern cuisine, while the Gnarabar Bistro is the cosier option with its open limestone fireplace and informal menu.

Margaret's Beach Resort, cnr Resort Pl and Walcliffe Rd, Gnarabar; (08) 9757 1583; open daily for lunch and dinner, and weekends for breakfast; www.gnarabar.com.au

SEA GARDEN CAFE $$
INTERNATIONAL

The Sea Garden is cosy in winter when wild waves crash onto the beach and relaxing during summer. The magnificent views and tasty menu ensure this cafe is popular year-round. The simple lunchtime menu includes salads and burgers and in the evening the house-made dips, fresh seafood and gourmet pizzas are favourites.

9 Mitchell Dr, Prevelly Park; (08) 9757 3074; open daily for breakfast, lunch and dinner; www.seagardens.com.au

SEA STAR CAFE & RESTAURANT $$
INTERNATIONAL

Sea views are on the menu at the Sea Star Cafe and Restaurant, not to mention hearty breakfasts, seafood and many outstanding regional wines. The laid-back beach mood inspires patrons to settle in for the day or night and watch the ever-changing scenery.

4 Bayview Dr, Gracetown; (08) 9755 5000; open daily for breakfast, lunch and dinner

UDDERLY DIVINE CAFE $
CAFE

An abundant selection of vegetarian options are available on the menu at this cleverly named cafe. Owner-chef, Trish Wray, prides herself on cooking everything on the premises. A dairy theme is also evident in the decor with paintings and mosaics of cows on the walls, while the real cows can be seen grazing in the distance, oblivious to their notoriety.

22 Bussell Hwy, Cowaramup; (08) 9755 5519; open daily for lunch

Meekatharra

THE ROYAL MAIL HOTEL $
INTERNATIONAL

Literally in the middle of nowhere is the small mining town of Meekatharra, which is where you will find the Royal Mail Hotel. Despite its remote location, the restaurant turns out meals comparable to any city hotel. Much of the produce is of premium quality and the menu is as seasonal as it can be, given its proximity to food suppliers. The hotel is air-conditioned and meals can be enjoyed in the restaurant or at the bar, where you're more likely to meet some of the colourful characters of this town.

Main St; (08) 9981 1148; open daily for dinner; www.royalmailhotel.com.au

Merredin

DENZIL'S RESTAURANT $
INTERNATIONAL

Situated halfway between Perth and Kalgoorlie, Denzil's Restaurant at the Merredin Olympic

---

BYO AVAILABLE   CREDIT CARDS ACCEPTED   DISABLED ACCESS   DRESS CODE APPLIES

Motel serves good food and a more than reasonable selection of wines. The restaurant is popular with locals as well as with tourists passing through town.

Merredin Olympic Motel, Lot 5 Great Eastern Hwy; (08) 9041 1588; open Mon–Sat for dinner; www.olympicmotel.com

MERREDIN MOTEL & GUMTREE RESTAURANT $

INTERNATIONAL

The dated 1960s decor may not be to everyone's liking, but the Gumtree Restaurant turns out a decent meal nonetheless. Popular with locals or guests of the motel, it is located conveniently close to the highway.

10 Gamenya Ave; (08) 9041 1886; open daily for dinner

Moora

MOORA HOTEL $

INTERNATIONAL

Situated on the banks of the Moore River, the small town of Moora is a popular stopover for travellers heading north. The Moora Hotel is a great place to refuel for the journey ahead, serving standard pub grub.

1 Gardiner St; (08) 9651 1177; open daily for dinner

Morawa

EVERLASTINGS RESTAURANT $$

INTERNATIONAL

In the heart of wildflower country, the small town of Morawa is where you'll find the modern Everlastings Restaurant. Part of the Everlastings Guest Homes, the restaurant serves a buffet and can also cater for functions.

10 Evan St; (08) 9971 1771; open daily for breakfast, lunch and dinner; www.everlastingsguesthomes.com.au

Mount Barker

BLUFF KNOLL CAFE $

CAFE

Situated in the Stirling Ranges, the Bluff Knoll Cafe caters to visitors touring the neighbouring mountains. Takeaway options are also available on its day-long menu.

Cnr Bluff Knoll Rd and Chester Pass rds, Borden; (08) 9827 9293; open Wed–Mon for lunch and Thurs–Sun for dinner

GALAFREY WINES $$

VINEYARD RESTAURANT

Overlooking the vineyard and views of the Porongurup and Stirling Ranges, savour Galafrey wines with a delicious gourmet platter. The vineyard platters at this family-run boutique winery feature fresh fruit, vegetables, trout, homemade mustard, double-smoked ham and their famous peach chardonnay chutney. It's seasonal produce, with freshness guaranteed since most of the ingredients are sourced locally.

432 Quangellup Rd; (08) 9851 2022; open daily for lunch; www.galafreywines.com.au

PORONGURUP TEAROOMS $

CAFE

About ten minutes east of Mount Barker, these tearooms are located at the entrance of Porongurup Range National Park. Established in 1937, the general store incorporates the tearooms and holds about 40 people. Serving traditional home cooking and using organic fruit, the menu is seasonal. Cosy up by the fire in winter and find a seat outside during the warmer months.

1972 Porongurup Rd, Porongurup; (08) 9853 1110; open daily for breakfast and lunch; www.porongurupinn.com.au

THE VINEYARD CAFE $$
VINEYARD RESTAURANT

The Vineyard Cafe's hilltop setting offers sensational views of the vineyard and valley below. Windrush Wines complement the delicious tasting plates and light gourmet lunches served here. Also available are decadent cakes as well as a choice of gluten-free, vegetarian and low-GI foods. The fireplace is a popular choice when it's too cold to relax on the verandah.

Windrush Wines, cnr St Werburghs and Hay River rds; (08) 9851 1353; open Fri–Sun for lunch; www.windrushwines.com.au

Mount Magnet

MOUNT MAGNET HOTEL $
INTERNATIONAL

With a glittering goldmining past, Mount Magnet boasts a main street as wide as its future once promised. But like many other towns that were set to prosper from a mining boom, World War I took priority and sadly, many of the miners didn't return home. Today, the Mount Magnet Hotel still stands proud and continues to serve counter meals and ales to its faithful clientele.

36 Hepburn St; (08) 9963 4002; open daily for dinner

Mundaring

LITTLE CAESARS PIZZERIA $$
PIZZA

Little Caesars has customers coming from all over Perth to try master pizza chef, Theo Kalogeracos', creations. The menu has every combination you can think of and includes vegetarian choices, soy cheese for the lactose intolerant and gluten-free options. However, it's the dessert pizzas that are most noteworthy, especially the Mudhoney, with chocolate mudcake on a pizza base and the New York Pecan Pie. Dine in or takeaway.

Shop 7, 7125 Great Eastern Hwy; (08) 9295 6611; open Wed–Mon for dinner; www.littlecaesarspizzeria.com.au

THE LOOSE BOX $$$$$
FRENCH

Nestled in the lovely Perth hills, 30 kilometres from the CBD, is the charming Loose Box restaurant. Offering one of the most exciting menus around, chef, Alain Fabregues, takes a spontaneous approach to his cooking by offering a degustation menu based on the best market produce of the day, with the fruit, vegetables and herbs picked from the rambling gardens as required. The wine list is extensive and includes several French gems not found in many Perth restaurants. And, if you're able to make a booking during the Manjimup Truffle Festival, from June to August, you will be fortunate enough to sample the elusive truffle.

6825 Great Eastern Hwy; (08) 9295 1787; open Wed–Sat for dinner and Sun for lunch; www.loosebox.com.au

---

BYO AVAILABLE   CREDIT CARDS ACCEPTED   DISABLED ACCESS   DRESS CODE APPLIES

ALFRED'S KITCHEN $
CAFE

No matter what day of the week or the weather, the fire blazes outside Alfred's Kitchen every night. This is Perth's longest-standing roadside hamburger joint, and the smell of grilled meat has hung over the historic town of Guildford since 1946. With 40 styles of hamburgers to choose from, arguably the best chips in Perth and their famous pea and ham soup, people in the know drive from all over the metropolitan area to dine here. And since it's open until 3am on Friday and Saturday nights, you never know who you might be sharing late-night tales with while huddling around the fire.

Cnr Meadow and James St, Guildford; (08) 9377 1378; open daily for dinner; www.alfredskitchen.com.au

BLACK SWAN WINERY & RESTAURANT $$$$
VINEYARD RESTAURANT

Overlooking vineyards and the odd farm animal, and with the Darling Ranges as a backdrop, the Black Swan Winery & Restaurant is the epitome of alfresco rustic dining. Where possible the ingredients are grown on-site or sourced locally, except for the wagyu beef and the Kurobuta pork which is flown in from the eastern states. To begin, a delicate soufflé or house-smoked chicken, followed by house-made pasta or duck breast l'orange. The winery makes a cheeky drop or two to complement your meal and other outstanding wines are also available. An added bonus is that it's open daily, which is refreshing in this neck of the woods.

8600 West Swan Rd, Henley Brook; (08) 9296 6090; open daily for lunch and Wed–Sat for dinner; www.blackswanwines.com.au

DARLINGTON ESTATE WINERY $$$$
VINEYARD RESTAURANT

There are not too many places in the world where you can enjoy award-winning wines and outstanding food while perched on the edge of a valley with endless bush views, just 25 minutes from the CBD. The temptations served here include oysters baked with crab and bacon, sesame-encrusted rack of lamb with chestnut potato mash and for dessert, a lime, raspberry and coconut tart served with spun sugar and blood orange sorbet. With new owners, the Darlington Estate Winery is an up-and-coming restaurant in the Perth area dining scene with an exciting future.

1495 Nelson Rd, Darlington; (08) 9299 6268; open Thurs for lunch, and Fri–Sun for lunch and dinner; www.darlingtonestate.com

DEAR FRIENDS $$$$$
MODERN AUSTRALIAN

New owners have injected life into Dear Friends, and owner-chef Kiren Mainwaring has drawn on his gourmet experiences in Europe and Asia to create the innovative menu. Dishes include many ingredients sourced locally and statewide, such as venison, hare, dhufish, quail and truffles. In case your mouth isn't already watering, the wine list is outstanding and the service is seamless.

100 Benara Rd, Caversham; (08) 9279 2815; open Wed–Sun for lunch and dinner; www.dearfriends.com.au

ELMAR'S IN THE VALLEY $$$
BREWERY RESTAURANT

Despite being licensed to seat up to 400 diners, this German-inspired brewery, restaurant, bar, and smallgoods shop is always busy. Situated in the heart of the Swan Valley and designed as a beer hall, the extensive lawned area to the

FAMILY FRIENDLY   LICENSED   OUTDOOR DINING   VEGETARIAN OPTIONS

rear often features families frolicking and the odd patron resting after over-indulging in the local brew. The rustic menu is consistently good and features Bratwurst sausages, pork schnitzel or shank and Kassler smoked pork chop. Lighter meals are available to leave room for the decadent desserts, which include a warm apple strudel and a chocolate plate for two.

8731 West Swan Rd, Henley Brook; (08) 9296 6354; open Wed–Sun for lunch and Fri–Sun for dinner; www.elmars.com.au

KAPPY'S $$$
ITALIAN

In the historic town of Guildford, the setting is cosy, the food unpretentious and the service friendly at Kappy's Italian Restaurant. Fresh pasta with hearty homemade sauces, lightly seasoned seafood and daily specials ensure this rustic restaurant is very popular. Not to worry if you can't get a table, as the takeout menu has a good selection from the main menu.

120 Swan St, Guildford; (08) 6278 2882; open Mon–Fri for lunch and Mon–Sat for dinner; www.kappys.net

KING & I $$
THAI

The King & I isn't your standard Thai restaurant. Here, crisp white tablecloths, comfortable chairs and opulent decor set the scene for authentic tasty Thai cuisine. The menu is extensive and the seafood curry and claypot dishes are highly recommended. Ample rice is served along with the friendly and helpful service, and BYO allows for a drop of your favourite wine. The takeaway menu is available from 5pm onwards.

147 James St, Guildford; (08) 6278 3999; open Tues–Sun for dinner

LE PARIS BREST CAFE & PATISSERIE $$
FRENCH

Complete with its own replica Eiffel Tower in the front courtyard, this French cafe is abuzz during the day with patrons sampling the mouth-watering pastries and light lunches. By night, it transforms into an intimate sanctuary for lovers to canoodle over innovative French fare. The decor is cheery French Provincial, making it a lovely spot to dine in the historic hillside town of Kalamunda.

Shop 9, Kalamunda Village Shopping Centre, 22 Haynes St, Kalamunda; (08) 9293 2752; open Tues–Sun for breakfast, lunch and dinner

LITTLE RIVER WINERY RESTAURANT $$$
FRENCH

For provincial French fare, the Little River Winery and Restaurant oozes rustic charm. While overlooking vineyards, you can pick away at tapas or a cheese platter, or order something more substantial like duck confit, their famous lamb pot pie or beef bourguignon, saving room for the sufficiently decadent handmade chocolate truffles. Using French winemaking techniques, the wine is extremely drinkable and suits the unpretentious menu.

2 Forest Rd, Henley Brook; (08) 9296 4462; open daily for lunch; www.littleriverwinery.com

RIVERSIDE @ WOODBRIDGE $
CAFE

On the banks of the Swan River, Riverside @ Woodbridge serves breakfast, lunch, morning and afternoon teas. The food served here is true home-style cooking, with roast dinners, bangers and mash, and homemade cakes that are so decadent it is pointless to resist. Located on the site of the heritage Woodbridge House, make a day of it and explore the mansion and grounds to immerse yourself in times past.

8254 Ford St, Woodbridge; (08) 9274 1469; open daily for breakfast, lunch and afternoon tea; www.riversidewoodbridge.com.au

ROSE AND CROWN $$$
INTERNATIONAL

Housed within the Rose and Crown Hotel, one of Australia's most iconic pubs and rumoured to be haunted with the spirits of convicts, you'll find the 1841 Restaurant and Posh Convict Bar & Grill. Having undergone an extensive renovation, this ageing beauty is often packed with locals in the labyrinth of rooms or in the immaculate beer garden. The 1841 serves delicious pub fare with a daily changing menu to include platters, steaks and tapas. The Posh Convicts Bar & Grill offers a full grill dinner menu and there is a spooky cellar available for functions.

105 Swan St, Guildford; (08) 9347 8100; open daily for lunch and dinner, and weekends for breakfast; www.rosecrown.com.au

SANDALFORD RESTAURANT $$$$
VINEYARD RESTAURANT

Dining in one of the state's oldest vineyards beneath a vine-covered patio is one of the most blissful ways to spend an afternoon in the Swan Valley. Equally special is savouring the European menu inside the rustic restaurant beside the enormous fireplace. The wine complements the consistently outstanding food. The giftshop is likely to tempt, especially after a generous tasting and taking a tour of the winery is sure to leave a lasting impression.

Romantic candlelit weddings alongside wine barrels are one of Sandalford's specialties.

Sandalford Wines, 3210 West Swan Rd, Caversham; (08) 9374 9301; open daily for lunch; www.sandalford.com

SITTELLA RESTAURANT $$$
VINEYARD RESTAURANT

The Sittella Winery and Cafe is in one of the most picturesque spots in the Swan Valley, with rolling vineyards cascading away through floor-to-ceiling windows. The accomplished menu includes classics such as seafood chowder, oven-roasted duck breast and rack of lamb. However, the long lunch is one of the few degustation menus available for lunch in Western Australia. Sittella Winery produces a range of red, white, sparkling and fortified wines sure to enhance your dining experience at this lovely restaurant.

Sittella Winery, 100 Barrett St, Herne Hill; (08) 9296 2600; open Tues–Sun for lunch; www.sittella.com.au

STEWART'S RESTAURANT $$$
MODERN AUSTRALIAN

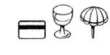

Horse enthusiasts will probably already know about Stewart's at Brookleigh's reputation. However, for those not in the know, this equestrian centre showcases an award-winning restaurant. Chicken breast filled with forest mushrooms, salmon saltimbocca, and duck and porcini risotto are just a few of the creations on offer. The surroundings are casually elegant and the wine list is extensive.

Brookleigh Estate, 1235 Great Northern Hwy, Upper Swan; (08) 9296 6966; open Wed–Sun for lunch and dinner; www.brookleigh.com.au

Nannup

NANNUP BRIDGE CAFE $$
MODERN AUSTRALIAN

Romance is on the menu at Hamish's Cafe, as lovers cosy up inside during the cooler months and dine alfresco when it's warmer. The country setting is conducive to rustic food, and oysters and steak are popular dishes in this lovely region of Western Australia.

1 Warren Rd; (08) 9756 1287; open Wed–Sun for lunch and Fri–Sat for dinner

MULBERRY TREE RESTAURANT $$
INTERNATIONAL

Diners enjoy country hospitality as soon as they arrive at the Mulberry Tree, located in an original homestead complete with pressed-metal walls. Situated in the main street, this charming cafe serves homemade food with old-fashioned, friendly service.

62 Warren Rd; (08) 9756 3038; open Wed to Sun for lunch and dinner

TATHRA RESTAURANT $$
VINEYARD RESTAURANT

Specialising in marron, trout and beef, it's no wonder the Tathra Restaurant has been operational since 1990. Situated in peaceful surroundings 14 kilometres from the township of Nannup, the property includes a winery, accommodation, a museum, wildlife sanctuary and cottage built in 1870. The verandah is a popular dining spot and you're sure to be visited by the friendly birds while feasting on the many local delicacies, including the winery's popular Tiger Port and Nannup Nectar.

Tathra Winery, Blackwood River Tourist Dr (Route 251); (08) 9756 2040; open daily for lunch; www.tathra.net

Narrogin

ALBERT'S RESTAURANT $$
INTERNATIONAL

Located in the charming Albert Facey Motor Inn, Albert's restaurant overlooks the hotel's pool area. Complementing the à la carte menu full of international flavours, the wine list includes many local favourites. The complex is centrally situated opposite Foxes Lair, 24 hectares of natural bushland and wildlife, and the Dryandra Woodland.

Albert Facey Motor Inn, 78 Williams Rd; (08) 9881 1899; open daily for breakfast and Mon–Sat for dinner; www.albertfacey.com

New Norcia

NEW NORCIA HOTEL $$
INTERNATIONAL

Patrons lounge on the impressive verandah for lunch, dinner or drinks at the historic New Norcia Hotel. The atmosphere is informal and the Sunday night roast is popular, as are the barbecues in summer. Try a glass of New Norcia Abbey Ale, a traditional ale laced with the scents of fruit and spice. A stroll around the town to admire the magnificent architecture before or after your meal is a must.

Great Northern Hwy; (08) 9654 8034; open daily for lunch and dinner; www.newnorcia.wa.edu.au/accommodation/new-norcia-hotel/

BYO AVAILABLE   CREDIT CARDS ACCEPTED   DISABLED ACCESS   DRESS CODE APPLIES

Newman

NEWMAN HOTEL MOTEL $
INTERNATIONAL

The Pilbara's Newman Hotel Motel includes accommodation, a restaurant and bar. The hotel is comfortably appointed and serves reasonable pub fare to its hearty clientele. Newman is the gateway to the outstanding Karijini National Park and also boasts the largest open-cut iron ore pit in the world.

Newman Dr; (08) 9175 1101; open daily for dinner; www.newmanhotelmotel.com.au

Norseman

NORSEMAN HOTEL $
INTERNATIONAL

In the middle of nowhere, well actually the Nullarbor Plain, Norseman is a town known for its enormous reserves of gold. And where there are miners, you can be sure to find a decent pub serving that all-time Australian favourite, cold beer and hearty counter meals. The Newman Hotel remains in the original colonial style it was built in at the turn of the last century.

90 Roberts St; (08) 9039 1023; open daily for dinner

Northam

3TWOTWO $$
INTERNATIONAL

In Northam's oldest pub, this restaurant serves seafood, steaks and homemade delights. Centrally located and built in 1858, the hotel has been restored to include many features of the era, such as wooden floors, high ceilings and open fireplaces, bringing a touch of style to the country.

Avon Bridge Hotel, 322 Fitzgerald St; (080 9622 1023; open Thurs–Sat for dinner; www.avonbridgehotel.com.au

CAFE BETHANY $
CAFE

In the heart of Northam, Bethany Cafe serves homemade food in relaxed surroundings. The interior is cheery and inviting and service is friendly, making it a popular spot with the locals. Payment is by cash only

175 Fitzgerald St; (08) 9622 3128; open Mon–Sat for breakfast and lunch

CAFE YASOU $
GREEK

A taste of Greece is an unexpected find in the country town of Northam. Cafe Yasou serves the Mediterranean flavours of Cyprus and Greece within a vibrant setting of lime green walls adorned with Greek goddesses. Located in the town centre, dining here is relaxed, the service is friendly and the coffee is the best in town.

175 Fitzgerald St; (08) 9622 3128; open Mon–Sat for breakfast and lunch; www.cafeyasou.com.au

Northampton

MINERS ARMS HOTEL $$
INTERNATIONAL

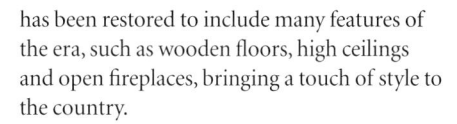

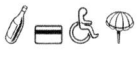

Originally built in 1868, with only a couple of the original walls remaining, the Miners Arms has been extended into the pub it is today.

FAMILY FRIENDLY   LICENSED   OUTDOOR DINING   VEGETARIAN OPTIONS

Claiming to be the oldest pub in town, even though the Railway Tavern reputably has the oldest licence in Western Australia, it was built by pioneer, Captain John Hoskins. The classic Australian pub fare is best savoured with a chilled ale.

Hampton Rd; (08) 9934 1281; open daily for dinner

THE RAILWAY TAVERN $$
INTERNATIONAL

Credited with the longest continuous licence in Western Australia, the tavern displays a fascinating history of the district on its walls. Serving wholesome food, the menu changes regularly and the pizzas are very popular.

71 North West Coastal Hwy; (08) 9934 1120; open Wed–Sun for lunch and dinner; www.railwaytavern.com.au

Northcliffe

THE DAIRY LOUNGE CAFE $
CAFE

Set among the rolling hills of the working dairy, Bannister Downs Farm, The Dairy Lounge Cafe's sumptuous morning and afternoon teas include homemade pies and cakes. The Top Paddock Platter served with a warm crusty cob loaf is a lunchtime favourite. On display is the farm's milk processing and packaging system.

Bannister Downs Farm, Muirillup Rd; (08) 9776 6300; open Sat–Thurs for lunch; www.bannisterdowns.com.au

Onslow

BEADON BAY HOTEL $
INTERNATIONAL

Located in the centre of town and close to the beach, this hotel is a very popular spot for socialising and also serves up reasonably priced counter meals. Known for its resilience, the pub has survived several cyclones.

Second Ave; (08) 9184 6002; open daily for lunch and dinner

NIKKI'S LICENSED RESTAURANT $$
INTERNATIONAL

The compact coastal town of Onslow is home to Nikki's Licensed Restaurant, where locals come for steak and fresh seafood. They apparently serve the best prawns in the state, which is believable considering Onslow's proximity to Mackerel Islands and its world-class fishing. Close to some of Western Australia's major oil reserves, this sleepy town is sure to soon make its mark on the tourist trail.

17 First Ave; (08) 9184 6121; open daily for dinner

Pemberton

HIDDEN RIVER ESTATE RESTAURANT $$$
VINEYARD RESTAURANT

Rumour has it that the owners of Hidden River Estate bribe the butcher with bottles of port for their fillet steak. Other mouth-watering dishes include the cheese fondue, smoked duck breast in black truffle and the chef's specialty, prawn laksa. The playground and kids menu also ensure parents will actually get the chance to enjoy their delicious lunch. The menu complements the Hidden River Estate wines wonderfully and it's not surprising that diners drop in for a morning coffee and are still there well into the afternoon.

Mullineaux Rd; (08) 9776 1437; open daily for lunch; www.hiddenriver.com.au

JARRAH JACKS BREWERY $$$
BREWERY RESTAURANT

All those ale lovers hankering for a beer in the midst of wine country will appreciate Jarrah Jacks Brewery cafe. Foodies won't have to endure standard fried fare, with impressive dishes like provincial duck sausage, Pemberton trout dip, and chicken and mushroom roulade on the menu. Overlooking picturesque scenery and with a kids playground, including an indoor play area, patrons can drop in any time of the day for a play, sample and a bite to eat.

Lot 2, Kemp Rd; (08) 9776 1333; open daily for lunch; www.jarrahjacks.com.au

KING TROUT RESTAURANT AND MARRON FARM $
SEAFOOD

Surrounded by magnificent karri trees, punters can be found fishing for their own lunch here. This makes for a great family activity and fishing aficionados can try out the special fly-fishing dam. Since you'll be catching your meal, freshness is guaranteed, and as a chef cooks up your catch you can sample the smoked trout or smoked trout pâté and marron. Rods can be hired and tours are available.

Cnr Northcliffe and Old Vasse rds; (08) 9776 1352; open daily for lunch; www.warrenriverresort.com.au

THE SHAMROCK RESTAURANT $$
INTERNATIONAL

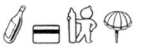

Before electricity came to town the Pemberton Mill was powered by batteries, which were housed in the building where the Shamrock Restaurant now resides. Built in 1911, the restaurant retains much of its charm from its humble beginnings. Best known for its marron and trout platters for two and steaks, the restaurant has been operational since the 1970s.

18 Brockman St; (08) 9776 1186; open daily for lunch and dinner; www.shamrockdining.com.au

Pingelly

THE EXCHANGE TAVERN $
INTERNATIONAL

The Exchange Tavern is an old-style hotel in a Federation building, well located in the centre of town. Serving counter meals, patrons can always rely on good old-fashioned fare and a cleansing ale.

1 Pasture St; (08) 9887 0180; open daily for dinner

Pinjarra

EDENVALE HOMESTEAD & HERITAGE TEAROOMS $
CAFE

Edenvale Homestead is home to a number of community groups, such as the visitor centre, arts centre, a museum and tearooms. Serving light meals and Devonshire teas, the

---

FAMILY FRIENDLY   LICENSED   OUTDOOR DINING   VEGETARIAN OPTIONS

tearooms are opposite the Pioneer Memorial Park and a lovely spot to soak up the historic charm of the building. Built in 1888, the homestead has had an interesting past, having functioned as a house of worship, a cemetery, a school, governmental institutions and a private dwelling.

1 George St; (08) 9531 2223; open daily for breakfast and lunch

RAVEN WINES $$$

VINEYARD RESTAURANT

The concept at the sleek Raven Wines Cafe is a revolving menu concept, aka 'Food Mood'. The menu reflects the quality of the many fine ingredients sourced from top suppliers in Perth and, of course, the Raven Wine cellar range. The Raven Platter comes highly recommended, as does the citrus-cured Atlantic salmon and loin of veal with fondant potatoes. However, don't be surprised if none of these delights are available on the day because the innovative menu changes constantly, which is commendable given this restaurant's comparatively remote location.

41 Wilson Rd; (08) 9531 2774; open Wed–Sun for lunch and weekends for breakfast; www.ravenwines.com.au

REDCLIFFE ON THE MURRAY $$

MODERN AUSTRALIAN

Settled in 1836 and situated on the banks of the Murray River, this fully restored barn serves modern Australian food and is a popular spot for weddings.

13 Sutton St; (08) 9531 3894; open daily for lunch

Port Hedland

ESPLANADE HOTEL PORT HEDLAND $$$$

INTERNATIONAL

If you're looking for a slice of Port Hedland culture, head to the Esplanade Hotel for hearty counter meals, where a local favourite is the grilled barramundi. Visitors can mingle with the locals in the generous courtyard or over a game of pool. The evening's entertainment includes exotic dancing.

2–4 Anderson St; (08) 9173 2783; open daily for lunch and dinner; www.theesplanadeporthedland.com.au

HEDDY'S BAR & BISTRO $$$

INTERNATIONAL

Dine by the stunning Indian Ocean at the All Season's bistro, where the alfresco dining is as popular as the local seafood. For a more casual experience, enjoy a counter meal at the bar or a cocktail by the pool.

All Seasons Port Hedland, cnr Lukis and McGregor sts; (08) 9173 1511; open daily for breakfast, lunch and dinner; www.accorhotels.com

THE PILBARA ROOM RESTAURANT $$

INTERNATIONAL

Centrally located and situated within the Hospitality Inn Port Hedland, the Pilbara Room Restaurant is one of the best dining options in town. Prime cuts of meat and fresh seafood complement the friendly service and atmosphere.

Hospitality Inn Port Hedland, Webster St; (08) 9173 1044; open daily for breakfast and dinner; www.porthedland.wa.hospitalityinns.com

BYO AVAILABLE   CREDIT CARDS ACCEPTED   DISABLED ACCESS   DRESS CODE APPLIES

WEDGE STREET COFFEE SHOP
$ CAFE

Inside a newsagency, the Wedge Street Coffee Shop is a popular place to stop for coffee and a magazine or to the sample the menu of salads, sandwiches and a selection of Asian-inspired fare. This busy spot also has a takeaway menu.

12A Wedge St; (08) 9173 2128; open daily for breakfast and lunch

Ravensthorpe

RAVENSTHORPE PALACE MOTOR HOTEL
$$ INTERNATIONAL

Situated in the quiet country town of Ravensthorpe, the stately Palace Hotel has been keeping locals and visitors well fed and hydrated since it was built in 1907. The upstairs verandah is a popular spot to watch the town's comings and goings.

28 Morgan St; (08) 9838 1005; open daily for lunch and dinner

Rockingham

BETTYBLUE BISTRO
$$$ INTERNATIONAL

With views as far as Garden Island, the unpretentious Bettyblue Bistro serves honest food, making it a favourite with locals and family groups. The portions are generous, steaks are cooked to perfection and the seafood is always fresh, with barramundi being a signature dish. A takeaway menu is also available.

Shop 3, 1 Railway Tce; (08) 9528 4228; open daily for breakfast, lunch and dinner

CHARLIE'S BISTRO
$$$ INTERNATIONAL

Charlie's Bistro continues the tradition of serving a tasty menu to locals and tourists alike. Barramundi and steak and chips are popular choices, and the children's menu includes standard favourites. The decor complements the hearty menu with its warm tones and welcoming atmosphere.

7 Railway Tce; (08) 9527 1777; open Tues–Sat for lunch and dinner, and Sun for breakfast

EMMA'S ON THE BOARDWALK
$$$$ MODERN AUSTRALIAN

With bay views from every table and a menu to rival any cosmopolitan restaurant, Emma's on the Boardwalk is deserving of its many awards. The grilled rock lobster is the signature dish, although the adventurous won't be able to resist kangaroo or crocodile. The wine list includes many outstanding Western Australian wines and the set menus will satisfy the indecisive.

Shop 7–8, 1–3 Railway Tce; (08) 9592 8881; open Wed –Sun for lunch and dinner; www.emmasontheboardwalk.com.au

SUNSETS CAFE BISTRO
$$$ MODERN AUSTRALIAN

As the name suggests, vibrant sunsets and ocean views make this bayside bistro popular. Blackboard specials include fresh delicacies such as duck and seafood. Whether meeting for a social gathering or a family meal, a booking is recommended.

The Boardwalk, Palm Beach; (08) 9528 1910; open daily for breakfast, lunch and dinner; www.sunsets.com.au

FAMILY FRIENDLY LICENSED OUTDOOR DINING VEGETARIAN OPTIONS

Y2K CAFE & RESTAURANT $$$
MODERN AUSTRALIAN

Tastefully decorated with modern decor and wooden floors, the Y2K Cafe & Restaurant offers views of the adjacent parklands and the waters of the Cockburn Sound. Famous for cooked breakfasts, head chef, Ralph Rains, serves quality food in relaxed surroundings. Naturally, the alfresco area is ideal during the warmer months.

57B Rockingham Beach Rd; (08) 9529 1044; open daily for breakfast, lunch and dinner

Roebourne

MOBY'S KITCHEN $
SEAFOOD

Rumoured to be offering the best fish and chips in the state, Moby's Kitchen overlooks the Indian Ocean, where it's quite likely some of the stars on the menu recently swam past. If seafood isn't part of your diet then steak and hamburgers are also on offer. What could be more relaxing than watching the sun set into the horizon while feasting on seafood caught from the ocean that day?

Bartley Crt, Point Samson; (08) 9187 1435; open daily for lunch and dinner

TATA'S RESTAURANT $$$
INTERNATIONAL

In the Point Samson Resort, diners at TaTa's Cafe chill out in typically leisurely Western Australian fashion. Offering an à la carte menu, the cafe serves international cuisine including hearty steaks and a sensational platter featuring seafood freshly caught that morning.

Point Samson Resort, 56 Samson Rd, Point Samson; (08) 9187 1052; open daily for dinner; www.pointsamson.com/tatas

TRAWLERS TAVERN $$
INTERNATIONAL

Situated on the first floor and offering never-ending views of the Indian Ocean, Trawlers Tavern is a popular weekend spot with its live entertainment. The menu includes bar snacks or more substantial meals such as fresh seafood.

Roebourne Port Samson Rd; (08) 9187 1503; open daily for dinner

RED ROCK CAFE $$
INTERNATIONAL

In the shire of Roebourne, the Red Rock Cafe caters to Wickham's lively mining community. The menu offers steak, pizza and the seafood the region is so well known for.

Mulga Way, Wickham; (08) 9187 1303; open daily for dinner

Rottnest Island

GEORDIE BAY CAFE $
CAFE

For a low-key dining experience – and let's face it, relaxing is what Rottnest Island is all about – the Geordie Bay Cafe serves light meals and great fish and chips. With views of Geordie Bay and its moored luxury vessels, the cafe is a great place to soak up the atmosphere.

Geordie Bay Rd; (08) 9292 5251; open daily for breakfast, lunch and dinner

MARLINS $$$
SEAFOOD

The island's premier restaurant serves a seafood-inspired menu, including crayfish when it's in season during summer. Situated in the

Rottnest Lodge, which started out as a colonial barracks and prison over 150 years ago, the complex still retains its rustic charm. For a romantic atmosphere, dine outside by the pool.

Rottnest Lodge, Kitson St, Thomson Bay; (08) 9292 5161; open daily for lunch and dinner

ROTTNEST BAKERY $
BAKERY CAFE

Indulging at the Rottnest Bakery has become a ritual for most visitors to the island. The smell of baked goods fills the air and it is almost impossible to resist sampling some of their famous bread, pies and rows of pastries. Recently refurbished, you can dine in or take your selections away and enjoy them by the beach.

Maley St, Settlement Mall, Thomson Bay; (08) 9292 5023; open daily for breakfast and lunch

ROTTNEST TEAROOMS BAR AND CAFE $$
CAFE

With views of the harbour, the Perth city skyline and beyond, and not to mention the Indian Ocean just metres away, it is no wonder this spot is busy year-round. In winter the meals are hearty, while in summer feasting on seafood out on the wooden deck epitomises the spirit of Rottnest Island.

Main Settlement; (08) 9292 5171; open daily for breakfast, lunch and dinner

Southern Cross

CLUB HOTEL $$
INTERNATIONAL

Southern Cross hovers between the border of the wheat belt and the Eastern Goldfields, giving the town a mix of wheat-belt and goldmining clientele. The Club Hotel is located on the main street of town and serves lunch and dinner. The hotel also has budget accommodation.

21 Antares St; (08) 9049 1202; open daily for lunch and dinner

PALACE HOTEL $$
INTERNATIONAL

Regally holding court over the main street of town, the Palace Hotel provides a glimpse of the town's former gold-rush glory. The hotel serves counter meals and offers accommodation upstairs.

Great Eastern Hwy; (08) 9049 1555; open daily for dinner

SOUTHERN CROSS MOTEL $$$
INTERNATIONAL

With its prime corner location in the northern part of town, the Southern Cross Motel is a good example of Federation architecture from the turn of the last century. The restaurant is fully licensed and caters well to visitors and locals. Accommodation is available upstairs and the playground makes this a popular spot for families.

Canopus St; (08) 9049 1144; open daily for breakfast and dinner

Tom Price

TOM PRICE HOTEL MOTEL $$$
INTERNATIONAL

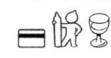

Known as a place of extremes, Tom Price is located 747 metres above sea level, making it the highest town in the state. Despite its remoteness, it's a town with modern facilities,

FAMILY FRIENDLY   LICENSED   OUTDOOR DINING   VEGETARIAN OPTIONS

including this bistro at the Tom Price Hotel Motel. The Sunday-night carvery is very popular and the children's menu is a hit with families.

Central Rd; (08) 9189 1101; open daily for breakfast, lunch and dinner

Toodyay

COLA CAFE AND MUSEUM $
CAFE

The themed Cola Cafe and Museum is a 1950s-style cafe offering an all-day menu. Located in the heart of town, diners sit on the terrace while enjoying a hearty breakfast, lunch or morning or afternoon tea. The museum features Cola memorabilia collected over 45 years, with over 6000 items on display.

128 Stirling Tce; (08) 9574 4407; open daily for breakfast and lunch; www.colacafe.com.au

VICTORIA HOTEL $$
INTERNATIONAL

Situated in the historic Victoria Hotel and built in 1888, the Vicarandah Room serves hearty meals and country hospitality. Located in the heart of town, patrons watch passers-by until they join in with the meandering to explore the charming town of Toodyay.

116 Stirling Tce; (08) 9574 2206; open daily for lunch and dinner

Wagin

THE PALACE HOTEL $$
INTERNATIONAL

Recently renovated, the Palace Hotel serves its faithful patrons seven days a week. The beer garden is a favourite spot, especially with those with little ones bursting with energy. The children's menu draws a family crowd and the pub is a relaxed place to enjoy one of the beers on tap or a coffee.

51 Tudhoe St; (08) 9861 1003; open daily for lunch and dinner

Walpole

THE NORNALUP TEAHOUSE RESTAURANT $$$
MODERN AUSTRALIAN

Situated in the heart of the Nornalup Valley and moments from the Valley of the Giants Tree Top Walk, the Nornalup Teahouse Restaurant serves a range of light to substantial meals. The menu features fresh seasonal produce like marron, scallops, scotch fillet, lamb and rabbit, plus there's a children's menu. The wine list includes many outstanding drops from the region as well some rarer varieties and a range of Bridgetown ciders.

6684 South Coast Hwy, Nornalup; (08) 9840 1422; open Wed–Sun for lunch and dinner; www.nornalupteahouse.com.au

THURLBY HERB FARM CAFE $
CAFE

Using ingredients from the farm, the cafe at the Thurlby Herb Farm serves fresh lunches and home-baked cakes for morning or afternoon tea. Visitors can breathe in all that fresh country air in beautiful surroundings while strolling through the herb farm from which they distil essential oils. Handcrafted products, gourmet food and imported gifts are sold in the shop.

Lot 3 Gardiner Rd; (08) 9840 1249; open Mon–Fri for lunch; www.thurlbyherb.com.au

---

BYO AVAILABLE | CREDIT CARDS ACCEPTED | DISABLED ACCESS | DRESS CODE APPLIES

TREE TOP RESTAURANT $$$
MODERN AUSTRALIAN

The Tree Top Restaurant is one of the few places in Walpole open for dinner, however that's not the only reason to dine here. Elegantly decorated, the restaurant isn't the usual run-of-the-mill bistro that you might find in a motel. Drawing on the region's local produce, the meals served here are fresh, well presented and mostly importantly of all, tasty.

Tree Top Walk Motel, Nockolds St; (08) 9840 1444; open daily for dinner; www.treetopwalkmotel.com.au

SLOW FOOD CAFE $$$
VINEYARD RESTAURANT

Situated between Denmark and Walpole, and nestled on the banks of the Kent River, the cafe at the Old Kent River Wines embraces the slow food movement. The cafe serves a hearty menu that takes pride in using fresh local produce, with ingredients like marron and lamb featuring regularly. The atmosphere is rustic and friendly, and the experience is incomplete without a visit to the boutique winery.

Old Kent River Wines, Kent River, South Coast Hwy; (08) 9855 1589; open daily for lunch; www.oldkentriver.com.au

Wickepin

WICKEPIN HOTEL $
INTERNATIONAL

The small wheat-belt town of Wickepin is most famous for the Albert Facey Homestead, which celebrates the life of the author and his best-selling novel, *A Fortunate Life*. The Wickepin Hotel serves light lunches and counter meals in its dining room every night and offers comfortable accommodation.

34 Wogolin Rd; (08) 9888 1192; open daily for lunch and dinner

Wyndham

WYNDHAM TOWN HOTEL $
INTERNATIONAL

Western Australia's most northern town, Wyndham is home to the saltwater crocodile, the Kimberley Prison Tree (a boab tree used as a holding cell) and some of the state's most magnificent scenery. The Wyndham Town Hotel is the best place in town for a meal and more importantly for a cold drink in this extreme corner of Western Australia.

O'Donnell St; (08) 9161 1003; open daily for lunch and dinner

Yallingup

AMBERLEY RESTAURANT $$$
VINEYARD RESTAURANT

Nestled in stunning scenery overlooking the Amberley Estate vineyard, this winery restaurant's modern Australian dishes are served according to the seasons. After an obligatory tasting of Amberley's exceptional wines, you could start with ham hock and foie gras terrine, then move onto the venison cutlets with spring vegetables, and end with a hot chocolate and orange fondant.

Amberley Estate, cnr Thornton and Wildwood rds; (08) 9750 1112; open daily for lunch and Sat for dinner

---

FAMILY FRIENDLY   LICENSED   OUTDOOR DINING   VEGETARIAN OPTIONS

LAKESIDE DINING, CAPE LODGE, YALLINGUP

CAPE LODGE RESTAURANT $$$$$
MODERN AUSTRALIAN

There's so much to rave about at Cape Lodge and the restaurant is no exception. It was voted among the Top Ten in the World for Food in *Condé Nast Traveller's* Gold List in 2008. As one would expect from the winner of such a prestigious award, the menu changes daily and the wine list includes 150 premium and vintage wines. There is also the opportunity to learn from executive chef, Tony Howell, by attending one of his cooking classes. Bookings are essential, if only to brag that you've experienced the sublime.

3341 Caves Rd; (08) 9755 6311; opening times vary according to the seasons; www.capelodge.com.au

CAVES HOUSE HOTEL $$$$
INTERNATIONAL

In the lovely heritage-listed complex that comprises Seashells Resort, Yallingup, diners thrive on the local produce brought to their table. The lovely dining room captures all the charm of the era and during the warmer months patrons relax on the timber decking overlooking the gardens.

Yallingup Beach Rd; (08) 9750 1500; open daily for lunch and dinner; www.caveshousehotel.com.au

FLUTES RESTAURANT $$$$$
MODERN AUSTRALIAN

After meandering through fairytale gardens to reach Flutes Restaurant, patrons are instantly charmed before surrendering themselves to chef Francois Morvan, who consistently delivers innovative creations to the table. The menu has a distinct Asian influence, like the char sui duck. There are also classic favourites like Butterfield beef fillet and braised cheek with potato mash and truffled butter, and Flutes' signature trio of Pemberton marron, Tasmanian salmon and wild Kimberley barramundi. Any dietary requirements will be met and on-site is the Brookland Valley winery, accommodation and an up-market giftshop.

Brookland Valley Winery, Caves Rd, Wilyabrup; (08) 9755 6250; open daily for lunch, and dinner by request; www.flutes.com.au

LAMONT'S MARGARET RIVER $$$$
MODERN AUSTRALIAN

Renowned cook Kate Lamont is a household name in Western Australian kitchens. Her restaurant in Yallingup overlooks a lake, invoking a sense of tranquillity, and her ever-changing menu is custom-made to suit this spectacular culinary area. The signature dish of Pemberton marron, however, is a constant. Kate Lamont's cooking classes are also a huge hit and regularly booked out.

Gunyulgup Valley Dr; (08) 9755 2434; open daily for lunch and Sat for dinner; www.lamonts.com.au

BYO AVAILABLE   CREDIT CARDS ACCEPTED   DISABLED ACCESS   DRESS CODE APPLIES

Yanchep

BLUE DOLPHIN RESTAURANT $$
INTERNATIONAL

Overlooking the Two Rocks Marina and the magnificent coast, the Blue Dolphin Restaurant serves a varied menu, including crayfish when in season. It's a relaxed place to relax with friends and family.

Two Rocks Shopping Centre, Two Rocks; (08) 9561 1469; open daily for lunch and dinner

CHOCOLATE DROPS $
CAFE

Specialising in quality handmade chocolates, Chocolate Drops sells its produce on-site but can also customise goodies to your specifications. Since the shop and tearooms are situated in the Yanchep National Park, it is only fitting that many of the chocolates come in shapes inspired by the resident wildlife. The quaint tearooms serve light country-style meals and have a good selection of teas, coffees and hot chocolate.

Yanchep National Park, Wanneroo Rd; (08) 9561 6699; open daily for lunch; www.chocolatedrops.com.au

LINDSAY'S RESTAURANT $$$
INTERNATIONAL

Club Capricorn's light and airy, contemporary-styled restaurant serves buffet and varied à la carte dishes from an international menu.

Club Capricorn, Two Rocks Rd; (08) 9561 1106; open daily for breakfast, lunch and dinner; www.clubcapricorn.com.au

THE TUDOR MANOR RESTAURANT $$$
INTERNATIONAL

Situated inside the heritage-listed Yanchep Inn, the Tudor Manor Restaurant serves a wide range of international dishes, catering to all tastes. The seafood platters are popular and a large selection of wines and imported beers are available. Wildlife spotting from the beer garden is a regular pastime.

Yanchep Inn, Yanchep National Park; (08) 9561 1001; open daily for breakfast, lunch and dinner; www.yanchepinn.com.au

York

CAFE BUGATTI $
ITALIAN

A local favourite for many years, Cafe Bugatti has a relaxed, informal atmosphere, with automobile memorabilia adding a fun element to the dining experience. Italian chef and owner, Nick Russo, delivers generous Italian fare to his lunchtime crowd. Many of his regular customers can be found relaxing at a sidewalk table or by the fire during the cooler months.

104 Avon Tce; (08) 9641 1583; open Wed–Mon for breakfast and lunch; www.yorkwa.com.au/Bugatti/home.htm

CASTLE HOTEL YORK $
INTERNATIONAL

The Castle Hotel York serves unpretentious pub fare in grand surroundings in one of the state's oldest hotels. With a choice of bar snacks and dishes from the à la carte menu, your meal can be enjoyed in the restaurant, at the bar

---

FAMILY FRIENDLY   LICENSED   OUTDOOR DINING   VEGETARIAN OPTIONS

area or in the courtyard, and the wood-fired pizza is a crowd pleaser. The hotel also has accommodation, a drive-through bottle shop and function rooms available for hire.

95–97 Avon Tce; (08) 9641 1007; open daily for lunch and dinner; www.castlehotel.com.au

RESTAURANT EBORACUM

$$$
INTERNATIONAL

Situated in the elegant Imperial Hotel in the heart of the charming town of York, Restaurant Eboracum is the finest dining option in town. Throughout the year the hotel hosts many promotions, including High Tea, book club meetings and themed cuisine nights. Upstairs luxurious suites await, and accommodation and dinner packages are available.

Imperial Hotel York, 83 Avon Tce; (08) 9641 1255; open Wed–Sun for lunch and dinner

YORK MILL BAKEHOUSE

$$
CAFE

Situated in an old flour mill, the bakehouse shares the premises with the York Mill Gallery. Inside are several cosy rooms, and the outdoor area is also very popular. The hearty meals are well prepared, and eating among the innovative artworks makes the experience all the more unique.

7–13 Broome St; (08) 9641 2447; open daily for breakfast and lunch, and Fri–Sat for dinner

AERIAL VIEW OF HOLIDAY INN BURSWOOD, PERTH

WHERE TO STAY A–Z

western australia

Town entries are ordered alphabetically, with places nearby listed at the end.

LEGEND
- $ = under $100
- $$ = $100–$150
- $$$ = $150–$200
- $$$$ = $200–$300
- $$$$$ = over $300

For low-season rack rate

- BREAKFAST INCLUDED
- CREDIT CARDS ACCEPTED
- FAMILY FRIENDLY
- FITNESS CENTRE
- ROOM SERVICE
- SWIMMING POOL

Perth

BROADWATER HOTEL & RESORT $$$$
Map ref. 6 D4

Just a few minutes out of the CBD, the Broadwater Hotel offers apartments catering to couples, groups, families and business people. The complex overlooks the Swan River and is close to public transport, the river foreshore, the Perth zoo and shops. There are one-, two- and three-bedroom apartments available, many with balconies overlooking the river. All are self-contained and stylishly decorated. On-site are tennis courts, bike hire, parking and a licensed restaurant.

137 Melville Pde, Como; (08) 9474 4222 or 1800 644 414; www.broadwaters.com.au

DURHAM LODGE B&B $$$$
Map ref. p. 7 E3

A few minutes from the centre of town, the Durham Lodge Bed & Breakfast is a purpose-built B&B with three stylish guest rooms, all with orthopaedic beds and ensuites and two with spas. Tourist information is available from your hosts, and the guest lounge features a cosy fireplace.

165 Shepperton Rd, Victoria Park; (08) 9361 8000; www.durhamlodge.com

GOODEARTH HOTEL PERTH $$
Map ref. p. 12

The Goodearth Hotel Perth offers well-priced accommodation in the heart of town. There are a variety of options available, including hotel rooms, self-contained apartments and multi-share rooms. There's also 24-hour reception, complimentary parking, grocery delivery service and internet access. Also, the use of shower facilities for guests arriving before or after check-in is a welcoming touch and is just one reason why this hotel has won so many awards.

195 Adelaide Tce; (08) 9492 7777;
www.goodearthhotel.com.au

HOLIDAY INN BURSWOOD $$$$
Map ref. 7 E3

Situated within the Burswood Entertainment Complex and all of its attractions, including the 24-hour casino, the affordable accommodation here is well appointed and interconnecting rooms are available. The CBD and airport are conveniently close by. Once you wander downstairs you will see the shores of the Swan River with the city as a backdrop.

Cnr Bolton Ave and Great Eastern Hwy, Burswood; (08) 9362 8888 or 1800 007 697; www.burswood.com.au

HOTEL NORTHBRIDGE $$$
Map ref. p. 6 D2

Built in 1912 and just across the railway line from the CBD, the boutique Hotel Northbridge is located in one of Perth's restaurant and entertainment districts. Each room includes a spa bath and the spacious penthouse suites include two bedrooms and are self-contained, including dining facilities for up to six guests. Reception is open 24 hours and the on-site 210 Restaurant & Cocktail Bar serves international cuisine for breakfast, lunch and dinner.

210 Lake St, Northbridge; (08) 9328 5254;
www.hotelnorthbridge.com.au

INTERCONTINENTAL PERTH BURSWOOD $$$$$
Map ref. p. 7 E3

With Perth's 24-hour casino, a world-class golf course, bars and several restaurants on your doorstep, sleeping may not be your first choice when visiting 'The Burswood', as the locals call it. Despite the ongoing excitement downstairs, the stylish rooms each with a king-sized bath and included valet parking, exude a feeling of tranquillity. There are a range of rooms and suites available, depending on your taste and budget. And, if you're after a bit of pampering, the day spa is one of the best in town.

Bolton Ave and Great Eastern Hwy, Burswood; (08) 9362 8888; www.ichotelsgroup.com/intercontinental/en/gb/reservations

MEDINA APARTMENTS $$$$
Map ref. p. 8

The Medina Apartments are situated in two locations in the Perth CBD. The Medina Grand and Medina Executive Barrack Plaza both offer studio, one and two-bedroom apartments, which are self-contained and have internet access. All apartments are modern and well appointed, and specialise in conference facilities. The CBD location ensures you have everything you could ever need on hand.

33 Mounts Bay Rd and 138 Barrack St;
1300 633 462; www.medina.com.au

MONT CLARE BOUTIQUE APARTMENTS $$$
Map ref. p. 12

Situated in cosmopolitan East Perth and just a few minutes' walk away from the city centre, these apartments are well appointed and offer a living room, a separate kitchen, private bathroom/laundry and one, two or three bedrooms. Free parking is included, and

BREAKFAST INCLUDED   CREDIT CARDS ACCEPTED   FAMILY FRIENDLY

the complex is secured and only accessible to guests.

190 Hay St, East Perth; (08) 9224 4300; www.montclareapartments.com

NEW ESPLANADE HOTEL PERTH $$$
Map ref. p. 8

Just a two-minute walk into the centre of town and situated on the Perth foreshore, the New Esplanade Hotel Perth has a choice of rooms with sensational river views. The deluxe rooms on floors seven and eight include a kitchenette and all rooms have private bathrooms and internet access.

18 The Esplanade; (08) 9325 2000; www.newesplanade.com.au

PARMELIA HILTON $$$$$
Map ref. p. 8

The Parmelia Hilton has an understated elegance and a range of guest rooms, from standard hotel rooms to swanky deluxe suites with separate dining and living areas. Downstairs are several dining and drinking options, including the Globe Bar and Restaurant, which serves excellent food. The fresh seafood is highly recommended.

14 Mill St; (08) 9215 2000; www1.hilton.com

PENSION OF PERTH $$
Map ref. p. 6 D2

Built in 1897, the Pension of Perth is a B&B in a historic home overlooking the lovely Hyde Park. All four of the guest rooms have ensuites and feature polished floorboards, high ceilings and open fireplaces. Every room is unique and decorated to suit the opulent era. This romantic B&B really is excellent value for money, as it includes a swimming pool, internet access, free off-street parking, touchpad keyless entry for late arrivals, and personal services like a visiting masseur or personal trainer can be arranged.

3 Throssell St; (08) 9228 9049; www.pensionperth.com.au

HYATT REGENCY PERTH $$$
Map ref. p. 12

Situated on the east side of town, the Perth Regency Hyatt has commanding views over the Swan River and beyond. Offering standard hotel rooms right up to the presidential suite with its own butler, all rooms are spacious and well appointed. There are several packages available; Romance, Relaxation, Bed & Breakfast and Local Discovery. The Hyatt has several outstanding eateries, excellent business services and function facilities.

99 Adelaide Tce; (08) 9225 1234; www.perth.regency.hyatt.com

QUEST ON JAMES $$$$
Map ref. p. 11

In the quieter end of Northbridge and slightly away from its bustling nightlife, the Quest Apartments offer a choice of one-, two or three-bedroom, fully self-contained apartments. The secured complex includes a swimming pool, spa and barbecue facilities, which are ideal for entertaining. Undercover secured parking and a restaurant delivery service are available.

228 James St, Northbridge; (08) 9227 2888; www.onjames.property.questwa.com.au

THE MELBOURNE $$
Map ref. p. 8

Built in the last century, The Melbourne has been lovingly restored into the boutique hotel it is today. All the rooms have private ensuites, some have balconies overlooking bustling Hay St and an apartment is also available.

FITNESS CENTRE   ROOM SERVICE   SWIMMING POOL

Downstairs is the elegant Melbourne Restaurant or the casual M Cafe, and on your doorstep are a plethora of dining options, shops, cinemas and theatres. The Swan River and Kings Park can be reached on foot in just a few minutes.

942 Hay St; (08) 9320 3333;
www.melbournehotel.com.au

THE OLD SWAN BARRACKS $
Map ref. p. 11

The Swan Barracks were built in 1896 and are one of the oldest buildings in Northbridge, one of Perth's premier entertainment districts. In January 2008 they were converted into budget accommodation and are close to nightlife and the CBD. The rooms are comfortable, clean and secure and there is a choice of shared dormitories or single, double and twin rooms, with female-only rooms also available. There is a 24-hour reception desk, lounge, dining and cooking areas, and computers with internet access. Cable TV, clean linen and breakfast are included in the rate.

2–8 Francis St, Northbridge; (08) 9428 0000;
www.theoldswanbarracks.com

LUXURY ROOM, THE OUTRAM, PERTH

THE OUTRAM $$$$$
Map ref. 6 C3

Known as one of Perth's most stylish places to stay, The Outram is situated in the city's elite West Perth district, close to eateries and boutiques. There are a range of rooms and apartments to choose from, and all rooms come with king-sized beds, LCD TVs and spa baths. The two-bedroom apartments include kitchens, suiting travellers who are lucky enough to stay a little longer.

32 Outram St; (08) 9322 4888;
www.wyndhamvacationresorts.com.au

THE RICHARDSON $$$$$
Map ref. 6 C3

Situated in the leafy suburb of West Perth, The Richardson is well positioned for the CBD, chic Subiaco and the bustling nightlife of Northbridge. The boutique hotel offers standard rooms, suites and penthouses and all are beautifully appointed and feature internet access, coffee machines, flat-screen TVs and balconies with views. The hotel includes one of Perth's best restaurants, Opus Restaurant, a day spa and a business centre.

32 Richardson St; (08) 9217 8888;
www.therichardson.com.au

PERTH CITY YHA $
Map ref. p. 8

It's no surprise this hostel won the Western Australia Tourism award for Best Backpacker Accommodation for 2008. Housed inside an Art Deco building right in the centre of the CBD, the hostel has been recently renovated. Facilities include those you'd find in a five-star resort, such as a swimming pool, library, well-equipped kitchen, travel desk, internet access, 24-hour reception and a funky cafe. The rooms are well appointed, with ensuite, family and shared rooms available.

BREAKFAST INCLUDED   CREDIT CARDS ACCEPTED   FAMILY FRIENDLY

300 Wellington St; (08) 9287 3333;
www.yha.com.au/hostels/wa/perth-city

MINDARIE MARINA $$$

Located about 30 minutes north of the city, the Mindarie Marina is perched on the edge of the Indian Ocean and offers restaurants, accommodation and a marina. Regardless of whether you book a one- or two-bedroom suite or the self-contained villa, a balcony with ocean and marina views is guaranteed.

Ocean Falls Blvd, Mindarie; (08) 9305 9305; www.mindariemarina.com.au

STARSAND LUXURY YACHT CHARTERS $$$$$

Spend the night aboard a 65-foot luxury ketch, where all you have to do is concentrate on having fun and relaxing. Accommodating ten people, there is a choice of double and single bunks, although sleeping on the deck under the stars is a popular option. The yacht departs from Fremantle and spends the night moored at Rottnest Island where the waters and island are at your disposal. All your meals are included and cruises up north are also available.

6 Brown St, East Perth; (08) 9316 3591; www.starsand.com.au

Fremantle

ESPLANADE HOTEL $$$
Map ref. p. 20

Situated in the historic town centre and opposite the harbour, the Esplanade Hotel is ideally located to enjoy the many cultural activities Fremantle has to offer. The impressive heritage building oozes all the charm of times past and has over 300 rooms and suites available. The rooms are elegantly appointed, and some offer a balcony and harbour views.

Cnr Marine Tce and Essex St; (08) 9432 4000; www.esplanadehotelfremantle.com.au

HERITAGE COTTAGE BED & BREAKFAST $$$

Located within walking distance to the beach and the heart of town, the Heritage Cottage Bed & Breakfast dates back to 1880 and is an adult-only retreat. Recently refurbished, the rooms include many of the features of this charming era, including high decorative ceilings, floorboards and open fireplaces, as well as the convenience of private bathrooms. Breakfast is served in the dining room or the courtyard, weather permitting.

273 South Tce, South Fremantle; (08) 9433 5946; www.fremantlebedandbreakfast.com.au

JILBA $$$
Map ref. p. 20

Jilba is a contemporary two-storey apartment with glass bi-fold doors opening onto a courtyard with quintessential limestone walls. Located in the west side of the town, just slightly away from the bustle, the apartment is still only metres away from all the action and is close to the train, cinema and restaurants.

Unit D, 49A, Pakenham St; (08) 9335 4623; www.fremantlewa.com.au/accom

LITTLE LEFROY STUDIO WAREHOUSE $$$

Encapsulating Fremantle's bohemian essence, the quirky Little Lefroy Studio Warehouse is located in the midst of all the action. The fully self-contained studio warehouse is warmly decorated with handcrafted materials and has a downstairs open-plan living area that leads to a courtyard ideal for chilling out. The couch opens out into a futon bed and upstairs is a spacious mezzanine bedroom and ensuite.

18 Little Lefroy La, South Fremantle; (08) 9848 3058

NEWPORT HOUSE $$$

With balcony views of the ocean and Rottnest Island, this three-storey home caters well to the discerning traveller. Featuring four bedrooms and two bathrooms, it is luxuriously appointed with a Tasmanian oak kitchen, good-quality appliances, a spa bath and off-street parking. The living area opens out onto the balcony and the ground floor patio includes a barbecue and outdoor setting. Town is just a short drive or leisurely stroll away.

4 Trafford St, Beaconsfield; (08) 9431 7878

OCEANIC APARTMENT $$$
Map ref. p. 20

Built in 1898, the Oceanic Hotel has recently been converted into the Oceanic Apartment. The decor is contemporary in style, but there are touches like the stained glass windows that pay homage to the era in which it was originally built. If you can tear yourself away from the sumptuous kitchen and flat-screen TV with cable, then explore the shops, eateries, harbour, markets and beach, which are on the doorstep of this centrally situated apartment. The apartment has three bedrooms and two bathrooms, a secluded private courtyard and private parking.

3/8 Collie St; 0423 099 030; www.oceanicapartment.com.au

PIER 21 APARTMENT HOTEL $$$$
Map ref. 6 A5

The Pier 21 Apartment Hotel is perched on the banks of the Swan River in an executive apartment block just a few minutes north of Fremantle. Choose from studio, or one- and two-bedroom apartments, all of which have balconies and most with river views. Tennis and squash courts are on-site, and cycling and walking trials meander around the complex and river.

7–9 John St, North Fremantle; (08) 9336 2555; www.pier21.com.au

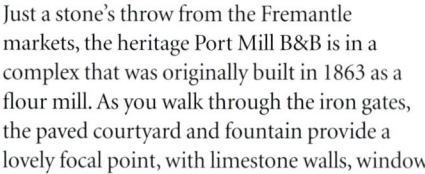

PORT MILL B&B $$$$
Map ref. p. 20

Just a stone's throw from the Fremantle markets, the heritage Port Mill B&B is in a complex that was originally built in 1863 as a flour mill. As you walk through the iron gates, the paved courtyard and fountain provide a lovely focal point, with limestone walls, window boxes overflowing with flowers and charming Juliette balconies. Located over several floors, each room has its own ensuite and balcony, and some rooms have views. There is also a self-contained apartment in the complex.

3/17 Essex St; (08) 9433 3832

Albany

FORESHORE APARTMENTS $$
Map ref. p. 52

In Albany's historic precinct and located on the first floor, the Foreshore Apartments enjoy lovely town and harbour views. Both one-bedroom apartments, Rembrandt and Vermeer, are fully self-contained and elegantly furnished, featuring high ceilings and fireplaces. If cooking in the fully equipped kitchen seems a chore, several metres away are local bars and restaurants. And for the indulgent, a delicious cooked breakfast can be delivered to your doorstep.

81–89 Proudlove Pde; (08) 9841 1506; www.foreshoreapartments.com.au

MIDDLETON BEACH HOLIDAY PARK $$
Map ref. p. 53

Adjacent to Middleton Beach and offering 500 metres of beach frontage, Middleton Beach Holiday Park is ideal for families. With the option of camping, caravan sites and one or two-bedroom chalets and cabins, guests can enjoy the park's facilities regardless of their budget. The kids will love the games room, playground, swimming pool and school holidays kids club. With restaurants and cafes in the area, you have the option of dining out or using the cooking facilities. At the end of the day, parents can relax in their chalet spas.

28 Flinders Pde; (08) 9841 3593 or 1800 644 674; www.holidayalbany.com.au

OLD SURREY $$$$
Map ref. p. 52

Built in 1841, this old-world manor is only a short stroll away from town or the beach. With its original stone construction, exposed beams and open fire, the Old Surrey retains its cosy charm. The whole family will have plenty of room to relax in the fully self-contained house, which includes four bedrooms and two bathrooms. Beautiful furnishings and the lovely hillside garden ensure a memorable stay.

55–59 Burt St, Mt Clarence; 0413 015 145; www.thepriory.com.au

THE PRIORY $$$$
Map ref. p. 52

Built in 1876, The Priory is adorned with antiques and artworks from the Victorian era. Each of the eight rooms includes private bathrooms and plush soft furnishings to complement the elegant fixtures and fittings. The boutique B&B is near to the town centre, a golf course, a national park and beaches. The mansion is ideal for couples seeking romance or groups looking to explore the region.

55–59 Burt St, Mt Clarence; 0413 015 145; www.thepriory.com.au

THE ROCKS ALBANY $$$$$
Map ref. p. 52

Built in 1882 and overlooking Albany's Princess Royal Harbour, The Rocks was once the governor's residence before becoming a home for returning soldiers in 1915. Several years later it had a variety of uses, including a maternity hospital, school, medical centre and hostel. Extensive renovations have returned this lovely building to its former glory. Each of the 12 guest rooms are unique, some offering harbour views and with romantic four-poster beds. Guests can wander through the cottage gardens or stroll into town.

182–188 Grey St West; (08) 9842 5969; www.therocksalbany.com.au

CAPE HOWE COTTAGES $$$

Cape Howe Cottages are nestled in a private retreat that's officially registered as Land for Wildlife by the Department of Conservation and Land Management. Spread over two adjacent 23-hectare bush properties, maximum privacy is ensured. Each of the cottages is self-contained and there are a range of options available for couples, families or friends. To make your stay special, ceremonies including weddings can be arranged, as can customised packages. Winner of countless tourism awards, Cape Howe Cottages guarantees a memorable stay.

322 Tennessee Rd South, Lowlands Beach; (08) 9845 1295; www.capehowe.com.au

THE LILY DUTCH WINDMILL $$

For a unique stay, The Lily Dutch Windmill is the only operational flour-producing windmill in Australia. Approximately 94 kilometres north of Albany and with views of the Stirling Range, the Lily is an ideal base to explore the region. All accommodation is self-contained, with a choice of The Winery Quarters, The Millers Quarters, The Dutch Cottage and The Dutch House. All options include an outside seating area, a Scandinavian wood heater, gas barbecue, laundry and mobile phone reception. The wholemeal stone-ground Spelt flour produced from the mill is used for the restaurant, which is housed in the 1924 Gnowangerup Railway Station. Also on-site is a private airfield and flying training facilities.

9793 Chester Pass Rd, Amelup; (08) 9827 9205 or 1800 980 002; www.thelily.com.au

STIRLING RANGE RETREAT $$

Fresh mountain air and views of Bluff Knoll are just the beginning of the ecotourism experience at Stirling Range Retreat, 90 kilometres north of Albany and sharing a boundary with the Stirling Ranges. Year-round walks or eco-tours offer enthusiasts the chance to explore the ranges, wildflowers and springs. The retreat offers a range of accommodation options, from camping to fully-self contained cabins. Regardless of your budget, facilities include a shuttle service for hikers, tourist information and meal packages.

Chester Pass Rd, Borden; (08) 9827 9229; www.stirlingrange.com.au

Augusta

AUGUSTA SHEOAK CHALETS $$

Situated just three kilometres from Augusta, the Sheoak Chalets offer panoramic rural views from the Leeuwin ridge. Karri trees tower above the four chalets that sleep from two to 16 guests. Each of the timber chalets is fully self-contained and Chalet 4 has been specifically designed with disabled customers in mind. The setting is so peaceful that kangaroos and blue wrens often visit in the hope of a free feed.

298 Hillview Rd; 0419 555 072; www.sheoakchalets.com.au

BAYWATCH MANOR $

For the budget conscious, Baywatch Manor makes for a relaxed stay. The modern Federation-style lodge is conveniently close to town and offers views of the Blackwood River, Southern Ocean and national parks. The lodge can house up to 36 guests and has a range of room options, including some with ensuites. The native gardens and lawns are the perfect place to enjoy a barbecue, and bikes can be hired. Also available for families, couples or small groups are the self-contained cottages situated along the Blackwood River.

9 Heppingstone View (rear of 88 Blackwood Ave); (08) 9758 1290; www.baywatchmanor.com.au

BREAKFAST INCLUDED   CREDIT CARDS ACCEPTED   FAMILY FRIENDLY

BEST WESTERN AUGUSTA GEORGINA MOLLOY MOTEL $$

The Georgina Molloy is centrally located to the region's attractions and a short stroll from Augusta's shops and cafes. Ideal for families, all rooms have cooking facilities, family rooms, interconnecting rooms and disabled facilities. On your doorstep is the Blackwood River en-route to the sea, making this is an ideal place to stay for soaking up the relaxing surroundings.

84 Blackwood Ave; (08) 9758 1255, 1800 180 288; www.georgianamolloy.bestwestern.com.au

BLACKWOOD RIVER HOUSEBOATS $$$$$

For an alternative option, why not test your sea legs and stay aboard a houseboat? An 'A'-class driver's licence is all you need to skipper once you've received your instructions. On board you'll have everything you need, including linen, bedding and a fully equipped kitchen. All you need to bring are your goodies (food, drink etc), clothes, fishing gear, activities, binoculars – and, of course, a camera to capture the wildlife, including dolphins, along the river. A dinghy is included and for a small fee goods can be delivered. There are three different vessels to choose from, depending on the number of guests. Exploring the Blackwood River, you will pass Molloy Island and 20 kilometres of unspoilt national park and if you're lucky you might be able to join a whale-watching tour.

Lot 450, Bussell Hwy, Westbay; (08) 9758 0181; www.blackwoodriverhouseboats.com

BRILEA COTTAGES AND B&B $$

Within a grove of peppermint trees, Brilea is nestled between Augusta and Margaret River. The two cottages, Rose or Lavender, are self-contained and both have two bedrooms, with a wood fire and spa adding a touch of luxury to your stay. The B&B offers a large bedroom with a queen-sized bed and a cooked breakfast is included. Overlooking a vineyard you'll be inspired to explore the region with a bushwalk or caving adventure, and connoisseurs won't be able to resist sampling the world-famous wines.

Bussell Hwy, Karridale; (08) 9758 5001

MOLLOY ISLAND HIDEAWAY $$

Molloy Island Hideaway is a lovely getaway as long as you don't mind the noisy neighbours, which consist of birds, kangaroos, lizards, frogs and possums. Sleeping ten comfortably, humans that is, it also has a separate section with its own entrance which makes it ideal for families or separate groups. With uninterrupted views of the tree canopy and walking trails, guests relish the natural surroundings of this very secluded island, which only homeowners and their guests have the privilege of visiting.

Fairlawn Pl, Molloy Island; 0403 338 813; www.molloyislandhideaway.com.au

Australind

AUSTRALIND TOURIST PARK $

Located on the Leschenault Estuary, the Australind Tourist Park is ideally situated for crabbing, and with Bunbury only seven kilometres away it's close to all amenities. On-site there are powered sites, cabins, vans and a motel. In the shady grounds are barbecue facilities and close by is a Chinese restaurant, tavern and the Bunbury golf course.

Lot 9, Old Coast Rd; (08) 9725 1206;
www.australindtouristpark.com.au

COOK'S PARK ON AUSTRALIND WATERS $$

The estuary location and 10 hectares of rural landscape make Cook's Park a tranquil getaway. With either water or rural views, both bedrooms can be booked as a single unit, making it suitable for families. After waking up to a fully cooked breakfast, guests can explore the grounds, including the original Cook's Cottage. Built in 1862, the cottage is made of mud and thatch and still stands in pre-restoration condition.

474 Cathedral Ave; (08) 9796 0505;
www.cookspark.com

LESCHENAULT INLET CARAVAN PARK $

On-site vans and cabins are situated on the shady sites at the Leschenault Inlet Caravan Park. Powered and unpowered sites are available, as are barbecues and cooking facilities. Pets are welcome. The campsite is only 50 metres to the beach for crabbing and prawning.

Lot 52, Cathedral Ave; (08) 9797 1095

Balingup

BALINGUP HEIGHTS HILLTOP FOREST COTTAGES $$$

Nestled within the forest, Balingup Heights has six timber cottages spread over 35 hectares, guaranteeing peace and privacy. Whether you're staying in the premium three-bedroom cottage, The Frog & Easel, traditional Settlers Cottage (also three bedrooms) set on 2.5 hectares, or in a one or two-bedroom cottage, groups of all sizes and requirements are catered for. All cottages are self-contained, include quality furnishings and linen, have wood fires and are fully insulated to ensure year-round comfort.

65 Nannup Rd; (08) 9764 1283;
www.balingupheights.com.au

BALINGUP JALBROOK COTTAGES & ALPACAS $$$

Whether you're after a romantic liaison or a family getaway, Balingup Jalbrook Cottages caters to all needs. If you're not too busy soaking in the spa with a glass of bubbly, enjoy the services of a masseur or beautician. Children are encouraged to help with farm chores like animal feeding, collecting eggs and fruit picking and if they're really lucky they might get to toast marshmallows by the bonfire in a storytelling or sing-along session. Log fires, crisp bed linen, air-conditioning and a range of movies, music, books and games will ensure a comfortable stay. Jalbrook is also a working alpaca farm and has alpaca products for sale in the Jalbrook Knitwear Gallery.

Lot 1, Jayes Rd; (08) 9764 1616;
www.jalbrook.com.au

BALINGUP ROSE B&B $$

Surrounded by forests and tranquil gardens, Balingup Rose B&B inspires relaxation. The original section of the house was built in 1927 and has all the charm of the era, including open fireplaces, jarrah floorboards and high ceilings. After curling up in front of an open fireplace in winter or chilling out on the verandah with

---

BREAKFAST INCLUDED   CREDIT CARDS ACCEPTED   FAMILY FRIENDLY

a glass of wine, you can stroll into the historic village of Balingup, settled in 1859. That's if you can bear to leave the valley views.

208 Jayes Rd; (08) 9764 1205; www.balinguprose.com.au

Balladonia

BALLADONIA CARAVAN FACILITY $

Boasting a population of less than ten people, you shouldn't have too much trouble finding a place to rest your head in Balladonia. The facility has powered and unpowered sites, dormitory accommodation and motel rooms. On-site is a camp kitchen, cafe, internet access and barbecue facilities.

Eyre Hwy; (08) 9039 3453

Beverley

BEVERLEY B&B $

Given the history of the town, it's only fitting that the Beverley B&B is housed in a heritage cottage. All five rooms are clean and comfortable and all double rooms have ensuites, while single rooms share a bathroom and kitchen. While staying in the town, which is known for the many architectural styles of its buildings, pay a visit to the museums and the lovely Avon River.

131 Forrest St; (08) 9646 0073; www.beverleybb.com

Boyup Brook

SCOTTS BROOK $

Within a tranquil vineyard in the Blackwood Valley, Scotts Brook has two queen bedrooms situated in a separate guest wing of this lovely homestead, with private access and lounge. After your gourmet continental breakfast, take a stroll around the farm and feed the friendly alpacas. Or visit the boutique Scotts Brook vineyard and learn more about winery activities. Of course, you can't leave without sampling the wines and dinner can be ordered by arrangement.

201B Scotts Brook Rd; (08) 9765 3014; www.scottsbrook.com.au

TULIP COTTAGE $

Overlooking the scenic Blackwood River Valley, the beautifully restored Tulip Cottage sleeps up to seven people in four bedrooms. Guests can relax on the verandah and in winter snuggle up by the fire. Just a few kilometres from town and close to the Blackwood River, activities include canoeing, bushwalks, birdwatching and farm visits.

30 Bridge St; (08) 9765 1223; www.tulipcottage.com.au

Bremer Bay

BREMER BAY BEACHES TOURIST RESORT CARAVAN PARK $

Nestled among shady peppermint trees, the Bremer Bay Beaches Tourist Resort Caravan Park is a four-star tourist park. Catering to all

FITNESS CENTRE   ROOM SERVICE   SWIMMING POOL

budgets, the park includes deluxe spa chalets, two bedroom chalets, cabins, ensuite vans, ensuite caravan sites and camping sites. The park includes a camp kitchen, shop, pool, tennis and basketball courts, barbecues and a children's playground. Situated at the western entry to the Fitzgerald National Park biosphere (one of only two in Australia), on your doorstep is flora, fauna and pristine Bremer Bay offering whale-watching, fishing, snorkelling, sand boarding and four-wheel driving.

Wellstead Rd; (08) 9837 4290;
www.bremerbayaccommodation.com

BREMER BAY RESORT $

The azure waters of Bremer Bay are just a two-minute drive or an enjoyable walk from this resort. The well-appointed accommodation includes a romantic Spa Suite with complimentary wine and chocolates and the River View and standard rooms each sleep three people. There is a two-bedroom, fully serviced and self-contained Family Villa that overlooks the inlet. Set in a rammed-earth building with high exposed-timber ceilings, the Mount Barren Restaurant overlooks natural bushland and the magnificent Bremer River.

1 Frantom Way; (08) 9837 4133;
www.bremerbayresort.com.au

QUAALUP HOMESTEAD WILDERNESS RETREAT $

Located 18 kilometres from Bremer Bay by four-wheel drive, the Quaalup Homestead Wilderness Retreat is nestled in the western part of the Fitzgerald River National Park, an ideal spot to see whales, birdlife and wildflowers. A range of basic accommodation options are available, from one-bedroom ensuite units, two-bedroom chalets, three-bedroom cabins, a caravan park and camping grounds. Nearby is the homestead, dating back to 1858, where guests are welcome to relax in the communal lounge room by an open fireplace. Breakfast and dinner can be arranged in advance.

Fitzgerald River National Park; (08) 9837 4124; www.whalesandwildflowers.com.au/quaaluphomestead

Bridgetown

FORD HOUSE RETREAT $$

Built in 1896, the elegantly appointed Ford House Retreat offers romance on the Blackwood River. Spread over four buildings, there's a choice of queen, double and single rooms with self-catering options available. Sweeping views, fresh flowers, open fires, spas, a library and lovely gardens add a special touch to this historic property. On-site is the boutique Tongue & Groove Cafe, open for breakfast and lunch can be arranged by request. Functions are held in the Feasting Barn and massages are available in your room or in the Wendy House overlooking the garden and river.

Eedle Tce; (08) 9761 1816;
www.fordhouse.com

MARANUP FORD $

Maranup Ford has a range of B&B, cottage, cabin, caravan and camping options. The five-bedroom cottage sleeps 12 and is ideal for families or large groups, whereas the one-bedroom cabin sleeps six. The caravan site is powered and has an excellent camp kitchen and ablution block. A Canadian-style canoe is available for hire and breakfast is served in the homestead. Dogs, horses, mountain bikes and a laid-back attitude are welcome.

Maranup Ford Rd; (08) 9761 1200

BREAKFAST INCLUDED   CREDIT CARDS ACCEPTED   FAMILY FRIENDLY

NELSON'S OF BRIDGETOWN $

Regardless of your budget, old-world charm is all part of the service at Nelsons of Bridgetown. Whether you stay in the heritage lodge, opt for a room with cooking facilities or indulge with a spa suite, all rooms are well appointed. The on-site restaurant serves breakfast, lunch and dinner, as well as offering conference and function facilities. Being centrally located, all the attractions of town are close by.

38 Hampton St; (08) 9761 1641 or 1800 635 565; www.nelsonsofbridgetown.com.au

TORTOISESHELL FARM $$$

Just 12 kilometres from town, Tortoiseshell Farm is hidden away in 40 hectares of tranquil forest. The accommodation includes two fully self-contained cottages and a homestead B&B. The cottages have facilities for leashed dogs and evening meals are available by request. Activities on offer include bushwalking, mountain-biking, birdwatching and horse riding (BYO horse and there's plenty of paddock space and trail rides). The owners have spent the past 30 years developing the farm into a sanctuary for people as well as for wildlife. Tortoiseshell Farm also runs a range of workshops throughout the year promoting local businesses and the environment.

Polina Rd; (08) 9761 1089; www.tortoiseshellfarm.com

Broome

CABLE BEACH CLUB RESORT & SPA $$$$
Map ref. p. 58

From humble beginnings as a few beachside bungalows, the Cable Beach Resort has grown into the integral Broome fixture it is today. The resort is situated minutes from the town centre and is across the road from Cable Beach, which many declare to be the most beautiful beach in Western Australia. Featuring corrugated-iron walls and polished wood floors, The Studios are ideal for couples. Designed for families, the Bungalows have open-plan living, kitchens and some have spas. The luxurious Villas include enclosed courtyards and private spas, and for pure indulgence the suites are adorned with original artworks, antiques and exotic artefacts. It's no surprise the Cable Beach Resort is the winner of so many awards as the ultimate tropical getaway.

Cable Beach Rd; 1800 199 099; www.cablebeachclub.com

KIMBERLEY KLUB BROOME $
Map ref. p. 58

In the middle of town and close to all the action, the Kimberley Klub has all the creature comforts in a relaxed and fun environment. Features include a poolside bar/cafe, book exchange, guest kitchen, laundry, games room, barbecues, an ATM and internet facilities. There are a range of air-conditioned dormitories and rooms, some shared and others private and one room is fully self-contained. A free daily bus shuttles to Cable Beach and the tour desk has plenty of local knowledge to enhance your stay.

62 Fredrick St; (08) 9192 3233 or 1800 004 345; www.kimberleyklub.com

MCALPINE HOUSE $$$$
Map ref. p. 58

Surrounded by lush tropical gardens, the beautifully restored McAlpine House boutique hotel was originally a pearler's home built in 1910. Personalised service is offered to each of its nine rooms, which can be booked

FITNESS CENTRE   ROOM SERVICE   SWIMMING POOL

individually or as a whole for a private gathering. All the rooms and suites are unique and have a dedicated lounge or courtyard garden, a bar, restaurant catering, library, barbecue facilities and a Chinese tea house. Also available is the luxurious, five-bedroom Captain Kennedy's House, which sleeps ten and has its own spa and private pool. Included in the tariff are airport transfers, gourmet breakfast and a personal laundry service.

55 Herbert St; (08) 9192 0510 or 1800 746 282;
www.mcalpinehouse.com.au

THE BUNGALOW-BROOME $$

Map ref. p. 58

The Bungalow Broome is a romantic one-bedroom hideaway in Cable Beach's residential area. Surrounded by tropical gardens, the air-conditioned bungalow has private decking where you can enjoy complimentary wine and goodies. Just a ten-minute stroll from pristine Cable Beach, a beach bag is provided with all the essentials such as sun umbrellas and beach towels and hampers can be arranged by your hosts. The stylishly decorated bungalow is separate from the main dwelling and has its own car park and entry.

3 McKenzie Rd; 0417 918 420;
www.thebungalowbroome.com.au

THE COURTHOUSE B&B $$$

Map ref. p. 58

Located in town and designed with family living in mind, the luxurious two-storey, three-bedroom Courthouse B&B offers a choice of indoor and outdoor areas to relax, socialise and work. The hosts' love of travelling and meeting new people inspired them to build the B&B in 2001, its decor embracing Broome's connection to Asia and its rich history. The full cooked breakfast is served by the pool or on the front balcony overlooking the historic courthouse.

10 Stewart St; (08) 9192 2733;
www.thecourthouse.com.au

KOOLJAMAN AT CAPE LEVEQUE $

Kooljaman at Cape Leveque is the epitome of paradise. Located 220 kilometres north of Broome on the Dampier Peninsula, access is only available by four-wheel drive or by air. A scenic flight to your remote beach safari offers magnificent views over the Buccaneer Archipelago and horizontal waterfalls. Once you've arrived, you have a choice of accommodation options from safari tents, cabins, campground units, tents or beach shelters. Some include ensuites, although you won't mind sharing the immaculate ablution block. The fully equipped safari tents are of particular interest as they are built on raised timber decks into the hillside and offer panoramic ocean views. Most of the activities focus around the spectacular bay, including boating, fishing, swimming, snorkelling, self-guided walks, whale-watching and ecological and cultural tours. Meal packages and bush butler services are available.

Cape Leveque; (08) 9192 4970;
www.kooljaman.com.au

Bunbury

ALL SEASONS SANCTUARY GOLF RESORT $$$

For the golfing enthusiast, the All Seasons Sanctuary Golf Resort offers the perfect blend of golfing and luxury just eight minutes from the CBD. All 37 of the apartments are set within

BREAKFAST INCLUDED   CREDIT CARDS ACCEPTED   FAMILY FRIENDLY

landscaped gardens, lakes and fairways. The studio suites have spacious bedrooms and the apartments are self-contained. For those seeking extra space, Villa on 8 overlooks the eighth green just a three-minute walk from the resort and has two bedrooms and two bathrooms. Considered to be the South-West's finest golf course, the Sanctuary Golf Course has 18 challenging holes strategically placed on 64 bunkers and an assortment of artificial lakes.

Cnr Old Coast Rd and Australind Bypass, Pelican Pt; (08) 9725 2777 or 1800 677 309; www.sanctuaryresort.com.au

BOATHOUSE B&B $
Map ref. p. 64

Right in the heart of Bunbury and located on the water's edge, the lovely Boathouse B&B has spectacular views at a ridiculously low price. While you're relaxing on the balcony watching the sunset, you might glimpse some of the dolphins that have based themselves in Bunbury. Those seeking seclusion should book the Jetty View Suite, with its own private balcony and luxurious decor. If you're on a budget you can cook up a feast in the kitchen.

11 Austral Pde; (08) 9721 4140; www.boathouseaccommodationbunbury.com.au

BUNBURY SILO ACCOMMODATION $$$$
Map ref. p. 64

Built for wheat in 1937, the historic grain silos have been transformed into luxury residential apartments. Situated close to the waterfront and Bunbury's tourist precinct, the three-bedroom apartment is fully equipped and well appointed, located within a secure complex overlooking Koombana Bay.

Off Casurina Dr, Marlston Waterfront; 0439 973 285; www.bunburysiloaccommodation.com

QUALITY HOTEL LORD FORREST $$$
Map ref. p. 64

Located among waterways, beaches and forests, guests escape to the country in style at the Lord Forrest Hotel. Offering a range of accommodation options, from standard hotel rooms to two-bedroom suites, the decor is contemporary. Offering cable TV, internet access, a cocktail bar and an à la carte restaurant open for breakfast, lunch and dinner, Bunbury's premier hotel is ideally situated to make the most of the township.

20 Symmons St; (08) 9726 5777 or 1800 097 811; www.lordforresthotel.com.au

Busselton

BEACHLANDS HOLIDAY PARK $

Trendsetting Beachlands Holiday Park is leading the way for holiday parks around the state with its makeover completed in early 2009. The self-contained bungalows, villas and cabins are all well appointed and some include flat-screen TVs and spas. The powered caravan and camping sites have cabling to ensure good TV reception and some of the caravan sites include private ensuites. The facilities include a water playground, heated swimming pool, jumping pillow, camp kitchen, internet access, barbecues and conference facilities.

10 Earnshaw Rd; (08) 9752 2107 or 1800 622 107; www.beachlandsresort.com.au

MANDALAY HOLIDAY RESORT AND TOURIST PARK $

Located between Busselton and Dunsborough in the midst of the Margaret River wine region, the Mandalay resort is directly across the road from the beach. The park is ideal for families and suits a range of budgets, offering camping to two-storey spa villas overlooking the beach and everything in between. Deemed as one of Australia's top tourist parks, the four and a half star facilities include shady sites, a camp kitchen, barbecue facilities, kid's entertainment galore for all ages, laundry facilities, internet access, a shop and bike hire.

Off Bussell Hwy at Lockhart St, Broadwater; (08) 9752 1328 or 1800 248 231; www.mandalayresort.com.au

MARTIN FIELDS BEACH RETREAT $$

Established in 1989 by current owners James and Jane Cummins and located 10 kilometres north of Busselton, the lovely Martin Fields Beach Retreat is as close to the water as the name suggests. All rooms have private ensuites and many have garden, river or ocean views. For a touch of luxury, why not book the three-course dinner, the spa suite or one of the beauty treatments on offer. The retreat can cater for small to medium groups and is also close to the many attractions of the Geographe region.

24 Lockville Rd, Geographe; (08) 9754 2001; www.martinfields.com.au

THE DOLPHIN HOUSE $$$$

Built on the canal, The Dolphin House promises absolute waterfront luxury. With views from every room, this three-bedroom home has all the features you would expect of a premier property: a chef's kitchen with complimentary provisions, a jacuzzi overlooking the sea, fireplace, plasma TV, PlayStation and direct canal access. Fishing enthusiasts will be thrilled at being able to fish and crab, while the kids will be entertained by the beach and parkland at the end of the street. Park your boat at your own private jetty at the end of a hard day of dolphin-watching and boating.

Port Geographe; www.stayz.com.au

Caiguna

JOHN EYRE MOTEL $

After travelling along the lonely highway the John Eyre Motel will seem like the Ritz. Perhaps a slight exaggeration, but the motel rooms are comfortable and the roadhouse is open 24 hours. There is also a caravan park with ablution facilities, a camping ground, licensed cafe and fuel.

Eyre Hwy; (08) 9039 3459

Carnamah

THREE SPRINGS TOURIST LODGE $

Situated halfway between Carnamah and Geraldton, the Three Springs Tourist Lodge offers B&B in tastefully decorated rooms with air-conditioning. Guests have the use of the communal lounge room with satellite TV. The BYO restaurant serves well-priced meals and there are barbecue facilities available for guests' use.

Three Springs; (08) 9954 1065; www.wildflower-bedandbreakfast.com

Carnarvon

CARNARVON CENTRAL APARTMENTS $$
Map ref. p. 68

Offering two bedrooms and all the comforts of home, the Carnarvon Central Apartments make for a relaxing stay. Located close to the centre of town and many of the region's attractions, the ideally located apartments are recently furnished, fully self-contained and include barbecue facilities.

120 Robinson St; (08) 9941 1317; www.carnarvonholidays.com

THE CARNARVON HOTEL $
Map ref. p. 68

Catering to all budgets, The Carnarvon combines motel and backpacker accommodation. Overlooking the waters and stately palms of The Fascine, the bay formed by the southern arm of the Gascoyne River, this is the ideal spot to watch the sunset. Featuring a sports bar and an affordable restaurant that takes advantage of its waterfront location, the hotel also caters for functions for up to 200 people.

121 Olivia Tce; (08) 9941 1181; www.thecarnarvon.com.au

WINTERSUN CARNARVON PARK $

Family owned and operated, the Wintersun Caravan and Tourist Park offers some of the best self-contained accommodation in town. Choose from powered sites, one and two-bedroom ensuite chalets, and grassed and shady caravan and camping sites. The whole family is catered for, with a playground, camper's kitchen, bowling green, internet and book exchange. During the winter months the park has an extensive social calendar, making this the perfect place to settle in and relax.

546 Robinson St; (08) 9941 8150 or 1300 555 585; www.wintersuncaravanpark.com.au

QUOBBA STATION $

Experience a real working station at the Quobba Station, 80 kilometres north-west of Carnarvon. The station has been in the Meecham family for 32 years, and runs around 10 000 sheep. With the harsh and jagged Indian Ocean coastline as its western boundary and Lake McLeod to its east, game fishing is renowned from the challenging rock platforms. The station offers a choice of rustic accommodation options, including chalets, cottages, transportable shacks, shearing quarters, caravans and camping. Also popular is surfing, beachcombing, whale-watching, wildlife in and above the sea, wildflower exploration and station tours.

Gnarloo Rd, 80 km north-west of Carnarvon; (08) 9948 5098; www.quobba.com.au

Cervantes

CERVANTES PINNACLES MOTEL $$$

Just a few kilometres from the ancient Pinnacles, the Cervantes Pinnacles Motel offers a choice of comfortable motel rooms, four family suites and deluxe rooms including a kitchenette. The motel is conveniently close to town.

7 Aragon St; (08) 9652 7145; www.cervantespinnaclesmotel.com.au

FITNESS CENTRE   ROOM SERVICE   SWIMMING POOL

PINNACLES CARAVAN PARK $

With the Pinnacles just a few minutes away, the pristine beachfront Pinnacles Caravan Park is the ideal seaside holiday spot. The self-contained cabins are well appointed and the camp and caravan park has shady and grassed areas, two camp kitchens, three amenities blocks, barbecues and a kids' playground. Fishing enthusiasts will be in for a treat as they can launch their lines from the beach, jetty, groyne or boat.

35 Aragon St; (08) 9652 7060;
www.pinnaclespark.com.au

Cocklebiddy

COCKLEBIDDY WEDGETAIL INN $

The town of Cocklebiddy is known for its sheep and extensive systems of caverns and lakes, which lie several hundred metres beneath the Nullarbor Plain. The Cocklebiddy Wedgetail Inn is not only within 10 kilometres of the caves, it's also a convenient stopover. As well as motel rooms, there is a caravan park, a licensed restaurant and a bar.

Eyre Hwy; (08) 9039 3462

Collie

PEPPERMINT LANE LODGE $$$$

Close to the scenic Ferguson Valley and Bunbury, the lovely Peppermint Lane Lodge has four cosy rooms, each with separate entrance and ensuite. All the water to the rooms is delicious UV-treated filtered rainwater. Wake up to the fresh country air and a hearty breakfast overlooking the dam and river. After a day of discovering the region's wineries, restaurants and galleries, lounge around the pool or soak in the spa and pre-order a delicious dinner. Don't forget to peruse the on-site art gallery or, if you're feeling creative, take an art class. Golf enthusiasts won't miss out either as there are several golf courses nearby.

351 Wellington Mill Rd, Wellington Mill;
(08) 9728 3138;
www.peppermintlanelodge.com.au

Coolgardie

COOLGARDIE MOTEL $

The centrally located Coolgardie Motel is a popular spot for travellers, and with single, double, triple and family units available, the facilities cater well to all requirements. The rooms are comfortable and include air-conditioning. On-site is a licensed restaurant and barbecue facilities, plus a swimming pool.

49–53 Bayley St; (08) 9026 6080

Coral Bay

BAYVIEW CORAL BAY $

Sunseekers drawn to the wonders of the Ningaloo Reef will appreciate the many accommodation options at the Bayview Coral Bay. The lodge provides self-contained bedsit-style rooms, while the self-contained Bayview Villas, Garden Villas, Chalets and Cabins sleep four to eight, depending on the configurations. The White House caters for a larger group with its four bedrooms, two bathrooms and balconies with views out over the bay. There are also powered and unpowered sites for camping and caravans. Facilities include a cafe, swimming pool, tennis courts, kid's playground, barbecues and laundry facilities.

Robinson St; (08) 9385 6655; www.coralbaywa.com

NINGALOO REEF RESORT $$$

You can practically taste the saltiness of Coral Bay and the Ningaloo Reef from the Ningaloo Reef Resort. Sleeping in paradise comes in a variety of options, from motel-style rooms to self-contained apartments and a romantic penthouse suite. If you tire of exploring the underwater dream, take a trip to the outback and investigate gorges, canyons and creeks by four-wheel drive.

1 Robinson St; (08) 9942 5934 or 1800 795 522; www.ningalooreefresort.com.au

THE NINGALOO CLUB $

The Ningaloo Club caters to those seeking a laid-back hostel with a range of accommodation options, including dormitories and twin and double rooms, some with ensuites. The bedrooms are located around the central swimming pool area and gardens and activities include table tennis and promotional events. Also available is an internet room, a communal kitchen and ablution facilities on both floors.

46 Robinson St; (08) 9948 5100 or (08) 9385 6655; www.ningalooclub.com

Corrigin

CORRIGIN WINDMILL MOTEL $

The Corrigin Windmill Motel has several motel rooms with private ensuites, plus a five-bedroom family lodge section with a shared bathroom, kitchenette and lounge room. Opposite the Rotary Park, the hotel is well placed to enjoy the historic attractions of this pretty wheat-belt town.

Brookton Hwy; (08) 9063 2390; www.corriginmotel.com.au

Cue

MURCHISON CLUB HOTEL $

Established in 1890 in the historic town of Cue, the Murchison Club Hotel was renovated in 2002. The hotel rooms in the original building are comfortably decorated and in a separate building there are self-contained motel units. Also in the main building is a licensed restaurant and beer garden.

Austin St; (08) 9963 1020; www.murchisonclubhotelcue.com.au

SWIMMING WITH A WHALE SHARK, NINGALOO REEF RESORT, CORAL BAY

FITNESS CENTRE   ROOM SERVICE   SWIMMING POOL

Denham

BAY LODGE ECONOMY BEACHFRONT $

Offering beachfront accommodation at affordable rates, the Bay Lodge Economy Beachfront offers self-catering rooms and dormitories with ensuites, a kitchenette and a living room. With the beach a few steps away and the dolphins of Monkey Mia beach close by; the lodge is a popular backpacker destination.

113 Knight Tce; (08) 9948 1278 or 1800 812 780; www.baylodge.info

DENHAM VILLAS $$$

Situated on the shores of Shark Bay and conveniently located close to the town centre, the Denham Villas are well equipped and simply decorated. The villas have two bedrooms, a separate living area, air-conditioning and kitchen facilities. Using the communal barbecue area is a great way to meet the other guests and share your travel tales about frolicking with the dolphins or about that fish that got away.

8 Durlacher St; 9948 1264; www.denhamvillas.com

HERITAGE RESORT SHARK BAY $$$

The Heritage Resort Shark Bay has well-appointed suites, which include all the usual hotel facilities but with the added bonus of magnificent views and gorgeous sunsets. The main attraction is the dolphins but fishing, watersports, cruising or four-wheel-drive tours will make your visit as busy as you like.

Cnr Knight Tce and Durlacher St; (08) 9948 1133; www.heritageresortsharkbay.com.au

MONKEY MIA DOLPHIN RESORT $

The Monkey Mia Dolphin Resort complex includes a resort, a lodge, caravan and camping facilities and some sites have a beachfront location. In the resort, many of the self-contained villas and hotel rooms have either a beachfront location or are set within the gardens. The lodge includes twin or family-style rooms, dormitories and a communal kitchen. Regardless of which style of accommodation you select, you will be in the heart of the Shark Bay World Heritage Area and all of its attractions.

Monkey Mia; (08) 9948 1320 or 1800 653 611; www.monkeymia.com.au

SHARK BAY VIEWS B&B $$

With your own private entrance, you can be sure you will be the only guests at the Shark Bay Views Bed and Breakfast. The simple accommodation is ideally suited to a couple or a single traveller and includes either a cooked or continental-style breakfast. Just a minute's walk to the beach and access to a courtyard, barbecue and outdoor dining will ensure you make the most of this beautiful spot.

58 Durlacher St; (08) 9948 1060; www.ozpal.com

Denmark

CHIMES SPA RETREAT $$$$

Would you enjoy lounging in a spa overlooking some of Western Australia's prettiest landscape?

BREAKFAST INCLUDED   CREDIT CARDS ACCEPTED   FAMILY FRIENDLY

Then book yourself into the intimate Chimes Spa Retreat and escape to an oasis of pampering. The spa has every treatment you could think of, either individually or with a partner. All the stylish suites have spa baths, many with views and there are a variety of room sizes and options, including a self-contained holiday house.

Mt Shadforth Scenic Dr; (08) 9848 2255; www.chimes.com.au

MISTY VALLEY COUNTRY COTTAGES $$

The Misty Valley Country Cottages really are the epitome of country cosiness. You'll be greeted by majestic karri trees, rolling hills and a basket of freshly baked muffins. The two and three-bedroom cottages overlook the picturesque lake and are ideal for groups, couples or singles. Fully self-contained with reverse-cycle air-conditioning, the timber cottages have an enclosed balcony with lovely views. The kids will love getting involved with farm activities like collecting eggs, bottle feeding the baby animals, pony rides, milking the friendly cow or a tractor ride.

52 Hovea Rd; (08) 9840 9239; www.mistyvalley.com.au

MT LINDESAY VIEW B&B $$

Mt Lindesay View Bed & Breakfast is perched on a lush hillside with picturesque scenery. The colonial-style homestead has a private entrance for the three suites, which are decorated in a quaint country style, and all the rooms have their own ensuite. Breakfast is served on the verandah and dinner can be ordered by arrangement.

Cnr Mt Shadforth Tourist Dr and McNabb Rd; (08) 9848 1933

PENSIONE VERDE $$

If you want to experience a slice of village life, then a stay Pensione Verde should satisfy. This intimate guesthouse and organic cooking school has nine hotel-style rooms and is situated in the heart of town. After your organic breakfast, which is served on the verandah overlooking the pretty village, guests can wander into the town's shops and restaurants or partake in one of the cooking classes on offer.

31 Strickland St; (08) 9848 1700; www.denmarkaccommodation.com.au

TREE TOPS $$$

With a lovely view over the Wilson Inlet, Tree Tops is a romantic getaway for two or a relaxing break for four. The timber A-frame holiday home is self-contained and includes a potbelly stove to snuggle up by in winter and a barbecue to enjoy during the summer months. On your doorstep are gorgeous beaches, wineries, treks and birdwatching.

21 Payne Rd, Weedon Hill; (08) 9364 1594; www.treetops.net.au

Derby

DERBY BOAB INN $$$

The Derby Boab Inn has comfortable motel-style rooms, including family suites, all air-conditioned with ensuites and wireless internet access. The inn includes a bar, beer garden, cafe, pool tables, live bands and entertainment and also exhibits the artworks of renowned artists.

100 Loch St; (08) 9191 1044

FITNESS CENTRE   ROOM SERVICE   SWIMMING POOL

JILA GALLERY APARTMENT $$

Conveniently located in the centre of town and close to amenities, the Jila Gallery Apartment is contemporary in style. The two-bedroom apartment is fully self-contained and includes barbecue facilities. Pets are welcome.

18 Clarendon St; (08) 9193 2560

KIMBERLEY COTTAGES $$$

Surrounded by peaceful bush, the Kimberley Cottages offer two or three-bedroom accommodation. The air-conditioned cottages are fully self-contained and comfortably appointed. There are also conference facilities for 20 people, and stress management and relaxation classes can be arranged.

18 Windjana Rd; (08) 9191 1114;
www.kimberleycottages.bigpondhosting.com

KIMBERLEY ENTRANCE CARAVAN PARK $

Situated on a shady bay, Kimberley Entrance Caravan Park offers powered and unpowered sites, as well as camping. Facilities include an undercover barbecue, a shop and three toilet blocks. The park is also within walking distance of the town and jetty.

2–12 Rowan St; (08) 9193 1055

KING SOUND RESORT HOTEL $$

In the town centre, the King Sound Resort offers hotel-style accommodation and all the rooms have ensuites. Within the resort is a bistro, cocktail bar, beer garden and a pool surrounded by tropical plants. The resort is a popular spot with anglers, since Derby has some of the strongest tides in the country.

112 Loch St; (08) 9193 1044

Dongara–Denison

DONGARA DENISON BEACH HOLIDAY PARK $

With its grassed sites and clean facilities, the Dongara Denison Beach Holiday Park delivers a relaxed seaside holiday only 5 metres from the beach. A range of accommodation options are available, from a waterfront chalet to a caravan or powered campsite. Facilities include internet access, a new playground, modern ablution block, basketball courts and camp kitchen. Regular functions are organised by management. Nearby are a plethora of water-based activities and historical buildings to explore.

250 Ocean Drive Rd; (08) 9927 1131;
www.ddbeachholidaypark.com

GETAWAY BEACH $$$

On the beach 12 kilometres from the town centre, the remoteness of Getaway Beach will appeal to the Robinson Crusoe in you. Both bedrooms have Indian Ocean views and the ensuite bathrooms have spas. Comfortably accommodating six, quality linen is provided and there's a well-equipped kitchen (including an espresso machine), barbecues and outdoor furniture. Canoes, fishing and diving gear are also available.

Off Brand Hwy; (08) 9927 2458;
www.getawaybeach.com.au

BREAKFAST INCLUDED   CREDIT CARDS ACCEPTED   FAMILY FRIENDLY

PORT DENISON HOLIDAY UNITS $$

The Port Denison Holiday Units offer clean and functional self-contained accommodation within close vicinity of the township. The one- and two-bedroom units are spacious and cater well to families or backpackers. Time your visit to marvel at the explosion of wildflowers from July to October, not to mention the year-round seaside activities and the opportunity to explore this historic region.

14 Carnarvon St; (08) 9927 1104; www.portdenisonholidayunits.com.au

SEA SPRAY BEACH HOLIDAY PARK $$$

Offering beachfront accommodation, the Sea Spray Beach Holiday Park has a range of accommodation options. The one- and two-bedroom apartments include well-equipped kitchens, air-conditioning, cable TV and internet access; some have balconies and all come with ocean views. Also on-site is a well-equipped caravan park.

79–81 Church St; (08) 9927 1165; www.seaspraybeachresort.com.au

Donnybrook

BORONIA FARM $

Donnybrook is home to the Lady Williams Apple and Boronia Farm, a 64-hectare organic farm, which includes gloriously scented native boronia. Fruit picking and participation in the farming activities is encouraged, as is canoeing on the dam. Built in the 1950s, the cottage has three bedrooms and is fully self-contained, with its original Meters No. 2 wood stove. The enclosed garden includes play equipment.

47 Williams Rd; (08) 9731 7154; www.boroniafarm.com.au

COUNTRY CHARM RETREAT B&B $$

Set within 17.5 hectares of countryside, the Country Charm Retreat Bed & Breakfast has two well-appointed suites both with ensuites and a private guest entrance. Catering for adults only, guests are welcome to relax in the gazebo or use the barbecue facilities.

629 Hurst Rd; (08) 9731 2010; www.countrychm.com

JARRAGON B&B $$

Jarragon Bed & Breakfast is a cosy three-bedroom cottage with environmentally friendly energy and water-saving facilities. Biodegradable cleaning products are used wherever possible and breakfast is cooked with organically grown local foods. The guest bathroom is well appointed and afternoon tea is provided on arrival. The cottage is centrally located, making it ideal to enjoy the many attractions of this historic town.

9 Collins St; (08) 9731 1930; jarragonbandb.mysouthwest.com.au

KIRUP KABINS FARMSTAY $$

With rolling hills aplenty, the kids can run for as long as their little legs will hold them at this farmstay. They might also like to help feed the farm animals or collect eggs, making Kirup Kabins a very family-friendly spot. The property has a licensed marron farm, so why not pick up a kilo or two to enjoy in your cosy cabin. The four cabins have two or three bedrooms and overlook the countryside.

Lot 3, Mailman Rd; (08) 9731 6272; www.kirupkabins.com.au

Dunsborough

BLUE ESCAPE $$$$$

Blue Escape is a stylish two-storey four-bedroom home just a short walk to the town centre, ocean and parks. The upper level takes advantage of the bay views, incorporating an open-plan living area and resort-style master bedroom. Downstairs are three more bedrooms and a games room for teenagers. The enclosed garden ensures the little ones can play safely, allowing the parents to relax on the balcony.

Private Properties (08) 9385 9385; www.privateprop.com/dun/dun39.php

DUNSBOROUGH RAIL $$
CARRIAGES & FARM COTTAGES

These lovingly restored jarrah rail carriages are a unique getaway. Tastefully appointed with modern fittings and self-contained, they suit couples or a small family. For larger groups, the cottages sleep eight and the farmhouse sleeps 13. The 40-hectare property is close to the South-West Cape region and all of its delights. Wildlife abounds among the peppermint and gum trees, including kangaroos and ponies – the kids will have a ball.

123 Commonage Rd; (08) 9755 3865; www.dunsborough.com

NEWBERRY MANOR $$$

Despite being built in 2000, Newberry Manor exudes the charm of a bygone era with the benefit of all the modern conveniences. The king-sized suites include spas, cable TV, internet access and private verandahs to the cottage garden, which has barbecue facilities. Within walking distance to the town centre, this B&B offers romantic accommodation in a convenient location.

16 Newberry Rd; (08) 9756 7542; www.newberrymanor.com.au

QUAY WEST RESORT $$$
BUNKER BAY

Luxuriously appointed villas, a day spa at your disposal and an outstanding restaurant all contribute to Quay West Resort Bunker Bay's five-star rating. Not to mention being perched above the world-class Bunker Bay. The studios and one and two-bedroom villas include deep baths, king beds and internet access. The secluded villas have separate living areas, cathedral ceilings and direct beach access.

Bunker Bay Rd, Bunker Bay; (08) 9756 9100 or 1800 010 449; www.mirvachotels.com/quay-west-resort-bunker-bay

WHALERS COVE $$$$

Within walking distance to town and a beachfront location, the Whalers Cove is the ideal seaside holiday location, catering equally well to groups and couples. Popular year-round, the villas are well appointed and each is uniquely designed. All are self-contained and have two, three or four bedrooms, cathedral ceilings, barbecues and outdoor settings. Arrangements can be made if your stay marks a special occasion or you just feel like some pampering.

3 Lecaille Crt; (08) 9755 3699;
www.whalerscove.net

Dwellingup

BANKSIA SPRINGS COTTAGES $$

Both Kurrajong and Kookaburra cottages are both self-contained, have well equipped kitchens and include linen and towels. Kurrajong has a queen-sized bed downstairs and a loft with two single beds upstairs, and a dormer window with views into the forest. The pretty two-bedroom Kookaburra Cottage is nestled into the 2 hectares of gardens and jarrah forest. Guests over the age of 16 are welcome.

Banksiadale Rd; (08) 9538 1880;
www.banksiasprings.com

DWELLINGUP BUNKHOUSES OUTDOOR ADVENTURE CAMP $

Purpose built for large groups, school camps or those seeking a challenge, the Dwellingup Bunkhouses Outdoor Adventure Camp sleeps over 60 people in dormitories and has facilities for another 30 campers. Also available is the chalet sleeping up to ten and a cubby which sleeps 12. Facilities include kitchens, ablution blocks and a dining/recreation room. Free activities include trampolines, BMX tracks, canoeing, an obstacle course and bushwalking. Adventure activities can be booked, including abseiling, rock climbing, canoeing/rafting, flying fox, archery, mountain-biking and paintballing, with instructors available for hire.

Lot 1379 Vandals Rd; (08) 9538 1314;
www.bunkhouses.com.au

DWELLINGUP CHALET & CARAVAN PARK $

The Dwellingup Chalets & Caravan Park offers caravans, self-contained chalets sleeping up to ten people and cabins sleeping five. Set on 13.5 hectares of natural surrounds, there are barbecue facilities and a kiosk. Dogs on leashes are welcome.

23 Del Park Rd; (08) 9538 1157;
www.dwellingupcaravanpark.com.au

TADDY CREEK $$$

Set on 1.5 hectares of rural land, Taddy Creek is a three-bedroom house appointed with a fully equipped kitchen, air-conditioning, potbelly stove and barbecue facilities. The property is in the process of being cultivated to ensure sustainability for future generations. Taddy Creek is a hit with the kids, as there is play equipment, an undercover blackboard, kids' movies, a winter creek for catching tadpoles and the property is fenced off from the road and dams so they can roam freely.

2379 Del Park Rd; (08) 9285 1727;
www.taddycreek.com.au

LAKE NAVARINO FOREST RESORT $

Surrounded by towering trees, Lake Navarino Forest Resort has cabins, cottages, park homes, a dormitory and powered sites. The timber cabins and cottages are self-contained and can sleep up to ten people; some have lake views. The park homes are more spacious than a caravan and the dormitory-style accommodation is available in the Bunk Hall and caters up to 20 people. Both the park homes and bunk hall have shared kitchen facilities and ablution blocks. For those

FITNESS CENTRE   ROOM SERVICE   SWIMMING POOL

really wanting to get back to nature, lakeside camping is available.

147 Invarell Rd, Waroona; (08) 9733 3000 or 1800 650 626; www.navarino.com.au

Esperance

BAY OF ISLANDS B&B $$

At the Bay of Islands Bed & Breakfast, every room overlooks the Southern Ocean and the islands of the Recherche Archipelago. There is a private spa area, internet access, barbecue facilities and balconies overlooking the archipelago. The town centre is a stroll away, West Beach is directly across the road, and Cape Le Grand National Park and Woody Island are in the area.

73 Twilight Beach Rd; (08) 9072 1995; www.bayofislandsbb.com

SEASCAPE BEACH HOUSE $$$$

Set in lush bush surroundings at West Beach, the Seascape Beach House has rugged sea views and is close to the beach and bike and walking trails. The architecturally designed house is solar powered and sleeps seven, with an open-plan living area, spacious outdoor entertainment area and barbecue facilities. A short drive or a leisurely walk and you will find yourself in the lovely town centre.

11 Cornell St; (08) 9071 3150

THE JETTY RESORT $$$

Located opposite Tanker Jetty and with views of the Bay of Isles, the Jetty Resort makes for a relaxing seaside holiday. Offering standard hotel rooms, spa suites with kitchenettes and fully-self contained two-bedroom apartments, the resort caters well to families and couples. The resort includes a heated pool, barbecues facilities, a charge-back facility to local restaurants and a children's playground.

1 The Esplanade; (08) 9071 3333; www.thejettyresort.com.au

WOODY ISLAND ECOSTAYS $

Woody Island is one of 100 islands in the Recherche Archipelago, with 240 hectares of nature reserve, 5 hectares of which has been developed for ecotourism. Choose from comfortable safari huts built on raised platforms or the rustic adventure huts, all sleeping five. Tents are available for hire in a variety of sizes and guests are also welcome to bring their own camping equipment. The island has a cafe, camp kitchen, toilet blocks and a children's playground. Activities include snorkelling, bushwalking, boating, fishing, swimming and birdwatching. Cruises to the island leave from the Taylor St Jetty in Esperance.

Via Mackenzie's Island Cruises, 71 The Esplanade; (08) 9071 5757; www.woodyisland.com.au

Eucla

EUCLA AMBER MOTOR HOTEL $

Just 12 kilometres from the South Australian border, and within the small community of Eucla, the Eucla Amber Motor Hotel has hotel rooms and a caravan park. In the hotel there's a choice of air-conditioned double rooms as well as budget rooms suitable for sharing.

BREAKFAST INCLUDED   CREDIT CARDS ACCEPTED   FAMILY FRIENDLY

The caravan park has powered sites and unpowered campsites.

Eyre Hwy; (08) 9039 3468

Exmouth

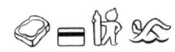

BEST WESTERN SEA BREEZE RESORT $$

Located next to the Historic Naval Base and deemed as the closest resort to the Ningaloo Marine Park, the Best Western Sea Breeze Resort is considered one of the best value resorts in Exmouth. The self-contained studios include cooking facilities, cable TV and internet access, and some of the studios cater for families. Lounge around the tropical pool or take advantage of one of the packages available and go diving, swimming with the whale-sharks or whale-watching.

116 North C St; (08) 9949 1800; www.seabreezeresort.com.au

EXMOUTH CAPE HOLIDAY PARK $

The Exmouth Cape Holiday Park offers a range of accommodation options such as cabins, chalets, powered caravan sites, camping facilities and the Blue Reef Backpackers Village. After you've explored the many attractions of the area, such as the Ningaloo Marine Park or the canyons, cool down in the swimming pool and let the kids run around in the playground. During the high season the outdoor cinema is open.

3 Truscott Cres; 1800 621 101 or 1800 621 101; www.aspenparks.com.au/holiday-destinations/western-australia/exmouth/exmouth-cape-holiday-park

NOVOTEL NINGALOO RESORT $$$$

Escape the winter blues and head for the Novotel Ningaloo Resort. Relax on the cheerily named Sunshine Beach or use the resort as a base to explore the Ningaloo Marine Park, the Cape Range National Park or swim with the manta rays and whale-sharks. With a choice of one, two- and three-bedroom apartments and bungalows, all the rooms include spas, king-sized beds and cable TV. The two and three-bedroom apartments include cooking facilities, although the fresh cuisine served at Mantaray's Restaurant should appeal to most tastes. The resort also caters well to conferences and functions, including weddings.

Madaffari Dr; (08) 9949 0000; www.novotelningaloo.com.au

SAL SALIS NINGALOO REEF $$$$$

Although the Ningaloo Reef Retreat doesn't claim to be a five-star resort, this is safari camping in style. Every tent has an ensuite, comfortable beds with 500 thread-count sheets, a choice of pillows and gourmet food on the menu. The price includes all meals, a selection of beverages, sea-kayaking, snorkelling, guided gorge walks, a cruise and national park entry, although star-gazing on the beach may be as active as you may wish to be. The main camp building is raised above the sand dunes, taking in the view of the coastal scrub. A contemporary Australian dinner is served against a burnt amber sunset.

North West Cape, Cape Range National Park; (02) 9571 6399 or 1300 790 561; www.salsalis.com.au

FITNESS CENTRE   ROOM SERVICE   SWIMMING POOL

Fitzroy Crossing

FITZROY RIVER LODGE $

Set within 20 hectares of unspoilt bush, seemingly in the middle of nowhere, the welcoming Fitzroy River Lodge is perfect for an overnight stopover or longer stay. The lodge provides a range of accommodation options, including modern hotel rooms, self-contained rooms, safari lodges with private facilities, caravan and camping facilities, and for a touch of luxury, river-view suites with spas. The lodge has several dining options, barbecue facilities, tennis courts, volleyball and internet access, plus tours can be organised.

Great Northern Hwy; (08) 9191 5141; www.kimberleyhotels.com.au/fitzroylodge

IMINTJI WILDERNESS CAMP $

There's no need to rough it here, as this campsite has proper beds with linen included, lighting and private ensuite bathrooms to ensure a civilised stay. Even with these little luxuries, the environment is preserved as the Imintji Wilderness Camp was designed with the ecosystem in mind. The shady site has wonderful views of the King Leopold escarpment and is well situated to explore the Bell, Galvans and Barnett River gorges.

Gibb River Rd; (08) 9277 8444 or 1800 889 389; www.kimberleywilderness.com.au

MORNINGTON WILDERNESS CAMP $

Six hours from Fitzroy Crossing, the Mornington Wilderness Camp is an ideal base to explore the Mornington Sanctuary and its spectacular gorges, Fitzroy River and King Leopold Ranges. The spacious safari tents include ensuites and balconies overlooking Annie Creek, although you're welcome to bring your own tent and camp by the creekside. The restaurant serves breakfast, lunch and dinner, and meal packages are available. Nature lovers will appreciate the diverse range of wildlife, and a variety of self-guided and organised tours can be arranged. All proceeds from your visit support the non-profit Australian Wildlife Conservancy, and the sanctuary is open between May and October.

Gibb River Rd; (08) 9191 7406 or 1800 631 946; www.australianwildlife.org

Gascoyne Junction

BIDGEMIA STATION $

Just 11 kilometres from Gascoyne Junction, Bidgemia Station is a working cattle station on the banks of the Gascoyne River. Stay in the five-bedroom lodge, which is fully self-contained and includes a swimming pool and a deck overlooking the river. Meals can be arranged in advance. For a more authentic farmstay, the Shearers Quarters are comfortably decorated and have shared facilities, or you can camp on the riverbank like they did in times gone by.

Carnarvon Rd; (08) 9943 0501; www.bidgemia.com

Geraldton

DRUMMOND COVE HOLIDAY PARK $

Situated on the Batavia Coast about 10 kilometres from Geraldton, Drummond Cove Holiday Park has a range of accommodation choices, from four-bedroom homes to unpowered campsites. A short stroll to one of

---

BREAKFAST INCLUDED   CREDIT CARDS ACCEPTED   FAMILY FRIENDLY

the best beaches in the area, the park also has a swimming pool, a children's playground, barbecue facilities and on-site shops.

North West Coastal Hwy; (08) 9938 2524; www.drummondcove.com

GERALDTON B&B $

The Geraldton Bed & Breakfast is just a short stroll to the beach and a little further to the CBD. All guests staying in any of the three bedrooms have access to the shared bathroom, living areas, swimming pool and outdoor entertaining area. If you're after a little more privacy, stay in one of the fully self-contained cottages which also have access to the pool. Both cottages have polished floorboards and are tastefully decorated, and one of the cottages has a spa overlooking the pool area.

183 George Rd; (08) 9921 6334; www.geraldtonbedandbreakfast.com.au

MANTRA GERALDTON $$$$

The tastefully decorated Mantra Geraldton has fully self-contained studios and one, two and three-bedroom apartments. The complex includes a secured carpark and an outdoor pool and spa. Within close vicinity to the CBD and Champion Bay Marina, Mantra is ideally located to explore the region and beyond, for short- and long-term stays.

221 Foreshore Dr; (08) 9956 1300 or 1300 987 604; www.mantra.com.au

MARINA VIEWS $$$$

Overlooking the marina, you could practically dive from your balcony into the water at the Marina Views. With outdoor lounge areas, leather couches and flat-screen TVs, the apartments bring a bit of glamour to the commercial fishing town of Geraldton. The double-story apartments have two bedrooms, two bathrooms and living areas on both floors. Fully self-contained, the kitchen is well equipped, although you might prefer to have a barbecue in one of the outdoor entertaining areas, which are well sheltered from the infamous Geraldton sea breeze.

Foreshore Dr; (08) 9938 3848; www.geraldtonaccommodationservice.com.au

OCEAN CENTRE HOTEL $$$$

The waterfront Ocean Centre Hotel overlooks Champion Bay, while only being a few steps from the CBD. Whether you're staying in one of the standard hotel rooms or the honeymoon suite, the hotel is tastefully decorated throughout and many have balconies to take advantage of those wonderful ocean views. There is also a charge-back facility to your room from several popular restaurants, and internet access is available in selected rooms.

Cnr Foreshore Dr and Cathedral Ave; (08) 9921 7777; www.oceancentrehotel.com.au

Gingin

BROOKSIDE $

Set in an idyllic country location, Brookside gives guests the opportunity to explore the region and its wineries, cafes, Moore River and many other rural activities. The modern chalets are fully self-contained and are suited to couples and families. The budget accommodation is dormitory style and has shared amenities.

1010 Chitna Rd, West Gingin; (08) 9575 7585; www.brooksideaccommodation.com.au

BINDOON'S WINDMILL FARM $

Fancy a break from city living? Then head to Bindoon's Windmill Farm, a 16-hectare property just an hour from Perth and home to native wildlife and plants. Both chalets here are ideal for group stays and every bedroom has its own private ensuite and air-conditioning. There are also two rooms available in the homestead, with shared facilities. Although the no-thrills accommodation is comfortable, experiencing a farmstay is the main attraction as guests interact with farm animals, learn about fruit orchards and tour the farm. Popular with international visitors.

Great Northern Hwy, Bindoon; (08) 9576 1136; www.ausbusiness.net/windmill

BURROLOO WELL FARMSTAY $$

If you're craving privacy, Burroloo Well Farmstay will satisfy since it's located on 280 hectares of farm. The double-storey house is set high in the Darling Range and has views across the Chittering Lake, with balconies taking full advantage of the stunning panorama. The cedar house is fully self-contained and has two bedrooms.

Great Northern Hwy, Upper Chittering; (08) 9576 1010

ORCHARD GLORY FARM RESORT $$$$

All 20 of the chalets at the Orchard Glory Farm Resort are fully self-contained, tastefully decorated and even have custom-made beds for the long-legged. Situated in the Chittering Valley and its many attractions, the farm itself has plenty to enjoy, whether it be exploring the waterfalls and vineyards, petting the farm animals, fruit picking or barbecuing by the lake. There are also conference facilities for up to 100 people, who can be comfortably accommodated in the chalets.

41 Mooliabeenee Rd, Bindoon; (08) 9576 2888; www.orchardglory.com.au

THE ORCHARD VILLA $$$

The architecturally designed, Mediterranean-style Orchard Villa is reminiscent of provincial France as lavender, olive trees and fruit orchards pepper the air. All four bedrooms are lovingly and plushly furnished, and the kitchen will inspire the chef in you. Outside there are lovely views from the terrace or find a quiet spot on the 2.5-hectare property to relax.

Great Northern Hwy, Bindoon; (08) 9271 2270; www.elizabethmoir.com

Greenough

ROCK OF AGES COTTAGE $

Originally built in 1857, the Rock of Ages Cottage has been restored to include three bedrooms with shared bathroom facilities. Also available is a guest lounge room with an open fireplace, a barbecue area and an outdoor spa. The cottage is located on the Greenough Flats and is just ten minutes away from Geraldton.

Phillips Rd; (08) 9926 1154; www.ozbnbdir.com/rock_of_ages_wa

---

BREAKFAST INCLUDED   CREDIT CARDS ACCEPTED   FAMILY FRIENDLY

Halls Creek

BEST WESTERN HALLS CREEK MOTEL $$$

The rooms at the Best Western Halls Creek Motel are set within beautifully landscaped gardens. All 30 of the rooms have been recently upgraded, and some include family facilities and spas. The motel is ideally situated to take advantage of the attractions of Halls Creek, including the Bungle Bungles.

194 Great Northern Hwy; (08) 9168 9600; www.hallscreek.bestwestern.com.au

KIMBERLEY HOTEL $$$

Retaining the colonial character of Halls Creek's gold-rush heyday, the Kimberley Hotel is one of the largest motels in the Kimberley. The spacious rooms are surrounded by green lawns and the hotel is a short walk from town. Halls Creek sits on the edge of the Great Sandy Desert and is an ideal base to explore the surrounding goldfields, Wolfe Creek Meteorite Crater or the home of the Bungle Bungle massif in Purnululu National Park.

Roberta Ave; (08) 9168 6101; www.kimberleyhotel.com.au

Harvey

BLUEHILLS FARMSTAY HARVEY $$

The stylishly designed chalets at Bluehills Farmstay sleep six and are fully self-contained. Nearby is the two-bedroom cottage at Uduc Brook Farmstay, situated in a tranquil environment and also self-contained. The kids will love feeding the farm animals, trying their hand at milking, pony rides and fishing, while all visitors delight in the region's rolling hills, pristine beaches and abundant produce.

Weir Rd; 0439 313 898; www.bluehillsfarmstay.com.au

HARVEY HILLS FARMSTAY CHALETS $$

With views over Harvey Dam, the four chalets of the Harvey Hills Farmstay sleep four to six people. Each of the chalets has a potbelly stove, air-conditioning and electric blankets. Ideal for families, there's a swimming pool, trampoline, farm animals to feed and 40 hectares of pastures to run wild in. For the energetic, climbing up the rolling hills gives views of the Indian Ocean and the dam is a drawcard for sailing, canoeing, windsurfing and picnicking.

Weir Rd; (08) 9729 1434; www.harveyhillsfarmstay.com.au

HARVEY RAINBOW CARAVAN PARK $

The Harvey Rainbow Caravan Park includes shady grassed camping areas and powered sites as well as on-site vans. There is an undercover barbecue area and a modern ablutions block. If you want a little more comfort, book into one of the chalets and enjoy the lovely surroundings of Harvey and its many features.

199 Kennedy St; (08) 9729 2239

HIGHLAND VALLEY HOMESTEAD $$$$$

Combining a blend of historical charm and modern comfort, the Highland Valley Homestead is set in 130 hectares. The original homestead was built in 1920 and was crafted from local jarrah. There is an assortment of pampering packages incorporating the day spa, and girls' weekends are well catered for.

402 Collie River Rd; (08) 9726 3080;
www.highlandvalleyhomestead.com.au

TOP PADDOCK COTTAGE $$$

If you're looking for a tranquil break, Vista Ridge Estate offers valley, vineyard and ocean views. Contemporary in style and fully self-contained, the two-bedroom Top Paddock Cottage also has a fold-out couch, dining facilities for six people and spa bath. Outside is a barbecue and outdoor seating under the trees overlooking the vineyard.

Vista Ridge Estate, 7 Newell St; (08) 9729 3240;
www.vistaridge.com.au

INDIAN OCEAN RETREAT & CARAVAN PARK $

Located 20 kilometres west of Harvey, the Indian Ocean Retreat is the ideal seaside holiday. Offering two and three bedrooms, all the chalets are fully self-contained and well appointed with ocean views; some include spas and others are built on the beach. The caravan park has powered sites, clean facilities, a shop, a playground, barbecues and also self-contained park cabins sleeping two to eight people.

Myalup Beach Rd, Myalup; (08) 9720 1113;
www.indianoceanretreat.com.au

Hyden

WAVE ROCK CABINS & CARAVAN PARK $

The Wave Rock Cabins and Caravan Park offers a range of accommodation options from powered and unpowered sites, on-site caravans and a variety of cottages. The holiday park includes a playground, internet access, a kiosk and barbecue facilities and Wave Rock is within walking distance.

Wave Rock Rd; (08) 9880 5022;
www.waverock.com.au/CaravanPark.htm

WAVE ROCK LAKESIDE RESORT $$

All 14 of the two-bedroom brick cottages at Wave Rock Lakeside Resort are fully self-contained. Situated 1 kilometre from the intriguing Wave Rock, the cottages are set along Lake Magic, where boats are available for hire. Although plans for redevelopment are planned for the future, guests are welcome to use the recreational facilities at the local caravan park and motel.

Wave Rock Rd; (08) 9880 5022;
www.waverock.com.au/resort

WAVE ROCK MOTEL HOMESTEAD $$

A mixture of units and suites are offered at the Wave Rock Motel Homestead, which includes three dining options and a heated poolside bar. The suites have spas and their own private courtyard. The guest lounge is a great place to relax with a drink, with its open fireplace, reading materials and games.

2 Lynch St; (08) 9880 5052;
www.waverock.com.au/motel.asp

Jurien Bay

APEX CAMP JURIEN $

Offering a range of accommodation options, like self-contained units, budget accommodation, camping sites and a beach house, the Apex Camp Jurien is ideal for groups. Located in secluded Jurien Bay, the campsite has a dining and function hall, a shaded barbecue area, a camp kitchen and recreation facilities.

15 Bashford St; (08) 9652 1010;
www.apexcampjurien.com.au

JURIEN BAY TOURIST PARK $

With a beachside location to one of Western Australia's favourite coastal regions, the Jurien Bay Tourist Park includes powered and unpowered sites, on-site vans and deluxe chalets. The chalets are well appointed, and include a fully equipped kitchen and air-conditioning. Within the park is a cafe, two camp kitchens, two barbecue areas, two ablution blocks and many children's facilities.

Roberts St; (08) 9652 1595;
www.jurienbaytouristpark.com.au

OCEAN VIEW RETREAT $$$$

Featuring five bedrooms and two bathrooms, the Ocean View Retreat is a fully self-contained beach house ideal for a group. The two-storey house sleeps 12 and has an open-plan living area and separate games room. While the kids are occupied, parents can enjoy a barbecue, chill out in one of the two lounges or relax in the spa in the ensuite. The beach and parks are a short stroll away.

6 Coubrough Pl; (08) 9255 2653;
www.oceanviewretreat.com.au

ON THE BAY B&B $

Boasting a beachside location, On the Bay Bed & Breakfast offers two queen-size bedrooms with shared bathroom facilities. Outside are barbecue facilities and a pool designed for lounging around. The town centre is a short walk away and the world-renowned Pinnacles are a 15-minute drive.

34 Grigson St; 0429 202 748 ;
www.jurienbayaccommodation.com

SEAFRONT ESTATE $$$

Within walking distance to town and the beach, Seafront Estate is located within a well-maintained complex. The modern three-bedroom and two-bathroom villa has a courtyard and there is also a communal barbecue and pool area for entertaining. The park opposite the complex is a bonus for families with small children.

Heaton St; (08) 9652 2055;
www.jurienbayholidays.com

Kalbarri

GECKO LODGE $$$$

Gecko Lodge is a boutique B&B offering adult-only accommodation. Although secluded, the lodge is close to the beach, the Murchison River, shops and cafes. Contemporary in design and purpose built, the lodge has four guest suites and two of the rooms have spas. All the rooms include an LCD TV and open onto the pool courtyard area.

9 Glass St; (08) 9937 1900;
www.geckolodgekalbarri.com.au

FITNESS CENTRE   ROOM SERVICE   SWIMMING POOL

KALBARRI MURCHISON VIEW APARTMENTS $$

Sitting at the mouth of the Murchison River, and just 100 metres from the beach and amenities, the Kalbarri Murchison View Apartments are ideally located to explore the region. The self-contained apartments have two or three bedrooms, overlook the gardens and have easy access to the pool and barbecue area. Book early to secure one of the apartments with ocean and river views.

Cnr Grey and Rustons sts; (08) 9937 1096; www.kalbarrimurchisonviewapartments.com.au

KALBARRI PALM RESORT $$$

Ideal for a family break or a romantic getaway, the Kalbarri Palm Resort is located in the town centre. The resort includes two pools, outdoor spa, cricket pitch, a tennis court and a playground. There are an assortment of hotel rooms, suites with spas and two-bedroom apartments.

8 Porter St; (08) 9937 2333 or 1800 819 029; www.kalbarripalmresort.com.au

KALBARRI SEAFRONT VILLAS $$$

Offering river and ocean views and a range of villas, the Kalbarri Seafront Villas are located in the heart of town. All apartments are spacious and self-contained, with internet access, cable TV and complimentary dinghy use. On-site is a guest swimming pool, a barbecue area and free parking for cars and boats.

108 Grey St; (08) 9937 1025; www.kalbarriseafrontvillas.com.au

KALBARRI TUDOR HOLIDAY PARK $

The Kalbarri Tudor Holiday Park is just moments away from all that Kalbarri has to offer. On-site are cabins, caravan and powered camping sites, a brand-new pool and camp kitchen. There's wireless internet throughout the park and an oval across the street.

10 Porter St; (08) 9937 1077 or 1800 681 077; www.tudorholidaypark.com.au

Kalgoorlie–Boulder

ALL SEASONS KALGOORLIE PLAZA HOTEL $$$

Map ref. p. 92

Located in the town centre, the All Seasons Plaza Hotel has 100 modern hotel rooms, some with balconies. The restaurant serves international cuisine and you can enjoy your meal by the pool or in your room. As soon as you step outside the hotel, you're in the midst of the wide streets of Kalgoorlie.

45 Egan St, Kalgoorlie; (08) 9080 5900; www.accorhotels.com/gb/hotel-1884-all-seasons-kalgoorlie-plaza-hotel

KALGOORLIE OVERLAND MOTEL $$

Map ref. p. 92

Offering comfortable motel-style rooms, the Kalgoorlie Overland Motel also has two-bedroom family rooms with cooking facilities. All rooms include ensuites and internet access is available to guests. Away from the busy town centre, you are only a few minutes away from the airport, public transport, shops and restaurants.

566 Hannan St, Kalgoorlie; (08) 9021 1433; www.overlandmotel.com.au

BREAKFAST INCLUDED   CREDIT CARDS ACCEPTED   FAMILY FRIENDLY

PALACE HOTEL $$

Map ref. p. 92

The Palace Hotel has a range of accommodation options, from basic rooms suited to backpackers to hotel rooms with balconies and apartments, including one with five bedrooms. Complimentary wireless internet access is available in most rooms, and the hotel is situated close to the airport and public transport.

137 Hannan St, Kalgoorlie; (08) 9021 2788; www.palacehotel.com.au

QUEST YELVERTON KALGOORLIE $$

Map ref. p. 92

The Quest Yelverton Kalgoorlie is the premier accommodation in town and is conveniently located within walking distance of all the action. It offers studios and one and two bedroom apartments, with internet access and cable TV. All the spacious studios and apartments are well appointed with kitchens, and some have spas. The hotel has a charge-back arrangement with many local restaurants.

210 Egan St, Kalgoorlie; (08) 9022 8181; www.kalgoorlie.property.questwa.com.au

RYDGES KALGOORLIE $$$$

Map ref. p. 92

Formerly the Broadwater Resort Hotel Kalgoorlie, the Rydges Kalgoorlie offers a range of accommodation options, including deluxe studios and one and two bedroom apartments. The modern rooms come with spa baths and air-conditioning, and the apartments are self-contained. Complimentary parking is available to all guests, and the hotel is ideally located to explore this historic town.

21 Davidson St, Kalgoorlie; (08) 9080 0800 or 1300 857 922; www.rydges.com

Karratha

BALMORAL HOLIDAY PARK $

Balmoral Holiday Park is ideal for those seeking long-term accommodation, but accommodates tourists on an overflow basis only. The caravan sites are paved, the ablution blocks are clean, and there are laundry facilities and an internet kiosk. The kids will enjoy the playground and the big kids can be found playing pool or table tennis, or watching TV in the recreation room.

Balmoral Rd; (08) 9815 3628; www.aspenparks.com.au/holiday-destinations/western-australia/karratha/balmoral-holiday-park

BEST WESTERN KARRATHA CENTRAL APARTMENTS $$$$

The Best Western Karratha Central Apartments provide modern and comfortable accommodation. There's a choice of self-contained studios and one and two bedroom apartments in a convenient central location. Within walking distance are restaurants with charge-back facilities to the resort. It's a relaxing place to take the family before launching off on your Pilbara adventure.

27 Warambie Rd; (08) 9143 9888; www.karrathacentral.bestwestern.com.au

PILBARA HOLIDAY PARK $

Cabins, chalets, powered caravan sites and camping facilities are all available at the Pilbara Holiday Park. On-site is a camp kitchen, barbecue facilities, laundry, an internet kiosk,

FITNESS CENTRE   ROOM SERVICE   SWIMMING POOL

a swimming pool and a recreation room with a pool table and table tennis.

Rosemary Rd; (08) 9185 1855 or 1800 451 855; www.aspenparks.com.au/holiday-destinations/western-australia/karratha/pilbara-holiday-park

DAMPIER ARCHIPELAGO $$$

If a luxurious adventure at sea appeals, then come aboard the 12-metre sailing ketch, Spinifex Spray. Only a few minutes from Karratha, Skipper Brad will reveal the many secrets of the Dampier Archipelago that most people will never discover. The warm waters off the coast include some 42 islands and 150 beaches, and when taken ashore you will view rare rock art that's unique to the area. Your overnight stay onboard will be intimate, with a maximum of only six guests allowed. The rates includes dinner and breakfast.

contact Karratha Visitor Centre; (08) 9144 4600; www.pilbaracoast.com

Katanning

NEW LODGE MOTEL $$

Spacious and comfortable accommodation is guaranteed at the New Lodge Motel. Situated in the gardens of The White House, a grand residence built in the early 1900s, the motel's function centre and conference facilities make it ideal for corporate or group stays.

170 Clive St; (08) 9821 1788; www.newlodge.com.au

WOODCHESTER B&B $

Housed in a lovely Cape Dutch colonial home, the Woodchester B&B is a hidden treasure in the country town of Katanning, known for its farming community. Built in 1927 and designed by a Dutch architect, each of the home's lovely rooms has its own ensuite. Woodchester's extensive collection of antiques, glassware and artworks make an interesting display, while the long verandahs opening onto lawns are inviting during the warmer months. The township is a short walk away, where you'll find restaurants, art galleries and the monthly farmer's market.

19 Clive St; (08) 9821 7007; www.tacawa.com.au

Kellerberrin

KELLERBERRIN CARAVAN PARK $

Situated in the heart of the wheat belt, the Kellerberrin Caravan Park offers inexpensive accommodation. All six of the caravan bays are powered and have grassed areas, and on-site is an ablution block, laundry and barbecue.

Connelly St; 0428 138 474

KELLERBERRIN MOTOR HOTEL $

All five of the non-smoking hotel rooms at the Kellerberrin Motor Hotel offer ensuites, TVs and fridges. Situated in the town centre and on the highway, it's a popular place to enjoy an imported ale in the beer garden or a live band.

108 Massingham St; (08) 9045 5000

BREAKFAST INCLUDED   CREDIT CARDS ACCEPTED   FAMILY FRIENDLY

THE PREV $

The Prev is ideal for corporate functions or group stays and offers bed and breakfast style accommodation in double, single, twin or dormitory rooms. Located at the base of Kellerberrin Hill, there are conference facilities that cater for up to 30 people.

1 George St; 0427 063 638

Kojonup

JACARANDA HEIGHTS B&B $$

A short drive from Kojonup, Jacaranda Heights offers well-appointed accommodation. The entire first floor of the homestead is available and includes two bedrooms, a lounge and a bathroom with spa. Your privacy is maintained as only single bookings are made. Families are welcome and small children are encouraged to interact with the farm animals.

14 Stock Rd; (08) 9831 1200; www.jacarandaheights.com

KEMMINUP FARM HOMESTAY $$

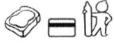

Surrounded by reserves bursting with wildflowers, birdlife and the gateway to the wonders of the south, Kemminup Farm Homestay is ideally situated. The homestead offers charming country-style accommodation furnished with antiques. Every room has its own ensuite and breakfast can be enjoyed in the cosy dining room. The working wheat and sheep farm will delight kids and parents alike. The children will love to feed and pet the farm animals, while parents can peruse the farm's museum with its collection of farm machinery and household memorabilia which has been in the family since 1900.

Kemminup Rd; (08) 9831 1286

KOJONUP B&B $

A barn has been transformed into accommodation at Kojonup B&B, around 160 kilometres from Albany and within walking distance of the centre of Kojonup. All four of the rooms are well appointed, and the master bedroom has its own ensuite. The other three rooms share a guest bathroom which includes a lovely claw-foot bath. The spacious living area is available to all guests.

47 Newstead Rd; (08) 9831 1119; www.kojonup.biz

Kulin

KULIN CARAVAN PARK $

Although offering standard powered camping and caravan sites, the Kulin Caravan Park also has air-conditioned Railway Carriages available for hire. On-site are barbecues and clean facilities, and the park is situated on the edge of the peaceful town.

Rankin St; (08) 9880 1053

Kununurra

DIVERSION CRUISES & HIRE $$$$$

On the upper reaches of the Ord River, experience the beauty of Lake Kununurra aboard a houseboat. With five moorings stretching over 35 kilometres, you'll have the opportunity to explore the stunning scenery and wildlife. The two-bedroom self-contained boat has a bathroom, kitchen, swim deck, upper deck, barbecue and air-conditioning.

1 Lily Creek Dr; (08) 9168 3333

HIDDEN VALLEY TOURIST PARK $

With the Mirimar National Park as the camp's backdrop, and a short distance to the town centre, the Hidden Valley Tourist Park is ideally located to explore the Ord River, Bungle Bungles and Lark Argyle. Savour the tropical weather and lounge by the pool or host a traditional Aussie barbecue. The camp kitchens and ablution blocks are well maintained and laundry facilities are available. The cabins sleeping four are self-contained and include air-conditioning and ensuites. Tents and caravans have powered and unpowered sites and the sites are grassed and shaded.

Weaber Plains Rd; (08) 9168 1790; www.hiddenvalleytouristpark.com

HOTEL KUNUNURRA $

Offering comfortable accommodation for excellent value, Hotel Kununurra has a convenient central town location and is the perfect base from which to explore the Kimberley region. The hotel has a range of accommodation options to suit all budgets, including single and double rooms, suites and family rooms. The Zebra Rock Bar & Restaurant serves international cuisine and is open daily for breakfast, lunch and dinner.

37 Messmate Way; (08) 9168 0400; www.hotelkununurra.com.au

KIMBERLEY CROC BACKPACKERS $

Although geared towards the budget traveller, guests at the Kimberley Croc Backpackers are always impressed by the standard of accommodation and facilities. All the rooms are clean, air-conditioned and secure, and they include linen. There are a variety of accommodation options available, including long-term stays. The outdoor lounge, swimming pool, barbecue facilities, professional kitchen and internet cafe give guests the opportunity to mingle. Socialising is limited in the new ablutions block as there are private and individual bathroom cubicles.

120 Konkerberry Drv; (08) 9168 2702; www.kimberleycroc.com.au

KUNUNURRA COUNTRY $$$
CLUB RESORT

Centrally located in the middle of town, the Kununurra Country Club Resort is only a few minutes from the airport. Standard hotel rooms, two-bedroom apartments and club rooms for a touch of luxury are available, and since the resort belongs to the Aspen Park group, travellers can be sure of high standards. On-site are bars, Kelly's Bar & Grill, a swimming pool and internet access.

47 Coolibah Dr; (08) 9168 1024 or 1800 808 999; www.kununurracountryclub.com.au

EL QUESTRO WILDERNESS PARK $

As if the sheer size of the El Questro Wilderness Park isn't unique enough – it's a million acres, or 400 000 hectares – it's the diversity of its landscape and wildlife that wows visitors. Luckily, El Questro offers a range of accommodation options to suit all budgets, from the luxurious adult-only homestead to the Emma Gorge Resort with its tented cabins at the base of the gorge. There is also the option of the Station Township, offering bungalows and riverside camping. A range of activities to suit outdoor enthusiasts are focused around the park's rugged beauty, with fishing, trekking, boating, horseriding, caving and helicopter flights just a few of the highlights on offer. For a more relaxed holiday, picnic on a cliff-top or by a rockpool, soak in the thermal springs or simply curl up under a tree with a book. The park is open from 1 April to 31 October and there are regular flights from Kununurra.

Gibb River Rd; (08) 9169 1777; www.elquestro.com.au

PRIVATE ROOM PERCHED OVER CHAMBERLAIN GORGE, EL QUESTRO WILDERNESS PARK, KUNUNURRA

Lake Grace

DAREAN FARM COUNTRY RETREAT $

Just a few minutes from town, Darean Farm is a self-contained timber cottage built to serve the early settlement of the area. Now, the two-bedroom cottage has undergone a renovation to include all the modern comforts, a private garden and a barbecue on the front porch. Situated on a working sheep and grain farm, your hosts are happy to give you the grand tour and guests are encouraged to participate in the farm activities. The area is teeming with photography opportunities or you can simply relax and enjoy the lovely sunsets over the lake.

Lot 4126, South Rd; (08) 9865 1068

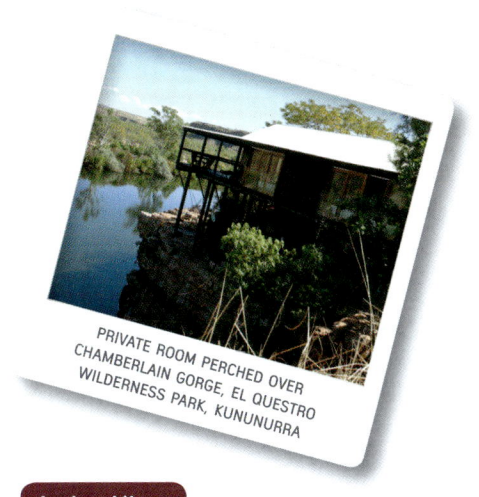

Lake King

LAKE KING CARAVAN PARK $

Situated five and a half hours east of Perth in the heart of the Golden Outback, the rustic Lake King Caravan Park has basic amenities including powered and unpowered sites, on-site caravans, camp kitchen and barbecue facilities. Pets are allowed.

Critchley Ave; (08) 9838 0052

LAKE KING TAVERN & MOTEL $$

Housed in a rammed-earth building with cathedral ceilings, the Lake King Tavern & Motel is popular among the locals for its pub fare (which changes daily), open fire and friendly atmosphere. The accommodation is in a separate building and has eight motel-style rooms with modern bathrooms. Guests leave feeling well rested before continuing their journey to Esperance, Kalgoorlie, Hyden or beyond.

165 Varley Rd; (08) 9874 4048; lakekingtavernmotel.com.au

FITNESS CENTRE   ROOM SERVICE   SWIMMING POOL

Laverton

DESERT INN HOTEL & MOTEL $

Once famous for its booming mining trade, nowadays Laverton has a reputation as being a frontier town, since it's the last pub before you hit Alice Springs. The self-contained units at the family-owned Desert Inn are comfortably appointed, and the pub serves hearty counter meals and cold beer.

2 Laver St; (08) 9031 1188

Leonora

HOOVER HOUSE B&B $$

Live like a mining tycoon and stay at Hoover House, the residence of the former mine manager of the Sons of Gwalia Mine. There are three uniquely decorated rooms, furnished in the era of the historic building, and all have private bathrooms. Don't forget to visit the Gwalia Historical Museum, which is part of the complex.

Tower St; (08) 9037 7122; www.gwalia.org.au

Mandurah

DOLPHIN HOUSE BOATS $$$$$

If you're looking for a holiday with a difference, give Dolphin House Boats a go. They're located in the Mandurah ocean marina but a skipper's ticket isn't required; however, assistance is on-call 24 hours a day should you need it. There are seven boats in the fleet and all are fully equipped with cooking facilities, bathrooms, bedding and rear decks with swimming platforms. As you explore the Peel Inlets, try your hand at snaring blue manna crabs; nets are provided.

Mandurah Ocean Marina; (08) 9535 9898; www.dolphinhouseboats.com

LAKESIDE HOLIDAY APARTMENTS $$$

Just 15 minutes from Mandurah's marina, restaurants and shops, these two-bedroom and two-bathroom apartments are situated on an ornamental lake, as the name suggests. Fully self-contained, relax on your deck while having all the comforts of home to hand. It's on the doorstep of the Peel tourist precinct, and just a short stroll away is the Clansman Restaurant, which prides itself on its Scottish fare, as well as boat launching facilities.

1 Lakes Cres, South Yunderup; (08) 9537 7634; www.lakesideholidayapartments.com.au

PEEL MANOR HOUSE $$$$

On 5 hectares of rural tranquillity, Peel Manor House boasts 16 king-sized suites, ensuring a private stay in warm and elegant surroundings. Some of the rooms have spas, and lake and garden views. Popular as a wedding and conference site, the Peel Estate and its awarding winning wines are nearby.

164 Fletcher Rd, Karnup; (08) 9524 2838; www.peelmanorhouse.com.au

SEASHELLS RESORT MANDURAH $$$$

Right next door to the Mandurah Ocean Marina, and situated on Comet Beach, Seashells Mandurah has well-appointed one, two and three-bedroom apartments and villas.

High-quality materials like granite, marble, wood and wool feature throughout. Some of the villas and apartments include spas and have ocean or marina views. The infinity-edge swimming pool is a nice touch, and the resort has meeting and conference facilities.

16 Dolphin Dr; (08) 9550 3000 or 1800 800 850; www.seashells.com.au

SILVER SANDS TIMESHARE RESORT $$$

The Silver Sands Timeshare Resort is an old favourite with visitors to the region. Close to town and many water attractions, the rates are very competitive. Fully self-contained one and two-bedroom apartments are available, and there are a range of family-friendly activities like tennis, squash, indoor and outdoor swimming pools, a large children's playground, minigolf and a games room. Being a timeshare resort, guests have the option of purchasing a share in the resort in exchange for holidays at Silver Sands or at other participating resorts worldwide.

Cnr Mandurah Tce and Adonis Rd; (08) 9535 7722; www.silversandsresort.com.au

Manjimup

DIAMOND TREE ANGUS STUD $$$

Set on 400 hectares, the Diamond Tree Angus Stud is located approximately halfway between Manjimup and Pemberton, giving guests the opportunity to explore wineries, restaurants, national parks, waterways, galleries and beaches slightly further afield. The two-bedroom farmhouse has wooden flooring, an open-plan living area, open fireplaces, cable TV, fully equipped kitchen and a luxurious bathroom. The wrap-around verandahs overlook the lush property and a dam that attracts wildlife, and since you will be the only guests there, your privacy is guaranteed. The farm is in current operation, housing approximately 500 breeding cows.

Channybearup Rd; (08) 9776 1348; www.diamondtreeangus.com.au

DINGUP HOUSE B&B $$

Originally established in 1870 as a three-room cottage, the Dingup House B&B has expanded into a historic homestead. Four of the guest rooms have private ensuite facilities and all are decorated with period fixtures and furnishings. Both living areas and the cottage gardens are lovely spots to meet other travellers, which is a time-honoured tradition as the house has been a place of social gathering since its humble beginnings. Just a few kilometres from town, the homestead can be booked out to groups, making it popular for special occasions.

114 Dingup Rd; (08) 9772 4206

FONTY'S POOL & CARAVAN PARK $

There aren't many places as ideal as this region of the state to set up a tent and savour the natural environment. Fonty's Pool Caravan Park is set in majestic surroundings and takes its name from the huge fresh spring-water pool. The accommodation consists of a self-contained two-bedroom cottage, cabins, and powered and unpowered sites. It's best to book early at this historic and picturesque caravan park so you don't miss out.

Seven Day Rd; (08) 9771 2105; www.fontyspool.com.au

KARRI GLADE CHALETS $$$

Surrounded by soaring karri trees and in the midst of the area's many natural attractions, the Karri Glade Chalets have two bedrooms, are fully self-contained and include spas, log fires and spring water flowing from the taps. The outside deck is the perfect place to appreciate the wonders of nature, and if the idea of messing up the kitchen disrupts your Zen-like state, then just stroll over to the Graphiti Cafe.

Graphite Rd; (08) 9772 1120; www.karriglade.com

WILGARUP LODGE B&B $$$

Situated on what was one of the first farms in the region, Wilgarup Lodge B&B has a chequered history sure to keep guests intrigued over breakfast. Many of the six rooms at the lodge include ensuite bathrooms, several with views, and all rooms are tastefully decorated. The four-bedroom cottage offers a self-catering option with its well-equipped kitchen and spacious living area. Breakfast is included with both lodge and cottage stays.

Lot 3, South West Hwy; (08) 9771 1991; www.wilgaruplodge.com.au

Marble Bar

IRONCLAD HOTEL $

Established in 1893, the Ironclad Hotel has become an icon in the hottest town in Australia, quite possibly because it prides itself on always serving a well-deserved cold beer. The name originates from the American miners who used to live in the town and regaled the locals with tales about the ironclad boats used in the Mississippi. The accommodation is basic but clean, and most importantly air-conditioned, and there are family and single rooms available. The restaurant serves breakfast, lunch and dinner and there are barbecue facilities and a games room.

15 Francis St; (08) 9176 1066

MARBLE BAR TRAVELLERS STOP $$

Once a thriving mining town of 5000, Marble Bar is best known now for its heat and isolation, which is perhaps what makes the Marble Bar Travellers Stop so accommodating for weary travellers. The simplistic double rooms provide cool relief from the rugged desert, and a base from which you can tour the town's mining history and visit the local swimming pools.

Halse Rd; (08) 9176 1166

Margaret River

BASILDENE MANOR $$$$

Map ref. p. 106

Set on 5.5 hectares of rolling hills, Basildene Manor is on the outskirts of the township and was built at the turn of the last century in the style of an English country manor. Decorated in old-world grandeur, the newer rooms in the Heritage Wing feature courtyards, balconies, spas and views. The grounds are lovely to stroll around, or you can find an inviting spot by the pool to ponder about your glorious surroundings.

Wallcliffe Rd; (08) 9757 3140; www.basildene.com.au

BREAKFAST INCLUDED   CREDIT CARDS ACCEPTED   FAMILY FRIENDLY

GILGARA RETREAT $$$

The Gilgara Retreat is a lovely replica of an 1870 station homestead, offering a range of accommodation options. The Main House is a traditional B&B featuring ornate high ceilings and a stylish main lounge for guests' use, and all rooms have ensuite bathrooms. The two-bedroom Lodge will suit families, while the individual Garden Suites are self-contained, with the bedroom and a two-person spa bath on the upper level.

300 Caves Rd; (08) 9757 2705; www.gilgara.com.au

STUDIO 9 $$$
Map ref. p. 106

Chic Studio 9 is centrally located in the Margaret River township. Luxuriously appointed, number nine represents love and matrimony in feng shui, and this one-bedroom love nest is luxuriously appointed with a spa, flat-screen TVs and kitchenette. Not that you will probably bother cooking, since cafes and restaurants are within walking distance and wineries are only a short drive away.

Bussell Hwy; (08) 9757 2871; www.accommodationstudio9.com.au

BEACH BARNACLE $$

Craving a traditional beachside holiday? Wake up to the roar of the sea at Beach Barnacle. Contemporary in style and brightly decorated, the beach house has three bedrooms and is fully self-contained. Although you will be more than comfortable staying indoors, the call of the sea will no doubt prevail, even if it just means watching the wild waves from the balcony while sipping a drink.

25 Wooredah Cres, Prevelly; (08) 9757 3519; www.beachbarnacle.com

BECKETT'S FLAT VINEYARD COTTAGE $$

Whether you're relaxing on the verandah or warming your toes by the fire, Beckett's Flat is a charming country retreat. The one-bedroom cottage is self-contained and includes linen and a well-equipped kitchen. On-site is the boutique Beckett's Flat winery and guests are more than welcome to visit the cellar door. Accommodation packages, breakfast and platters can be booked in advance.

49 Beckett Rd, Metricup; (08) 9755 7402; www.beckettsflat.com.au

BELL'S BEACH HOUSE $$$

Bell's Beach House is the epitome of a bungalow by the sea. It features a bright and airy interior with a large balcony to take in the wonderful bay views. Fully self-contained, there are three bedrooms and one bathroom and a modern kitchen. With just a short walk to the beach and shops, the beach house is ideally located for a relaxing family break.

Gracetown (address confirmed with bookings); (08) 9285 2100

BETTENAY'S $$$$

Situated within walking distance to the Margaret River Chocolate Factory and the award-winning Vasse Felix restaurant, Bettenay's is certainly well located. Featuring an apartment and two cottages overlooking a trout-filled lake; the cosy chalets are self-contained and have two or three bedrooms. The loft apartment is also self-contained, and includes luxury linen and a spa with views. Don't forget to visit Bettenay's cellar door to pick up a bottle or two.

Miamup Rd, Willyabrup; (08) 9755 5539; www.bettenaysmargaretriver.com.au

---

FITNESS CENTRE   ROOM SERVICE   SWIMMING POOL

CRAYTHORNE COUNTRY HOUSE $$$

Each of the four ensuite rooms is elegantly decorated and includes a full cooked country breakfast, with extra packages available offering extra goodies. Situated in the heart of gourmet and wine country, Craythorne is surrounded by woodland, and the immediate gardens feature hundreds of rose bushes, a lawned area and a view to the spring-fed dam.

180 Worgan Rd, Metricup; 9755 7477; www.craythorne.com.au

GRACETOWN CARAVAN PARK $

Ranging from camping to chalets, the Gracetown Caravan Park will suit most requirements. The kids will be delighted with the playground, with possums and kangaroos roaming around. Those seeking a bit of luxury will enjoy the fully self-contained multi-bedroom spa chalets. The ablutions block is conveniently located in the centre of the park, and the camp kitchen is well equipped.

Cnr Caves and Cowaramup Bay rds, Gracetown; (08) 97550 5301; www.gracetowncaravanpark.com.au

ISLAND BROOK ESTATE $$$$

Comprising of one- and two-bedroom chalets, the Island Brook Estate chalets are self-contained and all feature barbecues, outdoor settings and spas. The forest setting makes for a restful stay and after a day of wine-tasting your verandah or spa awaits.

7388 Bussell Hwy, Metricup; (08) 9755 7501; www.islandbrook.com.au

JUNIPER HOUSE $$$$

Juniper House is contemporary in style and full of features guaranteed to make your stay memorable. There are four bedrooms, two bathrooms, a large games room with pool table, darts and table tennis, and a well-equipped kitchen. However, it's the casual breezy atmosphere that just begs you to kick back and relax here. Plus the panoramic views will make the outdoor seating very hard to leave. Since it sleeps 12, it's ideal for a group getaway or for a family seeking space.

135 Walton Way, Gracetown; (08) 9285 2100; www.seasidehomes.com.au

LAKE VIEW SIESTA $

Considering the beach is only 300 metres away, the Lake View Siesta is extremely well priced. The bright and airy unit is fully self-contained, and separated from the bedroom is a spacious living area. Outside is a private courtyard and seating, and the town centre is within walking distance.

30 Lake View Cres, Prevelly; (08) 9757 2579

MERRIBROOK RETREAT $$$$$

Located a few minutes from the Indian Ocean, Cowaramup and Margaret River, and surrounded by the forest and lakes, the Merribrook Retreat is the ideal sanctuary for a tranquil escape. In keeping with the natural environment, the villas are architecturally designed using wood, stone and glass and the Luxury Lake House overlooks a private lake, creating a picturesque setting for guests as they enjoy the cooked breakfast that's included with the accommodation rates (the chocolate and banana bread is a must-try). As you

BREAKFAST INCLUDED   CREDIT CARDS ACCEPTED   FAMILY FRIENDLY

would expect from a retreat of this calibre, extra touches include in-room massages, heated pool, library, sauna, outdoor spa, lake and conference facilities. For keen bird and wildlife-watchers, a walking track weaves through the property.

Armstrong Rd, Gracetown; (08) 9755 5599; www.merribrook.com.au

PREVELLY SURF SHACK $$$$

The Prevelly Surf Shack is anything but a shack and more of an architectural delight that discreetly nestles into its rugged environment. The two-storey house has upstairs and downstairs sleeping and living areas. The upstairs kitchen will inspire greatness to the point where you might actually consider throwing a dinner party to make the most of the cooking facilities and the enormous dining table; or at least have a barbecue on the balcony with its unsurpassed ocean views. Cable TV, a Sony PlayStation, a games room, the enclosed garden, a nearby park and, of course, the beach ensure the whole family's needs are catered for year-round.

Prevelly Park, Surfers Point Rd, Prevelly; 0439 971 054; www.prevellysurfshack.com.au

REDGATE FARMSTAY $$$

Pet lovers who can't bear to leave their furry loved ones at home will be thrilled at finding a place where they're all welcome. But that doesn't mean the accommodation is less than luxurious. There is the option of one, two or three bedrooms, and all are well appointed and some include spas. The little ones will love the playground and feeding the farm animals.

81 Redgate Rd, Witchcliffe; (08) 9757 6400; www.redgatefarmstay.com.au

THE GROVE VINEYARD $$$

Nestled within The Grove Vineyard are two- and three-bedroom chalets and a honeymoon bungalow. All accommodation is self-contained and well appointed, and includes cable TV, outdoor entertaining areas overlooking the vineyard and private outdoor jacuzzis. It's ideally located to explore the region, but with so much to do here you may get no further than The Grove Vineyard itself. Wander down to the award-winning micro winery and sample its whites, reds and renowned sparkling wines, liqueurs and ports. If you're lucky you'll be served by Steven Hughes, the Grove's irreverent owner. Also on-site is the Yahava coffee roasters, who provide tastings as plentiful as the region's offerings.

Cnr Metricup and Carter rds, Wilyabrup; (08) 9755 7458; www.thegrovevineyard.com.au

THE NOBLE GRAPE GUEST HOUSE $$

Although built in recent times, The Noble Grape oozes old-world charm, being designed in the colonial style and decorated with antiques. The guest suites are in a separate wing and include ensuites, heating and wireless internet access. Breakfast is served overlooking the charming cottage gardens before you set out for the day to explore this delightful region.

29 Bussell Hwy, Cowaramup; (08) 9755 5538; www.noblegrape.com.au

THE ROOZEN RESIDENCE $$$$$

This luxurious, architecturally designed home has graced the covers of more than a few lifestyle magazines, so staying here may just be worth the splurge. Adjacent to the iconic Greek Chapel, and overlooking Prevelly's surfing

FITNESS CENTRE   ROOM SERVICE   SWIMMING POOL

beaches, you'll love the 180-degree views of the Indian Ocean. Stylishly appointed in minimalist style, included is a personal chef, a daily housekeeping service and tour arrangements. The expansive outdoor entertaining areas and all three bedrooms have views. The walls are adorned with contemporary artworks available for sale.

4 Chapel Pl, Prevelly; 0407 479 004; www.ronroozen.com.au

VILLA CRISAFINA $$$

The Mediterranean-style Villa Crisafina is ideal for couples seeking a beachside break. The fully self-contained villa has an upstairs bedroom, a balcony with amazing views, a fold-out sofa downstairs and a spa. However, its main appeal is the spectacular pool with ocean views and the beach just a short walk away.

45 Baudin Dr, Gnarabup; (08) 9757 1050; www.villacrisafina.com.au

Meekatharra

AUSKI INLAND MOTEL $

The modest Auski Inland Motel is clean and comfortable, and the ideal place to stay in town. All 28 of the units have private facilities and air-conditioning and the licensed restaurant turns out a hearty meal. Located in the centre of town, the motel is perfectly located to absorb Meekatharra's mining history and in winter the wildflowers are glorious.

Main St; (08) 9981 1433; www.hotelmotelnetwork.com.au/wa/west/auski_inland_motell

Merredin

MERREDIN B&B $$

Formerly a bank residence dating from the 1930s, the Merredin B&B is decorated in keeping with that era. Centrally located opposite the Cummins Theatre, the B&B is well situated in town and has three guest rooms that share facilities. The kitchen and living areas are available to all guests.

30 Bates St; (08) 9041 4358

MERREDIN TOURIST PARK $

One of the most highly regarded independent parks in the state, there are many accommodation options here. Whether you're staying in one of the self-contained villas, or in a caravan or tent, the barbecue facilities, children's playground and swimming pool are available to all. The camp kitchen and ablutions block are clean and well equipped, and the town and its amenities are just 1 kilometre away.

2 Oats St; (08) 9041 1535

MERREDIN OASIS HOTEL MOTEL $

Recently upgraded, the Merredin Oasis Motel Hotel has a range of standard rooms, executive suites and budget rooms. The parking and accommodation are located at the back of the establishment, away from the bustle of the highway.

8 Great Eastern Hwy; (08) 9041 1133

BREAKFAST INCLUDED   CREDIT CARDS ACCEPTED   FAMILY FRIENDLY

MERREDIN PLAZA ALL SUITES $

Considered to be the town's premier accommodation, the Merredin Plaza All Suites has been renovated to include one-bedroom suites with separate living areas and plasma TVs. Situated in the centre of town, it's close to cafes and shops.

149 Great Eastern Hwy; (08) 9041 1755

Moora

THE DROVERS INN $

Originally named the Commercial Hotel, this hotel was built in 1909 by Gus Liebe, famous for building the Budapest Opera House and His Majesty's Theatre in Perth. The rooms have been restored and there are also motel units available. A visit to Berkshire Valley Folk Museum, which includes many elaborate buildings from the mid-19th century, is highly recommended.

Cnr Dandaragan and Padbury sts; (08) 9651 1108

Morawa

EVERLASTINGS GUEST HOMES $

In the heart of wildflower country, the Everlastings Guest Homes has 20 modern rooms in a variety of sizes and all with private ensuites. Also available is a self-contained and well-appointed two-bedroom cottage with private access, which is available for short or long-term stays. Everlastings restaurant is open for breakfast, lunch and dinner.

10 Evan St; (08) 9971 1771; www.everlastingsguesthomes.com.au

MORAWA CHALETS $$

Opened in 2006, the air-conditioned Morawa Chalets are fully self-contained and well appointed. Both chalets have two or three bedrooms, and all linen is provided. The bedroom unit has disabled access.

White Ave; (08) 9971 1240

MORAWA MARIAN CONVENT B&B $

The Morawa Marian Convent B&B is an ideal stopover for travellers heading further north. Located opposite is the famous Old Presbytery and down the road is the local swimming pool, which may be of particular interest in the sweltering summer heat. The rooms are comfortably decorated and some have ensuites.

Davis St; (08) 9971 1555

Mount Barker

KARRIBANK COUNTRY RETREAT $$$

Do as the genteel folk once did and escape to the country at the Karribank Country Retreat. With the option of staying in the homestead or the self-contained chalet, the retreat caters to couples, families and groups. Originally established in the early 1900s, the property has features to complement the era including polished floorboards, high ceilings and cottage gardens. Porongurup National Park, wineries and local produce are close by, and the coast and its charming towns and seaside activities are 30 minutes away.

1983 Porongurup Rd, Porongurup; (08) 9853 1022; www.karribank.com.au

FITNESS CENTRE   ROOM SERVICE   SWIMMING POOL

KENDENUP LODGE & COTTAGES $$$

Although the township is only a few minutes' drive away, The Kendenup Lodge and Cottages are set on hectares of unspoilt bush and feel like a remote outback stay. The Great Stirling Range looms in the distance, and the region's history dates back to 1874 as having the state's first gold mine. The accommodation is charming, with two self-contained cottages (one including a spa) and lodge rooms with private ensuites available. The lodge is well designed for corporate and social functions, and a variety of events are hosted throughout the year.

217 Moorilup Rd, Kendenup; (08) 9851 4233; www.kendenup.com

THE SLEEPING LADY $$$$$

Guests will slumber soundly at The Sleeping Lady while surrounded by grounds reminiscent of the English countryside. The two-bedroom cottage has the right mix of character and modern conveniences, with its fully equipped kitchen, plasma TV, open fireplace, spa and picnic area. Overlooking the orchard and vineyard, couples and parents can relax on the deck while the little ones frolic in the children's playground.

2658 Porongurup Rd, Porongurup; (08) 9853 1113

CLOUD NINE SPA CHALETS $$$

With views overlooking the magnificent Stirling Ranges, both of the Cloud Nine Spa Chalets, Arcadia and Eden, offer well-priced up-market accommodation for couples, groups and families. The chalets are contemporary in design and decoration and include many little touches like electric blankets, complimentary champagne (from the winery next door), bath goodies, picnic set, barbecues, DVDs, outdoor day beds and a well-equipped kitchen that includes condiments. Arcadia includes an indoor two-person spa and Eden features a five-person hot tub and a sauna. Both chalets sleep five and a mobile beauty and massage therapist is available for bookings.

278 Moorialup Rd, East Porongurup; (08) 9853 1111; www.cloudninespachalets.com.au

STIRLING RANGE RETREAT $

The Stirling Range Retreat offers a range of accommodation, from chalets, cabins, dormitory rooms, caravans and camping. There is also a choice of activities to suit all tastes, including admiring the magnificent surroundings and wildflowers, relaxing by the pool or taking an eco-tour. For the really enthusiastic, Bluff Knoll is the highest peak in the state.

Chester Pass Rd, Borden; (08) 9827 9229; www.stirlingrange.com.au

Mount Magnet

WONDINONG PASTORAL STATION $

In an area rich in natural beauty, Mount Magnet is the state's longest continuously running gold mining settlement. Wondinong Pastoral Station is a working sheep and cattle station 72 kilometres north-east of Mount Magnet. Rooms are available, and caravans and campers are also welcome.

72 km north-east of Mt Magnet; (08) 9963 5823

BREAKFAST INCLUDED   CREDIT CARDS ACCEPTED   FAMILY FRIENDLY

Mundaring

THE LOOSE BOX $$$$$

With one of Perth's most famous gastronomic pleasures only a stumble away, the Loose Box cottages follow the same country chic style found inside the restaurant. Plush fabrics adorn the king-sized beds, the wood fire warms the cool night air and the large bath is a soothing post-dinner treat. Packages with or without a degustation meal are available.

6825 Great Eastern Hwy; (08) 9295 1787; www.loosebox.com.au

CATTON HALL COUNTRY HOMESTEAD $$$$

For many, the feeling of the Perth Hills is similar to that of the South-West, except it is only 40 minutes away from the city. Roselyn Cottage at Catton Hall Homestead is one example of country tranquillity, where pamper packages and a chauffeur service are available. The cottage is self-contained and decked out with antiques and all the luxuries you could want, including a heated outdoor spa to watch the sun set. The property includes a saltwater pool and tennis court and is a short stroll away from Carosa Winery, Lake Leschenaultia and walking trails.

Wilkins Rd, Mt Helena; (08) 9572 1375; www.cattonhall.com.au

CHAPEL FARM GETAWAY $$$

Chapel Farm Getaway is home to six themed rooms: the Australian Classic, Bali Paradise, Black & White, Beach House, African Safari and Oriental Delights. Although the rooms are similar in layout, they are all uniquely presented. A masseur is available on request and the licensed restaurant is open Thursday to Sunday for lunch and dinner.

231 Toodyay Rd, Middle Swan; (08) 9250 4755; www.chapelfarmgetaways.com.au

GRANDIS COTTAGES $$$$

Situated on 2 hectares in the gorgeous Swan Valley, with its many wineries and restaurants, the Grandis Cottages are surrounded by gum trees and rose gardens. The two-bedroom cottages are self-contained and include a full kitchen and a spa bath. Breakfast provisions are supplied and the alfresco area includes a barbecue.

45 Casuarina Pl, Henley Brook; (08) 9296 3400; www.grandiscottages.com.au

GRANDVIEW B&B $$

As promised, a grand view is indeed delivered, from the dining room, deck or by the pool, which is where you're welcome to take your breakfast. Like many hills properties, the Grandview B&B is full of character. The well-appointed rooms include ensuites, cable TV, electric blankets and air-conditioning. Wineries, bushwalks, restaurants and arts and crafts are all nearby, and the airport is just 15 minutes away.

30 Girrawheen Dr, Gooseberry Hill; (08) 9293 2518; www.grandviewbandb.com.au

GUILDFORD LANDING $$

At the Guildford Landing Function Centre there is a spa suite ideal for a bridal party to prepare for the big day or to unwind afterwards. There is also a self-contained unit for a more casual stay, with views from the balcony. Located in the heart of the

FITNESS CENTRE   ROOM SERVICE   SWIMMING POOL

historic town of Guildford, shops, cafes, public transport and the Swan River are all on your doorstep, with the wineries of the Swan Valley just a short drive away.

114 Swan St, Guildford; (08) 9377 1925; www.guildfordlanding.com.au

HIDDEN VALLEY ECO SPA LODGES $$$$$

Set within 5.5 hectares of tranquil jarrah forest, and just a few minutes from Mundaring, the Hidden Valley Eco Spa Lodges are luxuriously appointed, self-contained cottages, each featuring an outdoor heated Jacuzzi on a private deck. Adjacent to the cottages is the Hidden Valley's Farm Lodge, suitable for couples and small groups. The day spa is highly recommended for some extra pampering, as are the classes on exercise, Pilates, yoga, life coaching and art. Platters and gourmet packs can be pre-ordered if you don't feel like venturing out for food, although there are some lovely restaurants and wineries nearby. Revitalisation packages and tours can be tailored to your needs.

85 Carinyah Rd, Pickering Brook; (08) 9293 7337; www.hiddenvalleyeco.com

HOVEA RIDGE COTTAGE $$$$

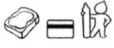

A quaint little stone cottage packed full of character awaits you here, complete with a claw-foot bath, a toasty potbelly, a daily delivery of baked goods and fresh fruit, polished floorboards, high ceilings, wrought-iron beds, French doors and valley views. Next door is John Forrest National Park, walking and cycle trails, and nearby are all the outdoor pursuits the area is famous for.

370 Margaret Rd, Hovea; (08) 9298 9493; www.hovearidge.com.au

KATHARINE SUSANNAH PRICHARD WRITERS' CENTRE $

Got a burning desire to retreat from the world and write that great Australian novel? The Katharine Susannah Prichard Writers' Centre is just the place to come for a night, a week or a month. The rooms are well appointed and include air-conditioning, ensuites and internet access, and the complex has cooking facilities. This is an ideal environment to interact with other writers, or simply find a quiet spot in the garden to express your inner voice. Members of the centre are entitled to a 45 per cent discount.

11 Old York Rd, Greenmount; (08) 9294 1872; www.kspf.iinet.net.au

ROSE & CROWN $$

The Rose & Crown has two types of accommodation: the Lodge and heritage rooms. The Lodge consists of 28 well-appointed modern rooms and are in a separate wing. The motel rooms have recently been refurbished with private ensuites, and there are also three family rooms with adjoining suites. Upstairs in the historic Rose and Crown hotel are sumptuous king-sized suites decorated in heritage style. Three of the four suites have spa baths.

105 Swan St, Guildford; (08) 9347 8100; www.rosecrown.com.au

SETTLERS REST FARMSTAY $$$

This country retreat is just 30 minutes from Perth. The three-bedroom cottage was built at the turn of the 20th century and has been beautifully restored to its former glory, including high ceilings, wooden floorboards and an open fireplace. Full of antiques and period furniture, it features all the modern conveniences while retaining its charm. Located on the banks of the Swan River (including a private jetty), visitors can marvel at the views of the Darling Ranges and the lovely sunsets over the vineyards from their verandah.

90 George St, West Swan; (08) 9250 4540; www.settlersrest.com.au

STRELLEY BROOK COTTAGE $$$

Strelley Brook Cottage is a historic mud-brick farmhouse built in 1860, and blends period decor with modern conveniences. The large estate is set on 4.5 hectares, ensuring privacy and seclusion. The rustic farmhouse was one of the first buildings in the area, and has two bedrooms and is fully self-contained. Surrounded by views of the Darling Ranges and vineyards, experience country life only 30 minutes from the CBD.

90 Lefroy St, Herne Hill; (08) 9296 1876; www.strelleybrook.com.au

TANNAMURRA $$$$$

If you're looking for a luxury home just 30 minutes from the CBD, then Tannamurra will not disappoint. Set within award-winning gardens, the huge property has several marron dams and guests are encouraged to catch their own freshwater crayfish. The luxurious four-bedroom Tuscan-inspired home is packed with European antiques, a chef's kitchen, an enormous open fireplace and a dining room table that seats 14. Located just five minutes from the lovely Swan Valley and its famous restaurants and wineries, the homestead is also within minutes of the Vines Golf Course.

Off Great Northern Hwy, via Lynward Park Estate; (08) 9430 9933; www.tannamurra.com.au

VINES RESORT & COUNTRY CLUB $$$$

For all you sinners out there, The Vines offers packages indulging in the Seven Deadly Sins: envy, revenge, lust, vanity, gluttony, sloth or decadence – just pick your vice and go for it. Otherwise play a round at the 36-hole championship golf course or enjoy the host of other facilities associated with a world-class resort. The accommodation includes resort rooms, some with a spa, and apartments backing onto the golf course.

Verdelho Dr, The Vines; (08) 9297 3000; www.vines.com.au

Nannup

BEYONDERUP FALLS $$

After relaxing in your spa on the deck overlooking the Blackwood River and green countryside, you might consider making that tree change a reality. All four of the two-storey timber chalets are completely private, and cater for adults only. The chalets are fully self-contained with log fires, air-conditioning and barbecue facilities, and a mobile masseur is available upon request.

Balingup Rd; (08) 9756 2034; www.beyonderup.com.au

CRABAPPLE LANE B&B $

The purpose-built Crabapple Lane B&B is tastefully decorated and has three bedrooms with ensuites. The communal lounge room is inviting and leads out to a pergola. It's near the Blackwood River and Kondil National

Park, where you will find alpacas, berry bushes, wildflowers and the lovely unspoilt village.

Barrabup Rd; (08) 9756 0017;
www.crabapplelane.com.au

REDGUM HILL COUNTRY RETREAT $$$$

Whether you're staying in the villa, which is in the guest wing of the homestead, or in one of the chalets, you'll find yourself on 4.5 hectares of magical grounds consisting of woodlands, ponds and gardens perched on the banks of the Blackwood River. The romantic two-storey chalets have wood fires and spas, and are self-contained. The retreat caters for adults only, and is very popular with honeymooners.

Balingup Rd; (08) 9756 2056;
www.redgum-hill.com.au

TATHRA HILL TOP RETREAT $$

Fresh air, playful blue wrens and double spas invoke romance at this adult-only retreat. The cottages at Tathra Hill Top Retreat are self-contained, and include luxurious bed linen and cosy living areas complete with a wood fire. If you need a reprise from lounging around in your pyjamas, change into your walking gear and hike to the Tathra Wildlife Sanctuary, take a stroll to the restaurant or forget about dressing for dinner altogether and have your meal delivered.

Blackwood River Tourist Dr (Route 251);
(08) 9756 2040; www.tathra.net

Narrogin

ALBERT FACEY MOTOR INN $

The Albert Facey Motor Inn brings a touch of modern luxury to the region with its spacious and comfortable rooms. The honeymoon suite includes a spa, and the hotel has corporate facilities and a restaurant overlooking the pool. Facing 10 hectares of Foxes Lair, an abundance of Australian bush and wildflowers is on your doorstep and the town's main street is a short walk away.

78 Williams Rd; (08) 9881 1899;
www.albertfacey.com

CHUCKEM FARM B&B $$

Chuckem Farm B&B consists of two bedrooms in the main homestead and an additional self-contained three-bedroom cottage. Situated on a grain and sheep farm, guests can enjoy a tour of the property, fish for yabbies, relax with a picnic or take a walk to marvel at the wildflowers during September and October.

1481 Tarwonga Rd; (08) 9881 1188

EDEN VALLEY FARMSTAY $$

Your hosts Jefferson and Barbara Harris welcome you to their working sheep, cattle and alpaca farm. A guided tour of the property and its varied birdlife and wildflowers is included with your stay. The two-bedroom cottage is in the original farmhouse and has been lovingly restored to its Federation glory, including the wood fire. Full board in the farmhouse is also available and meals are available by arrangement.

BREAKFAST INCLUDED   CREDIT CARDS ACCEPTED   FAMILY FRIENDLY

3733 Williams–Kondinin Rd; (08) 9881 5864; www.edenvalleyfarmstay.com.au

New Norcia

MONASTERY GUESTHOUSE $

Those seeking reflection will appreciate true Benedictine hospitality at the Monastery Guesthouse. Accommodating 24 guests, there is an assortment of single and twin rooms, some with shared facilities and others with ensuites. The room rate is regarded as a donation and is not a fixed price. Spiritual direction is available upon request, and a stay at the guesthouse really does define the phrase 'getting away from it all'.

Great Northern Hwy; (08) 9654 8002; www.newnorcia.wa.edu.au

NEW NORCIA HOTEL $

In Australia's only monastic town, you'll find a slice of Spain in this small country town's Benedictine community. Despite the simple accommodation available at the New Norcia Hotel, the grand building is impressive with its magnificent staircase, high arches topped by eight solid Roman pillars and wide, terrazzo-finished verandah.

Great Northern Hwy; (08) 9654 8034; www.newnorcia.wa.edu.au/accommodation/new-norcia-hotel

NIRRANDA FARMSTAY $$

Fancy some rural seclusion? The Nirranda Farmstay is a working grain, sheep and cattle farm on 2000 hectares. But don't worry, you won't be herding any cattle, just interacting with the farm animals, strolling down a country lane or taking a tour of the farm. The spacious four-bedroom homestead is comfortably decorated and includes a wood fire, barbecue facilities and a swimming pool.

9236 Great Northern Hwy, Wannamal; (08) 9655 9046; www.nirrandafarmstay.com.au

Newman

NEWMAN HOTEL MOTEL $

In the town centre, the Newman Hotel Motel is ideally located to discover the natural wonders of the Pilbara region. Offering standard motel rooms, there is also a pleasant swimming pool, barbecue facilities, bistro and bar.

Newman Dr; (08) 9175 1101; www.newmanhotelmotel.com.au

SEASONS HOTEL NEWMAN $

The Seasons Hotel Newman caters to all seasons of travellers. There are standard hotel rooms as well as interconnecting, disabled, self-catering and suites. The rooms are modern and well appointed, and include private facilities and air-conditioning. The Lodge has accommodation with shared facilities. On-site is a tropical swimming pool, restaurant, bar and minigolf course.

Newman Dr; (08) 9177 8666; www.seasonshotel.com.au

FITNESS CENTRE   ROOM SERVICE   SWIMMING POOL

Norseman

NORSEMAN GREAT WESTERN MOTEL AND GREAT WESTERN TRAVEL VILLAGE $$

Considered Norseman's premier hotel, this is a lovely spot to refresh and recharge the batteries before continuing on your way across the Nullarbor Plain. The rooms are comfortably appointed, and the rammed-earth hotel includes a pool and licensed restaurant.

Prinsep St; (08) 9039 1633;
www.norsemangreatwesternmotel.com.au

Northam

AVON BRIDGE HOTEL $

Enjoy a stay in not only a traditional Australian outback pub, but in fact Northam's oldest pub, built in 1858. Both the motel and hotel rooms include air-conditioning and the motel rooms have private ensuites. The pub has a beer garden and the restaurant has an à la carte menu.

322 Fitzgerald St; (08) 9622 1023;
www.avonbridgehotel.com.au

BRACKSON HOUSE B&B $$$

Brackson House was built in 1903, but the private guest wing is a recent addition and includes many of the original homestead's wonderful features. The four rooms include plush details like luxury linens, flat-screen TVs, internet access and individual decoration. The secluded courtyard includes a heated spa and the lawned area inspires one to curl up with a good book. Arrange dinner in the grand dining room, take a short stroll to the heart of the town or be adventurous and float in a hot-air balloon over the Avon Valley.

7 Katrine Rd; (08) 9622 5262;
www.bracksonhouse.com.au

EGOLINE REFLECTIONS $$

Set in beautiful grounds, Egoline Reflections is a classic homestead offering country hospitality. Built in 1850 and classified by the National Trust, B&B-style rooms and a self-contained cottage are available. Savour the surroundings or take advantage of the central location to explore the area.

Northam–Toodyay Rd; (08) 9622 5811;
Toodyay Rd; (08) 9622 5811

URALIA COTTAGE $$

Established in 1902, heritage-listed Uralia Homestead is a town landmark, showcasing the wealth of a bygone era. The period style has been carried through to self-contained Uralia Cottage, which has one bedroom and tranquil gardens that include a swimming pool.

Cnr 59 Gordon St and Uralia Tce;
(08) 9622 1742

MYSTIQUE MAISON $$$

With 14 bedrooms and six bathrooms, Mystique Maison is ideal for group retreats. Murder Mystery nights are a specialty, which isn't hard to imagine in this heritage-style homestead. Hopefully all the guests survive the night and are accounted for at breakfast.

10 Forrest St, Goomalling; (08) 9629 1673

BREAKFAST INCLUDED   CREDIT CARDS ACCEPTED   FAMILY FRIENDLY

Northampton

GLENORIE LOOKOUT LODGE $$

From your lodge, 2 kilometres from the main homestead, look out over Glenorie's working farm, the natural bushland and the Indian Ocean beyond. The cosy stone cottages sleeps four, is self-contained and well appointed with all the modern conveniences, except for a phone, bringing a sigh of relief to those seeking tranquillity. Spend your days meandering the 3600 hectare farm and from July to September witness the wildflowers in full bloom.

1697 Swamps Rd; (08) 9935 1017

OLD MINERS' COTTAGES B&B $

The Old Miners' Cottages B&B is set on established grounds watered by the Bowes River, which flows into the Indian Ocean. Long Cottage has two B&B rooms and can sleep up to eight adults, while Moyle's Cottage is self-contained. The property is heritage listed and ideally located for visitors wanting to explore the historic region of Northampton.

Brook St; (08) 9934 1864

Northcliffe

BIBBULMUN BREAK MOTEL $$

A popular rest spot for trekkers of the Bibbulman Track, which is only 100 metres away, the Bibbulum Break Motel has four rooms with ensuites. Close to the unspoilt coastline and national parks, guests will enjoy this rural getaway in the heart of town.

14 Wheatley Coast Rd; (08) 9776 6060; www.bibbulmunbreakmotel.com

NORTHCLIFFE HOTEL $

The Northcliffe Hotel has comfortable hotel rooms with all the standard modern conveniences required for a stopover. Included in the complex is a bar and a restaurant serving hearty counter meals.

Lot 8 Wheatley Coast Rd; (08) 9776 7089; www.northcliffe.org.au/accom.htm

RIVERWAY CHALETS $$

Accommodating two to six people, the four Riverway Chalets have a range of sleeping arrangements and the rammed-earth chalets are fully self-contained. Situated 7 kilometres from town and nestled in the forest, you can cosy up in peace by the fire or relax on the verandah and enjoy the wildlife.

Riverway Rd; (08) 9776 7183; www.riverwaychalets.com.au

WATERMARK KILNS $

The heritage-listed Watermark Kilns are 1950s tobacco kilns converted into accommodation. They have retained much of their character, including the gabled roof which has flaps that can be opened and closed to regulate the temperature inside. However, there are potbelly stoves for those cold days the region is known so well for. Accommodation is flexible, where guests can share with other travellers or hire an entire cottage. With self-contained facilities, guests are welcome to visit the

FITNESS CENTRE   ROOM SERVICE   SWIMMING POOL

permaculture garden and collect fresh eggs and since a marron farm is run on the premises, marron is available for sale.

Karri Hill Rd; (08) 9776 7349; www.watermarkkilns.com.au

Onslow

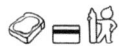

CLUB THEVENARD $$

Thevenard Island is one of the ten islands that make up the Mackerel Islands. The accommodation village, Club Thevenard, is a refurbished ex-mining camp that can cater for up to 55 guests, from singles and couples to families and groups. Alternatively, if you're after a bit more luxury, there are 11 beachfront cabins which range from two to five bedrooms and are fully self-contained.

Thevenard Island; (08) 9184 6444; www.mackerelislands.com.au

DIRECTION ISLAND $$$$$

Longing to escape to a deserted island? On Direction Island, seclusion is guaranteed since the only structure on the island is a beach cabin which sleeps six. Totally self-sufficient and only accessible by private vessel or charter boat, the island doesn't even have a jetty. There won't be a soul in sight except for your travelling companions. This truly is for the adventurous, and with your own private beaches and coral reef to explore, the snorkelling, diving and fishing opportunities are sensational. Don't forget to bring all your own linen and food, unless you're planning on catching it.

Direction Island; (08) 9184 6444; www.mackerelislands.com.au

ONSLOW MACKEREL MOTEL $$

With the Indian Ocean just metres away and the town within walking distance, the Onslow Mackerel Motel is ideally situated. The modern rooms are fully self-contained, with air-conditioning, internet access, barbecue facilities and boats available for hire. The motel is the perfect spot to stay on your way over to the Mackerel Islands or to explore the stunning Pilbara region.

Cnr Second Ave and Third St; (08) 9184 6586; www.onslowmackerelmotel.com.au

ONSLOW SUN CHALETS $$

Right on the beachfront in one of the north-west's few remaining seaside bush towns, these motel rooms and self-contained chalets are close to Onslow's attractions.

Second Ave; (08) 9184 6058; www.onslowsunchalets.com.au

Pemberton

CLOVER COTTAGE $$

Situated on the banks of the Warren River and with pastoral views, the limestone Clover Cottages make for a tranquil bush getaway. Fully self-contained, the cottages sleep up to six people and feature polished jarrah floors, wood fires and private spas. The property has several lakes stocked with brown and rainbow trout. Guided fishing tours of the lakes and rivers are available by arrangement.

251 Wheatley Coast Rd; (08) 9773 1262; www.clover-cottage.com.au

---

BREAKFAST INCLUDED   CREDIT CARDS ACCEPTED   FAMILY FRIENDLY

PEPPERMINT GROVE RETREAT $$$$

Nestled in Pemberton, birds abound as you relax on your private deck overlooking peppermint trees at elegant Peppermint Grove Retreat. The chalets feature king beds, twin spas and gas log fires. This 40-hectare, adult-only retreat ensures privacy and inspires romance and relaxation. If you can bear to tear yourself away from your room, pick up some local marron or trout for the barbecue.

Lot 5198, Channybearup Rd; (08) 9776 0056; www.peppermintretreat.com

PUMP HILL FARM COTTAGES $$

The Pump Hill Farm Cottages make for the ideal getaway, where the whole family can experience farm life the easy way. The rammed-earth two and three-bedroom cottages are self-contained and include a log fire. Couples may prefer the timber one-bedroom Forest Cottage nestled by the majestic karri forest. The three-bedroom Homestead sleeps eight and features a huge stone fireplace, claw-foot bath and lovely views of Pemberton. The little ones will love the playground, hay rides and feeding the friendly animals, while parents will appreciate the gourmet dinner platters of local fare.

Pump Hill Rd; (08) 9776 1379; www.pumphill.com.au

SALITAGE SUITES $$$$

Perhaps the attraction of the lovely Salitage Suites exudes from the very marri wood they've been crafted from, though many would argue that having their own private retreat nestled in old-growth forest is enough of a drawcard. The adult-only suites are fully self-contained, with king-sized beds and separate balconies. Salitage Winery is one of Western Australia's premier wineries and their reputation for outstanding quality is carried through into the suites.

Salitage Winery, Vasse Hwy; (08) 9776 1195; www.suites.salitage.com.au

WARREN RIVER RESORT $$$

Warren River Resort is surrounded by majestic karri trees and an abundant array of wildlife. Possum spotting, wildflowers in spring and fishing along the river are what it's all about on this 17-hectare property. Each of the private rammed-earth cottages are self-contained, with barbecue facilities, wood fires, birdfeeders and two or three bedrooms. Also on-site is a swimming pool, children's playground and games room.

713 Pemberton–Northcliffe Rd; (08) 9776 1400; www.warrenriverresort.com.au

Pingelly

PINGELLY ROADHOUSE AND MOTEL $

Although a small farming town, Pingelly makes a significant contribution to the state's wool and grain exports. Established in 1846, it provides insight into how the pioneers once lived and is a friendly community to visit. The Pingelly Roadhouse and Motel is the town's premier accommodation, and is comfortably appointed with a restaurant on-site.

8 Quadrant St; (08) 9887 1015

Pinjarra

LAZY RIVER BOUTIQUE B&B $$$$$

The suites at the Lazy River Boutique B&B include polished floorboards, high ceilings, plush bathrooms and lavish furnishings. All four suites have kitchenettes and sitting rooms opening out onto a deck. The grounds include a gazebo, a tennis court, and the Murray River, which is ideal for kayaking, fishing or lounging by. There's no need to face the public before your first coffee as breakfast is served in your suite and pre-dinner drinks and dinner can also be enjoyed in privacy.

9 Wilson Rd; (08) 9531 4550;
www.lazyriver.com.au

PINJARRA CABINS & CARAVAN PARK $

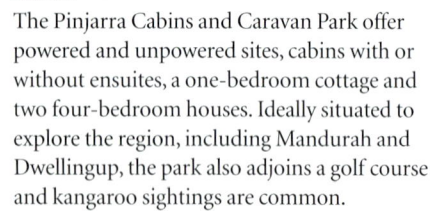

The Pinjarra Cabins and Caravan Park offer powered and unpowered sites, cabins with or without ensuites, a one-bedroom cottage and two four-bedroom houses. Ideally situated to explore the region, including Mandurah and Dwellingup, the park also adjoins a golf course and kangaroo sightings are common.

1716 Pinjarra Rd; (08) 9531 1374;
www.pinjarracaravanpark.com.au

NAUTICA LODGE $$

One hour south of Perth and situated halfway between Mandurah and Pinjarra, the Nautica Lodge B&B has two suites, one overlooking the river with a private terrace and the other able to be configured as a single, double or triple room. Both well-appointed rooms include private ensuites, air-conditioning and private entry. Enjoying the freedom of requesting breakfast when and where you so desire is a nice touch, as is the fact that your hosts can arrange transport for you to the local attractions, restaurants and pubs.

203 Culeenup Rd, North Yunderup;
(08) 9537 8000; www.nauticalodge.com

Port Hedland

ALL SEASONS PORT HEDLAND $$$$

All Seasons Port Hedland offers endless views of the Indian Ocean, but is also close to town. The rooms are comfortably appointed and include all-important air conditions. The hotel has conference facilities, a swimming pool and more ocean views for bistro patrons dining on the terrace.

Cnr Lukis and McGregor sts; (08) 9173 1511;
www.accorhotels.com

COOKE POINT HOLIDAY PARK $

With a variety of units and powered sites, the Cooke Point Holiday Park offers clean and modern accommodation and facilities. Geared well towards families, the park has a playground, swimming pool, recreation room, barbecue facilities and direct access to the beach, making this a great place to unwind and enjoy the Pilbara region.

2 Taylor St; (08) 9173 1271 or 1800 459 999;
cooke-point-holiday-park.wa.big4.com.au

HOSPITALITY INN PORT HEDLAND $$$

Offering motel-style accommodation, the rooms are air-conditioned, comfortable and clean. On-site are barbecue facilities, a licensed restaurant and a swimming pool. Centrally

BREAKFAST INCLUDED   CREDIT CARDS ACCEPTED   FAMILY FRIENDLY

situated, you are close to the beach, the conveniences of town and the many natural wonders of the region.

Webster St; (08) 9173 1044;
www.porthedland.wa.hospitalityinns.com.au

THE LODGE MOTEL $$$

The Lodge Motel is well located to the business district in South Hedland and offers standard hotel rooms and self-contained apartments. Included in the rate are meals, access to the gymnasium and swimming pool.

5–13 Hawke Pl, South Hedland; (08) 9172 2188

Ravensthorpe

RAVENSTHORPE PALACE MOTOR HOTEL $

Situated between Esperance and Albany, the Palace Hotel is one of those traditional heritage Australian pubs that reflect the state's rich mining history. The rooms are comfortable and downstairs the punters have their fill of hearty counter meals and cold beer. The gold and copper have long gone and now Ravensthorpe is known as a world-heritage conservation area famous for wildflowers, fauna and the imposing Ravensthorpe Ranges.

28 Morgan St; (08) 9838 1005

Rockingham

5 STAR @ ARIA $$$$$

Anyone for a penthouse on the beach? A stay here should suffice as the three-bedroom apartment also has never-ending ocean views interrupted only by Garden Island and Fremantle. The apartment is luxuriously appointed with elevator access, cable plasma TV, spa bath, a balcony with an outdoor setting and a well-equipped kitchen. Spread over the 8th and 9th floors, the Aria complex is secure and has undercover parking.

Rockingham Beach Rd; 0407 419 194;
www.rockingham-tourism.com

LUXURY @ NAUTILUS $$$

Situated within an apartment complex, this beachside accommodation is located just 40 minutes south of Perth. The two-bedroom apartment is stylishly decorated, with internet access, a well-equipped kitchen, barbecue and balcony with an outdoor setting.

18–24 Kent St; Rockingham Visitor Centre (08) 9592 3464

MANUEL TOWERS $$$

Despite an attempt at making a play on words, the only similarity between Manuel Towers and Fawlty Towers is that the B&B is run by an English lady and a Spaniard. The unique building features stone, recycled timbers, handcrafted furniture and other rustic materials, fooling you into believing that you are in the Mediterranean. All five rooms are beautifully decorated and have their own unique characteristics. One has a spa, another a balcony and there's also a room that caters for diasabled guests.

32A Arcadia Dr, Shoalwater; (08) 9592 2698;
www.manueltowers.com.au

PAYNE'S FIND $$$

Payne's Find is a well-appointed contemporary home right on the waterfront. Given its location, sensational views and direct access to the water, fun is guaranteed. Spread over three floors, there is plenty of space for the whole family, with a downstairs games room and a parents retreat upstairs.

171 Rockingham Beach Rd; Rockingham Visitor Centre (08) 9592 3464; www.rockinghamvisitorcentre.com.au

Roebourne

AMANI COTTAGE $$

With sea views, Amani Cottage is ideally situated to enjoy the beach and its many delights, including the harbour and seafood restaurants. Fully self-contained, the cottage includes air-conditioning, is comfortably decorated and has a cute garden.

1 McLeod St, Pt Samson; (08) 9187 1085

POINT SAMSON RESORT $$$$

Point Samson is possibly one of the last unspoilt places on earth. Thirty minutes from Karratha and just metres from the Indian Ocean, the resort hosts self-contained units and deluxe spa units. Set among tropical gardens, the swimming pool invites lounging with a cocktail. The picture-postcard beach on your doorstep offers swimming, snorkelling, fishing and relaxation.

56 Samson Rd, Pt Samson; (08) 9187 1052; www.pointsamson.com

SAMSON BEACH CHALETS $$$$

Situated in Point Samson, the Samson Beach Chalets are beautifully presented. Some are self-contained and include extras like outdoor showers, air-conditioning and internet access. The beach is nearby or you could just relax on one of the deck chairs by the pool.

44 Bartley Crt, Pt Samson; (08) 9187 0202; www.samsonbeach.com.au

SAMSON HIDEAWAY $$$

This holiday house is located in the centre of town and close to amenities, cafes and golf course, with the beach just a skip away. Comfortably decorated, the Samson Hideaway includes two bedrooms, air-conditioning and is fully self-contained.

49 Meares Dr, Point Samson; (08) 9187 0330

Rottnest Island

ALLISON CAMPING AREA $

The Allison Camping Area is the only campsite on the island. It is extremely popular, so early bookings by a ballot system are essential. Situated in Thomson Bay, the shady campsite is unpowered and includes barbecue facilities and an ablutions block.

Strue Rd; (08) 9432 9111; www.rottnestislandonline.com

HOTEL ROTTNEST $$$

Formerly the Quokka Arms, this Victorian building was originally the summer residence for the governors of Western Australia. Now it

BREAKFAST INCLUDED   CREDIT CARDS ACCEPTED   FAMILY FRIENDLY

accommodates tourists and every room has an ensuite. Downstairs is the island's favourite watering hole. Being right on the shoreline, the hotel is ideally situated to enjoy the numerous island attractions.

1 Bedford Ave; (08) 9292 5011;
www.hotelrottnest.com.au

KINGSTOWN BARRACKS $

The Kingstown Barracks includes two types of accommodation: the Kingstown Barracks, Rottnest Island Hostel and the Governor's Circle. The barracks have 17 dormitory rooms, some with ensuites and others with shared facilities. The hostel sleeps 50 people over several rooms and dormitories, and the facilities are communal. The Governor's Circle consists of self-contained cottages with an assortment of sleeping configurations.

Parker Point Rd; (08) 9432 9111;
www.rottnestisland.com

ROTTNEST ISLAND AUTHORITY HOLIDAY UNITS $

The Rottnest Island Authority Holiday Units include a variety of cottages, villas, units, bungalows and cabins. Available by ballot system, the holiday units are usually booked well in advance, but there is often some availability during the off-season. Recently renovated, the holiday units are situated in Thomson Bay, Kingstown, Geordie Bay, Longreach Bay and Fays Bay, and many have views.

(08) 9432 9111; www.rottnestisland.com

ROTTNEST LODGE $$$$

The Rottnest Lodge is the island's premier hotel and includes several historical buildings, including the original barracks and a prison. No longer thought of as an Alcatraz, a more up-market clientele is attracted these days with a range of rooms available. All rooms have ensuites, some with lakeside views, and the family rooms include two-bedroom apartments.

4 Kitson Way; (08) 9292 5161;
www.rottnestlodge.com.au

Southern Cross

SOUTHERN CROSS CARAVAN PARK & MOTOR LODGE $

Apart from being famous for being remote, Southern Cross is known for its gold history, farming and magnificent wildflowers. The caravan park includes powered and unpowered sites, park cabins as well as a motor lodge offering motel rooms where a light breakfast is included.

Great Eastern Hwy; (08) 9049 1212;
www.southerncrosscaravanpark.com.au

Tom Price

KARIJINI ECO RETREAT $

Located about an hour away from Tom Price, deep in spectacular Karijini National Park, the Karijini Eco Retreat offers a mixture of luxurious eco tents and more traditional campsites. Some of the eco tents have ensuites and the remaining tents have shared facilities, though rest assured that hot showers are available. Bush kitchens allow for self-catering although there is a bar and a licensed restaurant serving Australian fare. Explore the park's iconic unspoilt charm on foot and discover

FITNESS CENTRE   ROOM SERVICE   SWIMMING POOL

its fauna and flora as well as pools, gorges and treks with varying degrees of difficulty.

Off Weano Rd, Karijini National Park; (08) 9425 5591; www.karijiniecoretreat.com.au

Toodyay

AVONDALE ESTATE $$

If you're looking for a cosy country retreat in a historic building, don't overlook Avondale Estate. This romantic home, nestled on the Avon River, includes all the charm you would expect of the era with wooden floorboards, a claw-foot bath, fireplaces and high ceilings. Couples may prefer to treat this experience as a B&B in the guest wing, although the entire three-bedroom and two-bathroom homestead is available for hire.

9 Railway Rd; (08) 9574 4033;

BOSHACK FARM $$$

Live like the squatters used to in the bush at Boshack Farm, just 90 minutes from the CBD. Surrounded by bushland, the rustic cabins are nestled by the lake under a starlit sky. Pre-order a barbecue pack or BYO food and drinks. Alternatively, stay with a farming family and experience what it's like to live on a farm. The farmstay includes breakfast, dinner and an outdoor adventure tour. Your nights will be spent around the campfire sampling bush food. An ideal place for those seeking an authentic outback experience, and a popular venue for school camps and staff retreats.

Wattening Spring Rd, Bolgart; 0408 005 628; www.boshackoutback.com

IPSWICH VIEW HOMESTEAD $$$

Set on several hectares of countryside, 1890s Ipswich View Homestead has five guest rooms, all with ensuites, and there is also a self-contained unit. B&B includes a swimming pool, tennis court and minigolf.

45 Folewood Rd; (08) 9574 4038

MOUNTAIN PARK RETREAT $$$$

With uninterrupted views of rolling hills, Mountain Park Retreat is a two-storey Queenslander-style home that sleeps ten people. The five-bedroom and two-bathroom home is tastefully decorated and has several living areas, including a pool room. The master bedroom has a spa and there are commanding views from most rooms. It's suited to a group of friends or a large family, with an outdoor entertaining area and large dining room for socialising.

Cnr Dumbarton Rd and Nairn Dr; (08) 9255 2653; www.mountainparkretreat.com.au

TOODYAY FARMSTAY $$$

The elevated timber cottage here is an ideal rural retreat, situated 6 kilometres from town. The Avon River is only 200 metres away, where the Avon Descent white-water rafting competition flies past every year. The self-contained two-bedroom cottage has a sofa bed in the lounge room, a wood fire and reverse-cycle air-conditioning.

51 Leeder St, West Toodyay; (08) 9385 8824

BREAKFAST INCLUDED   CREDIT CARDS ACCEPTED   FAMILY FRIENDLY

Wagin

MORANS' WAGIN HOTEL $

Wagin is famous for its enormous statue of a ram overlooking the town, acknowledging its success with the wool industry. The town was established in the 1880s and today many of the grand buildings from the era not only still stand, but have been restored. The family-run Morans' Wagin Hotel was the first hotel built and offers hotel rooms and home-style food served downstairs.

77 Tudor St; (08) 9861 1017

Walpole

AYR SAILEAN $$$

Situated halfway between Denmark and Walpole, Ayr Sailean is a working sheep and cattle farmstay. The accommodation includes studio chalets, a three-bedroom cottage and house. The chalets are geared towards couples seeking a bit of luxury, with valley views from the bedroom and spas in the bathrooms. The renovated Wool Cottage was built in the 1930s and features an open fire in the lounge, while Inverell Home has sweeping views of the Frankland River.

1 Tindale Rd, Bow Bridge; (08) 9840 8098; www.ayrsailean.com

CHE SARA SARA CHALETS $

Nestled on the banks of the Frankland River, the Che Sara Sara Chalets are a tranquil retreat. The self-contained cottages have either two or three bedrooms and include an open fireplace or a potbelly. Bushwalking, canoeing, swimming, tennis and fishing for marron are some of the activities on offer. Pets are welcome and kennels are available and included in your rate. Nearby is the Valley of the Giants and Treetop Walk, inlets, circular pools, falls and Mount Frankland.

92 Nunn Rd, Hazelvale; (08) 9840 8004

HOUSEBOAT HOLIDAYS $$$$$

Explore the Frankland River aboard a houseboat and fish, swim or simply enjoy the natural beauty. There are three boats to choose from, varying in the number of berths and sleeping four to ten people. All include cooking facilities, outdoor furniture on the top deck and a motorised dinghy. Upon arrival you'll be given 'hands on' instructions, then left to discover your sense of adventure.

Lot 660 Boronia St; (08) 9840 1310; www.houseboatholiday.com.au

TREE ELLE RETREAT $$$$

The Tree Elle Retreat is one of those places that caters well to kids and yet hasn't forgotten about the adults. While a day spa, gourmet kitchens, king-sized beds, rural views and plush decor aren't exactly 'needs', they certainly have been raved about by the media and countless satisfied guests. The little ones will love interacting with the farm animals, collecting eggs and exploring the delightful grounds.

Lot 4, South Coast Hwy; (08) 9840 8471; www.treeelle.com

WALPOLE WILDERNESS RESORT $$

Soaking in a hot spa in the forest with stunning views and a wood fire are the ingredients for a cosy escape. The three-bedroom chalets at the Walpole Wilderness Resort are fully equipped, with barbecues and outdoor furniture on the deck. The resort is set on 70 hectares of towering trees and native flora and fauna, which you can discover along walking trails.

Gardiner Rd; (08) 9840 1481;
www.waresort.com.au

Wickepin

WICKEPIN HOTEL $

Wickepin was immortalised in Albert Facey's novel *A Fortunate Life*, which depicted the hardship of Facey's life during his time in the town. The Albert Facey homestead stands today in remembrance of the author. Nearby, the Wickepin Hotel offers standard hotel rooms and serves counter meals in the dining room.

34 Wogolin Rd; (08) 9888 1192

Wyndham

KIMBERLEY COASTAL CAMP $$$$$

You know you're really getting away from it all when the only way to get to your accommodation is by helicopter. Once you've landed at the Kimberley Coastal Camp and marvelled at the richness of the landscape, settle into your stylish guest gazebo with gulf views or relax in the pavilion with fellow travellers or a good book. Feast on seafood pulled from the ocean that day, or float in the swimming pool complete with those unmistakable Kimberley views. When you can't bear the luxury of uninterrupted relaxation, take a fishing expedition, explore ancient rock art, or meander along one of the walking trails. Depending on your luck, you might sight dingos, turtles, humpback whales, wallabies, birdlife and, yes, it is crocodile country. But what's a good Australian outback tale without a bit of drama?

Admiralty Gulf, access by air; 0417 902 006;
www.kimberleycoastalcamp.com.au

Yalgoo

TARDIE AND YUIN STATIONS $$$$

Six and a half hours from Perth, Yalgoo is known as the place where the outback starts. The homestead is comfortable and clean, but the real reason to visit here is to experience life on the station and get a sense of the outback's rugged, remote wilderness. Your hosts will welcome you into the family and their 16 000-hectare farm, which includes ancient Aboriginal sites, a disused mine, rivers, waterholes for swimming, sunsets, wildflowers and an amazing array of wildlife. All meals are included and guided tours can be arranged.

(08) 9963 7980

Yallingup

CAPE LODGE $$$$$

Winner of many hotel awards, Cape Lodge is the undisputed jewel in this famous wine region.

BREAKFAST INCLUDED   CREDIT CARDS ACCEPTED   FAMILY FRIENDLY

The fact that it has a helicopter landing pad gives you an idea of what a true five-star resort is really like. Whether you stay in the main lodge, in one of the suites, the two-bedroom cottage or the Vineyard residence (which caters for five couples), you can be sure your surroundings will be luxurious and the service impeccable. The restaurant overlooks the lake and serves only the freshest local produce to its discerning patrons. You may reluctantly leave the forest, parkland and manicured grounds of this country estate to partake in one of the lodge's wine- and nature-based tours.

3341 Caves Rd; (08) 9755 6311; www.capelodge.com.au

FOURWELLS $$$$$

Sleeping ten, Fourwells suits all requirements. Whether you're a large family or a group of friends, relaxation in this holiday house is unavoidable. All four bedrooms and three bathrooms are well appointed and the kitchen has all the modern conveniences you would expect, including a cappuccino machine. The landscaped gardens include an enclosed trampoline and a lawn for the children to run wild on, plus an outdoor Balinese shower to wash away the day at the beach. Other features include table tennis, barbecue, indoor spa, cable TV and internet access.

address confirmed with booking; (08) 9385 5611; www.privateprop.com

INJIDUP SPA RETREAT $$$$$

Injidup Spa Retreat combines accommodation with specialised spa treatments. The fully self-contained two-bedroom suites have heated polished concrete flooring, plunge pools, spa courtyard and decks with ocean views. Of course, a visit to the day spa is a must, with treatments especially designed after a private consultation.

Cape Clairault Rd, Injidup; (08) 9750 1300; www.injidupsparetreat.com

SEASHELLS RESORT YALLINGUP $$$

By the beach in the heart of the Margaret River wine region, Seashells Resort Yallingup is adjacent to the restored Caves House, built at the turn of last century. The studios and one- and two-bedroom apartments are designed in an Art Deco style, sympathetic to the era of the original complex. The studios include spas and the apartments are fully self-contained. Caves House has lovingly restored suites ideal for couples, and also hosts weddings and conferences.

Yallingup Beach Rd; (08) 9750 1500; www.seashells.com.au

SMITHS BEACH RESORT $$$$

Situated on pristine Smiths Beach between Cape Naturaliste and Cape Leeuwin, the stylish Smiths Beach Resort was built to have minimal impact on the environment. Floor-to-ceiling windows capture the magnificent setting, and the self-contained accommodation is luxuriously appointed, with a range of options depending on your budget. Everything is to hand – food, wine, tennis, a day spa and the spectacular coastline.

Smiths Beach Rd; (08) 9750 1200; www.smithsbeachresort.com.au

Yanchep

BOBBY JO'S B&B $

Just a short stroll from the beach, Bobby Jo's offers comfortable rooms, all with an ensuite and spa. Your hosts, Bob and Jo, will accommodate special requests to make your stay memorable, although watching the sun set into the Indian Ocean from your balcony is a given.

99 Two Rocks Rd; (08) 9561 5304; www.bobbyjostworocks.com

CASA DEL MAR $$

Located at Yanchep Lagoon and close to the region's attractions, Casa Del Mar is a beautifully appointed two-bedroom villa with a fully equipped kitchen, four-poster bed, entertainment system, air-conditioning, private courtyard and swimming pool. With the beach, national park, caves and golf course nearby and not to mention only an hour away from Perth, Casa Del Mar is the ideal weekend getaway.

10B Arney Crt; (08) 9298 9367; www.villayanchep.com

OCEANVIEW RETREAT $$$$

Superbly appointed, the Oceanview Retreat has five bedrooms, two bathrooms, a gourmet kitchen and those all-important ocean views. A stay here would suit groups or families wanting that homey feel and to make the most out of the area's many attractions.

address confirmed with bookings; (08) 9276 4257; www.oceanview-retreat.com.au

YANCHEP HOLIDAY VILLAGE $$

Golfing enthusiasts will enjoy a stay at the Yanchep Holiday Village, overlooking the championship golf course at the Sun City Country Club. The self-contained apartments have one, two or three bedrooms, private verandahs, air-conditioning and a store room for all your holiday gear.

St Andrews Dr; (08) 9561 2244; www.yanchepholidays.com

YANCHEP INN $$

The Yanchep Inn has a range of accommodation styles, with units in a freestanding building and rooms at the inn. The original units are located to the south of the inn and are comfortably decorated. Newer units overlook the lake and some have spa baths. Or why not stay in the historic inn itself, where the rooms are clean, the bathrooms are communal and apparently the ghosts are friendly.

Yanchep National Park; (08) 9561 1001; www.yanchepinn.com.au

York

IMPERIAL HOTEL YORK $$$

The fact that all of the rooms are named after champagnes should give you an idea that romance may be on cards at the Imperial Hotel. Built in 1886, the hotel has undergone a major renovation and is one of York's most prestigious buildings. Book in for an indulgence package, including a massage, candlelit dinner and complimentary champagne. Downstairs,

---

BREAKFAST INCLUDED   CREDIT CARDS ACCEPTED   FAMILY FRIENDLY

the Restaurant Eboracum prides itself on its simple yet sophisticated cuisine.

83 Avon Tce; (08) 9641 1255; www.imperialhotelyork.com.au

NOSH & NOD $$$

Situated next to the town hall and in the heart of this charming town, the Nosh and Nod offers hotel rooms and self-contained accommodation. Beautifully appointed, some of the rooms include spas and one room has a kitchenette. There is also a self-contained character cottage available for rent.

75 Avon Tce; (08) 9641 1629; www.noshnod.com.au

OLD ALBION B&B $$$$

Established in 1858, The Old Albion is heritage listed and is as charming as the day it was built. The stables have been converted into cottages from a bygone era and include antique furnishings, wood fires and ensuites, with the spa suite a favourite. Breakfast is served in the dining room each morning, and for the indulgent, the beauty retreat will complete your relaxing stay.

19 Avon Tce; (08) 9641 2608; www.oldalbion.com.au

QUELLINGTON SCHOOL $
HOUSE FARMSTAY

Quellington School House is situated on York's highest point, Quellington Hill, 20 kilometres from town. The school was originally built to educate the landowner's children and was opened up to the public in the early 1880s. The property has remained in the Gentle family for six generations, and nowadays the schoolhouse has been converted into accommodation. Sleeping seven guests, the cottage is fully self-contained and retains much of the charm of the era in which it was built.

Sees Rd, Quellington; (08) 9641 1343; www.yorkwa.com.au/Quellington

TIPPERARY CHURCH $$$

Located in the lovely Avon Valley, just 11 kilometres from York, the Tipperary Church was built in 1892 purely to serve Tipperary Farm, one of Western Australia's earliest farms. Today the church has been converted into a quirky B&B. This adult retreat is well appointed and features two bedrooms, both with ensuites and including a claw-foot bath in The Map Room, the upstairs master suite. The second bedroom, The Garden Room, opens onto the landscaped gardens and countryside. The grounds include a function room available for hire and the gardens are ideal for weddings.

2092 Northam Rd; 0439 965 275; www.tipperarychurch.com

FITNESS CENTRE　　　ROOM SERVICE　　　SWIMMING POOL

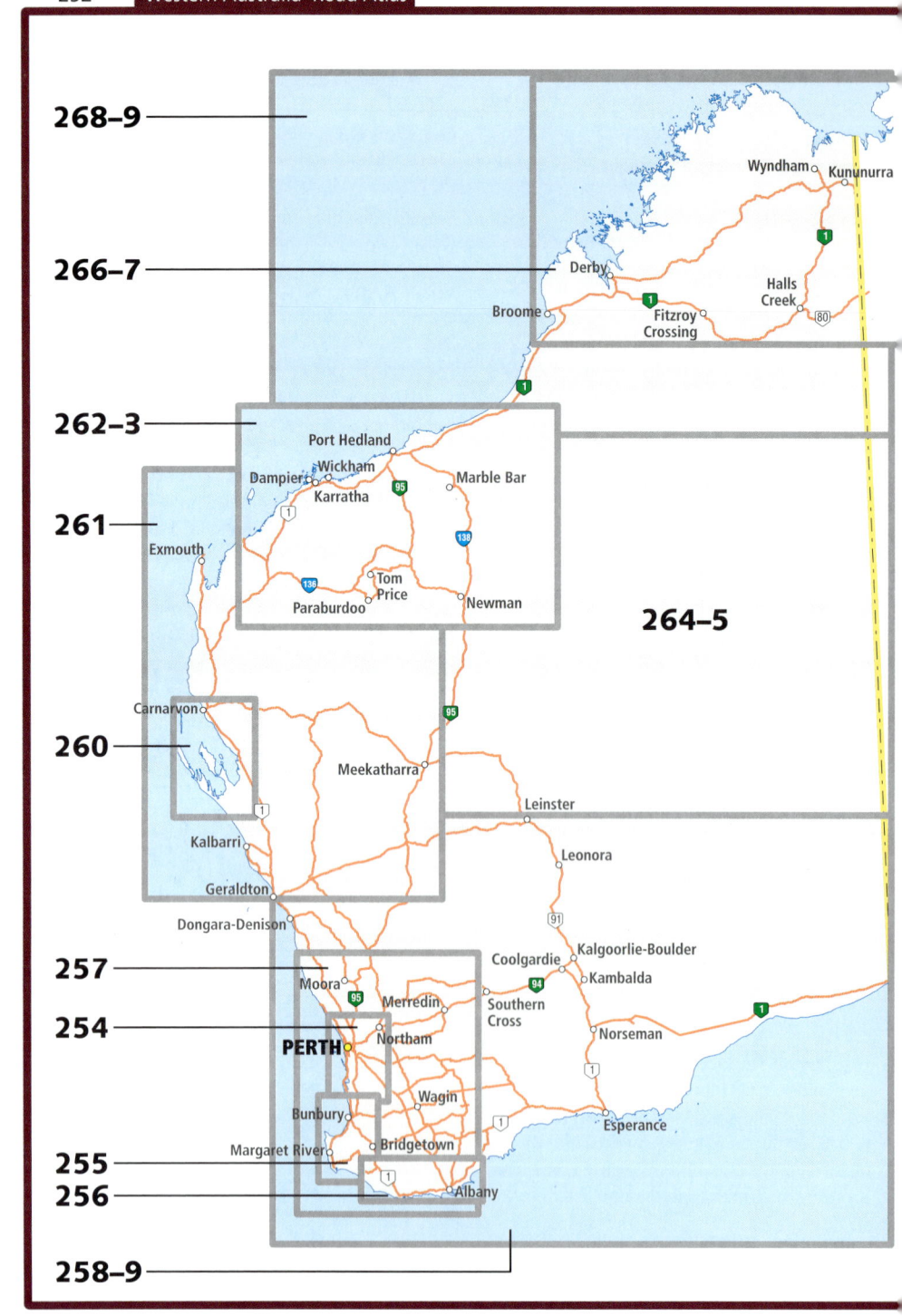

Western Australia Road Atlas

Legend

- Freeway, with toll
- **A1** **15** Highway, sealed, with National Highway Route Marker
- **M1** **83** Highway, sealed, with National Route Marker
- **A55** Highway, sealed, with State Route Marker
- Highway, unsealed
- **93** Main road, sealed, with State Route Marker
- Main road, unsealed
- Other road
- Walking track
- Railway
- ▼ 45 ▼ Kilometres between points
- State border
- **PERTH** ○ State capital city
- **MANDURAH** ○ Major city/town
- Yanchep ○ Town
- Gingin ○ Other population centres/localities
- Cundeelee ○ Aboriginal community
- Caiguna Roadhouse RH Roadhouse
- ONE TREE BRIDGE ○ Place of interest
- ⊕ Text entry in A to Z listing
- Lake, reservoir
- Intermittent lake
- National park
- Other reserve
- Aboriginal/Torres Strait Islander land
- Prohibited area
- ✈ Airport
- ★ Lighthouse
- ▲ Hill, mountain
- ● Gorge, gap, pass, cave or saddle

Maps are in a Lamberts Conformal Conic Projection
Geocentric Datum Australia 1994 (GDA94)

Perth & Surrounds	254
South-West Coast	255
South Coast	256
South Western Western Australia	257
Southern Western Australia	258–9
Shark Bay	260
Central Western Western Australia	261
Pilbara	262–3
Central Western Australia	264–5
Kimberley	266–7
Northern Western Australia	268–9

0 5 10 km
257
255
INDIAN
OCEAN
N
PERTH
Fremantle
Rottnest Island
ROCKINGHAM
MANDURAH
Pinjarra
Waroona
Yanchep
Two Rocks
Gingin
Bindoon
Chittering
Lower Chittering
Muchea
Bullsbrook
Toodyay
Northam
York
Mundaring
Kalamunda
Midland
Guildford
Armadale
Byford
Serpentine
Jarrahdale
Mundijong
Kwinana
Singleton
Halls Head
Dwellingup
Boddington
Wandering
Westdale
Quindanning
Yarloop
Wagerup
Hamel
Preston Beach
Lake Clifton
YANCHEP NATIONAL PARK
CRYSTAL & YONDERUP CAVES
NEERABUP NATIONAL PARK
WALYUNGA NP
AVON VALLEY NATIONAL PARK
JOHN FORREST NP
KALAMUNDA NP
SERPENTINE NP
YALGORUP NATIONAL PARK
HILLARYS BOAT HARBOUR, AQUARIUM OF WA (AQWA), SORRENTO BEACH
PERTH ZOO, INDIAN PACIFIC TRAIN, SWAN VALLEY WINERIES, BIBBULMUN TRACK, WILDFLOWERS, ADVENTURE WORLD
ROTTNEST ISLAND
HISTORIC TOWN
SWAN BREWERY, CANNING VALE MARKETS
STOCK ROAD MARKETS
C.Y. O'CONNOR MUSEUM
MUNDARING WEIR
ARALUEN BOTANIC PARK
TUMBULGUM FARM
ALCOA SCARP LOOKOUT
HOTHAM VALLEY TOURIST RAILWAY
ETMILYN FOREST TRAMWAY
LANE-POOLE RESERVE
CARTREF PARK COUNTRY GARDEN
WINDMILL HILL CUTTING
WANNEROO MARKETS
RAAF PEARCE AERODROME PROHIBITED AREA
INSTITUTIONAL RESERVE PROHIBITED AREA
GREAT NORTHERN HWY
GREAT EASTERN HWY
GREAT SOUTHERN HWY
BRAND HWY
TOODYAY RD
ALBANY HWY
BROOKTON HWY
SOUTH WESTERN HWY
KWINANA FWY
MITCHELL FWY
OLD COAST RD
WANNEROO RD
FORRESTFIELD
DARLING RANGE

0
10
20 km
N
INDIAN
OCEAN
SOUTHERN
OCEAN
254
257
256
YALGORUP NATIONAL PARK
Lake Preston
Yarloop
Lake Brockman
Warawarrup
Harvey Dam
FALLS BROOK NR
Mount Ross
LANE POOLE
CONSERVATION
Nalyerin Lake
RESERVE
Yourdamung Lake
Mount William
Murray R
MYALUP RD
Harvey
Wokalup
Stirling Dam
Harris River
Lake Ballingall
Myalup
Binningup
Binningup Beach
BENGER SWAMP NR
Benger
SOUTH WESTERN HWY
OLD COAST RD
DARLING RANGE
Buffalo Beach
Belvidere Beach
Brunswick
Beela
Bingham R
COLLIE RD
Leschenault
Leschenault Estuary
Brunswick Junction
Worsley
WILLIAMS
COALFIELDS
Allanson
Australind
Roelands
Koombana Bay
McKenna Point
Eaton
Burekup
WELLINGTON NATIONAL PARK
Collie
Shotts
Buckingham
Collie Burn
Collie Cardiff
Bunbury Lighthouse
Rocky Point
BUNBURY
Waterloo
Picton
Mount Lennard
Wellington Dam
Dardanup
Gelorup
Dalyellup Beach
Preston
HENTY PLAINS
Glen Mervyn Dam
Stratham
Stirling Beach
TUART FOREST NP
Boyanup
Mumballup
Lowden
BOYUP BROOK
McAlinden
Minninup Sand Patch
Peppermint Grove
Higgins Cut
Donnybrook
DONNYBROOK
Capel
Geographe Bay
TUART FOREST NP
Forrest Beach
Wonnerup Estuary
LIGHTHOUSE & MUSEUM
Cape Naturaliste
Bunker Bay
Cape Naturaliste Lighthouse
Sugarloaf Rock
BUSSELTON JETTY INTERPRETIVE CENTRE, UNDERWATER OBSERVATORY, BALLARAT ENGINE, BUSSELTON HISTORIC MUSEUM, ST MARY'S CHURCH
Rocky Point
Point Picquet
BANNAMAH WILDLIFE PARK
WONNERUP HOUSE
Vasse Estuary
Ludlow
GOODWOOD RD
Capel River
Thomson Brook
High Peak
Wilga
Grimwade
LEEUWIN-
Point Dalling
Dunn Bay
Dunsborough
BUSSELTON
Quindalup
Toby Inlet
Ruabon
Tutunup
Newlands
Kirup
Mullalyup
NATURALISTE
Mount Duckworth
Yallingup
Smiths Beach
CAVES RD
GUNYULGUP GALLERY
Marybrook
Vasse
Busselton Aerodrome
Yoongarillup
Balingup
OLD CHEESE FACTORY CRAFT CENTRE
NATIONAL
Cape Clairault
Carbunup River
North Jindong
Boallia
Walsall
VASSE HWY
Jarrahwood
Ferndale
PARK
Yelverton
BOOTLEG BREWERY
Jindong
Chapman Hill
Acton Park
WHICHER RANGE
SUES RD
Greenbushes
Cowan Dam
Metricup
BUSSELL HWY
NANNUP
BALINGUP NANNUP RD
Blackwood River
Bridgetown
Cowaramup Bay
Cowaramup Point
Gracetown
Cowaramup
Osmington
Nannup
BROCKMAN HWY
ELLENSBROOK HOMESTEAD
Mowen
MARGARET RIVER WINERIES, CAVES ROAD DRIVE, SURFING
Margaret River
Cape Mentelle
Rosa Glen
PIONEER SETTLERS MEMORIAL
Prevelly
EAGLES HERITAGE
MARGARET RIVER MARRON FARM
Marmaduke Point
Witchcliffe
DAVIDSON RD
Mount Mack
Palgarup
LAKE CAVE-MAMMOTH CAVE NR
MAMMOTH CAVE
LAKE CAVE
Forest Grove
Cape Freycinet
BORANUP GALLERY
GRAPHITE RD
ONE TREE BRIDGE
Manjimup
Deanmill
Scabby Gully Dam
Jardee
MUIRS HWY
North Point
Quoin Rock
BORANUP LOOKOUT
BORANUP MAZE
STEWART HWY
FONTY'S POOL
BUNNINGS DIAMOND WOODCHIP MILL, DIAMOND TREE FIRE LOOKOUT
Hamelin Bay
Hamelin Island
Foul Bay
Foul Bay Lighthouse
Knobby Head
Karridale
SCOTT NATIONAL PARK
GINGILUP SWAMPS NATURE RESERVE
D'ENTRECASTEAUX NATIONAL PARK
FOUNDERS FOREST
BEEDELUP NATIONAL PARK
Big Brook Dam
CLIFF SPACKMAN NR
MOONDYNE CAVE, JEWEL CAVE
Hardy Inlet
Augusta
HISTORICAL MUSEUM, RIVER CRUISES
Flinders Bay
Lake Quitjup
Lake Jasper
BIG BROOK ARBORETUM
GLOUCESTER NP
GLOUCESTER TREE
Pemberton
THE CASCADES
Barrack Point
WHALE RESCUE MEMORIAL
MATTHEW FLINDERS MEMORIAL
White Point
KING TROUT & MARRON FARM
WARREN NP
MARIANNE NORTH TREE & BICENTENNIAL TREE
BROCKMAN NP
BROCKMAN SAW PIT
Cape Leeuwin
CAPE LEEUWIN LIGHTHOUSE, WATER WHEEL
Seal Island
Saint Alouarn Island
Flinders Island
Black Point
Donnelly R
D'ENTRECASTEAUX NATIONAL PARK
Yeagarup Beach
Warren R
Northcliffe

0 10 20 km
257
255
Manjimup
Deanmill
Jardee
ONE TREE BRIDGE
PIONEER CAIRN, PIONEER CEMETERY, KING JARRAH
NYAMUP TOURIST VILLAGE
FONTY'S POOL
BUNNINGS DIAMOND WOODCHIP MILL, DIAMOND TREE FIRE LOOKOUT
FOUNDERS FOREST
BEEDELUP NP
BIG BROOK ARBORETUM
GLOUCESTER NP
GLOUCESTER TREE
Pemberton
THE CASCADES
MOON'S CROSSING
KING TROUT & MARRON FARM
WARREN NP
MARIANNE NORTH TREE & BICENTENNIAL TREE
BROCKMAN SAW PIT
D'ENTRECASTEAUX
Yeagarup Beach
NATIONAL
PARK
Warren Beach
Quinninup
MITCHELL
SOUTH WESTERN HWY
VASSE HWY
MUIRS HWY
PEMBERTON NORTHCLIFFE RD
MIDDLETON RD
Northcliffe
BOORARA TREE, LANE-POOLE FALLS
Mount Chudalup
WINDY HARBOUR RD
Black Head
Pebbley Beach
Sandy Peak
Point D'Entrecasteaux
Windy Harbour
Quagering Island
Sandy Island
Ledge Islet
West Cliff Point
SOUTHERN
OCEAN
Cow and Calf Rocks
SHANNON NATIONAL PARK
Shannon
Mount Burnside
Shannon Island
Sand Peak
Signal Point
Broke Inlet
Clarke Island
Cliffy Head
Chatham Island
PINGERUP PLAINS
Mount Pingerup
MOUNT FRANKLAND NATIONAL PARK
Mount Johnston
Granite Peak
Mount Mitchell
Mount Roe
Mount Frankland
FERNHOOK FALLS
Lake Muir
LAKE MUIR NATURE RESERVE
UNICUP NR
KULUNILUP NR
KODJINUP NR
QUINDINUP NATURE RESERVE
WINGEBELLUP RD
FRANKLAND CRANBROOK RD
Frankland
ROCKY GULLY FRANKLAND RD
RANDELL ROAD NR
TOOTANELLUP NR
Rocky Gully
PERILLUP RD
MT ROE-MT LINDESAY NATIONAL PARK
Mount Romance
GUM LINK ROAD NATURE RESERVE
SCOTSDALE RD
VALLEY OF THE GIANTS, TREE TOP WALK
WALPOLE-NORNALUP NATIONAL PARK
GIANT TINGLE TREE
Walpole
Nornalup
Nornalup Inlet
SOUTH COAST HWY
Irwin Inlet
OWINGUP NR
QUARRAM NR
Foul Bay
Peaceful Bay
Point Irwin
Boat Harbour
Point Hillier
Mandalay Beach
Mount Hopkins
Long Point
Lost Beach
Point Nuyts
Saddle Island
Bellanger Beach
Rocky Head
Goose Island
Rame Head

Tenterden
STOCKYARD RD
NUNIJUP RD
LAKE MATILDA RD
ALBANY HWY
Kendenup
STIRLING RANGE NATIONAL PARK
Mount Magog
Mount Gog
Mondurup Peak
STIRLING RANGE NATIONAL PARK
Quarderwardup Lake
Two Mile Lake
Wellstead
CHILLINUP NR
South Stirling
SOUTH STIRLING NR
METTLER LAKE NR
BASIL ROAD NR
TINKELELUP NR
MALLAWILLUP
WAMBALLUP NR
Kwornicup Lake
OLD POLICE STATION MUSEUM
Mount Barker
MUIRS HWY
LOOKOUT
Mount Barker (Pwakkenbak)
PARDELUP PRISON FARM
PARDELUP NR
ST WERBURGH'S CHAPEL
Mount Barrow (Yakarlup)
PORONGURUP NATIONAL PARK
PORONGURUPS RA
Woodlands
Kamballup
Narrikup
SHEEPWASH CREEK NR
The Springs
The Pass
SLEEMAN CREEK NR
REDMOND
Redmond
MILL BROOK NR
MILLBROOK
CHESTER PASS RD
BAKERS JUNCTION NR
Kalgan
Mount Boyle
King River
Albany Aerodrome
DENMARK MOUNT BARKER RD
Mount Lindesay
Mount Leay
Denmark
BARTHOLOMEW'S MEADERY
Mount Hallowell
MONKEY ROCK LOOKOUT
Wilson Inlet
Morley Beach
Pelican Spit
SOUTH COAST HWY
LOWER DENMARK RD
Marbelup
DOWN ROAD NR
ALBANY
HISTORIC TOWN, BIBBULMUN TRACK, WHALES
Mount Clarence
Melville
Princess Royal Harbour
King George Sound
Oyster Harbour
Mount Taylor
Nanarup
Mount Gardner
TWO PEOPLES BAY MARRON FARM
TWO PEOPLES BAY NATURE RESERVE
Two Peoples Bay
Manypeaks
MOUNT MANYPEAKS NR
WAYCHINICUP NP
Cheyne Beach
Hassell Beach
CHEYNE ROAD NR
NORTH SISTER NR
SOUTH SISTER NR
Normans Beach
North Point
South Point
Point Gardner
Coffin Island
Cape Vancouver
Ben Dearg Beach
Rock Dunder
Michaelmas Is
Breaksea Is
North Channel
Middle Channel
South Channel
Frenchman Bay
WHALE WORLD
Bald Head
FLINDERS PENINSULA
Isthmus Bay
TORNDIRRUP NATIONAL PARK
Peak Head
THE BLOWHOLES
Cave Point
THE GAP & NATURAL BRIDGE
Little Grove
Big Grove
Sharp Point
Stony Is
Port Hughes
Port Harding
Torbay
Dingo Beach
Shelly Beach
Torbay Head
WEST CAPE HOWE NP
West Cape Howe
Lowlands Beach
Knapp Head
Lights Beach
Wilson Head
Ratcliffe Bay
William Bay
WILLIAM BAY NP
North West Rock
South West Island
Eclipse Island
Cliff Head
Channel Point
Bald Island
BALD ISLAND NR
Mermaid Point
Twin Islands
SOUTHERN
OCEAN
Joins map above

South Western Western Australia

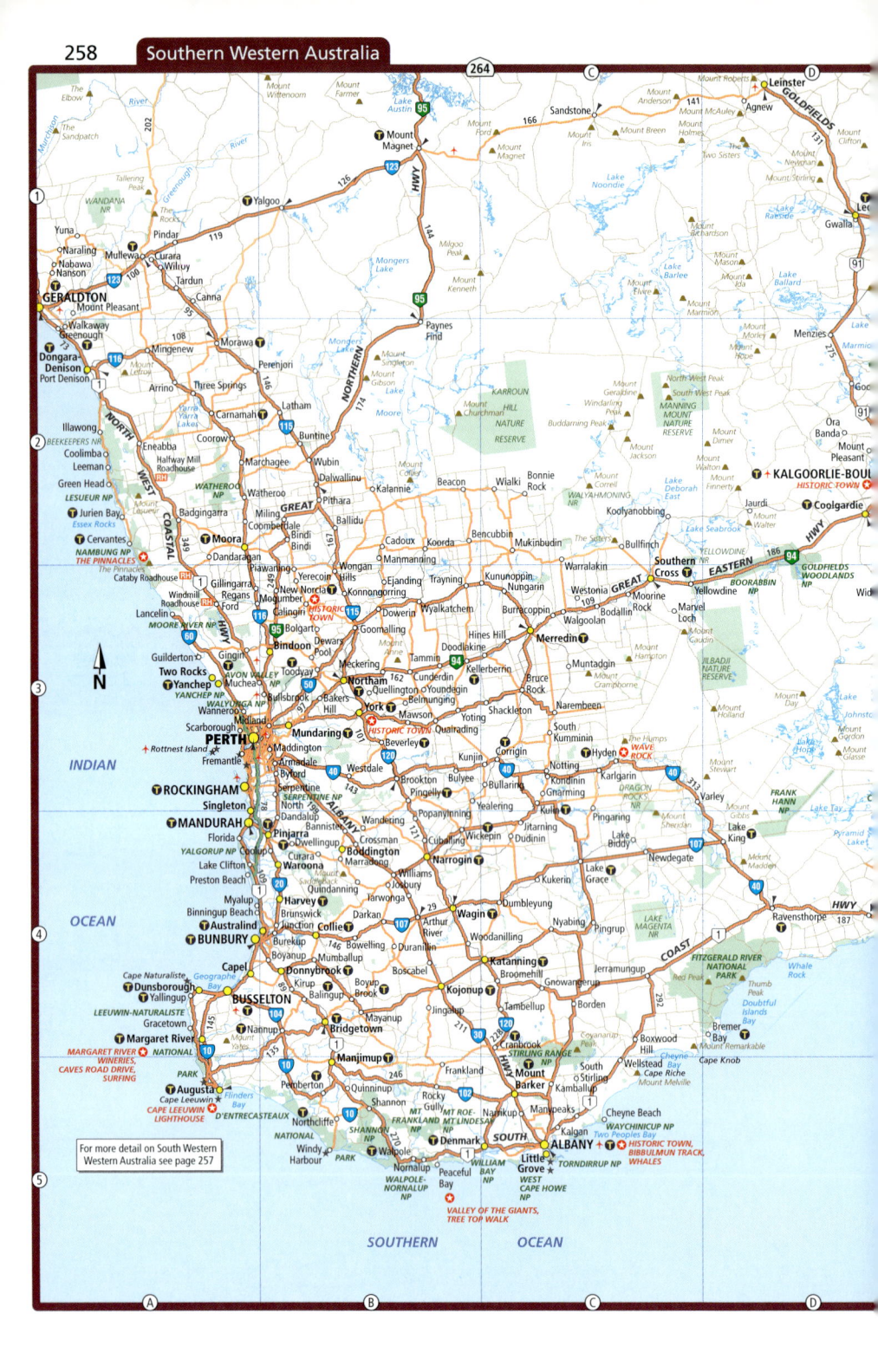

Southern Western Australia

WARNINGS: In outback Australia, long distances separate some towns. Travellers should familiarise themselves with prevailing conditions before departure and take care to ensure their vehicle is roadworthy. Adequate supplies of petrol, water and food should be carried at all times.

In central Australia, rainfall can make some roads impassable, even with a 4WD vehicle. Full information on road conditions should be obtained from local authorities before departure.

If visitors intend diverting off public roads within Aboriginal Land areas, a permit is required from the relevant Aboriginal authority.

0 10 20 km
261
South Bejaling Hill
Coollilee Hill
Pelican Hill
Coast Hill
Miaboolya Beach
ONE TREE POINT NATURE RESERVE
Anchor Hill
Carnarvon
Mangrove Point
Gascoyne Flats
SHARK BAY MARINE PARK
Grey Point
New Beach
Bush Bay
Cape Ronsard
Bernier Island
BERNIER AND DORRE ISLANDS NATURE RESERVE
Dorre Island
Cape St Cricq
Cape St Cricq Lighthouse
SHARK BAY
Gascoyne
River
ROCKY POOL RD
CARNARVON-MULLEWA
MEERAGOOLIA
Square Tank Outcamp
WINDERIE RD
CALLAGIDDY-
BUSH BAY RD
NORTH WEST COASTAL HWY
MARRON-YALBALGO RD
EDAGGEE
PIMBEE
Woomeral Seagrass Bank
Long Point
Cape Peron Flats
Cape Peron North
Cape Peron Lighthouse
NATURALISTE CHANNEL
Cape Inscription
Cape Inscription Lighthouse
Cape Levillain
West Point
Broadhurst Bight
Herald Bight
Guichenault Point
Herald Bluff
Denham Sound
PERON PENINSULA
FRANCOIS PERON NATIONAL PARK
Cape Lesueur
Cape Rose
Monkey Mia
DOLPHINS
Woomeral Seagrass Bank
DISAPPOINTMENT REACH
SHARK BAY MARINE PARK
Green Turtle Flat
Faure Island
Pelican Island
Wooramel
River
Wooramel Roadhouse
MEEDO
Carlaweelban Hill
Gladstone
Kopke Point
Middle Bluff
MONKEY MIA RD
Dirk Hartog Island
Quoin Head
Herald Bay Outcamp
FREYCINET
Bar Flats
Flag Hill
Denham
Knight Bank
DENHAM CHANNEL
SHARK BAY RD
Dubaut Point
Petit Point
Faure Flat
SEDIMENTARY DEPOSITS CONSERVATION RESERVE
L'Haridon Bight
Yaringa Point
CARBLA RD
BYRO-WOODLEIGH RD
Cape Bellefin
Cape Heirisson
Middle Flat
REACH
SHELL BEACH CONSERVATION PARK
SHELL BEACH
HAMELIN POOL MARINE NATURE RESERVE
STROMATOLITES
Overlander Roadhouse
Hamelin Outcamp
Steep Point
Cape Ransonnet
Shoal Flats
USELESS LOOP RD
Fork Flat
Henri Freycinet Harbour
Bibby Giddy Outcamp
Thunder Bay
INDIAN OCEAN
Pepper Point
Foster Outcamp
Giraud Point
CARARANG PENINSULA
Zuytdorp Cliffs
COBURN RD
Karkura Dunes
Natta Outcamp
Beethen Outcamp
Womerangee Hill
COOLOOMIA
ZUYTDORP NATURE RESERVE
N
A B C D
1 2 3 4 5

Central Western Western Australia

Pilbara

WITTENOOM: Due to the presence of blue asbestos in and around Wittenoom, townsite status has officially been removed. Electricity, water and postal services have ceased and there are no longer any licensed accommodation providers in the area. Any found to be offering accommodation are doing so without health permits.

0
20
40 km
268
264
Bedout Island
Eighty Mile Beach
Sandfire Roadhouse
GREAT NORTHERN HWY
KIDSON TRACK
Cape Keraudren
Point Poolingerena
Breaker Inlet
Poissonnier Point
Cartaminia Point
Larrey Point
Red Point
Mount Blaze
Pardoo Roadhouse
CAPE KERAUDREN RD
BORELINE RD
Ripon Island
GREAT SANDY DESERT
Goldsworthy
Mount Goldsworthy
Mount St George
Mount Grant
Shay Gap
Cattle Gorge
Kennedy Gap
Cundaline Gap
Kimberley Gap
Mount Woodhouse
DeGrey River
Coongan
Shaw
West
Mount Cecelia
MARBLE BAR RD
WARRAWAGINE RD
Muningarra
Coppin Gap
Kittys Gap
Talga Peak
Bamboo Creek
GORGE RANGE
Doolena Peak
Doolena Gap
The Pinnacles
The Sisters
Marble Bar
Ripon Mount Edgar
WOODIE WOODIE RD
GREGORY RANGE
Oakover River
Mount Newdegate
Lake Waukarlycarly
RIPON HILLS RD
Nullagine
Mount Sydney
TELFER MINE RD
Strelley
Strelley Gorge
Mount York
Glacier Valley
The Island Hill
Shaw Gorge
Warrawoona Peak
Horrigan Peak
Carawine Gorge
Upper Carawine Gorge
Yilgalong
THROSSELL RANGE
Mount Crofton
Emu Creek
Warrery Gap
Mount Elsie
Mount Olive
Mount Macpherson
Mount Webber
Yule River
SKULL SPRINGS RD
Hallcomes Peak
Mount Hays
Beaton Gorge
Nullagine
PILBARA
BLACK RANGE
Mount Maggie
Mount Cooke
Davis
Mount Rudall
Mount Hodgson
Meeting Gorge
KARLAMILYI NATIONAL PARK
Auski Roadhouse
MUNJINA
Mount Marsh
Mount McKay
Lynn Peak
Mount Lewin
Tongololo
Mount Lockyer
ROY HILL RD
TALAWANA TRACK
HORSETRACK RANGE
LITTLE SANDY DESERT
WALAGUNYA
HAMERSLEY RANGE
The Three Sisters
Marillana Creek
WEELI WOLLI SPRING
PUNDA POOL
HANCOCK RANGE
EAGLE ROCK FALLS
KALGANS POOL
Coondiner Creek
Jigalong Creek
Jimblebar Creek
Caramulla Creek
Fortescue River
Mount Meharry
Mount Robinson
WANNA MUNNA ROCK ART SITE
The Governor
Cathedral Gorge
Mount Newman
Newman
Jigalong
TROPIC OF CAPRICORN
Mount Ella
Spearhole Ck
Ophthalmia Dam
Capricorn Roadhouse
JIGALONG
Savory Creek
Perry Creek
Tunnel Creek
OPHTHALMIA RANGE

Central Western Australia

WITTENOOM: Due to the presence of blue asbestos around Wittenoom, townsite status has officially been [removed]. Electricity, water and postal services have ceased and [there are] no longer any licensed accommodation providers in the [area]. Any found to be offering accommodation are doing so [without] health permits.

For more detail on the Pilbara see pages 262–3

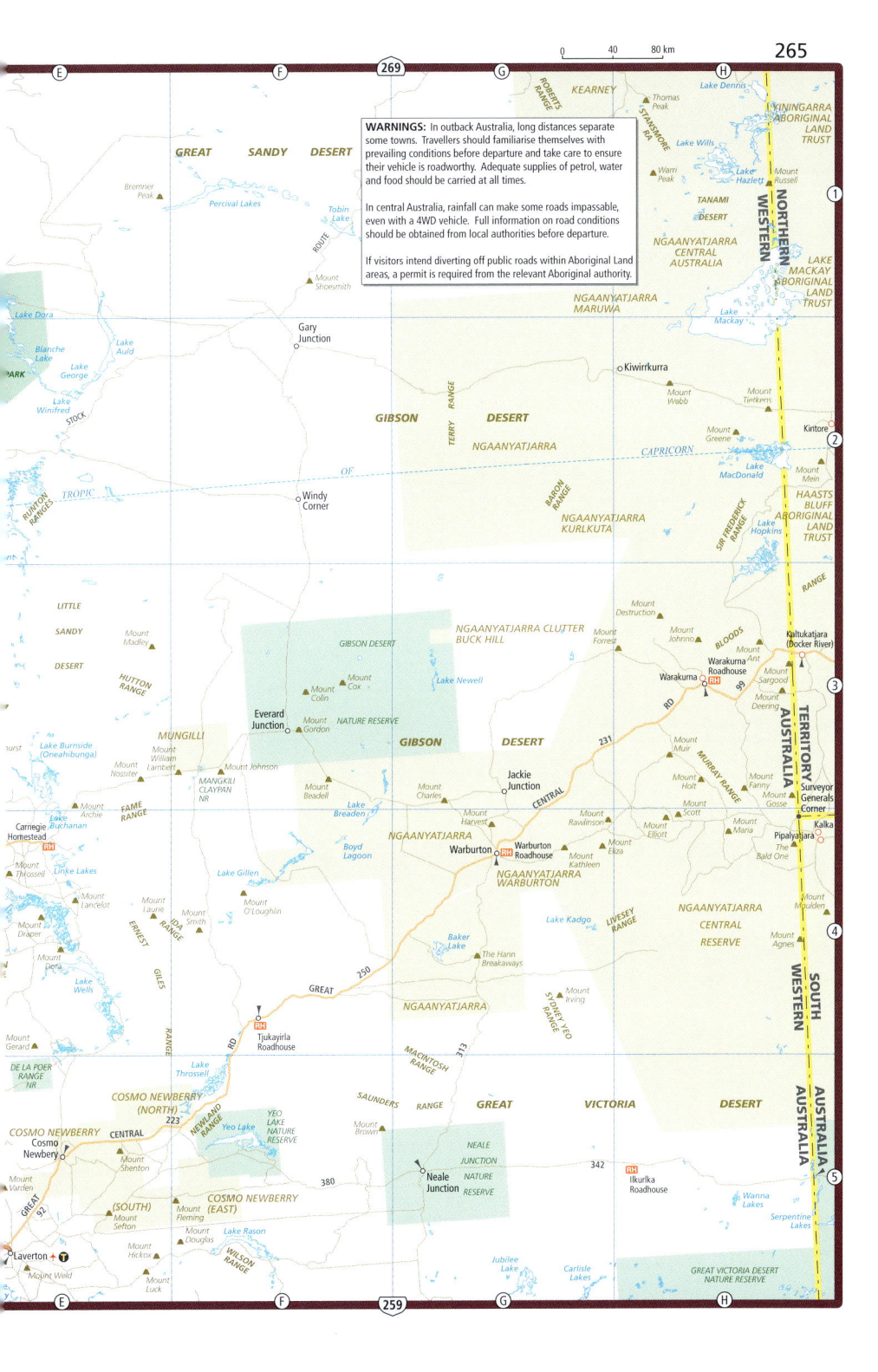

WARNINGS: In outback Australia, long distances separate some towns. Travellers should familiarise themselves with prevailing conditions before departure and take care to ensure their vehicle is roadworthy. Adequate supplies of petrol, water and food should be carried at all times.

In central Australia, rainfall can make some roads impassable, even with a 4WD vehicle. Full information on road conditions should be obtained from local authorities before departure.

If visitors intend diverting off public roads within Aboriginal Land areas, a permit is required from the relevant Aboriginal authority.

Kimberley

0 20 40 km
TIMOR SEA
JOSEPH BONAPARTE GULF
CAMBRIDGE GULF
Cape Londonderry
Cape Talbot
Lesueur Island
Glycosmis Bay
Koolama Bay
Cape Rulhieres
Governor Islands
Red Bluff
Cape Bernier
Cape Whiskey
Cape St Lambert
Reveley Island
Buckle Head
Thurburn Bluff
Cape Dussejour
Lacrosse Island
Cape Domett
Rocky Island
Pelican Island
Turtle Point
Cape Dombey
Hyland Bay
Tree Point
Cape Hay
Port Keats
Injin Beach
Port Keats (Wadeye)
Peppimenarti
MOYLE PLAIN
TABLE PLAIN
DALY RIVER / PORT KEATS ABORIGINAL LAND TRUST
MACADAM RANGE
Treachery Bay
New Moon Inlet
Swamp Point
Quoin Island
Keyling Inlet
QUEENS CHANNEL
Fitzmaurice River
BRADSHAW FIELD TRAINING AREA
KALUMBURU
Kalumburu
BARTON PLAIN
KIMBERLEY
OOMBULGURRI
Mount Casuarina
Mount Leeming
Mount Connelly
DRYSDALE RIVER NATIONAL PARK
Glider Gorge
Mount Keating
Worriga Gorge
Euro Gorge
ASHTON RANGE
Mount Nicholls
Sharp Peak
Mount Booton
Mount Burns
Mount Mongona
FORREST RIVER
Mount Fraser
Adolphus Island
Oombulgurri
Drayson Peak
MILLIGAN RANGES
NINGBING RANGE
Knob Peak
The Gorge
NOOGOORA BURR QUARANTINE AREA
ORD RIVER NR
PARRYS LAGOONS NR
PALM SPRINGS NR
Wyndham
PRISON TREE
The Grotto
Buttons Gap
Cave Spring Gap
WEABER PLAIN
Kununurra
Marralum
KEEP RIVER NATIONAL PARK EXTENSION (PROPOSED)
KEEP RIVER NP
Bullo Gorge
Karracumby Peak
The Tombs
River Peak
Bulla
East Baines Gorge
Desmonds Passage
PINKERTON
VICTORIA HWY
EMMA GORGE
ZEBRA ROCK GALLERY
CARR BOYD RANGES
Mount Beatrice
Mount Lawley
Mount Edith
GIBB RIVER RD
Palmer Pass
Grimwood Gap
Mount Todd
Salmond Gorge
VOYAGES EL QUESTRO WILDERNESS PARK
Dunham Pilot Dam
Carlton Gorge
ORD RIVER DAM, LAKE ARGYLE TOURIST VILLAGE
Lake Argyle
The Twins
Pimple Peak
Mount Sullivan
Scotty-Salmond Gorge
BEDFORD STOCK ROUTE
DOON DOON
GLEN HILL
Mount Evelyn
Mount Duncan
Amanbidji
NAGURUNGURU ABORIGINAL LAND TRUST
GREGORY NATIONAL PARK
ARGYLE DIAMOND MINE
Gordons Gorge
Mount Close
Mount Jarrad
Mount Kimon
MALNGIN 2 ABORIGINAL LAND TRUST
Mount Wickham
Warmun-Turkey Creek Roadhouse
Warmun
Mistake Creek
Mount Lush
Patterson Gorge
Mount Remarkable
VIOLET VALLEY
NORTHERN HWY
Mount John
Mount Elder
Mount Toby
Mount Besley
CONSERVATION RESERVE
BUNGLE BUNGLES
Mount Buchanan
PURNULULU NATIONAL PARK
MALNGIN ABORIGINAL LAND TRUST
DURACK RANGE
Crocodile Gorge
Mount Wells
Mount Ranford
Mount Napier
Mount Rose
DUNCAN RD
Tunganary Gorge
KIMBERLEY
Mount Frederick
LEOPOLD RANGES
Pyra Gorge
O'Donnell River Gorge
Mount Forster
Mount Coghlan
Crocodile Gorge
Marella Gorge
BUNTINE HWY
Mount Farquharson
Mount Archie
Nongra Lake
Mount Winifred
One Palm Tree Gorge
Neville Gorge
NICHOLSON PLAINS
Halls Creek
Mount Cummings
Mount Amherst
CHINA WALL
OLD HALLS CREEK
Mount Flora
Crowhurst Gorge
Saw Tooth Gorge
DUNCAN RD
BIRRINDUDU RANGE
NORTHERN TERRITORY
WESTERN AUSTRALIA
Mount Huxley
MUELLER
Eagle Hawk Crossing Gorge
Mount Ramsay
TANAMI RD
DENISON PLAINS
Mount Wittenoom
CREEK RD
Mount Dockrell
OLD BALLARA RD
STURT
GORDON DOWNS (RINGERS SOAK)
YINGUALYALYA ABORIGINAL LAND TRUST
CENTRAL DESERT ABORIGINAL LAND TRUST
TANAMI DESERT
GREAT NORTHERN
269

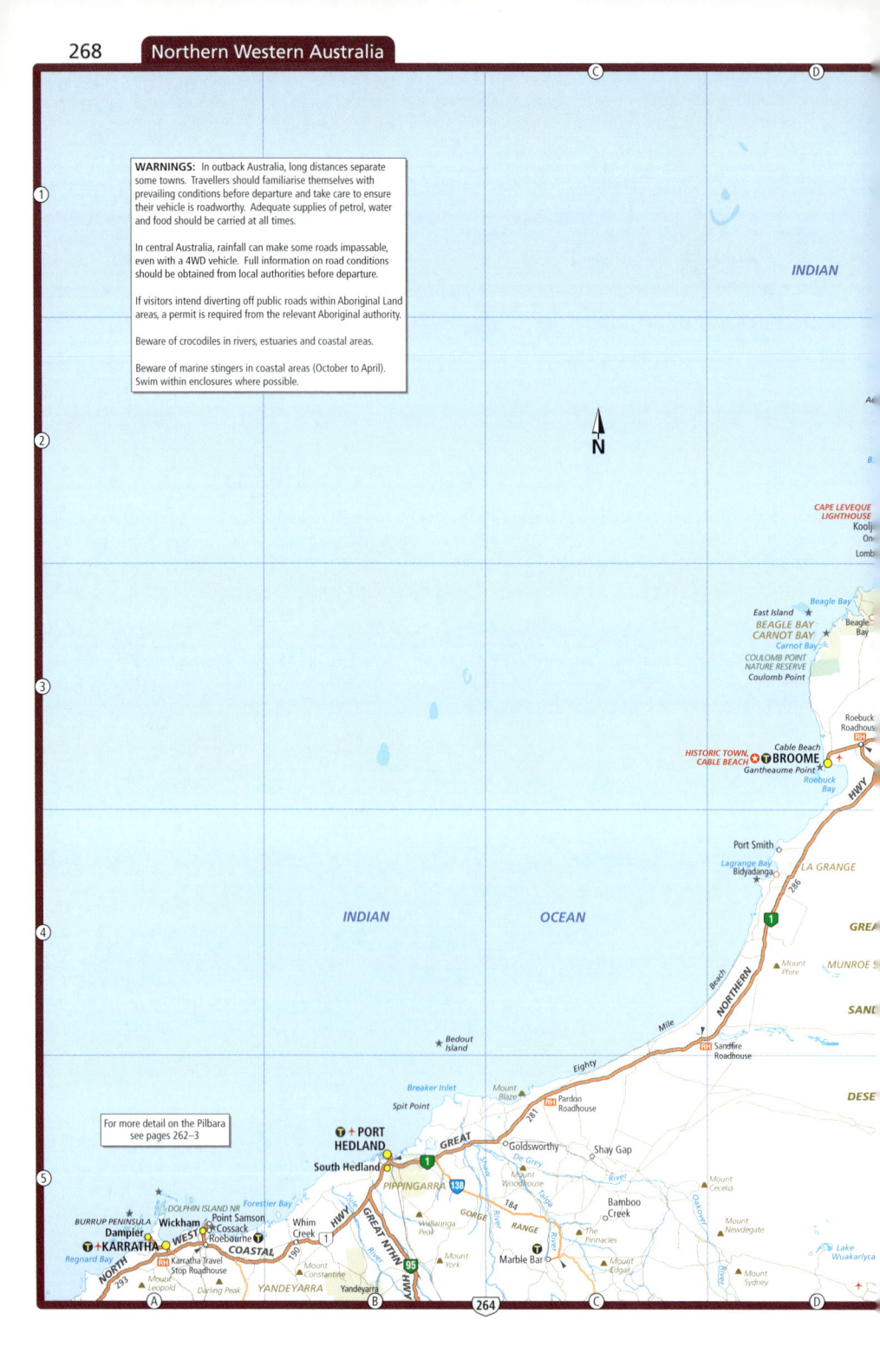

Northern Western Australia

WARNINGS: In outback Australia, long distances separate some towns. Travellers should familiarise themselves with prevailing conditions before departure and take care to ensure their vehicle is roadworthy. Adequate supplies of petrol, water and food should be carried at all times.

In central Australia, rainfall can make some roads impassable, even with a 4WD vehicle. Full information on road conditions should be obtained from local authorities before departure.

If visitors intend diverting off public roads within Aboriginal Land areas, a permit is required from the relevant Aboriginal authority.

Beware of crocodiles in rivers, estuaries and coastal areas.

Beware of marine stingers in coastal areas (October to April). Swim within enclosures where possible.

INDIAN OCEAN

For more detail on the Pilbara see pages 262–3

0 40 80 km

E
F
G
H
1
2
3
4
5
Cape Talbot
Cape Londonderry
Troughton Passage
Eclipse Islands
Long Reef
Gibson Point
Red Bluff
Oyster Rock Passage
Napier Broome Bay
KALUMBURU
Cape Rulhieres
Cape Bernier
Cape Whiskey
Voltaire Passage
ADMIRALTY GULF
Kalumburu
Cape Voltaire
CAPE BOUGANVILLE
BARTON PLAINS
Mount Casuarina
Buckle Head
JOSEPH BONAPARTE GULF
Cape Dombey
Hyland Bay
Cape Hay
Port Keats (Wadeye)
New Moon Inlet
Mount Connor
Mount Leeming
Mount Nicholls
Cape Dussejour
Turtle Point
Queens Channel
LAWLEY RIVER NATIONAL PARK
DRYSDALE RIVER NATIONAL PARK
OOMBULGURRI
CAMBRIDGE GULF
Bigge Island
Cape Pond
ADMIRALTY GULF
Kandiwal
Mitchell
Mount Keating
FORREST RIVER
Mount Fraser
Prince Frederick Harbour
MITCHELL RIVER NP
DOONGAN
Berkeley
Oombulgurri
NOOGOORA BURR QUARANTINE AREA
ASHTON RA
Cape Wellington
Hanover Bay
Mount Brookes
Mount Trafalgar
303
Marralum
Wildcat Reefs
Champagny Islands
PRINCE REGENT NATURE RESERVE
Drysdale
Mount Bertie
West Arm
Wyndham
KEEP RIVER NAT PARK EXTENSION (PROPOSED)
PARRYS LAGOON NR
MIRIMA NP
Kununurra
KEEP RIVER NATIONAL PARK
Mavis Reef
Hope Point
Deception Bay
Prior Point
Mount Eyre
KUNMUNYA
Mount Hann
Mount Beatrice
Mount Edith
RIVER
RD
55
102
VICTORIA
HWY
Cockell Reefs
Montgomery Reef
Montgomery Islands
Mount Methuen
Mount Hickey
GIBB
284
HWY
ORD RIVER DAM
Lake Argyle
Amanbidji
Doubtful Bay
BLYTHE CREEK
Mount Hindhaugh
Mount Lacy
Mount Sullivan
Mount Throssell
DOON DOON
Mount Duncan
Koolan
Collier Bay
Mount Daglish
MUNJA
Charnley
Mount Elizabeth
MAURICE CREEK
Durack
Salmond
151
Mount Evelyn
Isdell
Tabletop Mountain
Mount Page
Mount Nellie
Mount Dawson
YAMPI TRAINING AREA
Kupingarri
Mount Barnett Roadhouse
Chamberlain
RANGE
DUNCAN
MALNGIN 2 ABORIGINAL LAND TRUST
KING
Hann
KIMBERLEY
Wilson
Warmun-Turkey Creek Roadhouse
Warmun
PURNULULU CONSERVATION RESERVE
Mistake Creek
Stokes Bay
KING LEOPOLD
Mount Hart
LEOPOLD
RD
Mount Caroline
For more detail on the Kimberley see pages 266–7
DURACK
Mount Remarkable
VIOLET VALLEY
Mount Parker
Mount Elder
MALNGIN ABORIGINAL LAND TRUST
WATER RANGE
Mount Amy
375
RANGES
Imintji Store
Mount Buchanan
PURNULULU NATIONAL PARK
Mount Copley
Mount Eliza
Derby
Mount Lucy
RIVER
WINDJANA GORGE NP
CP
River
Mount Wells
Ord
BUNGLE BUNGLES
River
Mount Napier
WESTERN
NORTHERN
GIBB
Mount Rose
RANGES
Mount North
Mount Leake
Mount Frederick
Mount Laptz
161
TUNNEL CREEK NP
CURTIN AIR BASE
43
DEVONIAN REEF CONSERVATION PARK
Mount Sheba
Fitzroy
Mount Coghlan
HWY
BUNTINE
GREAT
BROOKING GORGE CP
GEIKIE GORGE CP
GEIKIE GORGE NP
Mount Amherst
RANGES
Oaks Mountain
80
RD
Willare Bridge Roadhouse
Camballin
219
Mount Cummings
Halls Creek
Fitzroy Crossing
Looma
Mount Wynne
Margaret
LINGA VALLEY
LOOMA
Mount Cedric
Mount Ball
MUELLER
Mount George
DUNCAN
Creek
Mount Wittenoom
Christmas
Onslow Peak
DENISON
Mount Arthur
Mount James
Mount Tuckfield
288
Mount Bertram
NORTHERN
TANAMI
GORDON DOWNS (RINGERS SOAK) PLAINS
YINGUALYALYA ABORIGINAL LAND TRUST
Mount Dockrell
GARDNER
Mount Jarlemai
Mount Fenton
Tulloch Peak
Mount Louise
Mount Talbot
Mount Hawick
WOLFE CREEK METEORITE CRATER NP
Mount Weekes
Mount Junction
PURTA ABORIGINAL LAND TRUST
RANGE
WORRAL RANGE
Ck
RANGE
Mount Bannerman
CANNING STOCK ROUTE
Sturt
MOUNT FREDERICK ABORIGINAL LAND TRUST
Lake Jones
Lake Betty
TANAMI DESERT
KOOLENA
Mount Erskine
ROUTE
Mount Mueller
404
RD
BILLILUNA
MINNIE RANGE
MT FREDERICK (NO.2) ABORIGINAL LAND TRUST
LAKE GREGORY
Mount Wilson
Balgo Hills
AUSTRALIA
Mount Ernest
STOCK
Lake Gregory
GREAT
SANDY
DESERT
Mount Elgin
Mount Elliott
KEARNEY
Mount Hughes
Lake Jeavons
Mount Tracey
YININGARRA ABORIGINAL LAND TRUST
Mount Fothringham
Mount Ford
ROBERTS RANGE
Thomas Peak
Lake Dennis
TERRITORY
CANNING
Lake White
Lake Wills
Warri Peak
Percival
Lakes
Bremner Peak
NGAANYATJARRA CENTRAL AUSTRALIA
Mount Russell
Tobin Lake
Lake Mackay
265

INDEX

USING THIS INDEX

This index includes all Western Australian towns, localities, national parks, major places of interest, eateries and accommodation options shown on the maps and mentioned in the text. In addition, it includes landforms and water features.

Place names are followed by an atlas page and grid reference, and/or the text page number on which that place is mentioned. A page number set in bold type indicates the main text entry for that place. For example:

Coolgardie 258 D2, 43, **71**, **202**

258 D2	– Coolgardie appears on this page in the atlas section
43	– Coolgardie is mentioned on this page
71, 202	– Main entries for Coolgardie

The alphabetical order followed in the index is that of 'word-by-word' – a space is considered to come before 'A' in the alphabet, and the index has been ordered accordingly. For example:

Green Lake
Green Mountains
Green Point
Greenacre
Greenacres
Greenbank

Names beginning with Mc are indexed as Mac and those beginning with St as Saint.

General Index

A

90-Mile Straight 41, 56
Abbey Church, New Norcia 114
Acton Park 255 B3
Adventure World, Bibra Lake 18
Aeronautical Museum, Beverley 56
Agnew 258 D1, 264 D5
Albany 256 B6, 257 D5, 258 C5, **52**, **139**, **190**
Albany Whaleworld, Albany 39, 54
Aldersyde 257 C3
Alexander Morrison National Park 257 A1, 258 A2
Alfred Cove 6 C5
Allanson 255 D2, 257 B4
Amanbidji NT 267 H3, 269 H2
Amphion 254 C5
Applecross 6 C5
Aquarium of Western Australia, Hillarys Boat Harbour 17
Araluen Botanic Park 33
Ardath 257 D2
Ardross 6 C5
Armadale 254 B3, 257 B2, 258 B3
Army Museum of Western Australia, Fremantle 27
Arrino 258 A2
Art Gallery of Western Australia, Northbridge 11
Arthur River 257 C4, 258 B4
Ascot 7 E2
Ascot Racecourse 7 E2
Ashfield 254 B2

Aspects of Kings Park, West Perth 26
Augusta 255 B5, 257 A5, 258 A5, **50**, **140**, **192**
Augusta Historical Museum, Augusta 51
Auski Roadhouse 261 D1, 263 E4, 264 B2
Australian Day Skyworks 24
Australian Prospectors and Miners Hall of Fame 95
Australind 255 C2, 257 B4, 258 B4, **51**, **193**
Avon Valley National Park 254 C1, 257 B2, 258 B3, 37, 126
Avondale Discovery Farm, Beverley 56

B

Baandee 257 C2

INDEX → BABAKIN – CAMBALLIN

Babakin 257 D2
Badgingarra 257 A1, 258 A2
Badgingarra National Park 257 A1, 258 A2
Badjaling 257 C2
Bakers Hill 254 C2, 257 B2, 258 B3
Balcatta 6 C1
Baldivis 254 B3
Balgo Hills 269 H4
Balingup 255 D3, 257 B4, 258 B4, **55**, **140**, **194**
Balladonia 259 F3, **56**, **141**, **195**
Balladonia Roadhouse 259 F3
Ballajura 254 B2
Ballaying 257 C3
Ballidu 257 B1, 258 B2
Bamboo Creek 263 F2, 264 C1, 268 C5
Bannister 254 D4, 257 B3, 258 B4
Barna Mia Animal Sanctuary, via Narrogin 113
Barracks Archway, Perth 9
Bay View Terrace, Claremont 24
Bayswater 7 E2
Beacon 257 C1, 258 B2
Beagle Bay 266 A4, 268 D3
Bedford 6 D1
Beedelup National Park 255 D5, 256 A1, 257 B5, 258 B5, 119
Beekeepers Nature Reserve 258 A2
Beela 255 C1
Belhus 254 B2
Belka 257 D2
Belmont 254 B2
Belmunging 257 C2, 258 B3
Bencubbin 257 C1, 258 B2
Benger 255 C1, 257 B3
Bentley 7 E4
Berndt Museum of Anthropology, Crawley 14
Bert Bolle Barometer, Denmark 75

Beverley 257 C2, 258 B3, **56**, **141**, **195**
Bibbulmun Track 53
Bibra Lake 254 B3
Bickley 254 B2
Bicton 6 B5
Bidyadanga 268 D4
Big Grove 256 B6, 257 D5
Bilbarin 257 D2
Billabong Roadhouse 261 B4
Bindi Bindi 257 B1, 258 B2
Bindoon 254 B1, 257 B2, 258 B3
Binningup 255 C1, 257 B3
Binningup Beach 255 C1, 258 A4
Binnu 261 B5
Blackwood Valley 34
Blessing of the Fleet, Fremantle 28
Blowholes, via Carnarvon 69
Boallia 255 B3
Bodallin 257 D1, 258 C3
Boddington 254 D5, 257 B3, 258 B4
Bolgart 257 B2, 258 B3
Bonnie Rock 257 D1, 258 C2
Boolading 257 C4
Boorabbin National Park 258 D2
Booragoon 6 D5, 254 B3
Borden 257 D4, 258 C4
Border Village SA 259 H2
Boscabel 257 C4, 258 B4
Boundain 257 C3
Bowelling 257 B4, 258 B4
Boxwood Hill 258 C4
Boyanup 255 C2, 257 B4, 258 B4
Boyup Brook 257 B4, 258 B4, 57, **142**, **195**
Bremer Bay 258 D4, **61**, **142**, **195**
Bridgetown 255 D3, 257 B4, 258 B4, **61**, **142**, **196**
Brierley Jigsaw Gallery, Bridgetown 61

Broad Arrow 258 D2
Brockman National Park 255 D5, 256 A2, 257 B5, 258 B5
Brookton 257 C3, 258 B3
Broome 266 A5, 268 D3, 49, **58**, **142**, **197**
Broomehill 257 C4, 258 C4
Bruce Rock 257 D2, 258 C3
Brunswick Junction 255 C1, 257 B4, 258 B4
Buckingham 255 D2, 257 B4
Bulla NT 267 H2
Bullaring 257 C3, 258 C3
Bullfinch 257 D1, 258 C2
Bullsbrook 254 B1, 257 B2, 258 B3
Bulyee 257 C3, 258 B3
Bunbury 255 B2, 257 B4, 258 A4, **64**, **144**, **198**
Bungulla 257 C2
Buntine 258 B2
Burekup 255 C2, 257 B4, 258 B4
Burns 254 A2
Burracoppin 257 D1, 258 C3
Burringurrah 261 C3, 264 A3
Burswood 7 D3, 254 B2
Burswood Entertainment Complex 7 E3, 13
Busselton 255 B3, 257 A4, 258 A4, **62**, **145**, **199**
Busselton Jetty, Busselton 35, 62
Butterabby Gravesite, Mullewa 111
Byford 254 B3, 257 B3, 258 B3

C

Cable Beach, Broome 59
Cadoux 257 C1, 258 B2
Caiguna 259 G3, **63**, **200**
Caiguna Roadhouse 259 G3
Calingiri 257 B1, 258 B3
Camballin 266 C5, 269 E3

Canna 258 A1, 261 C5
Canning Vale 254 B3, 257 B2
Canning Vale Markets, Canning Vale 24
Cannington 254 B3
Cantina 663 6 D2
Cape Arid National Park 259 E4
Cape Le Grand National Park 259 E4, 41, 80
Cape Range National Park 261 A2, 82
Capel 255 B2, 257 B4, 258 A4
Capricorn Roadhouse 263 F5, 264 C2
Carbunup River 255 A3
Carillon City, Perth 9
Carlisle 7 E3
Carnaby Beetle and Butterfly Collection, Boyup Brook 57
Carnamah 258 A2, **66**, **200**
Carnarvon 260 B1, 261 A3, **68**, **146**, **201**
Carnarvon Heritage Precinct, Carnarvon 68
Carnegie Homestead 265 E4
Carrabin 257 D1
Cascade 258 D4
Cataby Roadhouse 257 A1, 258 A3
Central Government Building, Perth 9
Central Greenough Historic Settlement, Greenough 86
Cervantes 257 A1, 258 A2, **67**, **147**, **201**
Chapman Hill 255 B3, 257 A4
Cheyne Beach 256 D5, 257 D5, 258 C5
Chidlow 254 C2
Chittering 254 B1, 257 B2
Christ's Church, Mandurah 102
Church of the Holy Cross and Old Presbytery, Morawa 109
Churchlands 6 B2
City Beach, Perth 6 A3

City Centre, Perth **8**
City of Perth Winter Arts Festival 24
Clackline 254 C1, 257 B2
Claremont 6 B4, 254 B2, 257 B2, 16
Claremont Museum, Claremont 16
Cliff Spackman Reserve 255 B5, 257 A5, 258 A5
Cocklebiddy 259 G3, **67**, **202**
Cocklebiddy Roadhouse 259 G3
Collie 255 D2, 257 B4, 258 B4, **70**, **202**
Collie Burn 255 D2
Collie Cardiff 255 D2, 257 B4
Collier Range National Park 261 D3, 264 C3
Comet Gold Mine, Marble Bar 104
Como 6 D4
Condingup 259 E4
Coolbinia 6 C2
Coolgardie 258 D2, 43, **71**, **202**
Coolgardie Cemetery, Coolgardie 71
Coolimba 258 A2
Coolup 254 B5, 257 B3, 258 B4
Coomalbidgup 259 E4
Coomberdale 257 B1, 258 A2
Coorow 258 A2
Coral Bay 261 A2, **72**, **147**, **202**
Cordering 257 C4
Corrigin 257 C2, 258 C3, **72**, **203**
Corrigin Pioneer Museum 72
Cosmo Newbery 265 E5
Cossack 261 C1, 262 C2, 264 A1, 268 A5, 47, 124
Cottesloe 6 A5, 254 B3, 16
Cottesloe Civic Centre, Cottesloe 16
Cowaramup 255 A3, 257 A4
Coyrecup 257 D4

Cranbrook 257 C4, 258 C4, **73**
Crawley 6 C4
Crossing Inn, Fitzroy Crossing 82
Crossman 254 D5, 257 B3, 258 B4
Cuballing 257 C3, 258 B4
Cue 261 D4, 264 B5, **73**, **203**
Culbin 257 C3
Cultural Heritage Museum, Balladonia 56
Cummins Theatre, Merredin 105
Cundeelee 259 E2
Cunderdin 257 C2, 258 B3
Curara 254 C5, 257 B3, 258 B4, 261 C5

D

Daglish 6 B3
Dalkeith 6 B4, 14
Dalwallinu 257 B1, 258 B2
Dalyellup 257 B4
Dalyup 259 E4
Dampier 261 C1, 262 B2, 264 A1, 268 A5
Dampier Archipelago 47
Dandaragan 257 A1, 258 A2
Dangin 257 C2
Dardadine 257 C3
Dardanup 255 C2, 257 B4
Darkan 257 C4, 258 B4
Darling & Swan region 32
Darling Range 27
Darlington 254 B2
Deakin 259 H2
Deanmill 255 D4, 256 A1, 257 B4
Denham 260 B3, 261 A4, **74**, **148**, **204**
Denmark 256 A6, 257 C5, 258 C5, **75**, **148**, **204**

D'Entrecasteaux National Park 255 D5, 256 C2, 257 C5, 258 B5
Derby 266 B4, 269 E3, **76**, **149**, **205**
Dewars Pool 254 C1, 257 B2, 258 B3
Dianella 6 D1, 254 B2
Dinninup 257 C4
Dirk Hartog Island 260 A3, 261 A4, 74
Dog Cemetery, Corrigin 72
Dolphin Discovery Centre, Bunbury 65
Dongara–Denison 258 A2, **77**, **150**, **206**
Donnybrook 255 C2, 257 B4, 258 B4, **78**, **150**, **207**
Doodlakine 257 C2, 258 C3
Doubleview 6 A2
Dowerin 257 C1, 258 B3
Drovers Cave National Park 257 A1, 258 A2
Drummond Cove 261 B5
Dryandra Woodland, via Narrogin 113
Drysdale River National Park 267 E2, 269 G2
Dudinin 257 D3, 258 C4
Dugongs, Shark Bay World Heritage Area 75
Dumberning 257 C3
Dumbleyung 257 D3, 258 C4
Dunsborough 255 A3, 257 A4, 258 A4, **78**, **150**, **208**
Duranillin 257 C4, 258 B4
Dwarda 254 D4
Dwellingup 254 C4, 257 B3, 258 B4, **79**, **151**, **209**

E

East Fremantle 6 B5
East Perth 6 D3, **12**
East Victoria Park 7 E4
Eaton 255 C2

Edenvale Complex, Pinjarrra 120
Edgewater 254 A2
Ejanding 257 C1, 258 B3
Elder's Building, Fremantle 21
Embleton 7 E1
Eneabba 258 A2
Esperance 259 E4, 40, **80**, **151**, **210**
Esplanade Hotel, Fremantle 21
Esplanade Reserve, Fremantle 22
Etmilyn 254 C5
Eucla 259 H2, 41, **81**, **210**
Eucla National Park 259 H2, 81
Eujinyn 257 D2
Everard Junction 265 F3
Exmouth 261 A2, **81**, **152**, **211**
Eyre Bird Observatory, Eyre 67

F

Fairbridge, Pinjarra 120
Ferndale 255 D3
Fire and Emergency Services Education and Heritage Centre, Perth 27
Fitzgerald River National Park 258 C4, 61
Fitzroy Crossing 266 D5, 269 F3, **82**, **153**, **212**
Floreat 6 B3, 254 B2
Florida 254 A4, 257 B3, 258 A4
Forest Grove 255 A4, 257 A4
Forest Heritage Centre, Dwellingup 79
Forrest 259 H2
Forrest Place, Perth 9, 24
Fortesque River Roadhouse 261 B1, 262 B3, 264 A1
Francis Burt Law Museum, Perth 27

Francois Peron National Park 260 B3, 261 A4
Frank Hann National Park 258 D3
Frankland 256 D1, 257 C4, 258 B5
Fremantle 254 A3, 257 B2, 258 A3, **19**, **137**, **189**
Fremantle Arts Centre, Fremantle 22
Fremantle Festival, Fremantle 28
Fremantle Markets, Fremantle 21
Fremantle Prison, Fremantle 22
Fremantle Prison Tours, Fremantle 26
Fremantle Street Arts Festival, Fremantle 28
Fremantle Technical College, Fremantle 21
Freo's West Coast Blues 'n Roots Festival, Fremantle 28
Furnissdale 254 B4, 257 B3

G

Gantheaume Point, Broome 60
Gary Junction 265 F2
Gascoyne Junction 261 B3, **83**, **153**, **212**
Geeralying 257 C3
Geikie Gorge National Park 266 D5, 269 F3, 49, 82
Gelorup 255 C2
Geraldton 258 A1, 261 B5, 45, **83**, **153**, **212**
Gibb River Road 49
Gibson 259 E4
Gidgegannup 254 C2, 257 B2
Gillingarra 257 B1, 258 A3
Gingin 254 B1, 257 B2, 258 A3, **85**, **154**, **213**
Gladstone 260 D3, 261 B4
Glendalough 6 B2, 254 B2

Gloucester National Park
    255 D5, 256 A1, 257 B5,
    258 B5, 119
Gnangara 254 B2
Gnarming 257 D3, 258 C3
Gnarojin Park, Narrogin 113
Gnowangerup 257 D4,
    258 C4
Golden Valley Tree Park,
    Balingup 55
Goldfields Exhibition Museum,
    Coolgardie 71
Goldfields region 42
Goldfields Woodlands
    National Park 258 D2
Goldsworthy 263 E1, 264 C1,
    268 C5
Goomalling 257 B2, 258 B3
Goongarrie 258 D2
Goongarrie National Park
    258 D2
Gooseberry Hill National Park
    254 B2, 257 B2, 258 B3
Gosnells 254 B3
Government House, Perth 24
Gracetown 255 A4, 257 A4,
    258 A4
Grass Patch 259 E4
Gravity Discovery Centre,
    Gingin 85
Great Australian Bight Marine
    National Park SA 259 H2
Great Ocean Drive, Esperance
    41, 80
Great Southern region 38
Great Southern wineries 39
Green Head 257 A1, 258 A2
Greenbushes 255 D3, 257 B4
Greenhill Galleries, Claremont
    27
Greenhills 257 C2
Greenmount 254 B2
Greenmount National Park
    254 B2, 257 B2, 258 B3
Greenough 258 A2, **85**, **155**,
    214
Gregory 261 B5

Gregory National Park NT
    267 H3
Grimwade 255 D3
Guilderton 257 A2, 258 A3
Guildford 254 B2
Gundaring 257 C3
Gwalia 258 D1, 101
Gwelup 6 B1

H

Haig 259 G2
Halfway Mill Roadhouse
    257 A1, 258 A2
Halls Creek 267 F5, 269 G3,
    86, **155**, **215**
Halls Head 254 B4
Hamel 254 B5, 257 B3
Hamelin Bay 255 A5, 257 A5
Hamelin Pool stromatolites,
    via Denham 74
Hamersley 254 D2, 261 C1,
    262 D4, 264 B2
Harrismith 257 D3
Harvey 255 C1, 257 B3,
    258 B4, **87**, **156**, **215**
Harvey Dickson's Country
    Music Centre, Boyup Brook
    57
Hassell National Park 256 D4,
    257 D5, 258 C5
Hay Street Mall, Perth 9, 24
Hazelmere 254 B2
Heartlands 36
Henley Brook 254 B2
Herdsman 6 B2
Highbury 257 C3
Hillarys 254 A2, 257 A2
Hillarys Boat Harbour 16
Hillman 257 C4
Hines Hill 257 D2, 258 C3
His Majesty's Theatre, Perth
    24
HMAS *Sydney* Memorial,
    Geraldton 84
Holly 257 C4

Holmes à Court Gallery, East
    Perth 27
Hopman Cup, Perth 24
Horrocks 261 B5
Houtman Abrolhos 261 B5
Houtman Abrolhos Islands
    84
Hutt 261 B5
Hyden 257 D2, 258 C3, **88**,
    156, **216**

I

Ilkurlka Roadhouse 259 H1,
    265 H5
Illawong 258 A2
Imintji Store 266 D4, 269 F3
Indigenart Mossenson
    Galleries, Subiaco 26
Inglewood 6 D2
Innaloo 6 B1
International Art Space
    Kellerberrin Australia,
    Kellerberrin 96
Irwin District Museum, Dongara
    77

J

Jackie Junction 265 G3
Jacobs Well 257 C2
Jandakot 254 B3, 257 B2
Japanese Cemetery, Broome
    59
Jardee 255 D4, 256 A1,
    257 B5
Jarrahdale 254 B3, 257 B3
Jarrahwood 255 C3, 257 B4
Jaurdi 258 D2
Jennacubbine 254 D1
Jerramungup 258 C4
Jigalong 263 G5, 264 D2
Jindong 255 B3
Jingalup 257 C4, 258 B4
Jitarning 257 D3, 258 C4
John Baxter Memorial, via
    Caiguna 63

John Forrest National Park 254 B2, 257 B2, 258 B3, 33
Joondanna 6 C2
Joondalup 254 A2, 257 A2
Josbury 257 C3, 258 B4
Jura 257 D2
Jurien Bay 257 A1, 258 A2, **88**, **156**, **216**
Jurien Bay Marine Park 88

K

Kailis Australian Pearls, Fremantle 27
Kalamunda 254 B2
Kalamunda National Park 254 B2, 257 B2, 258 B3
Kalannie 257 C1, 258 B2
Kalbarri 261 B5, **89**, **156**, **217**
Kalbarri National Park 261 B5, 45, 89
Kalgan 256 C5, 257 D5, 258 C5
Kalgoorlie–Boulder 258 D2, **43**, **92**, **157**, **218**
Kalka SA 265 H4
Kaltukatjara (Docker River) NT 265 H3
Kalumburu 267 E1, 269 G1
Kambalda 259 E2
Kamballup 256 B4, 257 D5, 258 C5
Kandiwal 266 D2, 269 F1
Karalundi 261 D4, 264 C4
Karawara 7 D4
Kardinya 254 B3
Karijini National Park 261 D1, 262 D4, 263 E4, 264 B2, 47, 125
Karlamilyi National Park 263 H3, 264 D1, 265 E1
Karlgarin 257 D3, 258 C3
Karonie 259 E2
Karrakatta 6 B4, 254 B2
Karratha 261 C1, 262 B2, 264 A1, 268 A5, **90**, **158**, **219**

Karratha Travel Stop Roadhouse 261 C1, 262 B2, 264 A1, 268 A5
Karridale 255 A5, 257 A5
Karrinyup 6 A1
Katanning 257 C4, 258 C4, **91**, **159**, **220**
Keep River National Park NT 267 G3, 269 H2
Keep River National Park Extension (Proposed) NT 267 H2, 269 H2
Kellerberrin 257 C2, 258 B3, **91**, **159**, **220**
Kelmscott 254 B3
Kendenup 256 A4, 257 D5
Kennedy Range National Park 261 B3, 83
Kensington 7 D4
Kenwick 254 B3
Keysbrook 254 B4, 257 B3
Kimberley 48
King River 256 B5, 257 D5
King Street, Perth 9, 24
Kings Park & Botanic Gardens, West Perth 6 C3, 13
Kings Park Indigenous Heritage Tour 26
Kings Park Walks 26
Kings Park Wildflower Festival 24
Kintore NT 265 H2
Kirkman House, Perth 24
Kirup 255 C3, 257 B4, 258 B4
Kitchener 259 F2
Kiwirrkurra 265 H2
Kojonup 257 C4, 258 B4, **96**, **159**, **221**
Kondinin 257 D3, 258 C3
Konnongorring 257 B1, 258 B3
Kookynie 258 D1
Koolan 266 B3, 269 E2
Kooljaman 266 A3, 268 D2
Koolyanobbing 258 C2
Koorda 257 C1, 258 B2
Korbel 257 D2

Kukerin 257 D3, 258 C4
Kulikup 257 C4
Kulin 257 D3, 258 C3, **97**, **159**, **221**
Kumarina Roadhouse 264 C3
Kumarl 259 E3
Kunjin 257 C2, 258 C3
Kununoppin 257 C1, 258 C3
Kununurra 267 G2, 269 H2, **98**, **160**, **221**
Kupingarri 266 D3, 269 F2
Kuringup 257 D4
Kweda 257 C3
Kwinana 254 B3, 257 B3
Kwolyin 257 C2

L

Lake Argyle 49
Lake Biddy 258 C4
Lake Cave 35, 107
Lake Clifton 254 B5, 257 B3, 258 A4
Lake Grace 257 D3, 258 C4, **99**, **160**, **223**
Lake King 258 D4, **100**, **160**, **223**
Lake Monger 6 C2, 15
Lancelin 257 A1, 258 A3
Landsdale 254 B2
Lane–Poole Reserve, Dwellingup 79
Latham 258 B2
Lathlain 7 E3
Laverton 259 E1, 265 E5, **100**, **161**, **224**
Lawley River National Park 266 D2, 269 F1
Lawrence Wilson Art Gallery, Crawley 14
Learmonth 261 A2
Leda 254 B3
Ledge Point 257 A2
Leederville 6 C2
Leeman 258 A2

Leeuwin–Naturaliste National Park 255 A4, 257 A4, 258 A4, 51, 79, 107
Leeuwin Ocean Adventure, Fremantle 22
Leinster 258 D1, 264 D5
Leonora 258 D1, **101**, **161**, **224**
Leschenault 255 C2
Leschenault Inlet, Albany 55
Lesmurdie Falls National Park 254 B2, 257 B2, 258 B3
Lesueur National Park 257 A1, 258 A2
Lionel Samson Building, Fremantle 21
Little Grove 256 B6, 257 D5, 258 C5
Lombadina 266 A4, 268 D2
London Court, Perth 9, 24
Looma 266 C5, 269 E3
Loongana 259 G2
Lowden 255 C2, 257 B4
Lower Chittering 254 B1, 257 B2
Ludlow 255 B3, 257 B4

M

Mcalinden 255 D2, 257 B4
Maddington 254 B3, 258 B3
Madora 254 B4, 257 B3
Madura 259 G3, **102**
Madura Roadhouse 259 G3
Malcolm 258 D1
Malyalling 257 C3
Mammoth and Lake Caves, Leeuwin–Naturaliste National Park 107
Mandurah 254 B4, 257 B3, 258 A4, **102**, **161**, **224**
Manjimup 255 D4, 256 A1, 257 B4, 258 B5, **103**, **163**, **225**
Manmanning 257 C1, 258 B2
Manning 6 D5
Manypeaks 256 C5, 257 D5, 258 C5

Marangaroo 254 B2
Marbelup 256 B6, 257 D5
Marble Bar 263 F2, 264 C1, 268 C5, 47, **104**, **163**, **226**
Marchagee 258 A2
Mardella 254 B3
Margaret River 255 A4, 257 A4, 258 A4, 34, **106**, **163**, **226**
Marradong 254 D5, 257 B3, 258 B4
Marralum NT 267 G2, 269 H2
Marrinup 254 C4
Marvel Loch 258 C3
Marybrook 255 A3
Mawson 257 C2, 258 B3
Mayanup 257 B4, 258 B4
Maylands 7 E2, 254 B2
Meckering 257 C2, 258 B3
Meekatharra 261 D4, 264 B4, **104**, **166**, **230**
Meelon 254 B4
Melros 254 A4
Melville 6 C5, 254 B3, 256 B6
Menora 6 D2
Menzies 258 D2
Merredin 257 D2, 258 C3, **105**, **166**, **230**
Metricup 255 A3
Middle Swan 254 B2
Midland 254 B2, 257 B2, 258 B3
Mid-west region 44
Miling 257 B1, 258 B2
Millstream–Chichester National Park 261 C1, 262 D3, 264 B1, 47, 90
Mingenew 258 A2
Minilya Roadhouse 261 A3
Minniging 257 C3
Minnivale 257 C1
Mirima National Park 267 G2, 269 H2
Mistake Creek NT 267 G4, 269 H3

Mitchell River National Park 266 D2, 269 F1
Mogumber 257 B1, 258 A3
Mokine 254 D1
Monkey Mia 260 B3, 261 A4, 45, 74
Moora 257 B1, 258 A2, **108**, **167**, **231**
Moore River National Park 257 A2, 258 A3
Moorine Rock 258 C3
Morawa 258 A2, **109**, **167**, **231**
Morley 7 D1
Mosman Park 254 B3
Moulyinning 257 D3
Mount Augustus National Park 261 C3, 264 A3, 83
Mount Barker 256 B5, 257 D5, 258 C5, **109**, **167**, **231**
Mount Barnett Roadhouse 266 D3, 269 F2
Mount Claremont 6 B3
Mount Frankland National Park 256 D2, 257 C5, 258 B5
Mount Hawthorn 6 C2
Mount Helena 254 C2
Mount Keith 264 D5
Mount Lawley 6 D2
Mount Magnet 258 B1, 261 D5, 264 B5, **110**, **168**, **232**
Mount Pleasant 6 D5, 258 D2
Mt Roe–Mt Lindesay 256 D2, 257 C5, 258 B5
Mowen 255 B4, 257 A4
Muchea 254 B1, 257 B2, 258 A3
Mukinbudin 257 D1, 258 C2
Mulka's Cave, Hyden 37
Mullalyup 255 D3, 257 B4
Mullewa 258 A1, 261 C5, **110**
Mumballup 255 D2, 257 B4, 258 B4
Mundaring 254 C2, 257 B2, 258 B3, **111**, **168**, **232**

Mundaring Weir 254 C2, 33, 111
Mundijong 254 B3
Mundrabilla Roadhouse 259 H3
Munglinup 258 D4
Municipal Museum, Esperance 80
Munster 254 B3
Muntadgin 257 D2, 258 C3
Muradup 257 C4
Murchison 261 C4, 264 A5
Murray Street Mall, Perth 9, 24
Museum of Performing Arts, Perth 27
Myalup 255 C1, 257 B3, 258 A4
Myaree 6 C5

N

Nabawa 258 A1, 261 B5
Nalya 257 C3
Nambung National Park 257 A1, 258 A3, 37, 67
Nanarup 256 C6, 257 D5
Nanga 254 C5, 257 B3
Nangeenan 257 D2
Nannup 255 C4, 257 B4, 258 B4, **112**, **172**, **235**
Nanson 258 A1, 261 B5
Nanutarra Roadhouse 261 B2, 262 A4
Napoleon Street, Cottesloe 24
Naraling 258 A1, 261 B5
Narembeen 257 D2, 258 C3
Naretha 259 F2
Narrikup 256 B5, 257 D5, 258 C5
Narrogin 257 C3, 258 B4, **113**, **172**, **236**
Naval Base 254 B3
Neale Junction 259 G1, 265 G5
Nedlands 6 B4, 14
Neerabup National Park 254 A2, 257 A2, 258 A3

New Norcia 257 B1, 258 B3, 37, **113**, **172**, **237**
Newdegate 258 C4
Newlands 255 C3, 257 B4
Newman 263 F5, 264 C2, **114**, **173**, **237**
Ningaloo Marine Park 45, 72
Nippering 257 C3
No 44 King Street, Perth 9
Nollamara 6 C1
Nornakin 257 D2
Nornalup 256 D3, 257 C5, 258 B5
Norseman 259 E3, **115**, **173**, **238**
North Dandalup 254 B4, 257 B3, 258 B4
North Fremantle 6 A5, 254 B3
North Jindong 255 A3
North Perth 6 C2
North Pinjarra 254 B4, 257 B3
Northam 254 D1, 257 B2, 258 B3, **116**, **173**, **238**
Northampton 261 B5, **116**, **173**, **239**
Northbridge 6 D3, **11**
Northcliffe 255 D5, 256 B2, 257 B5, 258 B5, **117**, **174**, **239**
Notting 257 D3, 258 C3
Nullagine 263 F3, 264 C2
Nullarbor National Park 259 H2
Nullarbor Plain 40
Nungarin 257 D1, 258 C3
Nurina 259 G2
Nyabing 257 D4, 258 C4

O

Ockley 257 C3
Ogilvie 261 B5
Old Court House, Perth 25
Old Gaol, Northbridge 11

Old Goldfields Orchard and Cider Factory, Donnybrook 78
Old Mill, South Perth 17
Old Perth Boys' School, Perth 25
One Arm Point 266 A3, 268 D2
One Tree Bridge, Manjimup 103
Ongerup 257 D4
Onslow 261 B1, 262 A4, **118**, **174**, **240**
Oombulgurri 267 F2, 269 G1
Ora Banda 258 D2
Orange Grove 254 B3
Osborne Park 6 B2
Osmington 255 B4, 257 A4
Our Lady of Mt Carmel Church, Mullewa 110
Outback Coast 44
Overlander Roadhouse 260 D4, 261 B4

P

Palgarup 255 D4, 256 A1, 257 B4
Palmyra 6 B5
Pannawonica 261 C1, 262 B3, 264 A2
Pantapin 257 C2
Paraburdoo 261 D2, 262 D5, 264 B2
Pardoo Roadhouse 263 F1, 268 C5
Parliament House, West Perth 15
Parkerville 254 B2
Paynes Find 258 B2
Peaceful Bay 256 D3, 257 C5, 258 B5
Peak Charles National Park 258 D3, 43
Peak Hill 261 D3, 264 C4
Pearl Luggers, Broome 59
Pedal Oz City Discovery Tour 26

Pemberton 255 D5, 256 A2, 257 B5, 258 B5, **118**, **174**, **240**
Penguin Island 254 A3, 257 B3, 258 A3, 123
Peppermint Grove 6 A4, 255 B2, 257 B4, 16
Peppimenarti NT 267 H1
Perenjori 258 A2
Perth 6 D3, 254 B2, 257 B2, 258 A3, **4**, **133**, **185**
Perth Cup 24
Perth–Fremantle River Cruise 26
Perth Institute of Contemporary Arts, Northbridge 12
Perth International Arts Festival 24
Perth Mint, East Perth 12
Perth Royal Show 24
Perth Town Hall, Perth 25
Perth Walking Tours 26
Perth Zoo, South Perth 17
Piawaning 257 B1, 258 B3
Picton 255 C2
Piesseville 257 C3
Pilbara 46
Pindar 258 A1, 261 C5
Pingaring 257 D3, 258 C3
Pingelly 257 C3, 258 B3, **119**, **175**, **241**
Pingrup 257 D4, 258 C4
Pinjarra 254 B4, 257 B3, 258 B4, **120**, **175**, **242**
Pioneer Museum, Northcliffe 117
Pipalyatjara SA 265 H4
Pithara 257 B1, 258 B2
Point Heathcote Reserve, Applecross 18
Point Samson 261 C1, 262 C2, 264 A1, 268 A5
Point Walter Reserve, Bicton 18
Popanyinning 257 C3, 258 B4

Porongurup National Park 256 B5, 257 D5, 258 C5, 109
Port Denison 258 A2
Port Hedland 262 D2, 264 B1, 268 B5, **121**, **176**, **242**
Port Keats (Wadeye) NT 267 H1, 269 H1
Port Smith 268 D4
Preston Beach 254 B5, 257 B3, 258 A4
Prevelly 255 A4, 257 A4
Purnululu National Park 267 G4, 269 H3, 49, 87

Q

Quairading 257 C2, 258 B3
Queens Gardens, East Perth 13
Quellington 254 D1, 257 C2, 258 B3
Quindalup 255 A3
Quindanning 254 D5, 257 B3, 258 B4
Quinninup 256 B1, 257 B5, 258 B5
Quinns Rocks 254 A2, 257 A2
Quokka country, Rottnest Island 31

R

Ranford 254 D5
Ravensthorpe 258 D4, **122**, **177**, **243**
Rawlinna 259 F2
Recherche Archipelago 41, 80
Red Bluff 261 A3
Red Bluff 267 E1, 269 G1
Red Bull Air Race 24
Redmond 256 B5, 257 D5
Regans Ford 257 A1, 258 A3
Reid 259 H2
Ringa 254 C1, 257 B2
Riverton 7 E5

Rivervale 7 E3
Robinson Street, Carnarvon 68
Rockingham 254 B3, 257 B3, 258 A3, **122**, **177**, **243**
Rocky Gully 256 D1, 257 C5, 258 B5
Roebourne 261 C1, 262 C2, 264 A1, 268 A5, **123**, **178**, **244**
Roebuck Roadhouse 266 A5, 268 D3
Roelands 255 C2
Rokeby Road, Subiaco 24
Roleystone 254 B3
Rosa Glen 255 B4, 257 A4
Rossmoyne 6 D5
Rottnest Island 254 A3, 257 A2, 258 A3, 27, **30**, **178**, **244**
Round House, Fremantle 21
Ruabon 255 B3
Rugby Union 26

S

Safety Bay 254 B3
St George's Cathedral, Perth 25
St George's Terrace, Perth 9
St James 7 E4
St John's Anglican Church, Fremantle 21
St Mary's Cathedral, Perth 25
St Patrick's Day Parade and Concert, Fremantle 28
Salmon Gums 259 E3
Salter Point 6 D5
Samson House, Fremantle 21
Sandfire Roadhouse 263 G1, 268 C4
Sandstone 258 C1, 264 C5
Sawyers Valley 254 C2
Scaddan 259 E4
Scarborough 6 A2, 254 A2, 257 B2, 258 A3, 16
Scarborough Fair Markets, Scarborough Beach 24

Scitech Discovery Centre, West Perth 6 C3, 15
Scott National Park 255 B4, 257 A5, 258 A5
Seabird 257 A2
Serpentine 254 B3, 257 B3, 258 B3
Serpentine National Park 254 C4, 257 B3, 258 B3
Shackleton 257 C2, 258 C3
Shannon 256 B2, 257 C5, 258 B5
Shannon National Park 256 C2, 257 C5, 258 B5
Shark Bay 45
Shay Gap 263 F2, 264 C1, 268 C5
Shelley 7 E5
Shenton Park 6 B3
Shipwreck Galleries, Fremantle 21
Shotts 255 D2
Singleton 254 B4, 257 B3, 258 A4
Sir James Mitchell National Park 255 D4, 256 B1, 257 B5, 258 B5
South Hedland 262 D2, 264 B1, 268 B5
South Kumminin 257 D2, 258 C3
South Perth 6 D4
South Stirling 256 C4, 257 D5, 258 C5
South-West, The 34
Southern Cross 258 C3, **124**, **179**, **245**
Spearwood 254 B3
Staircase to the Moon, Broome 59
Stairway to the Moon, Port Hedland 121
Stirling 6 B1, 254 B2
Stirling Gardens, Perth 10
Stirling Range National Park 256 D4, 257 D4, 258 C4, 39, 73
Stokes National Park 258 D4

Stoneville 254 C2, 259 E2
Stratham 255 B2, 257 B4
Subiaco 6 C3, 254 B2, 14
Subiaco Arts Centre, Subiaco 6 C3
Subiaco Pavilion Markets, Subiaco 24
Subiaco Station Street Markets, Subiaco 24
Sunken Garden, Crawley 14
Supreme Court Gardens, Perth 10
Swan Bells, Perth 10
Swan Brewery Tour, Canning Vale 26
Swan Valley 27
Swan Valley Wine Cruise 26
Swan Valley wineries 33
Swanbourne 6 A4, 254 B2

T

Tambellup 257 D4, 258 C4
Tammin 257 C2, 258 B3
Tardun 258 A1, 261 C5
Tarwonga 257 C3, 258 B4
Tathra National Park 258 A2, 66
Telecommunications Museum, Andross 18
Telegraph Station ruins, Eucla 81
Tenterden 256 A4, 257 C4
The Basin, Rottnest Island 31
The Berkshire Valley Folk Museum, Moora 108
The Cidery, Bridgetown 62
The Cloisters, Perth 25
The Markets @ Perth Cultural Centre 24
The Old Farm at Strawberry Hill, Albany 39
The Pinnacles 37
Thomson Bay 254 A3
Three Mile Valley, Wyndham 129
Three Springs 258 A2

Timber and Heritage Park, Manjimup 103
Tincurrin 257 C3
Tjukayirla Roadhouse 265 F4
Tom Price 261 D2, 262 D4, 264 B2, **124**, **179**, **245**
Toodyay 254 C1, 257 B2, 258 B3, **125**, **180**, **246**
Toolibin 257 C3
Torndirrup National Park 256 C6, 257 D5, 258 C5, 39, 54
Tourist Coal Mine, Collie 70
Tranby House 7 E2, 13
Trayning 257 C1, 258 B3
Trigg 6 A1
Tuart Forest National Park 255 B3, 257 A4, 258 A4, 63
Tuart Hill 6 C1
Tuckanarra 261 D4, 264 B5
Tunnel Creek National Park 266 D4, 269 F3, 77
Tutunup 255 B3
Two Rocks 254 A1, 257 A2, 258 A3

U

Ulva 257 D2
University of Western Australia, Crawley 6 C4, 14
Upper Swan 254 B2, 257 B2

V

Varley 258 C3
Vasse 255 B3, 257 A4
Victoria Park 7 E3

W

WACA, East Perth 6 D3, 13
WACA Museum, East Perth 27
Waeel 257 C2
Wagerup 254 B5, 257 B3

INDEX → WAGIN – YANDEYARRA

Wagin 257 C3, 258 B4, **126**, **180**, **247**
Wagin Historical Village, Wagin 126
Waikiki 254 B3, 257 B3
Walga Rock, via Cue 73
Walgoolan 257 D1, 258 C3
Walkaway 258 A2
Walpole 256 C3, 257 C5, 258 B5, **127**, **180**, **247**
Walpole–Nornalup National Park 256 D3, 257 C5, 258 B5, 127
Walsall 255 B3
Walyunga National Park 254 B2, 257 B2, 258 B3
Wandering 254 D4, 257 B3, 258 B4
Wangara 254 B2
Wanneroo 254 B2, 257 B2, 258 A3
Wanneroo Markets, Wanneroo 24
Warakurna 265 H3
Warakurna Roadhouse 265 H3
Warawarrup 255 C1, 257 B3
Warburton 265 G4
Warburton Roadhouse 265 G4
Warders' Quarters, Fremantle 21
Warmun 267 G4, 269 H3
Warmun–Turkey Creek Roadhouse 267 G4, 269 H3
Waroona 254 B5, 257 B3, 258 B4
Warralakin 257 D1, 258 C2
Warren National Park 255 D5, 256 A2, 257 B5, 258 B5, 119
Warup 257 C4
Waterford 7 E4
Waterloo 255 C2, 257 B4
Watheroo 257 B1, 258 A2
Watheroo National Park 257 A1, 258 A2
Wattle Grove 254 B2

Wattleup 254 B3
Wave Rock, Hyden 37, 88
Waychinicup National Park 256 D5, 257 D5, 258 C5
Wellington National Park 255 C2, 257 B4, 258 B4, 70
Wellstead 256 D4, 257 D4, 258 C5
Welshpool 254 B2
Wembley 6 B2
West Cape Howe National Park 256 A6, 257 D5, 258 C5
West End, Rottnest Island 31
West Leederville 6 C3
West Perth 6 C3
Westdale 254 D3, 257 B3, 258 B3
Western Australian Maritime Museum, Fremantle 21
Western Australian Museum, Northbridge 11
Western Australian Museum Geraldton, Geraldton 84
Westonia 257 D1, 258 C3
Whale World, Albany 39, 54
Whim Creek 261 C1, 262 D2, 264 B1, 268 B5
Whiteman 254 B2
Wialki 257 C1, 258 C2
Wickepin 257 C3, 258 B4, **128**, **181**, **248**
Wickham 261 C1, 262 C2, 264 A1, 268 A5
Widgiemooltha 258 D3
Wilga 255 D3, 257 B4
Willare Bridge Roadhouse 266 B5, 269 E3
Willetton 7 E5
William Bay National Park 256 A6, 257 C5, 258 B5, 75
Williams 257 C3, 258 B4
Wilroy 258 A1, 261 C5
Wilson 7 E5
Wiluna 264 C4
Windarra 259 E1, 265 E5

Windjana Gorge National Park 266 C4, 269 F3, 77
Windmill Roadhouse 257 A1, 258 A3
Windy Corner 265 F2
Windy Harbour 256 A3, 257 B5, 258 B5
Winthrop Hall, Crawley 14
Wireless Hill Park, Andross 18
Wishbone 257 D3
Witchcliffe 255 A4, 257 A4
Wittenoom 262 D4, 264 B2
Wokalup 255 C1, 257 B3
Wolfe Creek Crater National Park 269 G4, 49, 86
Wongan Hills 257 B1, 258 B3
Woodanilling 257 C4, 258 B4
Woodlands 6 B2, 256 B5, 257 D5
Wooramel Roadhouse 260 D3, 261 B4
Wooroloo 254 C2, 257 B2
Worsley 255 C2
Wubin 258 B2
Wundowie 254 C2
Wyalkatchem 257 C1, 258 B3
Wyening 257 B2
Wyndham 267 F2, 269 H2, **128**, **181**, **248**

Y

Yalgoo 258 B1, 261 C5, 264 B5, **129**, **248**
Yalgorup National Park 254 A5, 255 B1, 257 A3, 258 A4
Yallingup 255 A3, 257 A4, 258 A4, **130**, **181**, **248**
Yanchep 254 A1, 257 A2, 258 A3, **130**, **183**, **250**
Yanchep National Park 254 A1, 257 A2, 258 A3, 27, 131
Yandeyarra 261 D1, 262 D3, 264 B1, 268 B5

Yarloop 254 B5, 255 C1, 257 B3
Yarramony 254 D1
Yealering 257 C3, 258 B3
Yellowdine 258 C3
Yelverton 255 A3
Yerecoin 257 B1, 258 B3
Yokine 6 C2
Yoongarillup 255 B3, 257 A4
York 254 D2, 257 B2, 258 B3, **131**, **183**, **250**
Yornaning 257 C3
Yoting 257 C2, 258 B3
Youndegin 257 C2, 258 B3
Yuna 258 A1, 261 B5
Yunderup 254 B4

Z
Zanthus 259 F2

Where to Eat

1907 Restaurant and Cocktail Bar, Perth 132
3twotwo, Northam 173

A

Abrolhos Restaurant, Greenough 155
Albert's Restaurant, Narrogin 172
Alexanders Restaurant, Bunbury 144
Alfred's Kitchen, Guildford 168
Amberley Restaurant, Yallingup 181
Amirage Restaurant, Gingin 154
Annalakshmi on the Swan, Perth 132
Aquarium, Ascot 133
Aristos Waterfront, Bunbury 144

B

Balingup Bronze Cafe, Balingup 140
Balladonia Roadhouse, Balladonia 141
Balthazar, Perth 133
Barista 202, Kalgoorlie 157
Beachside Cafe, Albany 139
Beadon Bay Hotel, Onslow 174
Bettyblue Bistro, Rockingham 177
Black Rock Cafe, Kalbarri 156
Black Swan Winery & Restaurant, Henley Brook 169
Blackwood Bistro, Balingup 141
Blue Dolphin Restaurant, Two Rocks 183

Blue Duck, Cottesloe 6 A4, 133
Bluewater Grill, Fremantle 6 C4, 137
Bluff Knoll Cafe, Mount Borden 167
Boardwalk Bar & Bistro, Bunbury 144
Boatshed Restaurant, Geraldton 153
Bonaparte Seafood Restaurant, Esperance 151
Bridgetown Pottery Tearooms & Gallery, Bridgetown 142
Brookwood Estate, Cowaramup 163

C

C Restaurant, Perth 133
Cabernet Restaurant, Manjimup 163
Cafe Bethany, Northam 173
Cafe Bugatti, York 183
Cafe Carlotta, Broome 143
Cafe on the Dam, Jarrahdale 162
Cafe Pronto, Mandurah 161
Cafe Yasou, Northam 173
Cantina 663, Mount Lawley 133
Cape Lodge Restaurant, Yallingup 182
Capri, Fremantle 137
Carlaminda Wines Bistro, Ferguson Valley 145
Castle Hotel York, York 183
Caves House Hotel, Yallingup 182
Chapman Valley Wines Restaurant, Nanson 154
Charlie's Bistro, Rockingham 177
Che Sera Sera, Denmark 148
Chocolate Drops, Yanchep National Park 183
Chudacud Estate, Boyup Brook 142

Cicerello's, Fremantle 22, 137
Clairault, Willyabrup 165
Clarke's of North Beach, North Beach 139
Club Hotel, Southern Cross 179
Cola Cafe and Museum, Toodyay 180
Commercial Hotel, Kojonup 159
Cream, East Perth 134
Cullen Restaurant, Cowaramup 165

D

Darlington Estate Restaurant, Darlington 169
Dear Friends, Caversham 169
Deco Restaurant, Perth 6 D5, 134
Déjà vu Cafe, Manjimup 163
Denzil's Restaurant, Merredin 166
Derby Boab Inn, Derby 149
Dunsborough Bakery, Dunsborough 150
Dwellingup Community Hotel Motel, Dwellingup 151
Dwellingup Millhouse Restaurant, Dwellingup 151

E

Earl of Spencer, Albany 139
Edenvale Homestead & Heritage Tearooms, Pinjarra 175
Elmar's in the Valley, Henley Brook 169
Emma's on the Boardwalk, Rockingham 177
Esplanade Hotel Port Hedland, Port Hedland 176
Etcetera Brasserie, Karratha 158
Everlastings Restaurant, Morawa 167

F

Fin's Cafe, Coral Bay 147
Flutes Restaurant, Willyabrup 182
Fraser's Restaurant, West Perth 6 C3, 134
Freemasons Hotel, Beverley 141
Fre-Jac French Restaurant, Balingup 141

G

Galafrey Wines, Mount Barker 167
Geordie Bay Cafe, Rottnest Island 178
Gingin Hotel, Gingin 154
Gnarabar Restaurant, Gnarabar 166
Greenpool Restaurant, Denmark 149
Gulliver's Tavern, Kununurra 160

H

Hackersley, Ferguson Valley 145
Ha-Lu, Mount Hawthorn 6 C2, 134
Hearson's Bistro, Karratha 158
Heddy's Bar & Bistro, Port Hedland 176
Hidden River Estate Restaurant, Pemberton 174

I

Indiana Cottesloe Beach Restaurant, Cottesloe Beach 6 A4, 16, 134
Ivanhoes Gallery Restaurant, Kununurra 160

J

Jackson's Restaurant, Highgate 6 D2, 135
Jarrah Jacks Brewery, Pemberton 175
Just Wine and Tapas Bar, Como 6 D4, 135

K

Kalgoorlie Hotel, Kalgoorlie 157
Kappy's, Guildford 170
Kellerberrin Motor Hotel, Kellerberrin 159
Kelly's Bar & Grill, Kununurra 160
Kimberley Restaurant, Katanning 159
King & I, Guildford 170
King Trout Restaurant and Marron Farm, Pemberton 175
Kingsford Steak House, Carnarvon 146
Kulin Hotel & Motel, Kulin 159
Kyotmunga Estate, Lower Chittering 154

L

Lake Grace Hotel, Lake Grace 160
Lake King Tavern & Motel, Lake King 160
Lake Navarino Restaurant, Waroona 151
Lamont's Margaret River, Yallingup 182
Le Paris Brest Cafe & Patisserie, Kalamunda 170
Leeuwin Restaurant, Margaret River 163
Leuseurs Gallery Cafe, Jurien Bay 156
Lime 303, Albany 139
Lindsay's Restaurant, Yanchep 183
Little Caesars Pizzeria, Mundaring 168
Little Creatures, Fremantle 137
Little River Winery Restaurant, Henley Brook 170
Loose Goose, Esperance 151
Loretta @ Feddy, Katanning 159

M

Mantaray's Restaurant, Exmouth 152
Marble Bar Travellers Stop, Marble Bar 163
Marlins, Thomson Bay, Rottnest Island 178
Matso's Broome Brewery, Broome 143
Maya, Fremantle 138
Merredin Motel & Gumtree Restaurant, Merredin 167
Millbrook Winery Restaurant, Jarrahdale 162
Miners Arms Hotel, Northampton 173
Miss Sandalford, Perth 135
Moby's Kitchen, Point Samson 178
Mojo's Restaurant, Bunbury 144
Moora Hotel, Moora 167
Mount Barren Restaurant, Bremer Bay 142
Mount Magnet Hotel, Mount Magnet 168
Mulberry Tree Restaurant, Nannup 172
Must Margaret River, Margaret River 164
Must Winebar, Highgate 6 D2, 135

N

Nannup Bridge Cafe, Nannup 172
Nelson's of Bridgetown, Bridgetown 142
New Norcia Bakery, Mount Hawthorn 6 C2, 135
New Norcia Hotel, New Norcia 172
Newbliss Vineyard Cafe, Dwellingup 151
Newman Hotel Motel, Newman 173
Newtown House Restaurant, Busselton 145
Nicola's Ristorante, Bunbury 145
Nikki's Licensed Restaurant, Onslow 174
Norseman Hotel, Norseman 173

O

Oasis Bistro, Derby 149
Ocean Blues Restaurant, Esperance 152
Old Coast Road Brewery, Harvey 156
Old Goldfields Orchard & Cider Factory, Donnybrook 150
Old Pearler Restaurant, Denham 148
Opus Restaurant, West Perth 6 C3, 136
Other Side of the Moon Restaurant, Bunker Bay 150

P

Palace Hotel, Southern Cross 179
Porongurup Tearooms, Porongurup 167
Potshot Resort Restaurant, Exmouth 152

R

Raven Wines, Pinjarra 176
Ravensthorpe Palace Motor Hotel, Ravensthorpe 177
Red Cabbage, Perth 6 D4, 136
Red Manna Waterfront Restaurant, Mandurah 161
Red Rock Cafe, Wickham 178
Redcliffe on the Murray, Pinjarra 176
Restaurant Amusé, East Perth 136
Restaurant Eboracum, York 184
Riverside @ Woodbridge, Woodbridge 170
Riverside Restaurant, Fitzroy Crossing 152
Ronsard Bay Tavern, Cervantes 147
Rose and Crown, Guildford 171
Rottnest Bakery, Thomson Bay, Rottnest Island 179
Rottnest Tearooms Bar and Cafe, Rottnest Island 179
Ruocco's, Fremantle 138
Russian Jack's Restaurant, Halls Creek 155

S

Sailfish Bar and Restaurant, Exmouth 152
Sails Restaurant, Carnarvon 146
Sala Thai, Fremantle 138
Saltimbocca, Kalgoorlie 157
Sandalford Restaurant, Caversham 171
Sandpiper Bar & Grill, Jurien Bay 156
Schnappers, Carnarvon 147
Scusi, Halls Head 162
Sea Gardens Cafe, Prevelly Park 166

Sea Star Cafe & Restaurant, Gracetown 166
Shades, Coral Bay 148
Shun Fung on the River, Perth 136
Sittella Restaurant, Herne Hill 171
Slice of Heaven Cafe, Manjimup 163
Slow Food Cafe, Walpole 181
Soto Espresso, Mount Lawley 6 D2, 136
Southern Cross Motel, Southern Cross 179
Star Anise Restaurant, Shenton Park 6 B3, 137
Stewart's Restaurant, Upper Swan 171
Stringybark Winery & Restaurant, Chittering 155
Sunsets Cafe Bistro, Palm Beach 177

T

TaTa's Restaurant, Point Samson 178
Tathra Restaurant, via Nannup 172
Taylor Street Cafe, Esperance 152
The 1896 Cafe, Balingup 141
The Berry Farm Cottage Cafe, Margaret River 164
The Boughshed Restaurant, Monkey Mia 148
The Bridgetown Hotel, Bridgetown 142
The Club Restaurant, Broome 143
The Colourpatch Cafe, Augusta 140
The Cornwall, Kalgoorlie 158
The Dairy Lounge Cafe, Northcliffe 174
The Deck, Esperance 152
The Desert Inn Hotel, Laverton 161

The Equinox, Busselton 146
The Europa Anchor Restaurant, Cervantes 147
The Exchange Hotel, Kalgoorlie 158
The Exchange Tavern, Pingelly 175
The Freemason's Hotel, Geraldton 153
The Goose, Busselton 146
The Grass Tree Cafe & Restaurant, Kalbarri 156
The Jetty Seafood Shack, Kalbarri 157
The Junction Hotel, Gascoyne Junction 153
The Lily Railway Station Restaurant, Amelup 140
The Loose Box, Mundaring 168
The Margaret River Chocolate Factory, Margaret River 164
The Mediterranean, Dawesville 162
The Miami Bakehouse, Mandurah 162
The Naked Bean, Albany 139
The Nornalup Teahouse Restaurant, Nornalup 150
The Old Zoo Cafe, Broome 143
The Palace Hotel, Wagin 180
The Pilbara Room Restaurant, Port Hedland 176
The Point Restaurant, Derby 149
The Railway Tavern, Northampton 174
The Red Herring, East Fremantle 138
The Reef Cafe, Coral Bay 148
The Ridge, Collie 147
The Royal Mail Hotel, Meekatharra 166
The Season Tree, Dongara–Denison 150
The Shamrock Restaurant, Pemberton 175
The Southern End Restaurant, Denmark 149
The Tudor Manor Restaurant, Yanchep National Parl 183
The Vineyard Cafe, Mount Barker 168
The Wharf Restaurant, Broome 144
The Wild Duck Restaurant, Albany 140
Thurlby Herb Farm Cafe, Walpole 180
Tides of Geraldton, Geraldton 154
Tom Price Hotel Motel, Tom Price 179
Trawlers Tavern, Roebourne 178
Tree Top Restaurant, Walpole 181

U

Udderly Divine Cafe, Cowaramup 166

V

Vasse Bar Cafe, Busselton 146
Vat 2, Bunbury 145
Victoria Hotel, Toodyay 180
Voyager Estate Restaurant, Margaret River 164

W

Wave Rock Motel Homestead, Hyden 156
Wedge Street Coffee Shop, Port Hedland 177
Whaler's Restaurant, Exmouth 152
Whim Creek Pub, Whim Creek 158
White House Hotel, Leonora 161
Wickepin Hotel, Wickepin 181
Willowbrook Farm Tearooms, West Gingin 155
Wino's Margaret River, Margaret River 165
Wise Vineyard Restaurant, Dunsborough 150
Wyndham Town Hotel, Wyndham 181

X

Xanadu Restaurant, Margaret River 165

Y

Y2K Cafe & Restaurant, Rockingham 178
York Mill Bakehouse, York 184

Z

Zuytdorp Restaurant, Kalbarri 157

Where to Stay

5 Star @ Aria, Rockingham 243

A

Albert Facey Motor Inn, Narrogin 236
Alison Camping Area, Rottnest Island 244
All Seasons Kalgoorlie Plaza Hotel, Kalgoorlie 218
All Seasons Port Hedland, Port Hedland 242
All Seasons Sanctuary Golf Resort, Pelican Point 198
Amani Cottage, Point Samson 244
Apex Camp Jurien, Jurien Bay 216
Augusta Sheoak Chalets, Augusta 192
Auski Inland Motel, Meekatharra 230
Australind Tourist Park, Australind 193
Avon Bridge Hotel, Northam 238
Avondale Estate, Toodyay 246
Ayr Sailean, Bow Bridge 247

B

Balingup Heights Hilltop Forest Cottages, Balingup 194
Balingup Jalbrook Cottages & Alpacas, Balingup 194
Balingup Rose B&B, Balingup 194
Balladonia Caravan Facility, Balladonia 195
Balmoral Holiday Park, Karratha 219
Banksia Springs Cottages, Dwellingup 209
Basildene Manor, Margaret River 226
Bay Lodge Economy Beachfront, Denham 204
Bay of Islands B&B, Esperance 210
Bayview Coral Bay, Coral Bay 202
Baywatch Manor, Augusta 192
Beach Barnacle, Prevelly 227
Beachlands Holiday Park, Busselton 199
Beckett's Flat Vineyard Cottage, Metricup 227
Bell's Beach House, Gracetown 227
Best Western Augusta Georgina Molloy Motel, Augusta 193
Best Western Halls Creek Motel, Halls Creek 215
Best Western Karratha Central Apartments, Karratha 219
Best Western Sea Breeze Resort, Exmouth 211
Bettenay's, Willyabrup 227
Beverley B&B, Beverley 195
Beyonderup Falls, Nannup 235
Bibbulmun Break Motel, Northcliffe 239
Bidgemia Station, Gascoyne Junction 212
Bindoon's Windmill Farm, Bindoon 214
Blackwood River Houseboats, Westbay 193
Blue Escape, Dunsborough 208
Bluehills Farmstay Harvey, Harvey 215
Boathouse B&B, Bunbury 199
Bobby Jo's B&B, Yanchep 250
Boronia Farm, Donnybrook 207
Boshack Farm, Bolgart 246
Brackson House B&B, Northam 238
Bremer Bay Beaches Tourist Resort Caravan Park, Bremer Bay 195
Bremer Bay Resort, Bremer Bay 196
Brilea Cottages and B&B, Karridale 193
Broadwater Hotel & Resort, Como 6 D4, 185
Brookside, West Gingin 213
Bunbury Silo Accommodation, Marlston Waterfront 199
Burroloo Well Farmstay, Upper Chittering 214

C

Cable Beach Club Resort & Spa, Broome 197
Cape Howe Cottages, Lowlands Beach 191
Cape Lodge, Yallingup 248
Carnarvon Central Apartments, Carnarvon 201
Casa Del Mar, Yanchep 250
Catton Hall Country Homestead, Mount Helena 233
Cervantes Pinnacles Motel, Cervantes 201
Chapel Farm Getaway, Middle Swan 233
Che Sara Sara Chalets, Hazelvale 247
Chimes Spa Retreat, Denmark 204
Chuckem Farm B&B, Narrogin 236
Cloud Nine Spa Chalets, East Porongurup 232
Clover Cottage, Pemberton 240
Club Thevenard, Thevenard Island 240
Cockiebiddy Wedgetail Inn, Cockiebiddy 202
Cook's Park on Australind Waters, Australind 194

Cooke Point Holiday Park, Port Hedland 242
Coolgardie Motel, Coolgardie 202
Corrigin Windmill Motel, Corrigin 203
Country Charm Retreat B&B, Donnybrook 207
Crabapple Lane B&B, Nannup 235
Craythorne Country House, Metricup 228

D

Dampier Archipelago, Karratha 220
Darean Farm Country Retreat, Lake Grace 223
Denham Villas, Denham 204
Derby Boab Inn, Derby 205
Desert Inn Hotel & Motel, Laverton 224
Diamond Tree Angus Stud, Manjimup 225
Dingup House B&B, Manjimup 225
Direction Island 240
Diversion Cruises & Hire, Kununurra 221
Dolphin House Boats, Mandurah Ocean Marina 224
Dongara Denison Beach Holiday Park, Dongara–Denison 206
Drummond Cove Holiday Park, Geraldton 212
Dunsborough Rail Carriages & Farm Cottages, Dunsborough 208
Durham Lodge B&B, Victoria Park 7 E3, 185
Dwellingup Bunkhouses Outdoor Adventure Camp, Dwellingup 209
Dwellingup Chalet & Caravan Park, Dwellingup 209

E

Eden Valley Farmstay, Narrogin 236
Egoline Reflections, Northam 238
El Questro Wilderness Park, Kununurra 222
Esplanade Hotel, Fremantle 189
Eucla Amber Motor Hotel, Eucla 210
Everlastings Guest Homes, Morawa 231
Exmouth Cape Holiday Park, Exmouth 211

F

Fitzroy River Lodge, Fitzroy Crossing 212
Fonty's Pool & Caravan Park, Manjimup 225
Ford House Retreat, Bridgetown 196
Foreshore Apartments, Albany 190
Fourwells, Yallingup 249

G

Gecko Lodge, Kalbarri 217
Geraldton B&B, Geraldton 213
Getaway Beach, Dongara–Denison 206
Gilgara Retreat, Margaret River 227
Glenorie Lookout Lodge, Northampton 239
Goodearth Hotel Perth, Perth 185
Gracetown Caravan Park, Gracetown 228
Grandis Cottages, Henley Brook 233
Grandview B&B, Gooseberry Hill 233

Guildford Landing, Guildford 233

H

Harvey Hills Farmstay Chalets, Harvey 215
Harvey Rainbow Caravan Park, Harvey 215
Heritage Cottage Bed & Breakfast, South Fremantle 189
Heritage Resort Shark Bay, Denham 204
Hidden Valley Eco Spa Lodges, Pickering Brook 234
Hidden Valley Tourist Park, Kununurra 222
Highland Valley Homestead, Harvey 215
Holiday Inn Burswood, Burswood 7 E3, 186
Hoover House B&B, Leonora 224
Hospitality Inn Port Hedland, Port Hedland 242
Hotel Kununurra, Kununurra 222
Hotel Northbridge, Northbridge 6 D3, 186
Hotel Rottnest, Rottnest Island 244
Houseboat Holidays, Walpole 247
Hovea Ridge Cottage, Hovea 234
Hyatt Regency Perth, Perth 187

I

Imintji Wilderness Camp, Fitzroy Crossing 212
Imperial Hotel York, York 250
Indian Ocean Retreat & Caravan Park, Myalup 216
Injidup Spa Retreat, Injidup 249

Intercontinental Perth Burswood, Burswood 7 E3, 186
Ipswich View Homestead, Toodyay 246
Ironclad Hotel, Marble Bar 226
Island Brook Estate, Metricup 228

J

Jacaranda Heights B&B, Kojonup 221
Jarragon B&B, Donnybrook 207
Jila Gallery Apartment, Derby 206
Jilba, Fremantle 189
John Eyre Motel, Caiguna 200
Juniper House, Gracetown 228
Jurien Bay Tourist Park, Jurien Bay 217

K

Kalbarri Murchison View Apartments, Kalbarri 218
Kalbarri Palm Resort, Kalbarri 218
Kalbarri Seafront Villas, Kalbarri 218
Kalbarri Tudor Holiday Park, Kalbarri 218
Kalgoorlie Overland Motel, Kalgoorlie 218
Karijini Eco Retreat, Karijini National Park 245
Karri Glade Chalets, Manjimup 226
Karribank Country Retreat, Porongurup 231
Katharine Susannah Prichard Writers' Centre, Greenmount 234
Kellerberrin Caravan Park, Kellerberrin 220
Kellerberrin Motor Hotel, Kellerberrin 220

Kemminup Farm Homestay, Kojonup 221
Kendenup Lodge & Cottages, Kendenup 232
Kimberley Coastal Camp, Admiralty Gulf 248
Kimberley Cottages, Derby 206
Kimberley Croc Backpackers, Kununurra 222
Kimberley Entrance Caravan Park, Derby 206
Kimberley Hotel, Halls Creek 215
Kimberley Klub Broome, Broome 197
King Sound Resort Hotel, Derby 206
Kingstown Barracks, Rottnest Island 245
Kirup Kabins Farmstay, Donnybrook 207
Kojonup B&B, Kojonup 221
Kooljaman at Cape Leveque, Cape Leveque 198
Kulin Caravan Park, Kulin 221
Kununurra Country Club Resort, Kununurra 222

L

Lake King Caravan Park, Lake King 223
Lake King Tavern & Motel, Lake King 223
Lake Navarino Forest Resort, Waroona 209
Lake View Siesta, Prevelly 228
Lakeside Holiday Apartments, South Yunderup 224
Lazy River Boutique B&B, Pinjarra 242
Leschenault Inlet Caravan Park, Australind 194
Little Lefroy Studio Warehouse, South Fremantle 189
Luxury @ Nautilus, Rockingham Visitor Centre 243

M

McAlpine House, Broome 197
Mandalay Holiday Resort and Tourist Park, Broadwater 199
Mantra Geraldton, Geraldton 213
Manuel Towers, Shoalwater 243
Maranup Ford, Bridgetown 196
Marble Bar Travellers Stop, Marble Bar 226
Marina Views, Geraldton 213
Martin Fields Beach Retreat, Geographe 200
Medina Apartments, Perth
Merredin B&B, Merredin 230
Merredin Oasis Hotel Motel, Merredin 230
Merredin Plaza All Suites, Merredin 231
Merredin Tourist Park, Merredin 230
Merribrook Retreat, Gracetown 228
Middleton Beach Holiday Park, Albany 191
Mindarie Marina, Mindarie 189
Misty Valley Country Cottages, Denmark 205
Molloy Island Hideaway, Molloy Island 193
Monastery Guesthouse, New Norcia 237
Monkey Mia Dolphin Resort, Monkey Mia 204
Mont Clare Boutique Apartments, East Perth 186
Morans' Wagin Hotel, Wagin 247
Morawa Chalets, Morawa 231
Morawa Marian Convent B&B, Morawa 231
Mornington Wilderness Camp, Fitzroy Crossing 212
Mt Lindesay View B&B, Denmark 205
Mountain Park Retreat, Toodyay 246

Murchison Club Hotel, Cue 203
Mystique Maison, Goomalling 238

N

Nautica Lodge, North Yunderup 242
Nelson's of Bridgetown, Bridgetown 197
New Esplanade Hotel Perth, Perth 187
New Lodge Motel, Katanning 220
New Norcia Hotel, New Norcia 237
Newberry Manor, Dunsborough 208
Newman Hotel Motel, Newman 237
Newport House, Beaconsfield 190
Ningaloo Reef Resort, Coral Bay 203
Nirranda Farmstay, Wannamul 237
Norseman Great Western Motel and Great Western Travel Village, Norseman 238
Northcliffe Hotel, Northcliffe 239
Nosh & Nod, York 251
Novotel Ningaloo Resort, Exmouth 211

O

Ocean Centre Hotel, Geraldton 213
Ocean View Retreat, Jurien Bay 217
Oceanic Apartment, Fremantle 190
Oceanview Retreat, Yanchep 250
Old Albion B&B, York 251

Old Miners' Cottages B&B, Northampton 239
Old Surrey, Mount Clarence 191
On the Bay B&B, Jurien Bay 217
Onslow Mackerel Motel, Onslow 240
Onslow Sun Chalets, Onslow 240
Orchard Glory Farm Resort, Bindoon 214

P

Palace Hotel, Kalgoorlie 219
Parmelia Hilton, Perth 187
Payne's Find, Rockingham Visitor Centre 244
Peel Manor House, Karnup 224
Pension of Perth, Perth 6 D2, 187
Pensione Verde, Denmark 205
Peppermint Grove Retreat, Pemberton 241
Peppermint Lane Lodge, Wellington Mill 202
Perth City YHA, Perth 188
Pier 21 Apartment Hotel, North Fremantle 6 A5, 190
Pilbara Holiday Park, Karratha 219
Pingelly Roadhouse and Motel, Pingelly 241
Pinjarra Cabins & Caravan Park, Pinjarra 242
Pinnacles Caravan Park, Cervantes 202
Point Samson Resort, Point Samson 244
Port Denison Holiday Units, Dongara–Denison 207
Port Mill B&B, Fremantle 190
Prevelly Surf Shack, Prevelly 229
Pump Hill Farm Cottages, Pemberton 241

Q

Quaalup Homestead Wilderness Retreat, Fitzgerald River National Park 196
Quality Hotel Lord Forrest, Bunbury 199
Quay West Resort Bunker Bay, Bunker Bay 208
Quellington School House Farmstay, Quellington 251
Quest on James, Northbridge 187
Quest Yelverton Kalgoorlie, Kalgoorlie 219
Quobba Station, via Carnarvon 201

R

Ravensthorpe Palace Motor Hotel, Ravensthorpe 243
Redgate Farmstay, Witchcliffe 229
Redgum Hill Country Retreat, Nannup 236
Riverway Chalets, Northcliffe 239
Rock of Ages Cottage, Greenough 214
Rose & Crown, Guildford 234
Rottnest Island Authority Holiday Units, Rottnest Island 245
Rottnest Lodge, Rottnest Island 245
Rydges Kalgoorlie, Kalgoorlie 219

S

Sal Salis Ningaloo Reef, Cape Range National Park 211
Salitage Suites, Pemberton 241
Samson Beach Chalets, Point Samson 244

Samson Hideaway, Point Samson 244
Scotts Brook, Boyup Brook 195
Sea Spray Beach Holiday Park, Dongara–Denison 207
Seafront Estate, Jurien Bay 217
Seascape Beach House, Esperance 210
Seashells Resort Mandurah, Mandurah 224
Seashells Resort Yallingup, Yallingup 249
Seasons Hotel Newman, Newman 237
Settlers Rest Farmstay, West Swan 234
Shark Bay Views B&B, Denham 204
Silver Sands Timeshare Resort, Mandurah 225
Smiths Beach Resort, Yallingup 249
Southern Cross Caravan Park & Motor Lodge, Southern Cross 245
Starsand Luxury Yacht Charters, East Perth 189
Stirling Range Retreat, Borden 192
Strelley Brook Cottage, Herne Hill 235
Studio 9, Margaret River 106, 227

T

Taddy Creek, Dwellingup 209
Tannamurra, via Lynward Park Estate 235
Tardie and Yuin Stations, Yalgoo 248
Tathra Hill Top Retreat, Nannup 236
The Bungalow-Broome, Broome 198
The Carnarvon Hotel, Carnarvon 201
The Courthouse B&B, Broome 198
The Dolphin House, Port Geographe 200
The Drovers Inn, Moora 231
The Grove Vineyard, Willyabrup 229
The Jetty Resort, Esperance 210
The Lily Dutch Windmill, Amelup 192
The Lodge Motel, South Hedland 243
The Loose Box, Mundaring 233
The Melbourne, Perth 187
The Ningaloo Club, Coral Bay 203
The Noble Grape Guest House, Cowaramup 229
The Old Swan Barracks, Northbridge 188
The Orchard Villa, Bindoon 214
The Outram, Perth 6 C3, 188
The Prev, Kellerberrin 221
The Priory, Mount Clarence 191
The Richardson, Perth 6 C3, 188
The Rocks Albany, Albany 191
The Roozen Residence, Prevelly 229
The Sleeping Lady, Porongurup 232
Three Springs Tourist Lodge, Three Springs 200
Tipperary Church, York 251
Toodyay Farmstay, West Toodyay 246
Top Paddock Cottage, Harvey 216
Tortoiseshell Farm, Bridgetown 197
Tree Elle Retreat, Walpole 247
Tree Tops, Weedon Hill 205
Tulip Cottage, Boyup Brook 195

U

Uralia Cottage, Northam 238

V

Villa Crisafina, Gnarabup 230
Vines Resort & Country Club, The Vines 235

W

Walpole Wilderness Resort, Walpole 248
Warren River Resort, Pemberton 241
Watermark Kilns, Northcliffe 239
Wave Rock Cabins & Caravan Park, Hyden 216
Wave Rock Lakeside Resort, Hyden 216
Wave Rock Motel Homestead, Hyden 216
Whalers Cove, Dunsborough 208
Wickepin Hotel, Wickepin 248
Wilgarup Lodge B&B, Manjimup 226
Wintersun Carnarvon Park, Carnarvon 201
Wondinong Pastoral Station, via Mount Magnet 232
Woodchester B&B, Katanning 220
Woody Island Ecostays, via Mackenzie's Island Cruises 210

Y

Yanchep Holiday Village, Yanchep 250
Yanchep Inn, Yanchep National Park 250

ACKNOWLEDGEMENTS

Much of the material in this book originally appeared in *Explore Australia 2011*, published by Explore Australia Publishing in 2010, where full acknowledgements for individual contributions appear.

The publisher would also like to acknowledge the help of the following people in the production of this edition:

Publications manager
Astrid Browne

Project manager
Melissa Krafchek

Editor
Jane O'Connor

Design
Erika Budiman

Layout
Megan Ellis

Cartography
Bruce McGurty, Paul de Leur, Emily Maffei, Claire Johnston, Jason Sankovic

Indexer
Max McMaster

Photo selection
Melissa Krafchek

Pre-press
PageSet Digital Print & Pre-press

Writers
Introduction, Perth and towns by Heather Pearson; Where to Eat and Where to Stay by Carmen Jenner.

Photography credits
Cover
Camel rides on Cable Beach, Broome (Nick Rains)

Back cover
Pentecost River and Cockburn Ranges, Kimberley (© photolibrary)

Polaroid image
Luxury bathroom overlooking Chamberlain Gorge, El Questro Homestead, Kununurra (Caroline West)

Full cover background
©istockphoto.com/saffiresblue

Title page
Aerial view of Bungle Bungle Range, Purnululu National Park (Australian Scenics)

Contents
Jetty and fishing boats along harbour, Broome (Australian Scenics)

Other images (left to right where more than one image appears on a page):
Pages iv–1 & 3 CK; 4–5 NR; 9 Len Stewart/LT; 10 JL/LT; 15 © photolibrary; 17 Courtesy of Aquarium of Western Australia; 18 © photolibrary; 19 JL/LT; 29 (a) CK (b) JD; 31 JL/LT; 33 & 35 Andrew Davoll/LT; 37 John Baker/EAP; 39 JL/LT; 41 Bill Belson/LT; 43 DS/LT; 45 Clay Bryce/LT; 47 NR; 49 JD; 50 NR; 54 JL/LT; 60 JD; 65 DS/LT; 69 Australian Scenics; 94 Tim Acker/AUSCAPE; 107 Courtesy of Cape Mentelle; 132 Courtesy of 1907 Restaurant and Cocktail Bar; 138 Courtesy of Little Creatures Brewing; 140 Courtesy of The Lily Dutch Windmill; 143 Courtesy of Matso's Broome Brewery; 160 Courtesy of Kununurra Country Club Resort; 165 Courtesy of Clairault Winery & Restaurant; 182 Courtesy of Cape Lodge; 185 Courtesy of Burswood Entertainment Complex; 188 Courtesy of The Outram; 203 Courtesy of Ningaloo Reef Resort; 223 Caroline West.

Abbreviations
CK Colin Kerr
DS Dennis Sarson
EAP Explore Australia Publishing
JD Jeff Drewitz
JL Jiri Lochman
LT Lochman Transparencies
NR Nick Rains

Explore Australia Publishing Pty Ltd
85 High Street,
Prahran, VIC 3181

This second edition published by Explore Australia Publishing Pty Ltd, 2011

First edition published 2008

10 9 8 7 6 5 4 3 2 1

ISBN 9781741173284

Copyright © Explore Australia Publishing Pty Ltd, 2011

This material first appeared in *Explore Australia 2011* (29th edition) published in 2010.

All rights reserved. Without limiting the rights under copyright reserved above, no part of this publication may be reproduced, stored in or introduced into a retrieval system, or transmitted in any form or by any means (electronic, mechanical, photocopying, recording or otherwise) without the prior written permission of both the copyright owner and the above publisher of this book.

Printed and bound in China by C & C Offset Printing Co. Ltd

Publisher's Note: Every effort has been made to ensure that the information in this book is accurate at the time of going to press. The publisher welcomes information and suggestions for correction or improvement. Email: info@exploreaustralia.net.au

Publisher's Disclaimers: The publisher cannot accept responsibility for any errors or omissions. The representation on the maps of any road or track is not necessarily evidence of public right of way.

The maps in this publication incorporate data copyright © Commonwealth of Australia (Geoscience Australia), 2006. Geoscience Australia has not evaluated the data as altered and incorporated within this publication, and therefore gives no warranty regarding accuracy, completeness, currency or suitability for any particular purpose.

Copyright Imprint and currency – VAR Product and PSMA Data

"Copyright. Based on data provided under licence from PSMA Australia Limited (www.psma.com.au)".

Hydrography Data (May 2006)
Parks & Reserves Data (May 2006)
Transport Data (November 2009)

Disclaimer
While every care is taken to ensure the accuracy of the data within this product, the owners of the data (including the State, Territory and Commonwealth governments of Australia) do not make any representations or warranties about its accuracy, reliability, completeness or suitability for any particular purpose and, to the extent permitted by law, the owners of the data disclaim all responsibility and all liability (including without limitation, liability in negligence) for all expenses, losses, damages, (including indirect or consequential damages) and costs which might be incurred as a result of the data being inaccurate or incomplete in any way and for any reason.

Maps contain Aboriginal Land data (2005), which is owned and copyright of the relevant Queensland, Northern Territory, South Australia and Western Australia state government authorities. The authorities give no warranty in relation to the data (including accuracy, reliability, completeness or suitability) and accept no liability (including without limitation, liability in negligence) for any loss, damage or costs (including consequential damage) relating to any use of the data.

TRAVELLING TIMES & DISTANCE CHART

WESTERN AUSTRALIA

	Albany	Broome	Bunbury	Busselton	Carnarvon	Derby	Esperance	Eucla
Albany		31:00	4:45	4:35	16:05	33:00	5:40	15:30
Broome	2567		29:00	29:00	17:25	3:10	31:00	37:00
Bunbury	342	2354		1:05	13:30	30:00	8:55	18:25
Busselton	331	2404	54		14:20	31:00	9:15	19:05
Carnarvon	1298	1461	1082	1131		19:00	19:35	26:00
Derby	2720	221	2509	2558	1614		33:00	39:00
Esperance	480	2513	686	717	1584	2666		10:15
Eucla	1352	3011	1373	1589	2193	3164	908	
Geraldton	819	1929	603	653	479	2083	1104	1714
Halls Creek	3184	684	2972	3021	2077	547	3130	2824
Kalgoorlie	835	2123	739	794	1363	2276	391	888
Karratha	1931	832	1715	1764	643	986	2084	2582
Kununurra	3543	1044	3332	3381	2437	907	3490	3282
Mandurah	392	2255	107	156	983	2408	717	1490
Manjimup	212	2478	132	119	1205	2631	632	1504
Meekatharra	1157	1410	945	995	622	1563	1105	1603
Merredin	468	2066	407	462	1086	2220	540	1164
Narrogin	279	2261	174	229	1081	2415	529	1230
Norseman	648	2309	669	885	1491	2463	204	704
Perth	409	2185	174	223	913	2338	758	1427
Port Hedland	2030	611	1819	1868	870	765	1977	2475
Wyndham	3553	1054	3342	3391	2447	917	3500	3382

Distances between towns are shown below the white line (km). Travel ti
Distances/travel times on this chart have been calculated over main roads